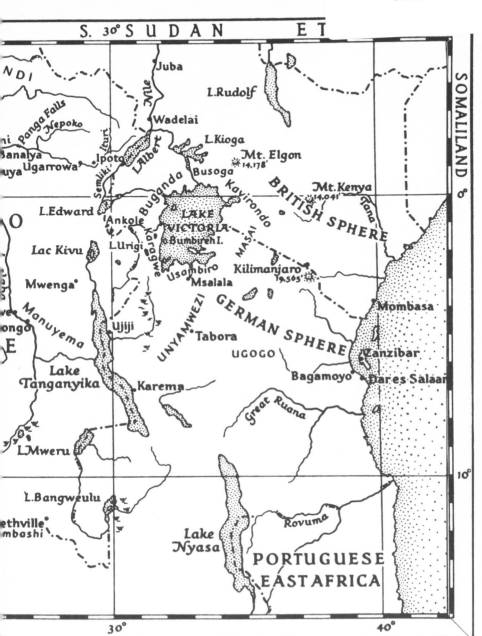

S. 30° S U D A N   ET

Juba

L.Rudolf

Panga Falls
Nepoko
Banalya
Ugarrowa
Ipoto
Semliki
L.Albert
Ituri

Wadelai

L.Kioga

Mt. Elgon
14,178'

Busoga

Buganda

Kavirondo

Mt. Kenya
14,041'

Tana

BRITISH SPHERE

SOMALILAND 0°

L.Edward

Ankole

LAKE
VICTORIA
Bumbireh I.

L.Urigi

Karagwe

Lac Kivu

MASAI

Kilimanjaro
19,565'

Usambiro

Msalala

Mwenga

Manuyema

Mombasa

UNYAMWEZI

GERMAN SPHERE

Ujiji

Tabora

UGOGO

Zanzibar

Bagamoyo
Dar es Salaam

Lake
Tanganyika

Karema

Great Ruana

L.Mweru

10°

L.Bangweulu

ethville
mbashi

Rovuma

Lake
Nyasa

PORTUGUESE
EAST AFRICA

30°   40°

Surgeon-Major Parke's African Journey 1887–89

Surgeon-Major Parke's
African Journey
1887–89

J. B. LYONS

The Lilliput Press

To Christopher Stoker

First published in 1994 by
THE LILLIPUT PRESS LTD
4 Rosemount Terrace, Arbour Hill,
Dublin 7, Ireland

A CIP record for this
book is available from
the British Library
ISBN 1874675 20 1

Jacket design by Ed Miliano
Set in 11 on 13 Dante by
Koinonia of Manchester
and printed in Dublin by
Colour Books of Baldoyle

Contents

Maps and Illustrations

front endpaper: The Nile System
back endpaper: Route followed from Banana Point to Zanzibar; Lake Albert and Equatorial Province
page 2: Detail from Ptolomey's map of Africa showing *montes lune*

between pages 130 and 131:
Parke's Castle, Dromahair, County Leitrim (Photo by author)
Clogher House, Kilmore, County Roscommon (Photo by author)
William Parke, JP, in Masonic dress (Courtesy the Secretary, Masonic Lodge, Mohill, County Leitrim)
Interior view of T.H. Parke Masonic Hall, Carrick-on-Shannon, with portrait of Parke over mantlepiece (Courtesy the Secretary, Masonic Lodge, Mohill, County Leitrim)
Thomas Heazle Parke, 'Bwana Doctari' (From *My Personal Experiences of Equatorial Africa*)
Statue of Surgeon-Major Parke by Percy Woods (Photo by Patrick Nolan)
Surgeon T.H. Parke (Courtesy RCSI, Stoker Donation)
Henry Morton Stanley and his officers, Ward, Barttelot, Jameson, Jephson, Nelson and Stairs (Courtesy RCSI, Stoker Donation)
Emin Pasha (Sketch by Dr R.F. Felkin)
Dr Parke with his pygmy servant (From *My Personal Experiences of Equatorial Africa*)
'The Execution' (From *The Graphic*)
'The Mountains of the Moon' (Sketch by Lt Stairs, *The Illustrated London News*)
'Farewell to Africa': Stanley and his officers leaving Mombasa in the steamship *Katoria*, Parke on *chaise-longue* (From *The Illustrated London News*)
'Rescued!' (From *Punch, or The London Charivari*, December 14, 1889)
'Between the Quick and the Dead' (From *Punch, or The London Charivari*, November 22, 1890)
Menu of dinner in Royal College of Surgeons in Ireland (Courtesy RCSI)

Acknowledgments

It is a pleasure to thank the Presidents and Councils of the Royal College of Physicians of Ireland and the Royal College of Surgeons in Ireland for grants-in-aid which made publication possible. I am particularly grateful to Anne McAllister who brought T.H. Parke's *Diary* to the College and to the Stoker family for making their acquisition possible; William K. Parke of Derry-gonnelly, County Fermanagh, permitted use of a 'family tree' brought to my attention by Mary McGowan in Parke's Castle at Lough Gill; Dr Arthur Dolan of Mohill was an informative guide at Kilmore and Drumsna; Mary O'Doherty facilitated my research in innumerable ways. Others to whom I am indebted include Hugh Brazier, James Brindley, Joseph Collins, Peter Costello, Beatrice Doran, Alec Elliott, John Garry, Larry Geary, Mark Holmes, Cecil Humphries, Aine Keegan, Vincent Kinane, Hazel Lidwell, P.M. Logan, Lorraine McLean, Robert Mills, Patrick Nolan, Francis J. O'Kelly, Conor O'Riordan, Desmond and Moira Payne, Geoffrey Popham, W.H. Reid, Martin Ryan, Ursula Sheridan, Gillian Smith and Christopher Stoker.

The staffs of the National Library, the libraries in the Irish Colleges of Physicians and Surgeons, the Royal Dublin Society and Dublin University have been most helpful. The illustrations were processed by the Photographic Departments of the RCSI and TCD. The pictures of William Parke, JP, and of the interior of the T.H. Parke Masonic Lodge, Carrick on Shannon, are reproduced by permission of the Secretary, Masonic Lodge, Mohill, and of the Grand Secretary, Molesworth Street, Dublin. Quotations from *The Diary of A.J. Mounteney Jephson* are permitted by the Hakluyt Society and Cambridge University Press. Map 1 is reproduced from Roger Jones's *The Rescue of Emin Pasha* by permission of Messrs Allison & Busby; the route map from Banana Point to Zanzibar is reproduced from *The Diary of A.J. Mounteney Jephson* by permission of the Hakluyt Society and Cambridge University Press. Quotations from Parke's diary and letters are made by permission of the Mercer Library, RCSI.

Acknowledgments

The final word of thanks goes to my dear wife Muriel, who cheerfully tolerated the presence in her home of yet another biographee, while sustaining the biographer with her customary thoughtfulness and occasionally wielding a discriminating blue-pencil.

J.B. Lyons, MD, FRCPI
Department of the History of Medicine,
Royal College of Surgeons in Ireland, Dublin

Foreword

In January 1887, bored by garrison life in the British army of occupation in Egypt, Surgeon Parke jumped at the chance of a place on Stanley's expedition to relieve Emin Pasha. Thomas Parke was an impecunious and adventurous Irish doctor – a veteran of Wolseley's unsuccessful attempt to relieve Gordon at Khartoum three years before. But he knew next to nothing about Stanley and of his plans to save Emin, the Governor of Equatoria on the Upper Nile, and the only one of Gordon's old lieutenants to survive the Mahdist' advance. If Parke had known more, he might never have joined him. The expedition proved to be the largest, longest, most expensive, and most controversial of all Stanley's expeditions. At the time it also seemed the most unsuccessful.

Stanley re-supplied Emin, hemmed in by the Mahdists to the north, and brought him safely back to the east coast, to Bagomoyo in the newly founded colony of German East Africa. But the expedition, which cost over £20,000 and the lives of more than 200 of its African members, and spread ruin among the Africans it encountered, brought no immediate imperial dividends to Stanley's motley backers.

The late 1880s were the climatic years of the Scramble for Africa. Three Great Powers (Britain, Germany and France) and one enterprising individual (King Leopard II of the Belgians) were competing for the dwindling blank spaces at the centre of the map of Africa. For various reasons their eyes had recently turned to the head waters of the Nile: to Equatoria in the Southern Sudan, and to Uganda. In fertile Uganda both Britain and Germany hoped to find a profitable hinterland to help finance their poverty-stricken colonies in East Africa. By taking control of the head waters of the Nile Britain also hoped to block a French advance from the west coast to the Nile, which they believed was a strategic threat to Egypt. This three-cornered struggle had been exploited brilliantly by King Leopold. Posing as an international philanthropist, and offering himself as a buffer between the contending Great Powers, he stretched out both his hands to grab the supposed riches of the Upper Nile.

Ever since 1878, Leopold had been Stanley's chief patron and employer. He had seized on Stanley's discoveries of the course of the River Congo in 1874–7 to create his own Congo State, with Stanley as his founding father. For the Emin Pasha Expedition he gave Stanley leave of absence provided he adopted the route by way of the Congo. He offered him free transport by the rivers steamers of the Congo State. But Leopold's generosity nearly sank the expedition. The steamers were inadequate for transporting the stores. Anyway the west coast route was far longer and more difficult, as it involved hacking a track hundreds of miles through tropical jungle.

Stanley's main financial backer for the expedition was a group led by Sir William Mackinnon. He was the head of a syndicate of businessmen and philanthropists who had recently founded the Imperial British East Africa Company to administer the new colony of British East Africa (later Kenya) under royal charter. They were hoping for a slice of Uganda, too.

The third backer was the Egyptian government, controlled, since the British landing in 1882, by the government in London. Egypt contributed £10,000 for the expedition. On the face of it this was to pay for repatriation of the Egyptian and Sudanese government employees marooned in the wilds of Africa. In practice, London was using the Egyptian tax payer to peg out a claim in central Africa. If Stanley could re-supply Emin, and Emin's garrison proved loyal, then in due course his base in Equatoria could become the base for the re-conquest of the Sudan from the south.

Such were the fond hopes that Stanley's backers reposed in Emin. But Emin proved a broken reed. Soon after Stanley's arrival – in effect precipitated by it – there was a mutiny among his Sudanese soldiers. After infinite frustrations, Stanley persuaded Emin to allow himself to be rescued. Worse still, from Stanley's point of view, was Emins behaviour when he reached the safety of the coast. In the excitement of the banquet to celebrate the expiation's arrival, Emin fell through the roof of a hut and landed on his head. On his recovery – and Dr Parke helped save him – he declared he would desert the Egyptian flag and throw in his lot with the German colonial service. (He was in fact a German by origin who had taken the name of 'Emin', 'The Faithful'.) Of course he was welcomed with open arms by the Germans, and received a telegram of congratulations from the Kaiser.

This was a farcical conclusion to all of Stanley's hardships and those of his companions. On his return Stanley hammered out a two-volume best seller claiming credit for the expedition's achievements. In fact it was Parke and a companion, not Stanley, who had discovered the Ruwenzori Mountains, alias the Mountains of the Moon. As for the disasters that had overcome the rear column of his expedition, killing most of its members, Stanley blamed these mishaps on the folly of its white officers. Naturally they – or their surviving relations – did not take this lying down. A storm of abuse burst over Stanley's head. To defend himself he turned to the four young officers of his main column, Dr Parke among them.

It was in this fevered atmosphere that Parke published his own account of the expedition in 1891, *My Personal Experiences in Equatorial Africa*. If Parke's aim was to take the heat out of the situation, he certainly helped to achieve it. The book is prosaic in tone, diplomatic in its comments. There is nothing but praise for Stanley. Facing fearful odds, the white men quite properly show the stiff upper lip. Black men die like flies, but this is the dark continent and black men are used to it. In short, Parke's book manages to make one of the great epics of Victorian travel sound decorously dull. Stanley did not object.

Dr Lyons has brought the story more clearly into focus with two intriguing literary discoveries. First, he has found 150 letters from Dr Parke which show that his original diaries were edited, re-written – and expurgated – by an Irish doctor friend, Dr John Knott. Second, he has found the original diaries themselves and published lengthy extracts from them in this scholarly volume.

As one would expect, the originals evoke some of the pungency of the jungle missing from the edited version. Stanley becomes more human and less attractive. Acts of violence towards Africans intensify. Punishments meted out by the white men would have been condemned as atrocities if they had been directed against fellow Europeans. And everywhere there is the stench of the sick, the awful tang of suppurating flesh, and the gallons of useless purges and enemas directed against dysentery and malaria.

From the point of view of empire-minded Englishmen, Parke had done a fine job editing his diary. The sanitized version helped the cause. In 1890 Germany did a deal with Britain, swapping Uganda (among other African loot) for Heligoland. Mackinnon's IBEA Company, threatened by bankruptcy, had thrown in the sponge.

Would Germany – or France – take over Uganda after all? Lugard and an ill-assorted lobby of imperialists and do-gooders appealed to British public opinion to prevent the scuttle. It was fortunate for them that Stanley's best seller, and Parke's travel book, had made the region familiar territory. Despite the row about the rear column, Englishmen tended to accept the assumption implicit in Stanley's and Parke's accounts: the poor heathen in Africa needed Britain's civilizing touch. (Stanley was forgiven for handing the Congo over to Leopold as he had offered it to Britain first.) Lugard stumped the length and breadth of Britain putting the case for an imperial take-over. And it was significant that Parke – the humane Irish doctor, the 'man who had saved Stanley' – played a useful role at Lugard's suggestion, in persuading the British public that only Britain could save Uganda from itself.

The following year Britain took over Uganda as a crown colony. But Parke was already dead. At thirty-five he had paid the price for his years of adventure, struck down by a parasitic worm he had picked up in Africa.

Thomas Pakenham
Tullynally, Westmeath,
November 1993

'What were we who had strayed in here? Could we handle that dumb thing, or would it handle us? I felt how big, how confoundedly big, was that thing that couldn't talk, and perhaps was deaf as well. What was in there?'

Joseph Conrad, *Heart of Darkness*

'Evil hangs over this forest as a pall over the dead; it is like a region accursed for crimes; whoever enters within its circle becomes subject to Divine wrath. All we can say to extenuate any error that we have fallen into is, that our motives are pure, and that our purposes are neither mercenary nor selfish. Our atonement shall be a sweet offering, the performance of our duties.'

Henry M. Stanley, *In Darkest Africa*

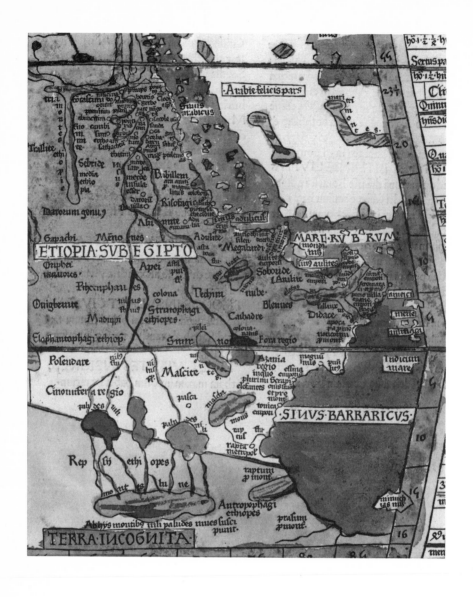

Introduction

After the death of Eleanor Knott, Professor of Early Irish at Dublin University, her relatives deposited certain of her father's papers at the Library of the Royal College of Surgeons in Ireland (RCSI). These included letters to Dr Knott from Thomas Heazle Parke (1857–93), Medical Officer to the Emin Relief Expedition, which unexpectedly disclosed the part played by John Knott in preparing Parke's book, *My Personal Experiences in Equatorial Africa* (1891), for publication. He was, in effect, its ghost-writer.

More recently the library acquired, almost fortuitously, the actual notebooks used by Knott, fair copies by Parke of diaries he had kept during his terrible African journey. Their collation with the printed version shows some differences of emphasis and facts which are discussed more fully later but seem sufficient to justify my study of Surgeon-Major Parke's fascinating career. Graduating from the Schools of Surgery in 1878–9, he held civilian posts briefly before being commissioned in the Army Medical Division in 1881. Experience of war in Egypt followed in 1882, and in 1884 he volunteered to join the forces sent to relieve beleaguered Khartoum. In the depths of Africa in 1888 he rediscovered the 'Mountains of the Moon', snow-capped giants known to Ptolemy.

The leader of the Emin Relief Expedition, H.M. Stanley (1841–1904), was at first cordially disliked by his white officers. Parke — *Bwana Doctari* to the afflicted Africans — wasn't an exception but with the other survivors he came to appreciate the explorer's better points. Had it been possible to send Stanley — *Bula Matari*,[1] the stone-breaker — to relieve Khartoum, would his determination have averted a tragedy? Parke certainly thought so.

His letters show that between his return to England in 1890 and his death on 10 September 1893, Parke had become something of a figure in high society and a guest in ducal houses. He remained unsettled and was looking for a congenial post that would enable him to retire from the army.

Since the publication in 1890 of H.M. Stanley's *In Darkest Africa*, the first and fullest account of the expedition, an extensive literature dealing with the subject has appeared.[2] It is not my primary intention to add still another account of the expedition to the existing plethora; the focus of my attention is its medical officer and his book. My principal source material is in Parke's diary – which he kept regularly from 20 January 1887 until 29 August 1889 when he discontinued it because of an eye complaint – and his letters to Knott and others. When quoting from these documents, spelling, punctuation and the use of capital letters have frequently been silently corrected. As biographical information is limited I have to be content to provide an outline of Parke's career rather than the ideal full 'Life'.

Present-day ease of travel and communication make it almost impossible to appreciate fully the hardships so stoically endured by Parke and his companions, out of contact with one another for months on end. Modern sensitivity to 'racist' attitudes together with the inevitable distortions of hindsight add to the difficulty of accepting the expedition's *bona fides* as a humanitarian venture, and in face of floggings and hangings can one do more than say *autres temps, autres moeurs*? Parke grew to manhood in an age which institutionalized violence. Flogging was not abolished in the British army until 1881. Death for mutiny or extreme disobedience was an accepted military norm. The story of the expedition's Congo journey exposes aggression in slow motion, entailing primitive, deliberate acts of individual violence but hardly differing in essence from the lightning-like strikes of the Gulf War. Western man then as now confronted a Third World populace with the assurance of superior strength. And as I write, conditions prevailing in Eastern Europe, the Middle East and Somaliland suggest that despite great technological advances human nature is still violent and imperfect, a curious mixture of political rigidity, brutality, cupidity and altruism.

As the Siege of Khartoum influenced T.H. Parke's life so decisively it is appropriate to present some information regarding Gordon and the Anglo-Egyptian events and conflicts that would have been familiar to my subject's contemporaries. One of Lytton Strachey's 'Eminent Victorians', Charles George Gordon (1833–85) served with the Royal Engineers in the Crimea and later earned the soubriquet 'Chinese' Gordon by suppressing the Taiping rebels. An austere, unsociable bachelor of religious disposition, neither money nor honours attracted him, a talented misfit in English society. Appointed next as British representative to the Danubian Commission to ensure that the Danube remained open to navigation, he was stationed at Galatz in Rumania. Here he renewed his friendship with Romolo Gessi, an Italian who had been an interpreter in the Crimea and was now running a Rumanian sawmill.

While visiting Constantinople in 1872 Gordon met Nubar Pasha, the Egyptian Foreign Minister (and a future premier), who told him that Sir Samuel Baker, Mudir (Governor) of the Khedive's Equatorial Province, was to retire. He suggested that Gordon might be a suitable replacement. The post was offered to him formally in 1873 and with the War Office's permission he accepted it. He selected Gessi as his second-in-command and, meeting in Cairo in 1874, they proceeded to Equatoria[3] where the new governor declared ivory to be a Soudanese government monopoly, attempted to abolish the slave trade, and recruited soldiers from the local tribes.

Gordon improved the province's administration and its agriculture; he moved his headquarters from Gondokoro to Lado and set up a chain of stations along the White Nile. Gessi circumnavigated the Albert Nyanza (Lake Albert) in 1876 and towards the end of that year the governor submitted his resignation and returned to London. He was not to escape his destiny, however, and early in 1877 he was back in Khartoum having accepted the position of Governor-General of the Soudan.

In Egypt, meanwhile, Khedive Ismail's prodigal spending had resulted in colossal borrowings at exorbitant interest rates. The mounting debt facilitated Disraeli's purchase from the Khedive of 40 per cent of the shares of the Suez Canal Company (1875) and finally the Commissioners of Debt, four in number, were called in to monitor the situation on behalf of Britain, France, Germany and Austria. The bankrupt Khedive was deposed in 1879 — replaced by his son, Tewfik — and a 'dual control' was imposed by Britain and France. The nationalist reaction was personified by an Egyptian colonel, Arabi Pasha (1840–1911),[4] who had brought the country to the brink of revolt by 1882 when on 8 January a 'Joint Note' sent to the Khedive in Cairo by British and French representatives intimated a determination to support His Highness in his position and to maintain order.

Rioters killed many foreigners in Alexandria's opulent European quarter on 11 June. A month later a British fleet bombarded the city's forts, occupied by rebels, an action provoking uproar among the volatile populace which burned and looted as it fled. Bluejackets and marines landed. The flamboyant commander of the gunboat, *Condor*, Lord Charles Beresford, second son of the Marquess of Waterford, was appointed Chief of Police and imposed drastic correctives, flogging looters and shooting incendiaries.[5] Arabi's soldiers, meanwhile, had withdrawn to an entrenched position at Kafr Dowar, some miles from Alexandria. This force was subsequently enlarged, but on 22 July the Khedive dismissed Arabi from his post as Minister for War, proclaiming him a rebel.

The British garrisons in Malta and Cyprus were strengthened by request of the Foreign Office and on 30 July the Scots Guards sailed from England leading a force that would eventually amount to about 40,000 men under the command of Dublin-born Sir Garnet Wolseley, prototype of 'the Modern Major-General' in *The Pirates of Penzance*. Some troops sailed from India.

The British attack was expected near Aboukir but instead, having taken control of the Suez Canal and Ismailia, there was a successful engagement at Kassassin followed by an early dawn attack at Tel-el-Kebir where Arabi's main army was overwhelmed on 13 September. Three days later Kafr Dowar was surrendered to Sir Evelyn Wood.

On 4 December Arabi Pasha, charged with rebellion against the Khedive, pleaded guilty. Condemned to death (a sentence immediately commuted to exile for life), he saluted the Court and sat down. Then, as the Court began to clear, a well-wisher presented him with a bouquet of white roses to symbolize his purity of purpose.[6]

A wave, or rather a flame, of nationalism was kindled in the deserts of the south by the presence on Abba Island in the White Nile of Mohammed Ahmed (1848–85) — the Mahdi ('the Expected Guide') — and his followers, the Dervishes. A succession of raids and military victories had supported his claim to invincibility, culminating in the annihilation near El Obeid in 1883 of a large Egyptian army commanded by a British officer, Hicks Pasha. The Mahdi was supported in battle by twenty thousand angels, he assured the faithful, and he claimed the power to turn Egyptian bullets into water.

Osman Digna, the Mahdi's deputy, a merchant whose business had been ruined by the anti-slavery drive, held much of the eastern Soudan; it seemed only a matter of time before Khartoum would be taken, and the question was should this be anticipated by evacuation of the city and the outlying garrisons. Sent to investigate the situation and to effect a withdrawal, Gordon was re-appointed Governor-General by the Khedive and before long was seen to be an isolated victim of circumstances, unable either to advance or to retreat and doomed unless relieved.

Many public figures seemed prepared to let fate dictate the outcome until, in response to popular demand, a relief expedition under the command of Lord Wolseley elected to follow the Nile to Khartoum rather than approach the city from the Red Sea via Souakin and Berber. Sir Charles Wilson commanded the small group of soldiers that finally reached Khartoum by steamer two days after its fall.[7] The provinces of Darfur and Bhar al-Ghazal had already fallen but in the remote south Emin Bey remained Mudir of

Equatoria. He was seen as Gordon's lieutenant and, like Gordon, he appeared powerless to leave his endangered province.

The Mahdi died (probably from natural causes) some months after the massacre in Khartoum. He was succeeded by the Khalifa, and the Dervishes were to retain control of the Soudan until defeated at the Battle of Omdurman on 2 September 1898 by Sir Herbert Kitchener, who was soon raised to the dignity of Baron Kitchener and awarded £30,000.

Dum-Dum bullets were used at Omdurman. 'The battlefield presented a sickening sight. The effect of the expanding bullet has been most deadly.'[8]

The Mahdi's tomb, a place of pilgrimage within the vanquished town, was destroyed, the body disinterred and burned in a steamer's furnace, the ashes thrown into the Nile. A British officer in an Egyptian regiment kept the head which was buried later at Wadi Halfa. Kitchener crossed the Nile to Khartoum in a gunboat. Gordon's palace lay in ruins, the staircase where he was killed no longer existing. The gardens were neglected and overgrown but there were shrubs in blossom and graceful citron, orange and pomegranate trees. The British and Egyptian flags were raised. The Guards' band played the 'Dead March' in Saul and after the chaplains' service the Soudanese band played 'Abide with me', Gordon's favourite hymn.

An Anglo-Egyptian Condominium was formed in 1899 to rule the Soudan as a separate state, having a Governor-General nominated by Great Britain and appointed by the Khedive. Lord Kitchener was succeeded as Governor-General by Sir Reginald Wingate, Bart, author of *Mahdiism and the Egyptian Sudan*, who introduced many economic and administrative reforms. The latter's successor, Sir Lee Stack, who proposed separation of Egypt and the Soudan, was assassinated by an Egyptian in Cairo on 19 November 1924.

The Graduates General Congress of Gordon Memorial College became the effective voice of nationalism which divided into moderates and radicals. The former group, the larger, had the Mahdi's posthumous son, Sayyid 'Abd al-Rahman al-Mahdi (d. 1959), as patron in the Ummah (Nation) Party, and later was strongly influenced by the Mahdi's Oxford-educated great-grandson, Sadiq al-Mahdi. The independent republic, with an elected parliament established by the Soudan in 1956, failed to create stability and after a bloodless *coup d'état* was replaced by a junta.[9]

Parliamentary rule, restored in 1986, was followed by the inception of the present military regime on 7 December 1989. Since 1983 civil war has existed between the government in Khartoum and the Sudan People's Liberation Army, but in recent years the situation in the south has been worsened by a split in the SPLA and tribal war between Dinkas and Nuer. It is highly ironic that the material condition of those governed by Emin Pasha in the 1880s appears to have been far superior to the plight of the starving thousands which the international relief organizations, with all their technical advantages, are unable to succour.

The Mahdists forced Emin to move south, vacating the very terrain across which more than a century later the Soudan's rebel factions are now fighting.

Notes

1 The correct spelling is 'Matadi' but the Zanzibaris softened the 'd' to 'r'.
2 Olivia Manning, *The Remarkable Expedition* (London 1947); Iain R. Smith, *The Emin Pasha Relief Expedition 1886–1890* (London 1972); Per Olof Sundman, *The Expedition* (London 1967); Peter Forbath, *The Last Hero* (London 1989), see also *The London Illustrated News*, suppl., April 1890; *The Graphic*, Stanley Number, March 1890; A.J. Mounteney Jephson, *Emin Pasha and the Rebellion at the Equator* (London 1890); J.S. Jameson, *The Story of the Rear Column* (London 1890); William Hoffmann, *With Stanley in Africa* (London 1938); Dorothy Middleton's 'Introduction' to *The Diary of A. J. Mounteney Jephson* (London 1969); Roger Jones, *The Rescue of Emin Pasha* (London 1972); Thomas Pakenham, *The Scramble for Africa* (London 1991), etc.
3 Annexed by Baker for the Khedive, Equatoria, an area south of the *Sudd*, the swampy area where profuse growth of vegetation makes the river impassable for 200 miles, extended to Lake Albert. Beyond lay, from east to west, Buganda (now part of Uganda), Unyoro and the Nile-Congo watershed. Equatoria's northern borders marched with those of Darfur and the Bahr al-Ghazal.
4 In *Khedives and Pashas* (London 1884) Moberly Bell, a *Times* correspondent, had nothing good to say of Arabi: 'Before he became notorious he used to be described by an expressive Arabic word which is inadequately translated by the English "muddleheaded" — not exactly a dreamer, nor yet half-witted, nor stupid nor yet unfortunate, but the sort of man of whom it will be predicated that everything he takes in hand will be wrong.' Wilfrid Blunt, Sir William and Lady Gregory were among the tiny 'disloyal' British minority that accepted him as 'El Wahid' — the 'One', an apostle of Egyptian nationalism. But Elizabeth Longford tells us that in Egypt during the Suez crisis (1956) 'the name of "Ourábi" was still a talisman'.
5 Charles Royle, *The Egyptian Campaigns*, 2nd edn (London 1900), p. 104.
6 Elizabeth Longford, *Pilgrimage of Passion* (London 1979). An unforeseen outcome of Blunt's and Gregory's pro-Arabi campaign was an affair between the poet and Sir William's young wife, Augusta, later the formidable 'Old Lady' of Dublin's Abbey theatre.
7 See Bernard Allen, *Gordon and the Sudan* (London 1931), *passim*.
8 Royle, *op. cit.*, pp. 532, 578.
9 P.M. Holt and M.W. Daly, *A History of the Sudan*, 4th edn (London 1988), *passim*.

Part One

1   The Voyage Out

Crossing the barrack square on his way to duty on 20 January 1887, Surgeon-Captain Parke recognized the lively figure of Major Barttelot approaching. The Irish doctor stopped to pass the time of day with Barttelot who said he had just arrived at Alexandria by P & O steamer, the SS *Mongolia*. He had been picked to serve in the Emin Relief Expedition led by Henry Morton Stanley, the explorer, and was on his way to Aden to collect thirteen Somalis. He suggested that Parke should join them.[1]

To Parke's eye, accustomed to making physical assessments, Edmund Barttelot, an officer of the 7th Fusiliers, was superbly fit; he radiated energy and obviously was delighted with the tasks ahead of him, passing clouds long forgotten. His CO had pitched into him during the Soudan campaign for a physical attack on a mutinous Somali soldier.[2] But who on earth was Emin Bey? The doctor put the question to Barttelot whose reply was extremely vague: 'Oh, some chap who wants to get out of Africa and can't manage to.' Hardly enlightening! But then, wasn't it the adventure, rather than the person, that really mattered?

When they parted, Barttelot's suggestion remained in Parke's mind. Alexandria was a busy station but there is a decided monotony in treating an endless series of venereal diseases.[3] Club life had begun to pall and there was a certain sameness in the city's social and sporting pursuits. An opportunity to cross Africa was a decidedly exciting possibility. And under Stanley's leadership the expedition was bound to be successful, not another ghastly Khartoum.

Hearing of H.M. Stanley's arrival in Alexandria on 27 January, Parke called at Abbat's Hotel and sent up Barttelot's note of introduction. Ushered into the great man's presence, he offered his services as medical officer to the expedition to be told curtly by Stanley 'that he could take no person except those he had already chosen'.[4] Stanley's manner did not invite further discussion. Parke left him his card and departed without being informed that the explorer was still negotiating for the post with a candidate or candidates who wished to impose their own self-interested conditions of service.[5]

Parke's outstanding social responsibility at that time was the mastership of the Alexandria Hunt Club. He was relaxing at the Khedivial Club on Friday evening (28 January) and looking forward to next day's meet when shortly before 10 pm he was handed a telegram. It was from Stanley: 'IF ALLOWED ACCOMPANY EXPEDITION WHAT TERMS REQUIRED ARE YOU FREE TO GO WITH ME.' His response was decisive: he sent a wire — 'YES COMING TO CAIRO TONIGHT' — arranged for a Major Wood of the Essex Regiment to look after the hunt and caught an express that left Alexandria at 10.30 pm. He reached Shepheard's Hotel at 6 am and supplemented his broken sleep in a chair in the reading-room. Then he took a bath and after breakfast was ready for his interview with Stanley at 9.30 am.

At their second meeting, Stanley was favourably impressed. Without delay, arrangements were set in train to obtain leave for Parke from the War Office. General Sir Frederick Stephenson, GCB, Commander of the British Forces in Egypt, received him at his house and urged the surgeon to consider 'the difficulties and dangers'.[6] Surgeon-General J. O'Nial signified that he had no objection. Unpaid leave was granted from 3 February 1887 and Parke signed an agreement to serve the expedition — which Stanley expected to take about eighteen months — without salary or remuneration other than an allowance of £40 for his outfit and £15 to buy surgical instruments.[7] He was also obliged to undertake not to publish anything connected with the expedition for six months after the issue of the official report.

By Sunday evening Parke was back in Alexandria where his news got a mixed reception at the Khedivial Club.[8] The next few days were spent getting his outfit and paying a number of farewell visits; he made his will and settled his accounts, including the gymkhana funds. On Tuesday the head of *The Eastern Telegraph* held a luncheon in his honour and on the following evening there was a farewell banquet. 'Many speeches were made and I felt I was parting from genuine friends.'[9] His Berber servant had promised to accompany him but 'funked' at the last minute and explained that his father did not wish him to go.

By now Parke would have learned something of the romantic story of Emin Bey, polyglot, naturalist, medical doctor and governor of Equatoria. The son of Lutheran parents, Eduard Schnitzer, as he was named originally, was born in Silesia in 1840. Short-sighted but intellectually bright, he possessed a disposition to be a wanderer. Having taken a medical degree in Berlin, he drifted in 1864 via Vienna, Trieste and Ragusa to Antivari in Albania, then a Turkish province. He obtained an official position as district medical officer and medical officer to the Quarantine Station in 1865. Some years later he became attached to the household of Ismail Hakki Pasha, the governor of Northern Albania, in which capacity he travelled throughout the Ottoman Empire. The governor's wife was young and pretty and predictably Dr Schnitzer fell in love with her. When she was unexpectedly widowed he became her protector. Running out of funds, he returned with his inamorata and her three children to his family home in Germany in 1875, but his ardour had cooled and he deserted her quite soon without having married her.[10]

Schnitzer embraced Islam in Egypt and attained fluency in Arabic. From Alexandria he moved to Cairo and Khartoum and thence he was called by Gordon to the Province of the Equator which was without a doctor. Known now as Dr Emin ('the faithful one') he settled at Lado and seemed impervious to the enervating heat and torturing mosquitoes. For some years he was Surgeon-General to the Forces and in 1878 Gordon appointed him Mudir of Equatoria. The African sun deepened his tan. The time spent awaiting audiences with local chiefs and the prolonged palavers increased his patience; the ritual exchange of gifts appealed to his generosity. 'Something of the native spirit passed into his blood, until he could accept a goat or bestow a shirt with equal gravity and dignity, seeing beneath the symbolic act the true fact of treaty.'[11]

The rise of the Mahdi and the spread of revolutionary fervour threatened colonial outposts with political annihilation. Lupton Bey, governor of the neighbouring Bhar al-Ghazal, was taken in chains to Kordofan where he died of typhus in the Mahdi's camp; Rudolf Slatin, removed from Darfur, submitted to Islam and survived.[12] Rumours of Emin's isolation reached England, still smarting from the tragic events at Khartoum, and it was generally agreed that an expedition must be sent to relieve him.

Parke would have known little of the convoluted discussions that preceded the formation of the Emin Relief Committee. Emin himself had merely asked for 'some paltry caravans of ammunition'.[13] Writing to his friend, Dr R.W. Felkin of Edinburgh, a former missionary, he represented himself as 'the last and only representative of Gordon's staff. It therefore falls to me, and it is my bounden duty, to follow up the road he showed us.' He indicated that they must not be left 'at the mercy of childish kings and disreputable Arabs' but that was all he demanded. 'Evacuate our territory? Certainly not!'[14]

But Felkin was also approached by others. He published a letter sent to him from Cairo by Dr George Schweinfurth, botanist and discoverer of the

Linkuku River, to whom it was addressed on 16 August 1886 by Dr Wilhelm Junker, the last European to have seen Emin Bey:

Must we believe that nothing will ever be done for the Equatorial Provinces? Write, write on, dear friend! Send forth words of thunder that will open the eyes of all the world! I am most urgent that Emin Bey should receive help without delay ... it would be a lasting shame if Europe should not attempt something for the help of Emin Bey ... it is with this hope alone that I essay to return to Europe.[15]

Attempts had already been made to relieve Emin but expeditions led by a German, Dr G.A. Fischer, from the East Coast, and by an Austrian, Oscar Lenz, approaching via the Congo (the present Zaire), were unsuccessful. The British cabinet resolutely refused to become involved, alert to the likelihood of finding itself obliged to rescue the rescuers but Sir Evelyn Baring (future Earl of Cromer) indicated that the Egyptian government, acknowledging a responsibility for Emin and the garrison, would contribute £10,000 towards an expedition which enabled him to withdraw from Equatoria. Mr (later Sir William) Mackinnon, founder of the British India Steamship Navigation Company, James F. Hutton, a Manchester businessman, Colonel Sir Francis de Winton, a Congo administrator, and some others undertook to raise the necessary funds without a public appeal. Their motivation was philanthropic, political and commercial: apart from the prime need either to remove Emin or to secure him in his province there were secondary opportunities to establish links between Mombasa on the coast and Wadelai on the Nile by making treaties with local chiefs. And besides, as Joseph Thomson, a young explorer, pointed out, Emin's stored ivory, if carried to the east, would more than suffice to pay the expedition's expenses.[16]

Opinion was divided only as to the route to be followed. The Emin Relief Committee,[17] over which Mackinnon presided, favoured a direct approach from the east coast, skirting the Victoria Nyanza, but Stanley argued for the more circuitous journey which would enable him to use the river-steamers of the River Congo (the Zaire). Finally the wishes of Stanley's master, Leopold II, King of the Belgians, had prevailed (he saw an opportunity for the Congo Free State to establish a frontier on the Nile) and it was decided to travel through the Congo and the Ituri Forest and establish contact with Dr Emin at the Albert Nyanza. Stanley would be the bearer of letters from the Khedive and the Prime Minister, and would also bring the notification of Emin's elevation to the rank of Pasha.[18]

★

Thomas Heazle Parke, a graduate of the Schools of Surgery of the Royal College of Surgeons in Ireland, was twenty-nine years of age when appointed to the Emin Pasha Relief Expedition. The second son of William Parke and his wife Henrietta Holmes, he was born at Clogher House, his parents' picturesque ivy-clad residence at Kilmore, County Roscommon, on 27 November 1857.[19] The Parkes were of Kentish stock: Roger Parke, the first of the line to flourish in Ireland, was brother-in-law to Sir Roger Jones, Constable of the Castle of Sligo in 1606, and father of two sons, Robert and William. The former, Captain Robert Parke, lived at 'Parke's Castle', near Dromahair, which has recently been restored.[20] His daughter married Sir Francis Gore, an ancestor of the Gore-Booth family of Lissadell. William Parke, High Sheriff of Sligo, settled at Dunally Castle and the Parkes of Kilmore were descendants of his line.[21]

In the nineteenth century the Parkes were no longer possessed of the wide domains they acquired by right of conquest when the hereditary lands of the O'Rourkes of Connacht were divided. William Parke, JP, of Kilmore owned 109 acres and rented additional pastures. He had ten children and if little is known of their upbringing it may be safely assumed that his sons devoted themselves to the favourite pastimes of the Anglo-Irish gentry, hunting, shooting and fishing.

T.H. Parke is said to have attended local schools before enrolling at an academy run by the Reverend Edward Power at 3 Harrington Street, Dublin, in 1869.[22] He entered the Royal College of Surgeons in Ireland six years later. This College was established by members of the Dublin Society of Surgeons anxious to sever their links with the barber-surgeons and was granted a charter in 1784. It had prospered during the Napoleonic Wars when it supplied surgeons for Europe's battlefields and its military tradition may have influenced the direction of Tom Parke's career.[23]

The presidents of the College during Parke's years of attendance included Robert McDonnell (1877), who was the first Irish doctor to transfuse blood successfully.[24] The chairs of surgery and medicine were held by Mr (later Sir) William Stokes and Dr James Little, respectively. The former was a fervent advocate of the system of antiseptic surgery recently introduced by Joseph (later Lord) Lister, an epochal advance which Parke would have seen used at the Richmond Hospital, where he was resident pupil after first attending the City of Dublin Hospital in Baggot Street. Henry Wilson, professor of ophthalmology, was Sir William Wilde's natural son.

His contemporaries in the College on St Stephen's Green included young men from all over Ireland and there was an understandable friendship between Parke and John Knott, a farmer's son from Kingsland, County Roscommon, his senior by four years and distinguished academically.[25] Knott's letters to his wife have survived and give us glimpses of a student's life at the College in the 1870s. He had digs at 12 Upper Camden Street and walked daily to the Richmond Hospital, a distance of some miles: 'So you see I am not likely to want for exercise. I must walk backwards and forwards with all speed I can assume for the clinical courses begin at 9 O'C and the College lectures at 12.' Professor (later Sir Charles) Cameron who taught chemistry left an unfavourable impression — 'a dull, most unintellectual chap, bustling about from one side of the laboratory to another and confusing the various operations of the different students.' Surgeon Stokes, on the other hand, earned Knott's admiration — 'son of *the* Stokes of Merrion Square ... Stokes Jnr is evidently an excellent surgeon as his cases (of amputations, fractures, abscesses, etc.) are almost all progressing favourably. He is also very gentle and tender'.[26]

Parke became a licentiate of the College (LRCSI) in 1878 and took the diploma of the King and Queen's College of Physicians of Ireland (LKQCPI) in the following year. He registered as a medical practitioner on 1 February 1879 and briefly held the posts of dispensary medical officer at Ballybay in County Monaghan and surgeon to the Eastern Dispensary at Bath. Then, having been coached by Dr John Knott, he passed the army entrance examination and was gazetted surgeon-captain on 5 February 1881. Physically he was well-built and handsome with a moustache, dark-brown hair and a frank open countenance.

He volunteered for service in Egypt to suppress the Arabi revolt and landed on 21 August 1882 at Alexandria where the city's most opulent quarter had been sacked. He was posted to No 5 Field Hospital at Ramleh with Woods' Brigade within three miles of the enemy's line. There were skirmishes every day; the insurgents' artillery seemed to him to be far more accurate than the British guns and several shells landed uncomfortably close to his tent but their explosive forces was somehow absorbed by the sand. He was present at the surrender of Kafr Dowar and received the Queen's Medal and the Khedive's Star.

His College friend John Knott heard from him towards the end of the year. 'Now that the war is over ...' Parke explained, 'I have time to drop a line to my old friends. I have been through everything during the campaign except Tel el Kebir.'[27] He was convalescing from fever on board HMS *Carthage*, and wishing he was back in Ireland — 'this is a miserable country, all desert' — but prepared to cheer himself by dwelling on forthcoming sporting events. 'We are to have horse races next month. I will ride my Chestnut horse and shall call him "Roscommon".'[28]

He repudiated the war-correspondents' stories of the neglect of the wounded: 'It is all a bundle of lies. The soldiers could not have been better treated all through the Campaign.' In Alexandria where the water-supply was grossly contaminated he often had fifty cases of typhoid under his care. At Cairo he was given charge of a surgical ward with 109 patients — 'which gives me more work than I can do.'

In July and August 1883 he was senior medical officer at Helouan Hospital near Cairo during the cholera epidemic in which 60,000 perished. He experimented with a saline infusion into an arm vein which was not yet an established and life-saving treatment — 'the patient recovered enough to speak but subsequently died.'[29] One of his closest companions, Surgeon C.B. Lewis, died after a few hours' illness.

Parke was stationed in Ireland with the 16th Lancers at Dundalk towards the end of 1883 and volunteered for active service again in the following year, wishing to join the Nile Expedition for the relief of General Gordon besieged at Khartoum by the forces of the Mahdi. He arrived in Egypt on 7 October 1884 and left Cairo for the front three days later. He was conveyed to Wadi Halfa in a steamer supplied under contract by Messrs Cook and son arriving on 3 November. The Nile Expedition's boats, built in England and transported to Egypt at great expense, took them on to Korti which they reached on 31 December; each boat carried twelve persons and the flotilla was successfully assisted by 380 of the *voyageurs* whom Wolseley had found so useful in his Red River campaign (1870) against the Canadian Métis, Louis Riel.[30]

Parke spent the next week attached to No 1 Field Hospital and then joined a convoy for Gakdul, a four-day journey across the Bayuda Desert. Charles Royle, historian of the Egyptian campaigns, has pictured their departure across an undulating, pebbly plain: 'It was a strange sight to see the camels with their necks stretched out like ostriches and their long legs, moving off in military array, until the rising dust first blended desert, men and camels in one uniform grey hue, and finally hid them from the sight of those who remained in camp.'[31] They proceeded through black mountain gorges to Gakdul where there were three wells at the northern end of a natural amphitheatre surrounded by tall, yellow sandstone rocks. Major Kitchener's Mounted Infantry had lately arrived having captured a convoy of camels with dates intended for the Mahdi.

Parke left Gakdul on 13 January as medical officer to the Naval Brigade under the command of the redoubtable Lord Charles Beresford who had some splendid racing-camels, Bimbashi, Beelzebub and Ballyhooley, which he had matched successfully against the best camels and horses of other officers on the journey to Korti, but now rode a big white donkey named 'County Waterford'.[32] They had their first sight of the enemy on 16 January gathering on the high, bare hills but fortunately the Mahdists did not venture a night attack. Parke slept as was customary beside his camel, its knees securely lashed. His head was protected in the angle between the beast's abdomen and hind leg. 'Yet I found to my disagreeable surprise, on awaking, that my living shield had moved off during my (evidently) sound sleep, leaving my person well exposed in the open.'[33]

The battle for the control of the Abu Klea wells, the following day, resulted in many casualties and Colonel Fred Burnaby, thrown from his horse, received a fatal sword-cut as his immense figure lay on the ground.[34] Major-General Sir Herbert Stewart was surprised on the night of the 18th to find the men of the bearer company who transported the wounded, and whose aid was then so badly needed, carried no arms; the home authorities believed them sufficiently protected by 'the Geneva Cross'. The battle of Gubat (Abbu Kru) on the 19th was a protracted bloody conflict in which General Stewart sustained a mortal wound (d. 16 February). They were ten hours under fire, the field hospital 'perched on an eminence' a pot shot for the enemy'.[35] After Sir Charles Wilson's unsuccessful attack on Metammeh, Parke was busy assisting Surgeon-Major W.H. Briggs at a long series of operations.

Lord Charles Beresford, himself a casualty, watched them amputate a leg and was surprised to see that there was no bleeding. They had used 'Esmarch's bandage', a device to prevent blood loss.

Parke was at Metammeh on 1 February 1884 when a *felucca* arrived from Khartoum with the news that the city had fallen. 'That calm, still morning on the banks of the Nile was one of sadness and disappointment.'[36] Wilson's up-river dash had been futile – many asked why he had not gone earlier.

Out of the five officers with the Naval Brigade two were killed, two were wounded — one severely, Lord Charles Beresford slightly — and Parke escaped without a scratch. He was next attached to the Guards' Camel Corps and returned with them to Alexandria where he took ship for home leave but just as the vessel was about to sail he was ordered to disembark for local service.

★

Early on 3 February 1887 a large gathering of friends saw Parke off at the railway station. His train for Suez which connected at Zagazig with the train from Cairo in which Stanley and Dr Wilhelm Junker were travelling. (The latter had worked with Emin in Equatoria and brought his despatches to the East Coast but did not join the expedition.) From Ismilia another of Emin's friends joined them, Giegler Pasha, Telegraph Inspector and later Deputy Governor-General of the Soudan. They put up at the Suez Hotel which was small, expensive and lacking in cleanliness.

Next day Parke went sailing with Bimbashi Roycroft of the Egyptian Army. Later he inspected the sixty-two Soudanese soldiers recruited by Barttelot and was impressed by their physical condition. Saturday was devoted to cricket. Roycroft and Parke played for the Suez team against 'Eastern Telegraph', and were beaten.

Stanley and Parke lunched with the British India Steamship Navigation Company's agent on the Sunday before going on board the SS *Navarino* in which Captain Robert H. Nelson, Arthur J. Mounteney Jephson and Lieutenant William Grant Stairs had sailed from London. They had brought with them the twenty-eight foot portable boat, *Advance*, the provisions donated by Fortnum & Mason of Piccadilly,[37] nine medicine chests the gift of Burroughs & Wellcome, canvas tents dipped in a copper sulphate preservative, rifles, ammunition, sappers' tools and numerous other essentials. William Bonny, another member of the expedition, a former NCO, missed the boat and sailed to Suez from Plymouth.

Parke supervised the stowing of the Soudanese soldiers' kit. Next morning he had his first patient, Mohammad Doud, a black NCO who held out the crumpled middle finger of his left hand. It had been badly fractured three weeks previously at Wadi Halfa and was so deformed that the surgeon had no option but amputation. When this had been effectively performed, Parke learned that his patient had come from Khartoum to Metammeh by riverboat on 21 January 1885 and could recall seeing the doctor there.

The *Navarino* steamed south into the heat of the Red Sea which at that time of year was quite tolerable; at noon on Tuesday there was a shower of rain, unusual in the region. Parke read *King Solomon's Mines* and took stock of his new companions.[38]

Stanley with his formidable reputation was as yet an enigma to his officers but presumably the best possible choice of leader for such an expedition associated in most minds with the 'discovery' of Dr Livingstone and as author of *Through the Dark Continent*. He was accompanied by a white servant, William Hoffmann, a young Londoner of German origin who spoke German and French fluently.

Parke found Stanley rather reticent but they are certain to have discussed the proposed route which had caused raised eyebrows when announced publicly on 13 January, on the occasion of the presentation of the Freedom of the City to the explorer at the Guildhall. Any attempt to travel by the shortest route from east to west would, he explained, be opposed by the Masai, 'the murderous Wakedi', or on the south-western route by the resolute Wahuma. Had Metesa still reigned, a passage through Uganda would have been readily permitted. 'But Mwanga, the son, was a person of very different disposition; he got drunk upon *bhang* [hashish]; he had already distinguished himself by the atrocious murder of Bishop Hannington, and the sight of a valuable convoy going to Emin Pasha would excite his cupidity.' For these reasons Stanley had gladly accepted the King of the Belgians generous offer of the free use of the Congo Free State's whole stock of steamers for ninety days.[39]

Lieutenant Stairs held a commission in the Royal Engineers. He was born in Halifax, Nova Scotia, on 1 July 1863 and educated locally and in Edinburgh. He had worked as a civil engineer in New Zealand before joining the British Army in 1885. He was present on 17 January 1887 at Thurlow Lodge, Norwood, the residence of Mr Maxim, who demonstrated the powers of the machine-gun he gave to Stanley.

Jephson, like Parke, belonged to the Irish landed gentry, the Jephsons of Mallow, County Cork, though he himself had been born to the manse at Hutton, Essex, in 1858. The tenth of twelve children born to the Rev. John Mounteney Jephson and his wife Ellen Jermy (daughter of the Recorder of Norwich), Arthur Jermy Mounteney Jephson was educated at Tonbridge School. Aspiring to a career in the merchant navy he served as a cadet in the *Worcester* but, changing his mind and his occupation, he became associated with the Comtesse de Noailles in her charitable activities. Stanley had regarded his application for a place in the expedition doubtfully, seeing him as too refined, too 'high class', but Hélène de Noailles supported her cousin's candidature with a donation of £1000.

Nelson, a native of Leeds, was a man of striking physique; he served with Methuen's horse in the Bechuanaland expedition and had fought in the Zulu campaigns. Sergeant Bonny had been a medical assistant in hospitals of the Army Medical Service and in Zululand, the Transvaal and the Soudan. He sailed in the second-class accommodation and the social barrier that separated him and Hoffmann from the other white officers was never quite broken down. John Rose Troup, the last man recruited in London out of more than 400 applicants, narrowly escaped a prison sentence for assaulting

20

a constable while on a spree, and had sailed independently from Liverpool to the Congo via Lisbon. He spoke Swahili fluently (having recently completed a three year stint as an employee of the Congo Free State) and was to be the expedition's transport officer. He was a son of General Sir Colin Troup of the Indian Army.

Parke slept on deck as it was too hot in the cabin; he took lessons from the first officer in reading the sextant. Perim, in the straits of Bab-al-Mendip, was passed on Friday, and in the small hours of 11 February the *Navarino* anchored at Aden, then a vital fuelling station for ships bound for India, Australia and the Far East. After breakfast the expedition, with its bulky cargo, was transferred to the SS *Oriental* where Barttelot and Jameson had preceded them. The latter, the expedition's naturalist, had come to Aden in the SS *Peshawar*.

James Sligo Jameson, grandson of John Jameson, a wealthy Dublin whiskey distiller, was born in Scotland on 17 August 1856. His mother, Margaret Cochrane of Glen Lodge, Sligo, died a few days after his birth. From an early age the boy evinced interest in natural history and in foreign lands. He studied for an army career but in 1877 the attractions of faraway places prevailed. His travels took him to Borneo where he collected birds, butterflies and beetles. He spent some years big-game hunting in South Africa and he fished the Limpopo River. The early 1880s found him with his brother, John A. Jameson, hunting in the Rocky Mountains of North America.

His marriage in 1885 to Ethel, daughter of Major-General Sir Henry Marion Durand, RE, KCSI, CB, did not allay his wanderlust and passion for collecting, and in January 1887 he offered his services to Stanley as naturalist. At first the latter demurred, 'He did not appear remarkably strong. We urged that, but he as quickly urged that as he had already spent a long time in the wilds of Africa, his experience disproved our fears.'[40] A more compelling argument was the candidate's willingness to subscribe £1000 towards the expedition's funds.

Actuated by a chivalrous nature, Jameson explained his motivation to Lady Durand: 'Ever since my childhood I have dreamt of doing some good in the world, and making a name which was more than an idle one, and now springs up the opportunity of wiping off a little of the long store standing against me.'[41] He also relished the expectation of making significant additions to his collections.

Barttelot, whom Parke had first met at Aswan in October 1884, served at Kandahar, Tel-el-Kebir and Abbu Klea. The second son of Sir Walter Barttelot, Bart, MP, of Stopham, Sussex, he was educated at Rugby and

Sandhurst and though bright and cheerful was notably impetuous and quick-tempered, but with an excellent record of enterprise and achievement. Writing to his sister, Barttelot mentioned his shipboard companions judging Stanley to be a man 'who improves decidedly on acquaintance', and must have many interesting stories to tell, but would be easily upset and very nasty when angry. Of Parke he wrote: 'I knew him up the river in '84 and '85. He is strong, bright and clever ... I am glad Parke has come, for it is always well to have someone who is not an entire stranger.'[42]

The *Oriental* was cheered by the passengers in the *Navarino* as she sailed for Zanzibar in the late afternoon. Next morning Parke detected the sinister signs of confluent smallpox in a Nubian soldier with high fever. He isolated Said Mohammad Abdul in a life-boat swung above the bulwarks and by vaccinating those at risk hoped to prevent a disastrous epidemic. Jephson, an anti-vaccinationist, refused to submit to the procedure. 'The doctor thought me mad [Jephson wrote] and I got chaffed for being eccentric ...'[43] William Hoffmann developed a sore and swollen arm which he said was worse than the disease.

They crossed the equator on 18 February. Parke watched the flying-fish; he drew up rules for the preservation of health in the tropics and gave instructions in first-aid. At Lamu he went ashore with Jameson who shot a brace of red-legged partridge. On display were the bleached bones of several hundred men killed on the battlefield by a former Sultan of Zanzibar.

The *Oriental* put into Mombasa for a few hours on 21 February ('a very pretty place with old fortifications' and a flourishing missionary station) and on the following day reached Zanzibar where Stanley had arranged to pick up 623 porters and additional cargo: ammunition, 28,000 yards of mixed cloth, 36,000 lbs of beads, several hundred bags of rice, a ton of metals and wire, forty pack donkeys and ten riding asses. It was here, too, that Parke was introduced to Tippu Tib, a massive figure, six foot two in height, an ivory-dealer and ex-slave-trader, whom Jameson, always prepared to see the best in everyone, described on first acquaintance as 'a fine old Arab, very lively, and a thorough old gentleman'.[44]

Tippu Tib was a virtual ruler in Central Africa. While Stanley might bluster and threaten to fight him if he opposed the expedition's freedom to travel in his territory, he was secretly empowered by the Belgian authorities to appoint the Arab as Governor of Stanley Falls (later called Stanleyville and Kisangani), an honour Tippu Tib sceptically accepted. He also agreed to sail with Stanley to the Congo with ninety-seven followers of whom thirty-five belonged to his harem, and he undertook to recruit 600 additional porters at Stanley Falls.

The Sultan's palace at Zanzibar was a large, square structure, imposingly ugly. The older, narrow streets were about five feet wide but the effect of the intricately-carved doors and windows, jet-black against pure white buildings, was striking. Parke inspected the SS *Madura*, the British India steamer chartered to take the expedition to the mouth of the River Congo. With Barttelot's assistance he supervised the transfer of men and equipment from the *Oriental*. He then called on Dr Hussey, the surgeon to the British Consulate; they drank champagne and discussed the demerits of English vaccination lymph. After dinner, Parke and Hussey strolled in the Sultan's gardens where a band was playing. They visited the tennis courts where many Europeans, including three ladies, were enjoying the warm evening.

The Zanzibaris came on board in lighters in groups of fifty. Their friends and relatives, a crowd of 2000 or more, assembled on the beach to see them off, and a score of canoes full of excited men and women plied between the shore and the ship creating a kind of pandemonium. The *Madura,* with its motley collection of races, had hardly put to sea when a furious conflict erupted between decks where the Soudanese felt oppressed by the Zanzibaris' superior numbers. Jameson helped the white officers to separate the combatants and, recalling how they fought like demons armed with clubs, he was reminded of 'an "Inferno" by Gustave Doré.'[45] It was then left to Parke to deal with a fractured arm and many contusions and lacerations. He also dispensed Eno's fruit salts for Tippu Tib and twelve of his seasick wives. These women were 'fairly good looking'; they were 'well developed in every way' and Parke thought Tippu Tib must have married them for love as they had no money and few possessions.[46]

There were now 812 persons attached to the expedition:

Stanley, his servant and seven British officers	9
Zanzibaris	623
Soudanese/Nubians	62
Somalis	13
Tippu Tib and followers	97
Additional (four officers and four men, including two interpreters joined later)	8

Parke noted that the Soudanese were tall, impressive men, averaging six foot in height, with Negroid features, but they seemed sulky and less adaptable than the Zanzibaris. The latter, though reckless and lacking in forethought, were excellent raconteurs and amusing company; averaging five feet nine inches they were extremely good-natured and in the hungry days ahead Parke found that 'if they had only three forest fruits they would share them with their companions'.[47] The Somalis were small, wiry, copper-coloured men measuring about five feet seven inches.

The enlisted men were divided into companies, each commanded by a white officer and with *Maniapara* or headmen over every dozen or so carriers. Parke took charge of thirteen Somalis and ninety-eight Zanzibaris in Company G. The officers undertook the duties of 'Officer of the Day' successively, wearing a sword and sash to indicate the special status of the duty officer. On Sundays, Parke read prayers and with some diffidence acted as clergyman. 'I did not know exactly where to commence and, once started, I experienced some difficulty in knowing where and how to stop.'[48] When acting as 'Officer of the Day', Parke supervised distribution of rations at 5 am, inspected the cleansing of the 'tween-decks area, accompanied the Captain on his morning rounds, and saw that all were in bed and lights out by 7 pm. A further visit of inspection was made during the night. Disinfectant powder was shaken 'tween-decks daily.

The Nile Expedition and Gordon's failure at Khartoum cropped up inevitably in conversation. Parke described the carnage at Abu Klea and Gubat vividly; he praised the men's firmness and courage and spoke of the marvellous air of the Bayuda Desert. Stanley resolutely refused to countenance Jephson's assertion that failure is sometimes nobler than success.

The *Madura* passed Durban on 4 March and Port Elizabeth two days later; heavy seas necessitated closure of all port-holes and entailed discomfort for the goats and donkeys, as waves broke over the deck, and long sick-parades for Parke. However, he found time to write to his mother, sister 'Harrie' and also to Jimmy Riddle of the 60th Rifles, to notify him that his brother's tombstone had reached Zanzibar safely. The doctor dined with Fleet-Surgeon Curtis at the Royal Naval Club, Simon's Bay, on 8 March; later he stretched his legs with Barttelot, Jameson, Stairs and Jephson before returning to the ship. The doctor spent most of the following day dealing with a bad head-injury. A young Zanzibari had fallen from the roof of a deckhouse in the early morning and was found lying prone and unrousable on the deck.

I found his face considerably swollen, unconscious, bleeding from mouth, symptoms of concussion. No fracture or dislocation. I gave him calomel grs vi, James's powder grs v, applied cold to his head and gave him some tea and milk. Arrived at Cape Town at 7 pm and dropped anchor.[49]

Parke refurbished his medical stocks and took charge of a case of surgical instruments sent out from London. He visited the hospital, dined with medical colleagues at the military mess and was advised by the PMO 'to use Quinine freely as a prophylactic certainly with the Europeans of the Expedition.' Quite a crowd assembled at the jetty to see the expedition's departure at 5.30 pm on 10 March. A cheer was raised for Stanley and the medical staff cheered for Dr Parke as the *Madura* steamed into a stormy sea.

By now the doctor had a number of seriously-ill patients under his care, with a variety of illnesses but he had difficulty in having them looked after properly, for men appointed as attendants walked away when his back was turned and on one occasion the concussed Zanzibari wandered into the saloon in a delirium. Soup ordered from the galley was wasted unless he waited personally until it was taken. The temperature in the humid space between decks was 100° F at 10 am. The first death occurred on 14 March resulting from dysentery and was followed within days by a death from pneumonia but Stanley consoled his medical officer with the observation that he lost twenty-eight men out of a total force of 250 on his last voyage from Zanzibar to the Congo.[50]

A third death was put down to heat-stroke. The unfortunate Sarboko Mackatubu, who had spent two hours washing his clothes, unprotected from the blazing sun, was buried in a clean white shroud at Banana Point, after the *Madura's* arrival at the sandy spit at the mouth of the River Congo on 18 March. Scanning the tombstones in the prominently-placed cemetery, Parke saw those of Sooks, a boy of nineteen, Dean, engineer to Stanley's previous expedition, and W.H. Sexton, MD, of Blessington Street, Dublin.

Notes

1 T.H. Parke's manuscript diary in Royal College of Surgeons in Ireland; henceforth, *Diary*.

2 H.M. Stanley, *In Darkest Africa*, Vols I and II (London 1890) — henceforth, *IDA* — Vol. I p. 124.

3 See A.A. Gore, 'A Medico-Statistical Sketch of Modern Alexandria', *Dublin Journal of Medical Science*; 1889; 88: 19–29. 'The more important admissions [to the military hospital over a five year period, 1883–8] were venereal, 2779; fevers, 1683; diarrhoea, 810; cutaneous diseases, 555 ... There were 566 admissions for wounds and injuries.' Total admissions, 10,779; deaths, 164.

4 *Diary*, 27 January 1887. Stanley's account of this interview (*IDA*, I, p. 49) is manifestly inaccurate: 'To try if he were in earnest I said, "If you care to follow me to Cairo, I will talk further with you. I have not the time to argue with you here."'

5 According to Roger Jones (*Rescue*, p. 93) the post was offered to Dr R. Leslie, an old Congo hand, who objected to the clause in the contract forbidding the officers to publish any account of their travels until six months after the appearance of the official record, and to the possibility that he might have to defer to Stanley in therapeutic decisions. Stanley referred to 'two most unpleasant experiences with medical men both of whom were crotchety, and inconsistent' (*IDA*, I, p. 49). Later (*The Lancet*, 1893, ii, 738) Stanley stated that the Emin Relief Committee had negotiated with a doctor who was 'demanding impossible pay and interpolating onerous conditions in his draft contract'.

Rolph Bidwell Leslie, MA, MD (Toronto, 1876), LRCP (London, 1879) served with the

Turkish army in the Turco-Servian and Russo-Turkish Wars and gained further experience during a smallpox epidemic in Constantinople. He held a hospital post in Port of Spain, Trinidad, and was a civil surgeon in the Zulu War.

    J.R. Troup had known Leslie in the Congo and recalled 'his extreme kindness in caring for those who came under his care'. *With Stanley's Rear Column* (London 1890), p. 30.

6 *Diary*, 30 Jan.

7 *Diary*, 29 Jan. Reply to Surgeon Gen. O'Nial from War Office: '29th yours today government is not responsible for Stanley expedition and cannot give official sanction to officers joining it Barttelot has been given leave of absence from his regiment without pay with leave to travel in Africa this is all that can be done to Parke.'

8 '... Some said lucky fellow and others poor devil'. *Diary*, 30 Jan.

9 *Diary*, 2 February.

10 Georg Schweitzer's *Emin Pasha: His Life and Work*, 2 Vols (London 1898) provides information that would have been unknown to Parke. Eduard Carl Oscar Theodor, s. of Ludwig Schnitzer, b. 28 March 1840 at Oppelen in the Prussian province of Silesia was reared at Neisse in the Protestant persuasion. From a local school he proceeded to the universities of Breslau, Berlin and Königsberg to read medicine. Even as a young man, according to his biographer, he tended 'to fluctuate between extremes, a mixture of equally groundless optimism and pessimism' (*op. cit.*, 1, p.3), and becoming engrossed in the practical aspects of his chosen profession he obtained the MD degree at Berlin but did not take the State examination essential for German practitioners. When he attempted to rectify the omission he was told that too great a time had elapsed. He reacted by leaving Berlin immediately instead of pressing his claim.

    Young Schnitzer tried unsuccessfully in Engand for an appointment in Africa; in Vienna he volunteered, again without success, to join an army being formed to accompany the Archduke Ferdinand Maximilian who had been made Emperor of Mexico. He went to Trieste, hoping for a post as ship's doctor, but even that humble job eluded him. Constantinople was his next intended destination but *en route* he availed of an opportunity to open a medical practice at Antivari, an Albanian seaport, where he arrived on 21 December 1864. He procured medicines from Berlin, was welcomed by the European colony and secured patients among the local community travelling widely on horseback throughout the region. He studied Illyric, Turkish and Greek and accepted the local customs in an area where everyone 'whether Turk, Gipsy, or Christian' took a long siesta in the middle of the day. His skin was deeply tanned and he adopted the local costume — 'White linen trousers (cream-coloured Russian linen), instead of braces a red silk sash, with fringed ends, wound three or four times round the body; a white shirt, a linen coat, a fez with a long tassel, a large moustache; there [he told his sister] you have my picture for the present, until the photographer comes round this way.' (*op. cit.*, 1, p. 11).

    In the evenings Dr Schnitzer sat in the moonlit garden with his friends, enjoying the wine, the excellent tobacco and the animated conversation with no wish to return to Germany's more rigid formalities. And besides, he was appointed MO to the quarantine station in July 1865. Every vessel arriving in the port was carefully examined and if suspected of coming from a country tainted with cholera it was quarantined for ten days or more. Letters, goods and parcels from the Levant were disinfected.

    Intellectual company was lacking but the doctor conversed with the well-informed skippers who called to the port. They brought him books from Trieste and he subscribed to the *Medizinische Zeitung* in Berlin. Before long he was a member of several learned bodies and, when invited to assist the Parisian *Société Asiatique*, he wrote an essay for it in modern Persian. He played chess well and was an excellent pianist.

Schnitzer distinguished himself by dealing with an epidemic from which other doctors had fled. 'Disease is disease [he told his sister]; and whether it be cholera or anything else it is our duty to combat it.' Having visited Scutari (Uskadur) towards the end of 1870 he was taken into the service of Ismail Hakki Pasha, governor of Northern Albania, and followed him to Asia Minor, Constantinople, Trebizond (to where the Pasha, falling into disfavour, was exiled) and subsequently to Janina where Ismail, restored to better fortune, was appointed governor under a new minister.

Writing to his sister from Trebizond in 1872, Schnitzer revealed that he had survived a revolt in Northern Albania. 'Today we are in the old Byzantine Imperial residence of Trebizond, on the banks of the Black Sea on Asiatic soil.' He had few duties 'beyond a daily visit to the harem'. He supervised the children's education and mentioned that Madame Ismail, two or three years younger than himself, was 'very kind and amiable'. They lived in some state at Trebizond with a household of servants including six slave girls. 'Everything is most picturesque. Circassians, Persians, Kurds, and Armenians, forming a motley crowd, fill the baazar and the Occident is far away.'

After Ismail Hakki Pasha's death, Schnitzer assumed charge of the widow's affairs. They moved to Arco in Italy before he took her to meet his family in Germany. But on 18 September 1875 on the pretext of visiting university friends in Breslau he left Neisse and failed to return, nor did he communicate again with his family for many years. In retrospect it is known that he was in Trieste on 15 October 1875; he reached Cairo on 23 October and arrived in Khartoum early in December.

11 A.J.A. Symons. *Emin Pasha, Governor of Equatoria* (London 1950), p. 14.

12 Still a prisoner in the Mahdi's camp when Khartoum fell, he was shown Gordon's head and asked: 'Is not this the head of your uncle, the unbeliever?' 'What of it?' Slatin replied. 'A brave soldier who fell at his post; happy is he to have fallen; his sufferings are over.' (Allen, *Gordon*, p. 432). Slatin Pasha eventually escaped and was with Kitchener when Omdurman was taken.

13 Cited by Smith, *Relief Expedition*, p. 35.

14 Ibid, p. 36.

15 R.W. Felkin, 'The Position of Emin Bey', *Scottish Geographical Magazine*, 1886; 2: 717.

16 *The Times*, 24 November, 1886.

17 The Emin Relief Committee: Mr William Mackinnon (chairman); Col. Sir Francis de Winton (secretary); Mr H.M. Stanley; Mr James F. Hutton; Sir John Kirk; Col. J.A. Grant; Rev. Horace Waller; Lord Kinnaird; Hon. Guy Dawnay; General Sir Lewis Pelly; Mr Burdett-Coutts; Mr Alex L. Bruce; Mr Peter Denny.

18 See Stanley, *IDA*, I, p. 57.

19 The house still stands but has lost its ivy and the servants' wing.

20 Betty MacDermot mentions in *O'Ruairac of Breifne* (Manorhamilton 1990) (p. 144) that Sir Brian O'Rourke's residence at Newtown was granted to Robert Parke. Citing Wood Martin's *History of Sligo*, she describes how in 1641 'Mr Parke was shut up and beleaguered in his castle of Newtown, between Dromahair and Sligo' until a detachment was sent to relieve him.

According to Archdeacon O'Rorke (*History of Sligo: Town and County*, 1986), Robert Parke, commonly called Captain Robert Parke, enjoyed a high position in the county, MP for Leitrim in 1661, and 'resided in the castellated mansion of Newtown ... which must have been built by himself, his father, or his uncle, Sir Roger Jones, and which is well situated at the head of Lough Gill, within a few hundred yards of the O'Rourke's old castle of Newtown.' (*op. cit.*, 1, p. 462). Although favoured by the Commonwealth establishment, he received estates in Sligo and Leitrim at the restoration, lands formerly in the possession of O'Conor Sligo and the O'Rourkes.

O'Rorke (*op. cit.*, 1, p. 463) believed it unlikely that Dunally, 'which is a fertile, well-timbered, and pleasant tract' on the right bank of the Kilsellagh River, is to be identified with the Dun Aille of the Four Masters where, in 1602, Caffar O'Donnell had his residence and fortress.

21 Roger Parke came to Ireland *c.* 1601 with Roger Jones of Denbeigh, Wales, whose sister Alice he married in 1609. Their sons were Robert (MP for Leitrim 1661) and William. The latter's sons were Roger (d. 1726); John (Lieutenant); and William (Ensign). Roger Parke (High Sheriff for Sligo in 1720) m. Isabella Ormsby: their sons were Roger (m. Alice Brown of Cork 1775) and Andrew.

Major Andrew Parke of the 8th King's Regiment d. 1803, leaving issue Major George Parke who owned plantations in Ceylon and married a Miss Joanna Kennedy. An element of uncertainty enters the record with the next generation in which Lt Col Roger Kennedy Parke of the 3rd Dragoon Guards inherited Dunally Castle: was he a brother or a cousin of Dr Thomas S. Parke and of William Parke (1820–93) of Clogher House, Kilmore?

Prior to her marriage with William, Henrietta (1830–95), daughter of General Holmes, lived at Newport House, Isle of Wight: their eldest son Benjamin (d. 1916) who married Edith Mary Newton Brady, daughter of the Resident Magistrate at Ennis, County Clare, became a bank manager in Galway. He eventually sold the lands of the Dunally and Kilmore estates to the Congested Districts Board; another son died penniless in the USA; Captain William (b. 1861) served with the Connacht Rangers in the Boer War and died France 1916 three weeks after his marriage to Rita Houston; Henrietta ('Harrie') lived in Cork after marrying George Stoker — their numerous descendants include Mrs Myrtle Allen of Ballymaloe, County Cork, Sir Michael Parke Stoker, FRCP, of Cambridge, his son Christopher, grandson Michael and many others; Emily married Herbert Malley, solicitor; Florence remained unwed; Isabel married Lt Beatty, RN; Laura married Edwards Nealon; Molly (1874–1900).

22 See *DNB*.

23 J.D.H. Widdess, *History of the Royal College of Surgeons in Ireland* , 3rd edn (Dublin 1984).

24 He was fortunate to take blood from a compatible donor for nothing was then known about blood groups.

25 See 'The Forgotten Scholar' in J.B. Lyons's, *'What Did I Die Of?'* (Dublin 1991), pp. 103–22.

26 Knott's correspondence with Mrs Knott, RCSI.

27 Knott's correspondence, RCSI (henceforth, *Letters*).

28 Ibid.

29 Parke papers, RCSI undated.

30 The recruitment of the *voyageurs* is alluded to in *The Habitant and Other French Canadian Poems* (1897) by Dr William Henry Drummond of Montreal who was born in Mohill, County Leitrim, in 1854 and became famous for his verses in dialect: 'Of course, de Irishman 's de bes', raise all de row he can,/But noboddy can pull batteau lak good Canadian man.'

31 Royle, *Egyptian Campaigns*, p. 333.

32 Lord Charles Beresford, *The Memoirs of Lord Charles Beresford*, 2 Vols (London 1914), Vol I, p. 254.

33 T.H. Parke, 'How General Gordon Was Really Lost', *Nineteenth Century*, 1892; 31: 787–94.

34 Author of *Ride to Khiva, On Horseback Through Asia Minor* etc (London 1876), Frederick Gustavus Burnaby (b. Bradford 1842), traveller, soldier and linguist, joined the Nile Expedition in a purely voluntary capacity, but was nominated to succeed Stewart as first in command in the event of the latter's death.

35 *Letters.*

36 Parke, *Nineteenth Century*, 1892, p. 31.

37 J.R. Troup was critical of this gift which should, he said, have contained vital, condensed foods — 'but what earthly use were *jam, red herrings, sardines and fancy biscuits* to support life while in the bush...' (*Rear Column*, p. 153).

38 *Diary,* 9 February 1887.

39 *The Times,* 14 January 1887.

40 *IDA,* I, p. 43,

41 Jameson, *Story of the Rear Column*, p. xxi.

42 Barttelot, Walter G., ed., *The Life of Edmund Musgrave Bartellot* (London 1890), p. 54.

43 See Dorothy Middleton, *Diary of A. J. Mounteney Jephson*, p. 71.

44 Jameson, *op. cit.*, p. 3.

45 Ibid, p. 4.

46 Parke papers RCSI undated.

47 Ibid.

48 *Diary,* 1 March.

49 *Diary,* 9 March. The powder containing antimony introduced by Dr Robert James (1705–76) was a popular remedy for more than a century; it was favoured by Dr Johnson and Mrs Thrale, but was thought to have hastened the death of Oliver Goldsmith, who insisted on taking it against his doctor's advice.

50 *Diary,* 12 March.

2   The Lower Congo

The disadvantage of relying on river-steamers was soon evident. The vessels chartered for the expedition were simply not available. Cables had not been received and surprise was expressed at the *Madura's* early arrival. A number of the state steamers were under repair; the largest was stranded helplessly on a sandbank. But Stanley refused to accept excuses and in a matter of hours he had hired sufficient transport to make a start the next morning.

Jameson and Nelson headed up-river at 9.30 am on 19 March with 232 men in the Dutch Company's steamer, *K.A. Nieman*. Parke, accompanied by Walker, an engineer who joined the expedition at Cape Town, followed in the *S.S. Governor Albuquerque* with 124 men and a large cargo. Stanley took about 300 men in the *Serpa Pinto*, and Barttelot and Jephson brought up the remainder in the *Kacongo* and the *Heron*.

Now that he was actually on the river, Parke was too close to it to appreciate fully the enormous, incessant power capable of carrying its presence for a distance of 200 miles into the stained Atlantic; on the map the Congo resembled a snake — 'an immense snake uncoiled, with its head in the sea, its body at rest curving afar over a vast country, and its tail lost in the depths of the land'.[1] The heat reflected from the brown muddy water was what the steamer's passengers were really conscious of, as their eyes lifted to watch the woods and distant green vegetation extending to the skyline. They reached Boma, sixty-three miles from the sea, at 6.30 pm and tied up for the night, proceeding the next morning against a rapid stream to Ango-Ango, from where Parke and Nelson marched with their men to Matadi, seven miles away.

This primitive river-port, linking the Congo to the ocean, was to be visited in 1890 by Joseph Conrad who featured it as 'The Common Station' in *Heart of Darkness*. A few wooden, barrack-like structures were the station's salient features and in one of these Captain Marlow, Conrad's surrogate, encountered the Company's chief accountant who kept his books in apple-pie order — 'Everything else in the station was in a muddle, heads, things, buildings'. The accountant worked steadily in his hot office, but, when an invalid on a truckle-bed was given temporary shelter there, he resented it. '"The groans of this sick person," he said, "distract my attention."' Parke, fortunately, was of different mettle and professionally attentive.

Above Matadi, the long series of cataracts collectively called Livingstone Falls made the river unnavigable for steamers for over two hundred miles. The projected railway to link Leopoldville to the sea was still in the planners' minds. The existing reality was man-power and the expedition faced its first long portage. The cargo deposited by the river-steamers was divided into manageable loads and, with a temperature of 98°F in the shade, Parke supervised the transfer of rice into small sacks. Ammunition was packed into boxes of convenient size and an endless supply of spades, shovels, axes and billhooks had to be accounted for; the twelve parts of the steel boat, *Advance*, were assembled. 'Men paraded at 6 am and continued to work all day in the sun. I sent a message by Stairs to Stanley to say that the sun was too hot for the men to continue fatigue duty, especially as the white officers had to be present, but he took no notice. I put 185 large bags of rice into the Congo Free State (CFS) storehouse.'[2]

Stairs earned the cognomen 'Bwana Mazinga' — the master of the Maxim — by giving a demonstration with the machine-gun which fired 330 shots a minute and astonished Tippu Tib and his men. Rifles were distributed and revolvers were given to the officers but Parke preferred to hold on to 'an old campaigning bull-dog' which had been with him on the Bayuda Desert march. Personal allowances were strictly limited; Jameson forfeited some wearing apparel so that his collector's gear and heavy rifle could be carried; Parke was unable to bring his full stock of Irish whiskey.

Within a week of the arrival at Banana Point there were four deaths and fourteen sick men had to be left at Matadi with Lieutenant Baert, a CFS official. A man who died from heart failure had an old dislocation of the right elbow, chronic orchitis and bronchitis.

Parke must have begun to wonder what criteria of fitness, if any, Dr Hussey had applied at Zanzibar when accepting the porters. The concussed patient made a full recovery and returned to duty.

At 5.15 am on 25 March a trumpeter in the Soudanese camp sounded reveille. An hour later Stanley marched out of Matadi at the head of a vanguard bearing the Egyptian flag and the various companies of the expedition followed in single file on a 'road' that was merely a track. Ahead of them, testing to muscles weakened by the voyage, the path was hilly and uneven and the mile-long column straggled up and down masses of broken quartz and cinder-like rock. Parke noticed that many of the men had imbibed palm wine and were drunk.[3]

The Soudanese soldiers carried only their rifles, rations and clothing but were hampered by hooded greatcoats. The Somalis were unable to understand why camels were not available. The Zanzibaris bore 60 lbs loads on their heads, carrying also rifles, rations, clothing and bedding mats. Tippu Tib and his men were attired in spotless white Arab robes and the women, with their faces piously concealed, draped their bodies in bright garments. Horned African goats were driven by lively Zanzibari boys and the burdened donkeys tensed sinews unaccustomed to labour. The riding asses were not yet ready to be mounted. Stanley provided a saddle for each officer but Parke, fussy in such matters, brought his own saddle with him from Alexandria.

Arriving at the thirty-yard wide Mpozo River, the steel boat was reassembled to ferry the expedition across in groups of fifty. They camped on the opposite bank and next morning at 5 am set off for Palabella which they reached by noon. The officers enjoyed luncheon and the hospitality of Mr and Mrs Clarke and Mr and Mrs Ingham at the Livingstone Inland Mission Station where the expedition camped until 28 March to allow recovery from the initial fatigue. Stanley had an enormous tent which required a special detachment of porters; each officer had a single tent, and there was a mess tent. Tippu Tib had a tent for himself and his wives. This was equipped with 'what might be called a large back-yard, enclosed with some light canvas or cloth, "to cheat surprising, prying eyes" from obtaining a glimpse of his numerous spouses whilst engaged in their domestic occupations'.[4] The Zanzibaris put up with simpler arrangements — 'They ran up small huts of sticks, roughly thatched with grass, just large enough for a man to crawl into; but the more fortunate ones, who were able to get possession of large pieces of thin sheeting-cloth, constructed impromptu tents.' The Soudanese usually found shelter under trees or bushes.[5]

The arduous journey from Matadi to Leopoldville took twenty-seven days to complete and was a paradigm of more terrible ordeals that lay ahead between Yambuya and the Albert Nyanza (Lake). Hunger and violence are inevitably encountered on long marches; even a semblance of order necessitates iron discipline—suffering and deaths are hardly to be avoided. The rewards, if any, are not to be reckoned in monetary terms; if travellers are to be repaid at all it is in the honing of courage, the warmth of comradeship, and possibly the lifting of nature's veil.

At times the column was stretched out over five miles and laggards were flogged to hurry them. The loss of a rifle or a load was severely punished and a number of Zanzibaris found themselves in chains. When the Soudanese soldiers, on short rations, grumbled to the point of mutiny Stanley said he would shoot the first mutinous man with his hand-gun. Assad Farran, a Syrian, protested that he had come as an interpreter or a servant but Stanley replied 'that his lot was cast with the Soudanese and he would share their fate'.[6]

Frayed tempers led to unpleasant incidents. A Soudanese almost strangled a Zanzibari because the latter had touched the soldier's shoulder with his load. Tippu Tib's brother-in-law, Selim, had an altercation with Jephson who threatened haughtily to throw him into the river. Delayed by a river crossing, Parke led his men through a pitch-black forest relieved to have a primitive light — 'Fortunately Tippu Tib gave me a candle so I managed to get my donkey along with me'.[7]

Supplies of rice and biscuits had been sent ahead from Matadi to Lukungu Station, where two Belgian officers were able to offer four days' rations of palm nuts, potatoes, bananas, brinjalls and Indian corn for 800 travellers. Hunger, nevertheless, eroded discipline and the Zanzibaris did not hesitate to throw down their loads and raid a plantation of bananas or a field of manioc. A Zanzibari chief, intent on plunder, was shot dead by a native who dared to defend his property. The latter, 'the murderer', was immediately slain by the invaders.

One of Tippu Tib's men had his left hand shattered by a bullet but wisely declined to let Parke amputate it. The doctor put eleven stitches into a leg lacerated by a hatchet; his patient continued the march as there was no alternative transport. Quite early on Stanley had an attack of violent diarrhoea which at first he ascribed to eating the guavas of Congo la Lemba and Parke labelled dysentery.

I gave him grs v of lead and opium. He had six rears [bowel movements] within $^1/_2$ an hour. I had him carried to the next camp as he was almost pulseless and quite blanched. Arrived at camp about 11 am, gave him rice, milk, beef-tea, arrowroot and 5 grs of Dover's [powder].[8]

Next day, though greatly improved, the MO insisted that the leader be carried in a hammock. By afternoon Stanley was well enough to remount his donkey.

This illness had an unexpected sequel affecting Stanley's relationships with Parke and Jameson. When the latter ventured to commiserate with his leader he was astonished by Stanley's response. 'I have only you to thank for it,' Stanley snapped and went on to blame Jameson, caterer for the week, for depriving him of meat. Indignantly, Jameson denied the charge and decided to have as little as possible to do with cooking arrangements in future.

Some days later, Stanley accused Parke of losing two rifles, which the MO denied. Told next day that he had lost nineteen rifles, he turned the accusation aside humorously, saying that at this rate he'd soon have lost all the expedition's guns.

Stanley seemed determined to put Parke in the wrong, anxious, perhaps, to re-assert his ascendancy following an embarrassing illness during which the MO's authority had prevailed. He called him to his tent in the evening to question him about the provision boxes. He explained silkily that the Zanzibaris told him that an officer had opened one of them. There had been similar occurrences, he added softly, on former expeditions leaving him with very little.

Parke did not attempt to conceal his annoyance. He replied curtly and factually. Stanley's present officers differed from his previous ones. The Zanzibari informers could surely have given him the name of the officer concerned. It was, indeed, Parke himself — he had opened a provision box to obtain milk, beef-tea and arrowroot for his patient.[9]

Defensively, Stanley riposted that it wasn't a matter to get angry about. But on the following evening, to make amends, the doctor was a guest in Stanley's tent. They smoked cigars and laughingly agreed that the report of Barttelot threatening to shoot Uledi, coxwain of the *Advance*, was a joke and not to be taken seriously, but they were actually underestimating the Major's uncontrollable temper.

Stanley remained a disturbing and unfriendly enigma to his officers. Jameson resented the way he rode 'straight ahead to the next camp' while the officers arrived hours later after work more suitable for slave-drivers.[10] Stanley, on the other hand, felt it was in his juniors' interest to get experience of directing the caravan. He claimed the role of mediator, skilled in intervening in disagreements between black men and white, but sometimes his interventions placed the officers in a false position.

On one such occasion when Jameson had reported that a man in his company was too ill to proceed, Stanley insisted that he should see that he went on. Obediently, acting against his better feelings, Jameson forced the man to rise and trudge on only to collapse after a few steps just as Stanley happened to pass by. The latter, seemingly full of concern, sent for Parke and told him to get the ailing man into a hut and look after him. To the onlookers, Jameson appeared to be a brute, Stanley a guardian-angel.[11] Stanley was *Bula Matari*, the 'stone-breaker', a cognomen earned in 1877; when coming

34

upon a group vainly attempting to break a boulder, he took up the sledge-hammer and judging the direction of the planes of cleavage correctly shattered the stone with a single blow. His 'General Orders', issued while on the *Madura*, decreed that 'for trivial offences a slight corporal punishment only can be inflicted, and this as seldom as possible'. But his own aggression lay so close to the surface that when the Soudanese and Zanzibaris had a row about a cooking-pot he amazed the bystanders by the way he ended it — 'by battering all round indiscriminately with a big stick'.[12] And yet, after a more pleasant social occasion, Jameson could say that Stanley 'when he throws off his reserve is one of the most agreeable of men and full of information'.[13]

The hills continued to present difficulty, especially when wet but the expedition also crossed beautiful, flat grasslands and passed through valleys filled with flowers and tropical vegetation, with gorgeously coloured foliage. Moments of despondency could be relieved, as Jameson found, when, having remonstrated for hours with refractory carriers, he came upon Parke seated under a tree. The doctor gave Jameson a drink of Irish whiskey *Jameson's Best Thirteen Years Old*, 'and then everything changed to a brighter hue'.[14]

Many rivers had to be crossed or forded. Sometimes a perilous wire suspension bridge was available, or it might be possible to improvise a bridge by felling trees to lie across the stream, an art in which Stanley excelled. The *Advance* was supremely useful when available but Stanley ordered Jephson and Walker to take it on with a crew and cargo to Manyanga.

Sometimes a dug-out canoe could be obtained locally and on an occasion when there was no other possible way to ford a rapid stream Stanley had a double rope stretched across it and 'the loads were passed from hand to hand, the men standing shoulder-deep holding the rope with one hand'. The entire column had crossed by 5 pm and the march continued until 9 — 'the last hour or so was spent trying to find our way through the forest which was pitch dark'.[15]

Stairs' donkey broke a leg coming down a steep bank and had to be shot. Parke's donkey fell when crossing a small river, drenching its rider. When going through a muddy marsh, Jameson's beast slipped into the mud, which filled the saddle-bags containing part of his collector's outfit.

Two weeks out from Matadi there had been thirty deserters and the doctor had left a number of ailing men at the mission stations along the way. By now the Europeans had brick-red faces ('vermilion' according to Stanley) and Parke's arms were blistered. He tried the palm wine 'which was as smart in going to my head as to my tummy'.[16] A number of elephants and antelopes were sighted and, at an elevation of 2000 feet, the nights were cold; the daytime heat was sometimes prostrating, even for the Africans, and the torrential rain hard to bear. Barttelot, unhappy with the sullen disputatious Soudanese, envied Jephson on the water in the *Advance* while the latter expressed a wish to be with the main body rather than on the turbulent river. Parke, in addition to his professional duties, supervised Jephson's men, Troup's men and his own company. He agreed to take over the duties of mess caterer from the disillusioned Jameson but suspected he was being imposed upon.[17]

Reached Lutete Missionary Station early [Parke wrote on 13 April] and dried our clothes. Beautiful tropical plants in the villages around... We were well treated by the Baptist Missionaries 5 or 6 in number. We were not asked to dinner. I left two sick, unable to march from remittent fever. Rice was distributed yesterday to carry us on to Stanley Pool, about eight or nine days ahead.

Struggling along within the caravan, Parke's attention was occupied fully by the effort to keep pace and to maintain order within his company but to any onlooker the long, brightly-coloured procession offered a deceptive air of pageantry. Herbert Ward, who had joined Troup and Charles Ingham on the American Baptist Mission to enlist porters for the expedition, described how he encountered the flag-bearer coming over the brow of a hill:

Behind him and astride of a fine henna-stained mule, whose silver plated trappings shone in the bright morning sun, was Mr Henry M. Stanley, attired in his famous African costume.[18] Following immediately in his rear were his personal servants, Somalis with their curious braided waistcoats and white robes; then came Zanzibaris with their blankets, water bottles, ammunition belts and guns; stalwart Soudanese soldiers with dark hooded coats, their rifles on their backs, and innumerable straps and leather belts around their bodies. Zanzibari porters bearing iron-bound boxes of ammmunition, to which were fastened axes and shovels, as well as their bundles of clothing, which were rolled up in coarse, sandy-colored blankets.[19]

Stanley waved Ward to a seat (on the ground), handed him a cigar taken from a silver case presented to him by HRH the Prince of Wales on the night before he left London, listened to the young man's expression of interest in the expedition and enlisted him (unpaid) on the spot. A widely-travelled artist with a knowledge of three African languages, Ward was the last of Stanley's recruits at officer level. He was an accomplished person by any standard and one wonders what slip of the pen, or the imagination, led Frank McLynn to refer to Stanley's lieutenants as 'an unprepossessing band'.[20]

When they camped at the Inkissi River on 16 April, Roger Casement, then working for the Sanford Exploring Expedition and very friendly with Ward, happened to be going in their direction. They saw a lot of Casement in the next few days. Barttelot thought him 'a real good chap' but just then Parke was 'very seedy' and not up to conviviality. Jephson admired Casement's spacious tent and envied his affluent retinue. 'It was delightful sitting down to a real dinner at a real table with a table cloth and dinner napkins and plenty to eat, with Burgundy to drink ... and this in the middle of the wilds.'[21]

Casement (b. Dublin 1864) was to play a major part in expedition work in Africa and beyond; he reported later on the inhuman treatment of native workers in the Belgian Congo (1904) and subsequently investigated conditions in the Peruvian rubber plants along the Putamyo River exposing the cruelty of the white traders. Sir Roger Casement was executed for treason in Pentonville Prison on 3 August 1916, attaining a place in the hagiography of Irish nationalism.

Reveille was sounded at daybreak on 21 April and after a long and wearying march the roofs of Leopoldville (Kinsasha) were sighted towards noon. Jameson described it as a 'a pretty spot, looking right up the Pool' but for Parke, feeling 'somewhat beaten' after a bout of fever and the exhausting march, the place itself was of little importance — 'there are only a few rather primitive huts here and, including missionaries, traders and CFS officers, about a dozen white men in all'[22] — but it offered the promise of re-embarkation and the expectation of relief from fatigue.

As something approaching famine conditions prevailed at Leopoldville, Jameson was sent to shoot hippos for meat. The men were installed in comfortable green huts but Nelson and Parke were laid up with fever. For several days the latter had been 'going at both ends'; now he moved to a straw-and-mud hut near the river. He handed his company over to Bonny and stayed in bed, taking 'all sorts of medicines'[23] and sustaining himself with nutrient enemas of milk and arrowroot. He returned to duty on 24 April.

Notes

1 Joseph Conrad, *Heart of Darkness*.
2 *Diary*, 23 March 1887.
3 *Diary*, 25 March.
4 Troup, *Rear Column*, p. 72.
5 Ibid.
6 *Diary*, 8 April. Obliged to remain with the rear-column, Assad Farran was an unreliable witness to the happenings at Yambuya.
7 *Diary*, 30 March.
8 *Diary*, 31 March. A preparation containing opium, *Pulvis Ipecacuanhae Compositus*, is a

celebrated remedy introduced by Thomas Dover (1660–1742) which was still in use well into the present century. Dover saw his patients at the Jerusalem Coffee House, in London. A sometime buccaneer, his fame as a physician is rivalled by his rescue of Alexander Selkirk (prototype of Robinson Crusoe) from the island of Juan Fernandez in the South Pacific.

9   *Diary*, 10 April.
10   Jameson, *Story of Rear Column*, p. 14.
11   Ibid, p. 20.
12   *Diary*, 13 April.
13   Jameson, *op. cit.*, p. 33.
14   Ibid, p. 19.
15   *Diary*, 30 March.
16   *Diary*, 12 April.
17   *Diary*, 7 April.
18   Stanley wore 'a Norfolk jacket, with continuations in the shape of knickerbockers ... his head-gear was a large flat-topped cap with a peak in front, such as is worn by officers in the German army' (Troup, *Rear Column*, p. 89).
19   Herbert Ward, *Five Years With the Congo Cannibals* (London 1890), p. 33. It will be noted that Stanley has been promoted from a donkey to a mule.

    An avid reader of travel books in boyhood, Herbert Ward embarked on his own travels at the age of fifteen at the risk of being disinherited. Before taking service as a transport officer on the Lower Congo he had spent some years in New Zealand, Australia and Borneo moving from one job to another, stock-rider, circus performer and miner. He was a talented painter and sculptor.
20   Frank McLynn, *Hearts of Darkness* (London 1992), p. 103.
21   Jephson's *Diary*, p. 88.
22   *Diary*, 21 April.
23   *Diary*, 22 April.

3 The Upper Congo

Stanley sensed a reluctance on the part of local officials to provide steamers, and the Church Mission's incumbent did not wish to deal with 'a man whose life was accursed before God, and whose every act was one of cruelty'.[1] But he stressed the urgency of the situation and by sheer will-power and reminding influential persons that they were indebted to him, he hired three wood-burning vessels, the *Stanley*, the *Peace* and the *Henry Reed*; also a barge, *En Avant*, and the hull of the *Florida*, whose engine was being repaired.

Parke and Barttelot left Leopoldville on 25 April, with most of their men in the *Stanley*, under orders to send the boat back from Lishar and to proceed overland to Mswata. After five-and-a-half hours steaming they stopped at an American mission station to cut wood, a chore to which Parke returned on the following morning at 4.30 am, continuing until he suddenly experienced a chill and felt ill. Barttelot was also febrile, his temperature 101°F.

When they disembarked at Lishar the natives, accustomed to the depre-dations of the CFS officers who had burned their villages, fled into the bush. Parke followed them, unarmed, with an interpreter and managed to calm their fears. A palaver followed and having given the chief thirty-nine matakas Parke was provided with guides.

Next day the guides refused to go any further and new ones were ob-tained. On 30 April they completed a march of sixteen miles and halted at a morass in the centre of a large, grassy plain where peaty drinking water was available. Parke shot a few pigeons which they ate. Mswata was a day's march away.

On 1 May Jameson embarked up-river in the *Stanley*, which had the Florida lashed to its side to increase its capacity. The flotilla put out into the stream and the expedition was on the move after unconscionable delays. Jameson regretted that so far his general duties had left him without leisure to devote to vocational interests. He found the expedition gloomy and devoid of enjoyment. If something did raise a laugh it seemed to die abruptly. The scenery, admittedly, offered compensations and his naturalist's eye picked out the geese, the soaring eagles, the solemn cranes standing on the river-bank, the kingfishers darting out of the forest to hover over the water, the gorgeous bee-eaters 'their colours glittering in the sun'.[2]

At Mswata on 5 May Jameson found Parke and Barttelot flourishing. 'Their tent was pitched right in the centre of the town, if it may be so called, amidst quantities of bananas.'[3] The pair merited their rest, for despite spells of fever they were now told to march to Kwamouth from where the *Stanley* would take them to Bolobo. Not, indeed, that they had been prodigal with their leisure time; they had amassed a great quanity of wood for the devouring furnaces, a gift for which they got no thanks from Stanley.[4]

Finding Jephson and Nelson ill, Parke dispensed an appropriate remedy. A man in Jephson's company had died and the doctor arranged for three sick men to be taken on board in exchange for three of his own men who were glad to return to him.

The quick-tempered Major did not favour the soft approach: 'I went to King Gondana and told him, giving him a smart prod with a stick, that unless guides were forthcoming in five minutes the soldiers would burn his village.'[5] Parke and Bartellot resumed their march at 5.30 am and spent the night at the hospitable French Mission. At Kwamouth where the Kassai River was darker than the Congo, the saws and axes were again plied energetically so as to have enough wood for the *Stanley*. The steamer arrived on 12 May and two days later Parke did his sick rounds at Bolobo; he dressed Jephson's palmar abscess and dealt with Jameson's broken nail.

Ward had joined the expedition 'in the hope of stirrings adventures with gun and pencil',[6] but because shipping space was at a premium Stanley decided to leave 128 of the weaker men at Bolobo where there was an abundance of bread, fish and bananas. He selected Ward, at ease in Swahili, to take charge of them, with Bonny as companion. They would follow on when the *Stanley* returned. Parke went on board the *Henry Reed* and Barttelot with his Soudanese joined the *Stanley*. After the overland journey the change should have been restful, but for Parke the voyage was spoiled:

I found extremely uncomfortable quarters on board the *Henry Reed* as there was only one cabin, and eleven filthy dirty highly smelling women of Tippu Tib's harem occupied it by day and I was obliged to sleep in this den at night. I spent most of my time on deck to get fresh air and retained a quarter of the cabin which I partitioned off by a blanket for myself to wash and dress in.[7]

It was customary for the Africans to sleep on shore, going on board after daybreak to permit an early start. Parke's disgust at the crowded conditions remained unmitigated and when Tippu Tib consulted him about a minor ailment the doctor availed of the opportunity to recommend that he should have his women washed. These ladies 'lounged and lolled about in the saloon in a dreamy, sickly state', but they were assertive and knew how to have their own way.

I got all the heavy baggage and boxes etc., etc., which I could collect and barricaded off a quarter of the saloon for myself but these beasts of women would force their legs through between the boxes exposing their legs up to their hips so as to lie at full length. Sometimes with their united strength they would push all my barricade of boxes down and squeeze me into a corner until I would have to scream for mercy.[8]

If he retaliated by sticking them with a pin 'their snarls and yells' brought their lord and master down from the deck to defend them. Parke's appeal to the Captain for olfactory relief was referred to Stanley, as to a Solomon, for a decision, but letting the side down the leader settled the matter in favour of Tippu Tib and his women.[9]

The overhanging branches of trees growing on the undermined banks made landing difficult when, towards afternoon, wood was needed. Tracks of elephants and buffalo were seen. Hippopotami and crocodiles were numerous. The river broadened to more than eleven miles above Bolobo; it was divided by islands into many streams and every now and then one or other of the steamers went aground.

Parke's diary is a factual record written by a man of average descriptive powers with little art to highlight his encounter with the primeval. Stanley, struck by the monotonous panoramas of unending forest, likened the sun-burnished channels of calm water to 'rivers of quicksilver', an uninspired metaphor. The same reach of river is recalled in reverie by Joseph Conrad's surrogate, Captain Marlow, in *Heart of Darkness* :

Going up that river was like travelling back to the earliest beginnings of the world, when vegetation rioted on the earth and the big trees were kings. An empty stream, a great silence, an impenetrable forest. The air was warm, thick, heavy, sluggish. There was no joy in the brilliance of sunshine. The long stretches of the waterway ran on, deserted, into the gloom of overshadowed distances... The broadening waters flowed through a mob of wooded islands; you lost your way on that river as you would in a desert, and butted all day long against shoals, trying to find the channel, till you thought yourself bewitched and cut off for ever from everything you had once known — somewhere — far away — in another existence perhaps.

The Baptist Mission at Lukolela was reached on 19 May, a straw hut where two very agreeable young Englishmen lived in what Parke described as 'solitary innocence of what is going on in Europe', perfectly content to proselytize the natives. Jameson and Nelson were 'seedy' with what the doctor called 'catarrh of the intestines and stomach' and distinguished subtly from dysentery.[10] He gave them milk and medicines and dosed several other sick men for a variety of complaints.

There was a blazing row at Lukolela when Stanley sided with a group of Zanzibaris who alleged that they had been punished unfairly by Stairs and Jephson. The officers said they had merely confiscated plunder obtained by unjustifiable looting, but Stanley insisted that, nine times out of ten, in disagreements of this kind the black man was right, the white man wrong. He had only to raise a finger, he warned Stairs, and the Zanzibaris would rush on him and club him to death.

Carried away by the pain of his infected hand, Jephson told his chief not to speak so loudly as he wasn't deaf, his upper-class accent amplifying his insolence. Outraged, Stanley lost his temper completely: 'You damned son of a sea-cook', he shouted, 'God damn you, you come here with a lie in your mouth you damned puppy. You are tyrants. Look how I deal with my men.' He challenged his juniors to put up their fists and fight him, upbraided them scurrilously and declared that they were dismissed and might as well go off into the bush. He ended his tirade by telling the Zanzibaris that should there be a recurrence they were to take the white men and tie them to a tree.

The startled missionaries said they never wanted to hear such foul language again and when the storm subsided Parke ventured to speak on behalf of his colleagues who were, he insisted, 'loyal and useful men'. The doctor was taken aback to be told by the irate and unrepentant leader that he and Barttelot had escaped the same fate narrowly when Barttelot struck a man with an iron bar during their march from Mswata. 'I collapsed entirely and sloped off', Parke noted in his diary, but at his suggestion Stairs and Jephson swallowed their pride and apologized to Stanley.[11] Peace was thus restored and when the journey was resumed at daybreak the dismissals were forgotten.

There was a profusion of vegetation on the river-banks where the swinging and jumping of hundreds of monkeys made a diverting picture, but wood-cutting and the purchase of provisions took precedence over this attractive spectacle.

Each officer was allowed four mattakas a day to buy food but, as that amount bought only a very small chicken, Parke reflected that 'we shall soon be in racing condition'. And besides, fowls were scarce. Parke, the captain of the *Henry Reed* and Walker, the engineer, certainly would not have existed comfortably on two chickens for four days if the captain had not added beans and rice to the menu. Goats were purchased occasionally, permitting a feast, but during Ramadan the Soudanese and Tippu Tib's followers abstained from food until after sunset.

By now an accumulation of difficulties had confirmed Stanley's decision to form an advance party of strong and fit men, carrying light loads, to proceed as rapidly as possible to the Albert Nyanza, leaving a rear column based at Bolobo and Yambuya. Ward and Bonny, as we have seen, stayed behind at Bolobo and Major Barttelot was to be placed in charge of an entrenched camp to be established at Yambuya on the Aruwimi River more than 1300 miles from the sea. They would follow on later when the men were stronger and Tippu Tib had provided additional porters.

Barttelot accepted the command under protest but Stanley insisted that he was the senior officer and reminded him, flatteringly, of his distinguished record in Afghanistan and the Soudan campaign and his achievement in leading a column of a thousand men from Kosseir on the Red Sea to Keneh on the Nile. One suspects that Stanley disliked Barttelot. They rarely saw eye to eye and Barttelot in Stanley's opinion was too aggressive and lacked forbearance. Nevertheless, he allowed him to nominate a second-in command and Barttelot selected the naturalist James Sligo Jameson.[12]

'Very well, sir', Jameson said, accepting this unwelcome commission without further comment, but in his diary he wrote: 'It is frightfully hard luck on me.'[13]

Arrived at Equator Station [Parke wrote on 24 May] 1½ miles north of the Line about 5.30 pm. This Station consists of two houses, one occupied by the Baptist Missionaries one of whom is an Irishman, the first up this far on the Congo. The 2nd house is occupied by Mr Glave of the Sanford Expedition and Captain Vangel [sic] of the CF State. Ivory is the chief trade, it is bought for forks and spoons, plates, beads, cloth etc etc. This ivory is afterwards sold for 10/- per lb and realizes a couple of hundred per cent.

The officers dined with Glave and Vangèle and greedily relished the unaccustomed luxury of bread, salt, mustard and sugar. On 25 May Parke was transferred to the *Stanley*, the largest steamer, which carried 350 men some of whom were mortally ill. Five days later at Bangala, Parke saw some cases of elephantiasis, a grossly disfiguring disorder causing swelling of limbs and scrotum. This was the furthest point up-river at which white men were stationed. After dinner, on 30 May, Stanley made a speech and King Leopold II was toasted with Bangala's last bottle of champagne.

Next morning Barttelot set off in the *Henry Reed* to deposit Tippu Tib and his contingent at Stanley Falls and rejoin the expedition. The other vessels resumed the tedious journey to Yambuya and steaming away from Bangala, following the *Peace* which had Stanley on board, Parke felt they were now leaving 'civilization' and entering an unknown and possibly hostile region.

There had been three predicted deaths and both Jephson and Jameson were feverish.

The latter recorded an expectation of early recovery in his diary on 3 June: 'Bad night; had to lie up again all day, but got better towards evening thanks to old Parke who has given me the right medicine to begin with, and topped it up with arrowroot, milk and brandy.' On the following evening at dusk some hippopotami, the first seen for many days, came close to the steamer. Parke shot at one of them with his rifle but the bullet went over the submerging head and a flight of owls passed by undisturbed.

At Upoto 'the men came on to the shore in full force all armed with spears and shields' but, after a lengthy palaver, Stairs went through the ceremony of blood-brotherhood with the chief; then food was offered generously by the natives and they were permitted to cut wood. The *Peace* was late to arrive, having steamed ahead the previous day and, passing out of sight, had taken a different channel. When Stanley came ashore he was furious to have wasted time searching for the companion vessel. He addressed them, quite unreasonably, as 'deserters' and threatened to treat them as such. 'You call yourselves gentlemen to do this?' But the *Peace's* captain told Parke privately that the separation had decidedly been Stanley's fault.[14]

Though Parke must have seen Dublin's daughters in their natural state at the maternity hospitals he was embarrassed by the female nudity which increased in completeness as they went up the Congo. At Bangala the women had worn 'picturesque fringes of brown bark cloth – like little kilts';[15] elsewhere they tied large banana-leaves cut into narrow strips around their waists, the bright green making an effective contrast to their dark skins. At Upoto, where they wore 'no Clothes whatever', they 'come up to you with baskets of manioc and mealies in the most unreserved and shameless manner'.[16]

Two days later, Parke reports: There was a terrible catastrophe owing to the centre deck houses falling over to one side, as they support the upper deck which was crowded with our men and was not strongly enough made. Supports were cut and placed in the weakest places. Passed a large village where the natives showed fight but as we all had plantains, manioc, goats and chickens we were not obliged to come into contact with them.[17]

Cannibalism flourished in the neighbourhood of Upoto. Pagan idols were sold and 'they sell necklaces and ornaments made from dried fingers and the teeth of those they devoured'.[18] It seems to have held a morbid fascination for Jameson, the gentlest of the officers. Captain Hausen of the CFS Service told him how three of his Houssas (native soldiers), captured by natives near the mouth of the Aurwimi, were tied to a tree and crammed with food to fatten them. Two were eaten, but the third, a scrawny middle-aged fellow, managed to escape. The Rev. William Holman Bentley of the Baptist Mission knew of the existence of cannibalism in areas above Stanley Pool, sometimes confined to those who had been killed for witchcraft. 'When remonstrated with, the natives have replied, "You kill your goats, and no one finds fault with you; let us kill our meat then."'[19] At their ghastly feasts, parents gave choice morsels of cooked human flesh to the children who thus acquired a taste for it.

Progressing slowly up-river they continued to see armed natives on the banks, their bodies covered with bright-red clay, and passed war canoes in the water each manned by fourteen men. Wood-cutting continued until late into the night against the illumination provided by blazing fires, which created a macabre spectacle as the animated, ebony figures of glistening axemen with white flashing eyes were outlined against the still frieze of the dark forest.

They passed a burned village which they learned had been destroyed by a neighbouring tribe because of a dispute over a woman, and made camp for the night, on 12 May, opposite Basoko, an island at the confluence of the Congo and Aruwimi Rivers. The frightened natives now remained hidden in the long grass and refused to trade. Fourteen months previously the *Stanley* had carried men from the Congo Free State who raided the village. Parke performed an operation to remove a piece of dead bone from the arm of a Zanzibari, accidentally wounded by a hatchet.

The natives' timidity concealed their latent aggression, creating a dilemma that did not need philosophic debate in an Africa where might was right.

Last night we commenced our first loot. Having stopped opposite a small village the men went on shore but could find no provisions except the plantains. We stopped for the night and the natives fled into the bush. Tom-toms and horns were sounding high in all the villages around so as to prepare all the inhabitants for the war path. Two minutes after pushing off from the bank this morning the natives swarmed to the banks with their shields and spears ready. They had been waiting in ambush [hoping that] by concealing themselves in the bush they would noiselessly collect in such numbers that they would finally surround us and resistance would be futile.[20]

Looting had to be a calculated policy for an expedition obliged to live off the land. Cowries, beads, brass rods and white or red handkerchiefs were the acceptable currency for barter but if the trade-goods were refused, or the distrustful natives refused to parley, necessity ruled and whatever was available was taken forcibly. A well-cultivated village could be expected to pro-

vide fields of manioc and sugar cane, herb gardens and Indian corn, plantations of bananas and plantains. If fortune smiled, goats and fowls were an
added bounty, but flesh meat was usually unobtainable.

At Yambuya, which was reached towards evening on 15 June, the river
was not more than 500 yards wide and a cataract marked the upper level of
navigation for steamers. The *Peace* and the *Stanley* were made fast to the
bank opposite the village and its occupation was planned. They were to have
steam up at 6 am. The *Peace* would cross the river while the *Stanley* just kept
headway in the centre of the stream. If the unwelcoming natives refused
permission to land, the *Peace* would sound its steam-whistle as a signal for the
Stanley to join her. Stanley and Jephson would then force an immediate
landing and Stairs, if necessary, would add support with the machine-gun
from the *Stanley's* upper deck.

In the event, however, the village was taken without bloodshed: after a
long palaver permission was refused, but when the steam-whistle blew and
the advance party's men scrambled up a steep bank the natives fled.[21] The
next twelve days were devoted to entrenching Yambuya and building a
stockade 350 paces in circumference to secure it against attack. Stairs completed a clearing around the camp; Jephson's men cut wood for the steamers;
Parke searched the neighbourhood for manioc plantations.

I was sent with a reconnoitring party to discover the extent of the manioc fields. I
found they were of extensive size ... and will sustain the garrison which we leave,
but there is little or no prospect of getting any other provisions as game is scarce, on
account of the river bank being very high which prevents the animals coming down
for water. Hippos also seem scarce. The natives refuse to sell any food but perhaps
may change their minds ... when they see that they will be paid and not robbed of
their goods as they have been accustomed to.[22]

Houses were built for the officers and as there was no meat available they
lived on rice, manioc cakes and beans with biscuits.[23] Supervising the construction of the stockade, Stanley spurred them to greater efforts and with
pleasure watched Parke, a competent carpenter, making the main gate,
cheerful and smiling but concentrating 'as though he were at a surgical
operation'.[24] On 20 June the *Stanley*, generously provided with wood, started
for Leopoldville, where the stores left there with Troup were to be loaded.
Then, returning up-river, Ward and Bonny with their men and cargo would
be collected from Bolobo and taken on to Yambuya.

Tuesday, 21 June – No natives have as yet come in, although a few paddle their canoes
close to the bank and sell fish to our men. Nearly all the natives who deserted this
village have gone and settled on the opposite side of the river close to the water. My

boy has broken one of my water bottles which is a nuisance as water may be scarce on the march.

Barttelot made a delayed arrival from Stanley Falls in the *Henry Reed* on 22 June much to the relief of Stanley who feared he had met with misfortune. He brought with him two fine fat goats. Alexander, the second interpreter, died of dysentery and one of the Soudanese was attacked by a native while foraging for food. The penetrating abdominal injury dismayed Parke but he dealt with it effectively and his patient recovered. The departure of the *Peace* with the *Henry Reed* for Leopoldville was an opportunity to send letters and gifts. Parke sent home ivory, two spears and shields, a paddle with an ivory-tipped handle and a native woman's fringe skirt.

The 'obstinate' natives, quite understandably, remained unfriendly and unforgiving towards this veiled imperialism. Their drums expressed their unease and anger, but there was no attack. They refused to trade for food, despite gifts of beads, but the outlook seemed more auspicious when a local chief went through the ceremony of blood-brotherhood with Barttelot. The latter sought an interview with Stanley and ventilated his misgivings about the trustworthiness of Tippu Tib. He expressed surprise at the way in which Stanley favoured the Arab, to be told immediately how vital it was that this should be done.

Stanley squashed his subordinate. 'Why, how can you — grown to the rank of Major — ask such questions, or doubt the why and wherefore of acts which are as clear as daylight?' Without Tippu Tib's continuing approval they could not have existed for a single week in his territory and for that reason, and for no other, Stanley had 'shared the kid and the lamb with him.'[25]

Thursday, 23 June – Alexander, our second interpreter (with the Soudanese), died from acute dysentery supervening on a very weak debilitated constitution. Cut wood to bring the *Peace* and *Henry Reed* down river. Some of the Soudanese went out foraging and one got severely wounded by a spear which penetrated the abdomen and glanced along the illium. I brought the parts together with hare lip pins. He lies in a very precarious condition.

Stairs ran a high temperature for several days. Parke dosed him with quinine and gave him Warburg's tincture but without benefit.[26] Then, suspecting typhoid fever, he told Stanley that Stairs was unfit to travel. In that case, Stanley decreed, the doctor should stay with his patient and Jameson must hold himself ready to go in his place. But to the latter's disappointment Stairs 'was full of hope for a speedy recovery', and, changing his diagnosis to malaria, Parke altered his prognosis and felt that the change would be beneficial.[27] Stanley, reflecting fatalistically that 'if death is the issue, it comes as easy in the jungle as in the camp', agreed that Stairs should accompany them.[28]

Barttelot was given explicit written orders. The *Stanley* was expected back in Yambuya before 10 August with stores from Leopoldville and Bolobo — ammunition, provisions and trade-goods required as currency when travelling in the region beyond the lakes. The steamer should also bring the men left with Ward and Bonny, and Tippu Tib had promised to supply 600 carriers. When the officers of the rear column felt 'sufficiently competent'[29] to do so they should follow closely the route taken by the advance party (which would be indicated by blazed trees and marked saplings) and use its bomas or make-shift defensive barricades. As soon as Stanley had contacted Emin Pasha and ascertained his intentions, he would march towards Yambuya to reunite the expedition.

Should Tippu Tib fail to send enough porters they must use their discretion as to what might be discarded, but ammunition, trade-goods (beads, brass wire, cowries etc.) and sappers' tools were to be regarded as of prime importance. If after a reasonable reduction of loads the caravan still could not proceed it would be better to make short marches twice over than to discard the vitally important stores.[30]

Warned against hostile natives and marauding Arabs, Barttelot was left in no doubt that the loss of men and stores would spell ruin for the expedition. His detailed orders could have directed him, had things gone according to plan, but Stanley had not reckoned on Tippu Tib's fatal delay in providing carriers or his own failure to return as promised in November; these circumstances were to make the Major doubt his competence to advance and oblige him to exercise his legitimate discretion, month after month, to remain at Yambuya.

Notes

1 Barttelot, *Life*, p. 67.
2 Jameson, *Story of Rear Column*, p. 41.
3 Ibid, p. 37.
4 *Diary*, 5 May 1887.
5 Barttelot, *op. cit.*, p. 91.
6 Ward, *Five Years*, p. 31.
7 *Diary*, 14 May.
8 *Diary*, vol. 4, undated.
9 Barttelot, *op. cit.*, p. 93.
10 *Diary*, 18 May.
11 *Diary*, 20 May.

12 *IDA*, I, p. 102.
13 Jameson, *op. cit.*, p. 43.
14 *Diary*, 6 June.
15 *Diary*, 30 May.
16 *Diary*, 7 June.
17 *Diary*, 9 June.
18 *Diary*, 7 June.
19 W. Holman Bentley, *Life on the Congo* (London 1893), p. 64.
20 *Diary*, 14 June.
21 This detail re-echoes in Conrad's *Heart of Darkness*.
22 *Diary*, 18 June.
23 Jameson, *op. cit.*, p. 73.
24 *IDA*, I, p. 126.
25 *Ibid*, pp. 119–20.
26 While residing in Demerara in 1834, Dr Charles Warburg discovered what he regarded as an almost certain cure for fever, far superior to quinine. A commission appointed in Vienna in 1848 to examine the remedy chemically concluded that it was a compound of aloes, camphor, saffron and sulphate of quinia. It appears to have been widely used but many denounced it as a secret nostrum.
27 *Diary*, 27 June.
28 *IDA*, I, p. 130.
29 *IDA*, I, p. 116; Barttelot, *op. cit.*, p 137.
30 Jameson, *op. cit.*, pp. 378–81.

4   The Ituri Rain Forest

As Parke walked out of the stockade at 6 am on 28 June he must have been struck by the irony of his position: Barttelot, who had introduced him to the expedition, remained at Yambuya, while he had this opportunity to challenge the enormous wilderness. Stanley bade his disappointed officers a genial good-bye: 'Now Major, my dear fellow, we are for it. Neck or nothing ... And, Jameson, old man, the same to you.'[1] Barttelot (who later offered a significantly different version of the brief *adieu*)[2] vowed gloomily to follow at the first possible opportunity, while Jameson consoled himself by the prospect of a leisure period that would enable him to draw, paint and write long letters to his wife.[3]

Nelson commanded a defensive rearguard. Stairs, still very ill, was carried in a hammock. Jephson was responsible for the dismantled steel boat which could be used above the cataract and was carried meanwhile on poles. Parke took charge of Number 1 Company of Zanzibaris and was responsible for 113 men and 99 rifles. Stanley, accompanied by his European servant William Hoffmann, was in over-all command of the advance party consisting of 389 men with 357 rifles.[4]

The terrain they now entered was natural forest with great trees matted together by creepers and lianas, soaring giants with criss-cross entangled branches that screened the light effectively and a canopy of leaves that hid the sky, a dense wall of living wood encumbered with vegetation and burdened, too, by the vast trunks of fallen timber, casualties of age and tempest. Whatever serpiginous tracks had penetrated this formidable barrier must now be enlarged with axes and billhooks to which end a select group of suitably equipped, strong-muscled men headed the column. They hacked and hewed, they tore a way through the forest, progressing faster, just a little faster, than the proverbial snail.

The humid equatorial heat was little modified by torrential rain that fell for hours, or days, and continued to drip from the multitudinous foliage until replaced by a steamy mist that clung to the intruders, who felt as if in a

50

Turkish bath, 'a conservatory of malaria'.[5] They were beset, too, by numerous hazards which included the poisoned arrows of natives hidden behind trees; deep pits intended to trap wild animals into which an incautious man might fall; short pointed sticks (*makongas*), grooved at the neck to break off within the flesh, placed cunningly on forest pathways to penetrate the feet of unwary travellers or longer sticks to impale the body of a man jumping from a fallen log; the nests of wasps and hornets. Hunger, of course, was a constant attendant.

When two Zanzibaris were wounded by arrows during the first march the natives were made to pay for their aggression, some of them falling to rifle bullets. Next day Parke treated men with wounded feet and he himself experienced a bout of high fever. 'My temperature ran up to 106. I felt above boiling point. Injected pilocarpine hypodermically which in a few minutes drenched me in perspiration.'[6]

By the end of the first week's march Stairs had improved but, on most days one or other of the officers was feverish. They encountered villages burned by Arab slave-raiders and in the evenings cut thorn-bushes to place around the camp as a make-shift boma. Sentries were posted and the howling natives did not venture to attack.

Now and then the broad tracks of elephants made the going easier but the boat sections slowed progress by catching in the creepers and the donkeys sank in the swamps. The fleeing natives took all moveable food with them at the advance party's approach; manioc (cassava) was the sole remaining edible. Parke was impressed by the standard of hygiene he saw in the silent villages. Beds were kept off the ground and there were well-designed ash-pits and refuse-pits — 'in some villages they have got very well-made latrines even to sit on. They are much cleaner than Irish villages.'[7]

Changing their direction they marched northwards and reached the Aruwimi where on the opposite bank they saw a canoe containing a goat. They hastened to assemble the *Advance* and during the long, tedious process of screwing it together Stanley watched the canoe through his binoculars and shot at anyone who dared approach it. When the steel boat was ready they crossed the river to claim the prize. They also managed to commandeer a few large canoes from a nearby island, shooting two natives in the ensuing fracas.

Stairs was still weak and Stanley took him with him in the *Advance*. The main party kept close to the bank where most of the scattered inhabitants lived and there was likely to be food. Chivalry was overborne by hunger and no opportunity was lost to kidnap a woman and hold her, hoping for a ransom in the form of goats or fowls. Parke alluded to an incident in which a captured mother managed to escape and 'ran away and left her baby, age about four years, in camp with us. The wretched child of course was left as we had no milk for it. I saw it last as we marched out of the camp lying on a mat near a fire chewing some leaves. Perhaps its mother returned for it, if not it surely was eaten by the cannibals.'[8]

On 3 July, Parke and Jephson, marching with the rear-guard, fell behind and were unable to keep up with those in front. They made tea in an old milk tin and cooked manioc in the embers of the fire — 'it is very good done so & not unlike baked potatoes.'[9] Parke led the advance party on 7 July but according to Jephson he 'cut the path all wrong so that we wandered about all the afternoon in the manioc fields going in any direction but the right one' until finally at 5.30 pm they struck the river again. Speaking to Nelson and Jephson one of the headmen said 'when either of you two white men lead us we go straight but when the "Doctari" leads us we go round and round'.[10] Jephson complained of a pounding headache and checking his temperature Parke's thermometer recorded 101°F. The doctor gave him quinine and offered him a hammock but the thought of the jolting this would entail made Jephson stay on his feet until he could crawl into bed.[11]

Friday, 8 July – Left at 6.30 am Nelson in advance. The bush is very dense and difficult to cut through. I did not leave the camp with the rearguard until 9.30 am which gives an idea of how difficult it is to get on, for the baggage was only a few yards ahead. Stanley went in a canoe and Stairs in the boat as he is still weak and feeble on his legs at the end of the day. We did about five miles having passed through three deserted villages. Bananas and manioc for dinner. No prospect of meat for some time as the natives desert their villages on our approach and carry away everything they possess. Their intelligence department rivals that of the British army on the Nile.

It was Parke's turn again to lead the advance party on 13 July. They left the camp at 9 am halting an hour or so later for cold rice and coffee. In the afternoon, struggling to join Stanley on the Aruwimi they were drenched and buffetted by a tornado. Nelson and Jephson failed to reach camp that night and slept in the bush with the Zanzibaris. By 15 July, Stairs was well enough to march. Exemplary punishment was meted out to a Soudanese soldier for forgetting his rifle — 100 lashes and thirty days in chains.[12]

When a native was shot through the thigh, severing the main artery, Stanley sent a Zanzibari running to summon Parke but the doctor arrived too late. The unfortunate man had bled to death. 'I was very sorry as it was a nice case to ligature and his life would have been saved.'[13]

Torrential rain continued and the forest streams were so swollen that when fording them the men were up to their necks in water. The noise of the caravan disturbed a hornet's nest and the punitive insects inflicted their agonizing stings gratuitously. Things seemed to be changing for the better on 20 July when natives arrived in canoes to sell twelve chickens. Parke scolded the cooks for not boiling the drinking-water and for not frying the manioc sufficiently. Undercooked manioc is highly toxic. Another trial sent to test their fortitude were white ticks with a predilection for the nasal mucous membrane, needing removal with a forceps.

The natives traded intermittently until one of them was seized and held in an effort to extract information about the area. Their mood changed then and furiously they shot arrows at the intruders. An interpreter attempted to explain the latter's plight. They were almost dying of hunger, he told them, and wished to buy three goats and whatever else they could purchase. Their man would be released unharmed.The natives remained unconvinced but when shots were fired they shouted their assent provided 'we took away that thing meaning the rifle'. They failed, alas! to return with the food 'so we were obliged to take it and loot the village, but we did not burn it'.[14]

Early in August a member of Jephson's company died of acute dysentery and two men were given '180 with the stick' for straying from the camp. Parke and Nelson went foraging but found only green stuff and plantains. The boat party captured two goats allowing them to taste meat again but a canoe was overturned by the turbulent waters below Panga Falls causing the loss of fourteen rifles, several boxes of ammunition and eight boxes of beads and cowries. An attempt to recover the items was made by divers and five rifles were salvaged.

Panga Falls, thirty feet high, extended up-river for a mile and Stairs, the expedition's engineer, cut a tunnel through the bush to facilitate portage of the canoes and the *Advance*. When this was completed and the flotilla was again on the water Stanley reconnoitred and returned with nineteen goats, a fortunate contribution, for Parke was worried by the men's gradual debilitation. 'They have not had manioc since the 28th; numbers suffer from ticks in the nose and gastro-intestinal catarrh but by far the most formidable malady is the enormous ulcers which the men get arising from the very smallest abrasion.'[15]

Wednesday, 10 August – All fit left camp today to forage for food. I remained behind to look after the sick, and dry my medicines, lint etc and look after the Camp. Two natives brought back by Stairs say that there was a fight here yesterday and when the villagers returned they found that we had occupied their village. They say that there is no food for two days. Nelson crossed the river for food. He had a fight and brought back some bananas and spears. The men forsook their women and the women in their turn dropped their children and fled. Jephson also brought in some bananas. One of his men had a spear driven through the wind-pipe and gullet [and died].

Food shortage caused a crime wave as the men began to steal from the officers and from their comrades. Thinking of home on 12 August, Parke made a nostalgic entry in his diary: 'grouse shooting begins but I'm afraid our grousing is of another sort.' An old woman promised to get them food 'but after walking us for 12 miles she could not find any, despite our threats to shoot her and even eat her'. At a village so recently deserted that the fires were still lighting Parke shot three chickens with one cartridge. 'I had a good square meal – one of the first for some time.'[16]

Next morning they left camp at 6 am, Jephson leading, Nelson (who had developed an ulcer) in the middle of the column and Parke in charge of the rearguard. They were halted by a fifty-yards wide river and used the *Advance* and a canoe to cross it and made camp at a village named Avisibba. An hour or so later a strong body of natives assembled on the opposite bank, a war party whose attack with poisoned arrows elicited an immediate response with rifle fire. The main attack faltered but the incensed warriors hid behind trees and stepped out agilely to launch their envenomed missiles.

With the intention of crossing the river to drive them away, Stairs went to the boat but was struck by an arrow.

I immediately returned [Parke wrote], took Stairs by the arm, examined him and brought him up to Camp in the Village about 150 yards off. He was very blanched and suffered from shock. There was a little haemorrhage and a punctured wound just below the apex of his heart and one inch below left nipple. But just as he was hit he knocked the arrow to one side, breaking it and leaving a couple of inches in the wound but this was so concealed behind the rib and covered by the overlapping intercostal muscles that I could not find it with the probe and to cut down and hunt for it would be unjustifiable surgery.[17]

Realizing that the arrow-poison had penetrated beyond the reach of his antiseptic, Parke decided that the best hope of averting its lethal consequences lay in sucking it out. 'I sucked with my lips until I considered that I had removed a good part if not all the poison. I then washed out my mouth with a disinfectant solution of Carbolic acid.' He touched the wound with silver nitrate, bandaged it and gave morphia hypodermically for Stairs was faint and anxious.

The wounded officer had an ague-like attack during the evening and next day was feverish but otherwise tolerably well though pain in the left shoulder alerted Parke to the possibility that the diaphragm was involved. He repeated the morphia injection. The camp, meanwhile, had enjoyed the fruits of victory and feasted on bananas and goat-flesh.

When the march resumed on 15 August Parke arranged for Stairs, his temperature now normal, to travel sitting on an inclined chair placed in a canoe. This enabled him to breathe more comfortably than in a horizontal position. 'I wished him to be carried down to the riverside but he insisted on walking the last 20 or 30 yards for he abhors to be considered or treated as an invalid unless he is actually prostrate.'[18] He avoided further probing for the arrow-head, hoping for its spontaneous extrusion.

The column now left the river, Jephson leading, Nelson in the centre position and Parke in the rear. They marched until dark and despite wet clothes, Parke and Nelson sharing a waterproof sheet, slept the sleep of the exhausted, 'opposite a roaring fire under a tree in the forest'.[19] Jephson had gone ahead with the vanguard but he returned about midnight to warn them that the path was pitted with game-traps.

After daybreak they spent hours trying to get around a wide river but were unable to avoid crossing it. They finished their last grain of rice and made do with roasted bananas. Then the officers pondered their whereabouts and discusssed the direction to take. On this ocasion Jephson had to admit that he had been led astray by the misguidance of a local woman and had then relied unwisely on the advice of an over-confident Zanzibari reputed to have an inspired sense of direction in the forest.

Things are very serious [Parke wrote on 17 August] we are lost in the forest with almost the entire expedition. There is no food and Stanley is anxiously waiting and wondering what has become of us. Stairs and about thirty sick men many of whom were wounded in the engagements of the 13th and 14th are without assistance. After we had been marching through a wilderness for miles until 2 o'clock, I thought that it was time to do something to make our position better, if possible, so I wrote a letter to return back the same way we had come. Nelson, Jephson and myself then held a consultation.

As they talked they decided to retrace their steps but just then shots were heard which they answered. Presently Saat Tato, Stanley's chief hunter, came bursting through the bush with six other Zanzibaris. They had been searching for the missing expedition and caught up with them by taking short cuts. They would now guide them back to the Aruwimi.

Saat Tato had shot three natives *en route* when they attacked his party and there were to be repercussions on the march to the river during which the rain fell in torrents. Six sick men had to be carried, one of whom died in the hammock. Parke pitied the Zanzibaris, unsuited to cold and wet weather which caused them to suffer physically and psychologically. They shivered miserably, developed goose-flesh, and turned a greenish-yellow colour. They developed chest complaints, coughed and were feverish with stiff and useless limbs.

At 11 am, having halted to eat roasted plantains, they were attacked from both sides by natives hidden among the trees. One man sustained a deep arrow-wound in the back and Parke and Nelson stayed behind with a few men to help him while the column went ahead. They remained under cover for to disclose how few they were in number would have invited direct attack. After a few shots the natives vanished into the bush and Parke's little contingent hurried after the column which was resting at a village where Jephson had goat-soup and hot tea ready for them. Some men, disobeying orders, went foraging for food and one was mortally wounded by an arrow in the liver. There were two agonizing deaths from tetanus.

The Aruwimi was reached at nightfall on 18 August, but Stanley's camp was higher up and Parke did not reach it until 21 August:

Jephson returned early this morning with orders from Stanley that he and Nelson were to go for bananas and that I was to go on to Stanley's Camp which I did and found many sick. One man, Msa, has died from dysentery and 2 from tetanus (from descriptions of their ailments from Stanley); 28 others were lying helpless from sickness in Camp. Stairs looked remarkably well, temperature normal, a purulent discharge from the wound but no sign of the Arrow. Stanley seemed depressed but did not lose his temper as I expected.[20]

Stairs had slept at the back of Stanley's tent during the doctor's absence and Parke gathered that he had had rather a miserable time until Stanley's servant fixed him up with blankets.

For some days they had only unripe bananas to eat and were tormented on the march by ants and hornets. Stairs had severe neck pain on 24 August which worried Parke, anxious now lest this symptom portended the onset of tetanus. Fortunately he was better next day but Parke suspected that 'some of the periosteum is rubbed off the rib' which would delay full recovery. Many men now had ulcerated legs.

On 27 August, Juma of No 1 Company was carried into camp having sustained a gunshot wound which shattered the right foot, the bullet entering at the heel, destroying many bones, before lodging under the little toe. Parke decided that 'all the small bones ... were so comminuted' that the foot could not be saved. He advised operation above the ankle. When Stanley had explained this 'in his usual calm and persuasive way' to Juma and his nearest relative, the surgeon operated while there was still light, under a chloroform anaesthetic given by Nelson.

An amputation distresses both patient and doctor and though the former's temperature was normal Parke's next diary entry was unusually sombre.

Juma's temperature is normal and he feels well; his stump was dressed yesterday in carbolized gauze. This perpetual marching through an apparently never-ending dark unbroken forest has a very depressing effect on the men. They think that we shall never see the open plain again and are all looking worn-out. Of our 6 donkeys which we brought from Yambuya on 28th June, now only three are alive and one of those I think I may safely say is not out of danger yet. These three deceased donkeys simply succumbed from starvation and hard marching for they have never carried anything except the saddle which indeed like all English equipment for hot climates is much too heavy.[21]

Stanley gave Parke a 'blowing up' when through unfavourable circum-stances his arrival in camp on 29 August was delayed. 'Nelson was seedy yesterday so I put him in a canoe. He is better today. Stanley shot a native.'[22]

Men fatigued by carrying heavy loads could evade the rearguard by just stepping a few yards into the bush where they were instantly hidden. They stayed out all night when so inclined, dropping in one by one in the morning, but sometimes loads were lost and Parke was particularly exasperated when the last box of biscuits had not arrived despite the efforts of a search party.

This is simply a judgement of Providence for keeping these provisions and thus courting starvation. Now the emergency has come but where is the box of biscuits? I have come to the conclusion long ago that it is much wiser to eat European provisions while you can get them for to keep them means that somebody else eats them when you want them yourself.[23]

Next morning, Parke had an exciting chase after a native woman:

She jumped into the river and as none of the men would follow her, as they were afraid of being drawn under by her or carried away by a crocodile, I took off my clothes and swam in after her but she made for the middle of the stream which ran about 2 miles an hour and simply left me behind as she could give me 20 yards in 100 and beat me. Although I had a man firing in front of her to stop her and the bullets dropped close to her she was too terrified of me to take any notice of the bullets. Occasionally she would sink and pretend she was drowning so as to get me down the river.[24]

Nine men speaking Swahili arrived at the camp in the afternoon bringing gifts of fowl and a goat. They welcomed the travellers and said they were

Manyuema serving Ugarrowa whose settlement, with several hundred armed men, was about eight marches up-river. The Zanzibaris were glad to speak their own tongue again and Parke thought the newcomers looked 'smart and clean'[78] but Stanley knowing more about them than the others was filled with mistrust. They were slave-traders and rapacious dealers in ivory and their arrival was a portent of evil.[26]

At a village lately occupied by the Manyuema, which they reached next day, they saw three children fatally speared by the raiders and inside the palisade a woman lay dead. The expedition spent two days in camp and Parke availed of an opportunity to dry his clothes, medicines and surgical dressings. The entire group of white men was suffering from diarrhoea for which the doctor was inclined to blame a cold wind blowing from the swamp but Stanley attributed more correctly to contaminated water.

Within an week of the encounter with the Manyuema there were ten desertions and an element of demoralization had entered the expedition leading to a loss of loads, the opening of boxes and thefts of ammunition. Hoping to control the situation, Stanley mustered the men, delivered a homily and ordered the removal of springs from the rifles of sixty men whose loyalty was not vouched for by the headmen.

On 7 September they camped on a bluff at an angle of the Ituri River overlooking a cataract, a picturesque and beautiful spectacle. But the rapids demanded herculean labours as the loads had to be removed from the steel boat and canoes, and these craft awkwardly man-handled over the long portages via tunnels cut through the bush. In this arduous manner Bafaido Rapids and the Amiri Falls were bypassed enabling the long march to continue under appalling conditions that varied little in severity from day to day. They remained exposed to tropical heat and tropical rainfall and were defenceless against a myriad of insects; hunger weakened them and they feared the spears and arrows of an indigenous population angered and frightened by their alien presence. They were, besides, increasingly uncertain of the extent of the apparently limitless forest. Parke knew that Stanley had expected to reach Wadelai on the Albert Nyanza by 15 July but now it was clear that it would take at least another two months to reach the lake. No wonder that having been on his feet from 7 am to 6 pm he felt entitled to open a bottle of brandy from the medical stores to lace the officers' tea.

Desertions and death were threatening to decimate the expedition. An increasing number of sick men, emaciated by protein loss from weeping ulcers, constituted an immediate problem in logistics. Some could be carried on the water but when an advanced state of helplessness was reached the only solution, however brutal and drastic, was to favour the survival of the fittest and leave the dying behind in the bush, pitiable skeletons barely conscious of their fate.[27]

On 16 September, when Parke had led the column for a distance of about eight miles, the sound of gun-fire was heard, reports unlike those of Winchester or Remington rifles. An attack was feared but it transpired that the shots were sounds of salutation from Ugarrowa's people. A welcoming party had crossed the river accompanied by musicians including women who sang happy songs of greeting. 'This was a pleasant surprise [Parke wrote ingenuously] meeting with civilized people in these parts.'[28] Ugarrowa's settlement was reached next day, an elaborate and well-constructed fort — 'a comfortable, compact village of wood and straw huts with large verandahs'.[29]

As a youth, Ugarrowa was tent-boy to Captains Speke and Grant and later had grown rich and powerful by selling slaves and ivory. Nine months earlier, accompanied by his Manyuema followers, the Arab trader moved from the Lualuba River to establish a station on the Ituri. They had devastated the neighbouring villages where 'the pagans' hindered their pursuit of ivory. Their established policy was to slay the adult aboriginals, sparing young women and children: females were sold into slavery in the harems of East Africa and Arabia; the growing boys were instructed in martial arts and indoctrinated as menials and foot-soldiers of a nefarious commerce.

Ugarrowa's flotilla of canoes arrived at Stanley's camp to a roll of drums, paying an official call. On the following afternoon, Stanley punctiliously donned his best suit, buckled on his sword and called on the Arab chief. It was agreed that for payment at the rate of five dollars per month for each man the sick could stay at Ugarrowa's and that deserters should not be harboured. The Arab also promised to send couriers with a letter to Barttelot who would reward him generously with gun-powder.

While this interchange of civilities was taking place between the leaders, bartering went on busily at a lower level. Bananas and other edibles were offered by the Manyuema for beads, cowries or clothes, and hunger drove the Zanzibaris to strip themselves almost naked. Watching these transactions, Parke deplored the contrast 'in the appearance of these firm burly fat sleeky men compared with our skeletons who have a peculiar ashy grey skin and sickly look'.[30]

On 18 September the companies were fallen in while Stanley and Parke inspected the sick. Forty-eight were selected to be left temporarily with the Arabs and the doctor could not forget how the other men looked at them rather enviously as if they, too, would have been glad to stay behind rather than to have to start what must have seemed to them a hopeless march through a purgatorial forest. Juma, the amputee, was among those left behind; he recovered fully and was eventually repatriated by sea to Zanzibar.

Notes

1 *IDA*, I, p. 134.
2 See Troup's version of Stanley's parting words as given to him by Barttelot at Yambuya: 'As Mr Stanley passed out of that gate his last words were, "Good-bye, Major; I shouldn't be a bit surprised to see you here when I return. I shall be away five months giving myself three months to go up to Kavalli and two to return, so I will be back in November."' (*Rear Column*, p. 14). Did Stanley have a presentiment of the rear-column's inability to move without his support?

   Barttelot's own account of Stanley's leave-taking is given in a letter to a friend: 'He said to me, "Good-bye, Major; shall find you here in October, when I return"' (*Life*, p. 116).
3 Jameson, *Story of Rear Column*, p. 72.
4 *IDA*, I, p. 131.
5 *Diary*, 29 June 1887.
6 *Diary*, 29 June.
7 *Diary*, 5 July.
8 *Diary*, 12 July. This incident may have been the basis for the hardly credible allegation recorded by Jameson (*op. cit.*, p. 111) that Stanley ordered a baby to be thrown into the water.
9 Jephson's *Diary*, p. 116.
10 Ibid, p. 120.
11 Ibid, p. 123.
12 *Diary*, 15 July.
13 *Diary*, 16 July.
14 *Diary*, 1 August.
15 *Diary*, 8 Aug.
16 *Diary*, 12 Aug.
17 *Diary*, 13 Aug.
18 *Diary*, 15 Aug.
19 *Diary*, 16 Aug.
20 *Diary*, 21 Aug.
21 *Diary*, 28 Aug.
22 *Diary*, 29 Aug.
23 *Diary*, 20 Aug.
24 *Diary*, 31 Aug.
25 *Diary*, 31 Aug.
26 *IDA*, I, p. 188.
27 *Diary*, 16 September.
28 *Diary*, 17 Sept.
29 *Diary*, 19 Sept.
30 *Diary*, 19 Sept.

5 The Journey to Ipoto

Three hundred and eighty-nine men had left Yambuya on 28 June and now eighty-three days later 271 filed out of Ugarrowa's to march in the direction of Ipoto, towards the station of another 'robber-baron', Kilonga Longa, a distance of five marches according to some, while others hazarded ten. With the smaller group of fitter men it was hoped that progress would be speedy but this was to leave hunger — 'the empty belly and the crying stomach'[1] — and the devastated countryside out of the equation. So fallible, indeed, are human planners that it was to take just under a month before they reached their destination.

Ugarrowa saw Stanley off in the *Advance* and gave him a parting gift of a 'large tray of exquisitely cooked rice, and an immense dish of curried fowl'[2] which Jephson complained later was not shared with the officers. The expedition's flotilla was accompanied for some miles by canoes with Arabs singing and beating drums, a cheering and heart-lifting escort. A few hours later these canoes were again sighted and catching up with them Ugarrowa's men handed over three wretched deserters who had been flogged on discovery.

These despondent, unrepentant men, ex-slaves of petty Zanzibaris officials, were tied to a tree overnight and in the morning Stanley decided that in order to keep the expedition intact he must make an example of them. Before a general assembly he assumed the dual role of prosecutor and judge and with remorseless, and as he believed, justifiable logic argued for a death sentence which was passed without dissent. The grim scene is well described by Parke.

Early in the cold morning all the Companies were formed into a square and the three deserters, wretched sullen-looking creatures were placed in the centre and all were doomed to be hanged. They drew short and long who should go today, the next tomorrow and the third on the following day. Mabruki was the first to go so a rope was placed around his neck and he was hanged. The greatest order and silence prevailed and he was pulled up by his comrades who were prisoners in irons. First a thin tree was pulled down and he was tied to the top, but as the tree cracked and would not rebound, he was hanged after the most modern approved style recommended by the Rev. Samuel Haughton, MD. Stanley said: 'Doctor, is he dead?' I replied 'Yes' and immediatly afterwards the column filed off and out of camp leaving Mabruki hanging lifeless to the tree.[3]

One of the two remaining condemned men escaped during the night but when the other was led out in the morning to expiate his crime the headmen appealed to Stanley who had indicated privately that he was open to a plea for clemency. 'Why should we wonder', Stanley asked forgivingly, 'that the servant runs away from his master when he cannot feed him?'[4] A sage question and had he posed it in poor Mabruki's defence that unfortunate's ending need not have been so peremptory. The escapee was driven back to the camp before nightfall by the terrors of the forest and Stanley earned a reputation as a caring father by pardoning him. 'Death to him who leaves Bula Matari!' they called. 'Show the way to the Nyanza.'[5]

Despite their hopes to the contrary, progress remained slow in the almost impenetrable forest covering a hilly terrain, and also on the river where long stretches were spoiled for navigation by broken water, churning and boiling through the jagged cataracts; it was delayed further by the need to spend time foraging widely in a largely uninhabited area where Arab raiders had created recent havoc, burning villages and pillaging crops, achieving a merciless spoliation which the white officers thoroughly deplored but did not hesitate to repeat when it was a matter of self-survival. Parke felt relieved that so many sick men had been left at Ugarrowa's, for the daily task of treating them was undermining his own health.

Each foraging party was supervised by a white officer, an arrangement the Zanzibaris disliked; they loved to wander and said that the officer's repetitive call to 'fall in' was too restrictive. Parke's plans to shoot game came to nothing as he found the forest a total wilderness, 'huge gloomy trees and dense thick bush beneath. Nothing can be shot in this forest as you can only see a few yards ahead'.[6] Stanley shot at an elephant but lacking a sufficiently powerful gun just wounded the great beast.

More often than not they returned empty-handed and went through the day without food other than, perhaps, fungi, red phrynia berries and crimson amoma fruit. An early detachment led by Parke and Stairs had better fortune and brought back enough plantains to distribute forty to every man. Now and then they stumbled on an untouched grove of bananas and when reduced to a total absence of conventional edibles the Zanzibaris did not hesitate to eat grubs, slugs, caterpillars and white ants. 'Inshallah!' they said. 'We'll find food either to-morrow or the next day.'[7]

Most mornings were breakfastless and held little expectation of luncheon, but there were gala days. An abundance of banana trees was discovered on 27 September and the welcome fruit was devoured in bulk with 'as great a relish as a Mansion House dinner'.[8] Parke ate twenty bananas at a sitting having spent most of the day dressing ulcers. An unexpected bonus was provided, too, when Stanley's terrier 'Randy' (so named for Lord Randolph Churchill) caught a guinea fowl that quickly went into a feeding-pot for his master and the officers. Another day of plenty for the officers occurred when Stairs came upon an antelope in a game-trap and a visiting party of Manyuema sold them rice at a high price.

During the march on 28 September an inhabited native village was seen on an island. As the flotilla had been delayed by broken water they lacked the canoes to make a mass landing but, intent on loot, a party went a little up-river to reach a point from which the huts were within range of rifle-fire.

I shot two men who were in a canoe [Parke wrote] as I thought they were escaping with a goat, but the canoe went downstream. Stairs shot a man dead against the central hut. When the island was well cleared some of our men swam across but found nothing to eat except dried pieces of elephant meat.[9]

Starvation deprived them of energy and in the mornings the men approached their loads and lifted them onto their heads with great reluctance. Hunger prompted individual efforts to find food and despite Mabruki's execution 'Abdullah the humped' deserted and was followed off by others. There were two deaths from dysentery and Wadi Asman — 'a grave man, faithful, and of much experience in many African lands'[10] — was drowned when he tried to swim a river with his Winchester on his back.

Having weeded out the unfit, much was expected from the remainder whose constitutions, already undermined by chronic starvation, tropical infections and physical exhaustion were, of course, by no means unassailable. Before long Parke was dealing with a new group of invalids which included Nelson, emaciated after several bouts of fever and seriously hampered by leg ulcers. Those unable to walk were carried in the *Advance* and the canoes.

'Our men are starving [Parke wrote on 1 October], they have been away all day looking for food but got little or none. However two men of No 1 Company accidentally came across a banana plantation on their meanderings and brought in some good specimens.' He was leading the advance party on 5 October when it reached the confluence of the Ihuri and the Ituri. Above this point the Ituri was no longer readily navigable and a difficult decision could no longer be postponed. Accordingly, after a *shauri* (conference), it was agreed to sink the canoes and that Rashid, chief of the headmen, should go on to find food with a few other unencumbered men, while Nelson, himself unable to proceed on foot, should remain behind with fifty-two incapacitated men and eighty-one loads; this starving group of invalids were to be supplied with food at the first possible opportunity, for in the meantime they would have nothing to eat other than what those few still able to walk a little could find by local foraging.

Our position could not be more trying having to abandon our white companion and so many faithfuls, each one of whom had already risked his life [many times] a day for the relief of Emin. The camp, as [we] marched away, looked the picture of loneliness and death. There was not a mouthful of food to be got for days around and the continual loud pealing noise of the cataract made the locality more melancholy. It was the most sickening, heart-rending good-bye I ever experienced.[11]

A doctor learns to live comfortably close to mass suffering, but if a relative, dear friend or colleague is affected his armour is no longer protective. No exception to this rule, Parke resumed the desolate trek lacking his customary equanimity but he was determined not to leave Nelson behind for an hour longer than necessary. With Stairs and Jephson, he took up a position in the rear of the column, for the men had to be chided and cajoled to keep them going. He was existing now on two teaspoonsful of arrowroot a day, supplemented by forest fruits, fungi and the leaves of the pepper plant.

Next day Parke went off with Stairs to shoot game but they got nothing. Some men found a patch of corn on an island and the doctor received his share, 'two milk tins full'. He suggested to Stanley that a donkey should be shot and eaten but the leader reluctantly postponed this extreme measure when an old native woman collected large brown beans which she scraped and, making little cakes with the scrapings, toasted them in the fire.

Things look blacker now than ever [Parke wrote on 10 October] as the party who went off for food yesterday have not yet returned, we have done our best to get a shot but have failed and feel quite exhausted. Stairs trying to fish and succeeded in pulling up three like gudgeon. Our position is really desperate: to go back is certain starvation and to go forward is most dismal. The foraging party returned but with very little food. This is 'Starvation Camp'.

A group of men who went to an island to fetch grass for the donkeys walked into an ambush and Ferruzi Ali, a Zanzibari chief, was struck with a knife which penetrated the skull and depressed the bone. There was quite an affray in which a few natives were shot and fourteen women captured. The fate of the latter is not discussed explicitly but can be imagined at the mercy of men sex-starved despite their debilitation.

A *shauri* open to all was held on 12 October to discuss whether they should not discard the boxes and return to Ugarrowa's, but finally it was decided to continue the march with all the loads they could carry. Parke, in the rear, had difficulty in getting started for the men kept wandering off in all directions in search of food and fungi.

The *Advance* was again on the water and Jephson brought a small quantity of Indian corn from an island. He also had a few small fish which he distributed to the white officers having given a basketful to the boatmen. A woman wearing beads given to her by Arabs was captured but as she had no sense of time or distance it was not possible to get any idea from her of the Arabs' whereabouts. Four men, presumably deserters, were absent at muster and one of them had absconded with Parke's bag containing most of his clothes and his sword.

Still alive but showing signs of brain compression, Feruzi Ali was a great worry to Parke who lacked a trephine which might have enabled him to deal with the depressed bone fragment. He did not dare to attempt to lift the bone using a mallet and chisel, for in the almost certain event of the headman's death (he died a few days later), the crude operation would be blamed. To sublimate his emotions, he stayed in camp preparing a dinner of forest fruits, beans and fungi using the leaves of a pepper plant as a condiment. He was put out by the loss of his clothes, being left with 'two pairs of stockings, 2 pairs of old boots, one ragged pair of knickerbockers, 2 shirts, 1 blanket and a waterproof sheet. All the rest are gone and there is no fig tree in the land.'[12]

The situation was eroding Stanley's self-confidence. 'Ah, it was a sad sight', he wrote, 'unutterably sad to see so many men struggling on blindly through that endless forest, following a white man who was bound whither none knew, whom most believed did not know himself.'[13] Asked if he had experienced such grim conditions in previous travel, he replied: 'Not quite so bad. We have suffered but not to such an extremity.' He took his meals, such as they were, alone and did not socialize with his officers but kept them under an appraising eye — Parke 'ever striving, cheerful and gentle'; Stairs and Jephson totally dependable.[14]

Friday, 14 October – The boat arrived early as Jephson was obliged to leave it a few hundred yards down river last night as it was so dark ... Jephson's indian corn is keeping us on our legs. Today we cross the entire expedition over the river which is about 100 yards in this place. At the crossing we blazed trees and put broad arrows and finger posts so as to show the chiefs and others where we have crossed. Also wrote on the trees that the Expedition had crossed. All the men are in a fainting condition for food.

Stanley shot his donkey on 15 October to feed the desperately hungry men each of whom was given a pound of flesh. The officers received a larger allowance, four pounds apiece. Parke enjoyed his meal and watched the ravenous men struggling 'like pariah dogs' for the hide, hooves and blood. The tidbit was the tongue.

When the donkey flesh was consumed forest fruits and a kind of porridge made from bean scrapings replaced the solid fare so briefly available. Starving men fell to die by the wayside and Parke knew that all that could be done was to take care of the rifles and trudge on. One is reminded of a terrible scene from Conrad's *Heart of Darkness*:

Black shapes crouched, lay, sat between the trees ... in all the attitudes of pain, abandonment, and despair ... They were dying slowly — it was very clear. They were not enemies, they were not criminals, they were nothing earthly now, — nothing but black shadows of disease and starvation, lying confusedly in the greenish gloom.

A second encounter with hornets added to the general grief and when rain fell torrentially the cavernous holes in the decayed trunks of the giant trees were favoured places of refuge.

The prospect of managing the *Advance* over further long portages had become insupportable and Stanley was prepared to abandon it but Uledi, the indefatigable coxwain, volunteered to take charge of it with his crew and get it around the rapids one way or another while the main party continued its journey.

Parke dispensed quantities of 'forced march tablets' to the officers but found them useless, certainly less beneficial than the last of the brandy which he doled out sparingly to his colleagues in this starvation period. Knowing that somebody had stolen his corn, the doctor stayed awake on 17 October until he heard the 'popping' sound of corn toasting on a fire. The thief turned out to be his own 'boy', sentenced immediately to twenty-four lashes.

An hour after starting the march on 18 October, shots were heard by ears straining for sounds of welcome and soon afterwards from the brow of a tall hill they were delighted to see that they were approaching a large forest clearing, the site of a well-designed village amply surrounded by green and golden fields of rice and corn, a bountiful area abounding in the beans and sweet potatoes, the fowls and goats and all the nourishment they so sorely needed. But armed sentries were posted there to deter the Zanzibaris from instinctive acts of plunder.

This apparently thriving village where the Manyuema sang at their work was Ipoto, a station set up for Kilonga Longa by his headmen, Ismailia, Khamisi and Sangeramani, as a centre from which to seek ivory. Strongly

66

armed and with well-stocked granaries, Ipoto presented a rich contrast to the devastation the raiders had created in its neighbourhood from which their goats and fowls had been stolen.

And so they hoped to rest and fill their bellies with goat-flesh and corn generously presented by the welcoming hosts. They gorged unwisely, accepting bloated stomachs as the lesser of two evils. But the quickly emptied cornucopia was not to be readily replenished and within a day or so the seemingly open-handed Manyuema showed reluctance to offer unlimited largesse, and displayed a parsimony dictated by disappointment not to have received the rich gifts they expected in return. Most of the expedition's trade-goods were still at Yambuya; a load of first-class beads lay on the river-bed below Panga Falls; the gold-braided Arab *burnouses* had disappeared with a deserter.

Wednesday, 19 October – Yesterday we had a good rest and such big feeds of indian corn and goat that no stomach could stand it for long. We were able to purchase beans and fowls for any little thing we had such as needles, camphorated chalk etc. After a feed of beans one felt like a balloon, the distension was indescribable. The people bought quantities of corn etc. etc. in exchange for clothes but as all mine were gone I was obliged to sponge on the others. In the evening Stanley told Jephson that he was to go back for Nelson and the 81 loads and return to this Camp. The boat was to be taken to pieces and left here with Nelson and Jephson. Last night Stanley and the three of us had a long talk over our tribulations for the last few weeks.

Next day Stanley arranged for a general issue of corn but the Manyuema's manner towards the Zanzibaris was overbearing. The former were suspicious of their light-fingered guests and sometimes they came to blows. Parke dealt with a nasty spear-wound through the chest and Stanley learned with alarm that his men were being induced to sell their ammunition and rifles for food. This was intolerable. An unarmed man could not expect to survive in Central Africa. Deprived of its arms the expedition would be immediately overwhelmed.

A muster was called. Five men who appeared without weapons were sentenced to exemplary flogging. With the aid of the Manyuema headmen the bartered rifles were recovered and when the main culprit was identified he was hanged as a terrible warning to others.

Ipoto had a vast population of rats which scurried over Parke in the night and in the mornings his boy picked lice of his shirt by the score. Ticks were troublesome adhering painfully to the nasal lining.

Uledi arrived triumphantly with the *Advance*. Rashid and his emaciated party, having gone astray, also arrived. Food was now available on commercial terms and Parke sold a scarlet mess-jacket and waistcoat for which he received fifty-six head of corn, a little honey and a chicken.

Sunday, 23 October – Stanley not well yesterday or today. I recommended him to change from his hut and get under his tent as the floor of his hut was quite damp and soft and spongy. I had his tent pitched and he moved in. I gave him some quinine and orange wine; he is also troubled with a boil posteriorly. I asked him for food as we have only had 117 head of corn amongst 3 of us since the 18th. He asked me in return if I had nothing to sell for food although in the Contract we were to be fed by the Expedition. He told me he had arranged with the Arabs or Manyuema to go back for Nelson and the boxes.

After a number of delays Jephson started out at last for Nelson's camp on 26 October with a strong party of Zanzibaris and Manyuema porters. It was now ordered that Parke should remain at Ipoto to take care of the sick, the boat and the loads, while Jephson, having returned with Nelson (if still alive), should follow on after the advance party. This decision disappointed Parke. He did not question it but felt he would be a prisoner — 'a pledge until redeemed by the payment of cloth, which is to be brought on by the rear column, and due for corn etc, which the men have had.'[15] Neverthless he packed, as requested, a chest of medicines and bandages that the officers might need.

Just then, Stanley was out of favour with Parke who was bewildered by the leader's attitude — 'he says we have all lost our senses although we work like slaves and assist him in every way, yet receive no pay and no food.'[16] He took no steps to get Parke a hut to live in but claimed to have made arrangements that he should be supplied with food and as a measure of good-will went through a ceremony of blood-brotherhood with Ismailia.

Stanley promised to relieve Parke in about three months and accompanied by Stairs, who had sold a shirt and clothes to get food, he left Ipoto on 27 October with 147 men all reluctant to re-enter the forest and commence the last stage of the outward journey to the Albert Nyanza. He gave Ismailia a gold watch and chain as security pending payment of guides who were to go with him for a few days but offended the doctor by omitting to say good-bye to him.

Notes

1 *IDA*, I, p. 204.
2 Ibid, I, p. 198.
3 *Diary*, 22 September 1887. The hanging was, of course, a travesty of Haughton's method. Samuel Haughton (1821–97) held doctorates in divinity, science and medicine and was

registrar of the medical school at Trinity College, Dublin. His purpose in calculating the drop that would convert judicial hanging from slow strangulation into instantaneous death from damage to the brain stem was entirely humanitarian but his macabre achievement attracted to him a certain notoriety commemorated by the term 'Haughton's drop'. See W.J.E. Jessop, 'Samuel Haughton: a Victorian Polymath', *Hermathena*, 1973, CXVI, 5–26; Davis Coakley, *Irish Masters of Medicine* (Dublin 1992), pp. 181–8.

4   *IDA*, I, p. 204.
5   Ibid, p. 205.
6   *Diary*, 1 October.
7   *IDA*, I, p. 215.
8   *Diary*, 27 Sept.
9   *Diary*, 28 Sept.
10 *IDA*, I, p. 217.
11 *Diary*, 6 Oct.
12 *Diary*, 13 Oct.
13 *IDA*, I, p. 220.
14 Ibid, p. 223.
15 *Diary*, 24 Oct. 'Poor Parke takes it very badly indeed & cannot make up his mind to the inevitable, though I must say it is hard to do so under the circumstances.' Jephson's *Diary*, p. 172.
16 *Diary*, 26 Oct.

6   With the Manyuema

'Now I am all alone at the mercy of these savages', Parke wrote in his diary. He accepted that 'although Stanley appeared cruel' no other course was open to the leader. Parke was in charge of twenty-eight ailing Zanzibaris but he believed that only two or three of them were 'sick' in the conventional meaning of that word: the others were *starving*, pitiably emaciated objects, 'simply bags of bones'.[1] He held the Manyuema ivory hunters in low esteem. 'They are slaves to Arabs and live like pigs. Everywhere all around the village is covered with filth of the foulest description. Men and women squat down together within a few yards of their dwellings.'[2]

His situation was unsatisfactory for he had not actually seen a written agreement between Stanley and Ismailia and the former had assured him evasively that he 'would get his food by smiles'. In a different context, Jephson mentioned Parke's 'insinuating smile, which would have charmed a bird off a twig'.[3] This failed to beguile the Arabs but he finally managed to have a hut allocated to him with a site close by for a tent in which to store the rifles. To his intense relief, news arrived on 2 November that Nelson was still alive but of the few other survivors two were dying and had to be left behind. Next day Nelson walked into Ipoto, haggard and hollow-cheeked. Choking with emotion at the realization of what his colleague had endured, Parke gave him a chair to sit on and disappeared behind the hut to dry his eyes.[4]

Before setting out from Ipoto to rejoin Stanley and the advance party, Jephson gave Parke some idea of the horror of his return to Nelson's starvation camp. Travelling with thirty Manyuema and forty Zanzibaris carrying food with them, and helped by the blazed trees their pace was much faster than on the outward march but they were not spared the daily spectacle on the wayside of the skeletons of those who had fallen down, victims of exhaustion and starvation. Grinning skulls, picked clean by birds and insects, leered at them from the undergrowth, silent sermons on mortality.

Accompanied by just one man, Jephson pressed ahead on 29 October determined to reach camp that afternoon, consumed by anxiety as to what he might find in it. Entering the empty camp, silent except for the groans of the dying, he was overjoyed to see Nelson sitting there but at the same time he was saddened by his friend's dejected, worn appearance. 'We clasped hands, then, poor fellow! He turned away and sobbed, muttering something about being very weak!'[5]

Nelson had existed on the fruit and fungi procured for him by his two boys. Despite this privation, the long rest allowed the ulcers to heal and he declared himself capable of proceeding on foot to Ipoto. Only five men remained of the fifty-two left behind by Stanley; a small group was out foraging, the others were dead or had deserted. It was necessary to leave thirteen boxes of ammunition and seven other loads behind, burying them for later retrieval.

Jephson realized how cut up Parke was to be left at Ipoto; he expressed their mutual dislike, at this phase of their awful journey, for their leader:

Stanley himself, so Parke tells me, took quantities of food & great numbers of chickens. He did not even take the trouble to say good-bye to Parke when he went, which, to put it mildly, was ungracious. It is really quite wonderful how little Stanley seems to care about the welfare of his officers, he seems to take no interest whatever in what they do or how they manage to get on. I think it is a mistake his having European officers under him, he should merely have Zanzibar chiefs & see to all the work himself. He expects [from] his officers too much to understand what he wants without telling them & is constantly giving orders to the men without letting the officers know that such orders are given, the result is often an absurd confliction of ideas & Stanley gets furious & completely loses his head & says things which he must sincerely regret saying when he comes to his senses. He has left Parke & Nelson entirely dependant for food & housing on the charity of the three Manyuema chiefs who are themselves merely the slaves of Abed bin Salim, a Zanzibar Arab who is now in Mecca. They are a very low class of men, so the white men's look out is not a pleasant one whilst they stay with the Manyuema, which I'm afraid will be for a good many months to come. On hearing of the poor state of Parke's commissariat I at once sold a shirt for a couple of chickens & one of the bottles out of my dressing case for some Indian meal & beans so that Nelson might have a good meal when he came in. He had expressly asked me to tell Parke to have a good dinner ready for him & I did not want him to be disappointed — poor old Nelson, he's a terrible one for his food![6]

Nelson was soon to realize that he had exchanged one starvation camp for another. Parke and he had *shauri* after *shauri* with the Manyuema headmen who refused to feed the boys, sent minuscule portions to the officers and insisted that if the men were to be fed they must work. Hoping to reduce the problem a little, Parke sent off as many of his men as possible with Jephson when the latter left to re-join Stanley on 7 November. Twenty-four sick men and three boys remained with the officers at Ipoto. The dismantled *Advance* was in a place of safety on the river bank, its screws and rubber washers etc. stored in a box in Parke's hut.

Monday, 31 October – This morning after some persuasion I got Ismailia to come and select a better hut and a site for the Tent in which I shall store the ammunition for fear of fire. Every hut I fancied was not theirs! However there is one which belongs to Khamis who is away and which I hope I shall get. The chiefs say that they feed us all and get nothing in return and now I want a hut. So that I see a storm brewing. I am in an excessively awkward position as Stanley did not show me any conditions of agreement with the Chiefs and, when I asked him if he had arranged for my food, replied that I should pull well with them and get my food by smiles. I am simply in bondage, held here by the savage Manyuema as a hostage for 3 bales of cloth which Stanley promised the Chiefs. I do not speak their language and vice versa and I am to be fed by smiles.

Summoned in his professional capacity to see a badly injured child who had fallen from a tree, Parke said it would die and a few hours later the accuracy of his prognosis was confirmed. He availed of every opportunity to offer medical skills to his hosts, blatantly determined to use this means of ingratiating himself and glad to receive even a head of corn or a cup of beans as a reward. 'And if the urgency of the case demands such strong measures as the inhalation of ammonia carbonate an extra fee is expected.'[7]

He hoped the ammonia would not lose its strength for it was an excellent placebo and might help to keep the doctor alive whatever about his patients. When Khamis was threatened with pneumonia, Parke paid him every attention, including a whiff or two from the mysterious bottle, expecting to be given a chicken at least, for his services. But having recovered the ungrateful patient sent nothing at all. To make matters worse the doctor soon tore his pyjamas accidentally and was obliged to resort to a pair of knickerbockers he had worn crossing the Bayuda Desert.

When Parke and Nelson forced an interview with the headmen, Ismailia again insisted he was feeding them at his own expense. Khamis produced a document in Stanley's handwriting with a shorter version in Arabic. The contract in English stipulated that the sick-men and officers were to be supplied with provisions but the chiefs disputed this and said that Stanley had lied to them. They explained that their supplies had diminished and that very little remained in their store-rooms.

By experience the white men learned to keep to the fore and make their salaams when raiding-parties returned to Ipoto. Their courtesy was often rewarded with a chicken or other edibles. They also found it profitable to drop in on their hosts towards noon as sometimes they were invited to sit down to a midday meal of curried chicken and rice, a repast which they enjoyed with the reservation that they were obliged to share a dish into which a dozen Arabs were dipping their hands. Their own quarters attracted numerous visitors whose avaricious eyes ranged over their possessions and whose robes left behind them rich deposits of vermin.

Walked round with the Chief [Parke wrote on 7 November] who offered us another hut which we agreed to take when it was cleaned out. Nelson bought a chicken which gave us a dinner. We never leave the ammunition etc. etc. only one of us can go away at a time for these Manyuema are evidently intent on relieving us of some of the rifles. Constantly we are asked to go and shoot elephants in the plantations and other methods to induce us away from the loads so that they may steal. Several small things have been stolen by the men putting their arms through the bars of the back door.

They were tormented by lice; sleep was generally delayed by the irresistible need to scratch until blood ran. Parke used a compact group of boxes of rifles as a bed for, despite their vigilance, thieving was rampant and stores were at constant risk. Rifles and ammunition were especially coveted. Attempts were even made to steal them when the officers were asleep and in this context Nelson's insomnia had a positive value. It was he who alerted Parke and the boys, hearing the first crackling of burning wood and straw, and frustrated the would-be arsonists who one night attempted to burn their hut, presumably hoping to make off with much booty at the height of the confusion.

Presents were expected in return for donations of food. Parke promised Ismailia a box, but when he sent him an empty Fortnum & Mason provisions box it was indignantly returned. The doctor looked about him for a better box and emptied a medical chest which pleased the chief. It was coloured and had a lock and key.

Sometimes they went an entire day without eating. Parke shot a hawk for the pot. He waited in vain with his rifle for wild pigs and his boy, to be sure of food, deserted him and went off to work for the Manyuema. By mid-November Nelson's condition had deteriorated; the ulcers recurred and he spent hours in a hammock. Parke could hardly bear to see such a splendidly athletic man — the Zanzibaris used to call him 'Pandalamona', the big strong man — reduced to an 'infirm, decrepit-looking skeleton'.[8] They bought whatever food was offered to them and Nelson sold a splendid scarlet waistcoat to Khamis for seven cups of meal. Parke had little clothing left but found himself quite comfortable with a towel around his waist — 'Most of the men and women wear nothing at all so we see a great deal of each other.'[9]

Ismailia started on a tour among the Washenzies this morning [Parke wrote on 14 November]. Each of these 3 Chiefs has a third of the surrounding country allotted to himself for his meanderings in search of plunder. They pillage the native villages for ivory and take whole families as slaves; indeed ivory trade and slave trade are synonymous, for the captors are returned in exchange for ivory only to be recaptured again to carry the same ivory to the Coast. We bought a little indian corn today.

Towards evening on 24 November there was a commotion throughout Ipoto and the women commenced an alarming ululation. News had filtered through from the advance-party that Stanley had killed the three guides and one of the Zanzibaris came to the officers to warn them not to sleep that night as the Manyuema were planning revenge. Parke and Nelson dared not think of the unimaginable tortures this might entail and decided that if they were to die they would die quickly. Taking refuge in the bush close to the tents Parke had his revolver and Nelson carried with him a more than adequate dose of strychnine.

Eventually the howling ceased, the village became quiet and the officers returned to their tents. Next morning the Manyuema chiefs explained that the initial rumours had been corrected and that the guides were slain by local tribesmen. [This encounter occurred *c.* 12 November but news moves slowly in the forest.][10]

Parke's 30th birthday on 27 November was a frugal occasion. Nelson had bought a goat to celebrate but in the expectation of an invitation (which did not materialize) to a mourning-feast for the dead guides they decided to save the beast. They killed it two days later and cooked the liver and kidneys immediately. So delicious were they that their palates demanded further gracious titillation, whereupon Parke produced a bottle of quinine-and-orange wine from a medicine chest. It made them quite tipsy and as a bonus they sold the empty bottle for corn. Next day they smoked the remaining goat-flesh.

They had a further *shauri* with the headmen on 1 December but when they offered two bales of cloth prospectively from the rear-column's stores the chiefs said they had no food to give. This led Parke to observe sourly how strange it was that there was always food to sell. He knew by now that the chiefs' strategy was directed towards forcing them into a plight in which they would be obliged to sell the rifles and ammunition, the talisman of power in Central Africa.

They managed to sow a small patch of beans and corn and Parke under-took the three-hour walk to the river to assure himself that the sections of the *Advance* were safe. The theft of Nelson's blankets and pyjamas from his tent was reported and having investigated the matter the chiefs found that Sarboko, a Zanzibari, had offered the blankets for sale. 'We hung him up by one arm to a tree for half-an-hour and he then confessed to having stolen the blankets and also two boxes of ammunition and a rifle.'[11]

Next day Sarboko retracted the confession and another Zanzibari was charged with stealing rice from the Manyuema chiefs. When the wretched man was tied tightly to a tree he howled so continuously that during the night Parke's boy, Sherif, decided to gag him. 'But so successfully did he do so that we found him dead in the morning.'[12]

Parke received three cups of beans from Sangeramani for medical atten-tion and on 6 December a chief's wife consulted him for a gynaecological complaint. Khamis was treated for constipation with such success that he remarked that two tablets, rather than four, might have sufficed.

Parke read Edwin Arnold's *The Light of Asia*, a favourite poem of J.S. Jameson, and dried the cartridges. At this time Nelson's condition had wors-ened. He was feverish, irritable and given to saying dispiritedly that they would never see their homes again. Eventually they agreed to open a bale of goods intended for Emin Pasha's personal use and sold a few 'shop-soiled' articles of clothing. For a coat and trousers they were given thirty head of Indian corn in what was, alas, a buyers' market. A Marino vest fetched seventy head of corn, a more satisfactory transaction.

Inevitably, Parke wondered if by now (9 December) Stanley had estab-lished contact with Emin Pasha and, of course, he had no way of knowing that after resting for several days at Ibwiri, where food was plentiful, to allow Jephson to catch up, the advance-party finally emerged from the forest on 4 December. It had then proceeded under a blue sky across a verdant plain towards the eastern hills, menaced from distant slopes to either side by angry natives. On the very day that Parke bartered the vest, Stanley, who on the previous evening read the exhortation of Moses to Joshua in *Deuteronomy* — 'Be strong and of good courage; fear not, nor be afraid of them' — had halted, prepared to chasten Mazamboni's bellicose warriors if they insisted on *Kurwana* (war) rather than the *Kanwana* (peace) he offered. Next day Stairs and Jephson led their companies into an action in which their modern arms assured them of victory. The banana planta-tions were scoured and the villages burned. Two days later the Albert Nyanza was sighted.

At Ipoto, on the path leading to the river, Parke found 'the bleached bones of Hatib Balyosi', a deserter from the advance-party, who had died of hunger within two miles of the camp. The ants had stripped whatever flesh remained. From time to time those diligent and disciplined insects took over the officers' tents forcing them to leave and stand within a circle of fire the red-hot embers of which provided the only impenetrable barrier. The ants, meanwhile, travelled fast, marching in mile-long columns through the tents; they had their generals and staff, their scouts and commissariat and being free, Parke noted, from the hindrance of 'red-tape', constituted a formidable enemy.

Wednesday, 14 December – The chiefs have commenced to build a new village at the opposite end of the *chamba*. Even they cannot bear the stench and filth. They commence building their own huts first and are building them of mud with thatched roof of leaves and verandah about 15 yards in length by 5 in breadth and 10 in height with a loft or granary to store away rice or corn. The framework of the huts is made of poles of different sizes with rods interwoven and clay between. There is also a boma of interwoven saplings about 6 feet high surrounding the back of the house where the women *twanga* or pound and also grind the corn on stones. Also a latrine consisting of the usual Arab fashion viz a deep hole covered over, with the exception of a hole about a foot square. There is also the harem enclosure. Nelson, poor chap, often talks of never getting home which helps to enliven the surroundings.

For some months Parke had enjoyed tolerably good health but in mid-December he developed a skin infection which he diagnosed as erysipelas (but J.C. Shee suggests it may have been a filarial infection),[14] which affected his left thigh spreading painfully to involve the lower abdomen and was accompanied by a large mass of septic glands in the groin. Parke knew instinctively that it would take about a month to resolve and that sooner or later the abscess would have to be lanced.

I am here exactly two months [he wrote on 18 December] and I sincerely hope that no other white man will ever be left amongst these barbarous Manyuema for so long a time. They have plenty of food but will not give it to us although we have sold them everything that we can possibly dispense with. Nelson is in such a weak condition that he will certainly die if he is attacked by any acute disease for he has no strength left and no food for him. It is really heart-rending. I'd much prefer to be by myself although not socially than see him wretched from day to day.

Having given himself an injection of cocaine as a local anaesthetic on 19 December, Parke prevailed upon Nelson to lance the abscess making a deep incision two inches long. The procedure gave great relief but he remained 'quite unstrung' because of their immobility which left them so open to

76

thieves. The loss of their rifles and ammunition would be an irremediable disaster.

On 21 December Parke got eight heads of corn 'for professional services' and accepting that 'the stomach governs the world' he decided, as the month advanced, that it would be justifiable to sell a Remington rifle in order to buy a goat and some 'nice things' for Christmas. The goodies they laid on included 'a lot of insects, half bees and half grubs which are found in the ground and are said to be good' and a *nousoir* made from pounded white ants which tasted like caviare. By 23 December Parke was improved but still febrile and unable to walk more than ten yards. He spent Christmas Day lying on the ammunition boxes with a soaring temperature. Nelson, feeling better, served goat and rice for dinner.

Parke regretted that he did not have a few of the bales of inferior calico that lay uselessly at Yambuya. With those to sell they could have lived 'like fighting-cocks'. As it was they were reduced to selling Emin's clothes, the disposal of which sometimes caused new problems. Having offered just four shirts for comparatively little, other potential buyers complained when no more shirts were available and vowed to wreak vengeance on the boys when they went for water. The officers knew that such threats were by no means idle. Ismailia had chopped off a slave-girl's hand for a petty offence and a young Zanzibari caught stealing received a fatal spear wound. Twelve Zanzibaris had disappeared and Parke seriously suspected that some of them had been eaten.

The imminent arrival of Kilonga Longa led him to hope for improved conditions but the headmen warned him to buy ten days' provisions as Ipoto would be reduced to starvation rations by an enlarged population. He was also told that he must give up the hut which was their only protection against the heat of the day.

Our position here is not without its comic side [he wrote on 27 December] for we are all crippled, 5 including our boys, and we are in the worst humour aggravated by fever, illness, dirt, starvation and the Manyuema who push into our tents, squat on our beds and covet everything they see. We purchased some bananas for some needles and pins. These Manyuema make a very serviceable cloth which they dye a variety of colours and sew it with grass with a needle made of rattan cane with eye complete.

Nelson was improving and the crops were a foot or so above the ground, but the milch goat was holding her milk. A tornado augmented their discomforts and the Old Year petered out dismally for Parke with a relapse of 'erysipelas' and a temperature of 104°F. Khamis had no food for them and once more they were eating leaves and fungi. 'Happy New Year to all relations and friends [Parke wrote in his diary] ... we have two onions and a cup of rice to see the five of us through the day. In the evening we sold a Remington rifle for 500 head of corn and some rice. I calculate it will be eighteen months before we get home.'[15]

The early days of 1888 saw Parke improving but Nelson was prostrated by fever and Sherif had stolen two bottles of Dover's powder and ipecachuana, some spoons and ammunition. The boy ran away when his master brandished a revolver. Parke had no intention whatsoever of shooting at him but actually proposed to hang him up by an arm until he confessed. A pair of Emin's drawers was exchanged for a chicken and as they needed meat so badly they decided to kill the goat.

Saturday, 7 January 1888 – Sangalamani brought us some rice (one cupful), goat's kidneys and liver which gave us a very excellent breakfast. This man has more gratitude in his composition than the others. We have arranged with Khamis to build us a house for our boys and also a boma for which we gave him a rifle and 70 rounds. It will be necessary to keep out Kilonga-Longa's rabble when they arrive.

Salvos of musketry, the beating of drums and a variety of cacophonies welcomed the approach of Kilonga Longa on 9 January 1888. He had been delayed when one of his wives went into labour but he now entered Ipoto with full ceremony, a small wiry man with sharp intelligent eyes, accompanied by some 400 travel-weary followers, men, women and children. In common with the expedition they had experienced hunger in the forest during the long trek north from Manyuema. They brought along with them Umari and the Zanzibari foraging-party missing from Nelson's starvation camp when Jephson relieved it. Kilonga-Longa had found them starving in the bush.

That evening the newly-arrived Zanzibaris visited the officers who took their rifles for safe keeping. The poor fellows were virtual skeletons but Parke and Nelson noticed with suspicion how their eyes took stock of everything in the tents. During the night Parke was roused by a peculiar scraping that ceased when he moved on his creaking bed only to recommence again and again in the silence. Suspecting an intruder he left the tent quietly and creeping around to where he expected a thief might be lying he rolled over 'a cold and slimy mass of bones covered by integument'.

It was a returned Zanzibari, Montgomery Kamaroni, who had almost removed a Remington through a hole cut in the canvas. Calling Nelson and the boys they tied him to a tree. The impulse to shoot him immediately was resisted; next day he was condemned to be hanged but accepting that the crime was committed under the spur of intolerable hunger the capital sentence was commuted to a flogging. 'I flogged him [Parke wrote] with rods until I was tired (which was not very severe).'[16]

Parke was asked to attend some of Kilonga Longa's invalids, including a woman who had just had a miscarriage and carried a tiny foetus to him wrapped in a banana leaf. The lately-arrived Zanzibaris were allowed to work for food. Kilonga Longa wore his sword when he paid a formal visit to the officers on 12 January. Parke, whose sword was stolen and whose mess-jacket was sold, felt a little at a disadvantage. It seemed a good opportunity, nevertheless, to discuss provisions but when Umari translated the English contract Kilonga Longa substituted the Arabic version which none of them could read. The Arab claimed to have known Stanley on the Congo and said he was not a good man. He had bought bales of cloth years ago from Salim ibn Abado in Manyuema but failed to pay for them in Zanzibar. Kilonga Longa had himself given Stanley thirty tusks of ivory in exchange for arms but was sent poor powder and inferior guns. Despite his animadversions the Arab chief sent them two days' rations of rice and despatched a raiding-party to comb the neighbourhood for food and ivory.

Torrid heat and torrential rain alternated and after the latter, as if newly created in a sea of slime, every inch of ground, every dirty heap of vegetable rubbish swarmed with little white maggots and other amorphous animalcules. A new moon, a clean silver sliver, graced the forest clearing, its sublimity insuffi-cient to obliterate the moral offence beneath; its directional powers were unable to assuage tides of human cupidity resulting in the hunger and the horror of enslaved possessors of the land bound to cruel Arab masters, themselves en-slaved to a mania for ivory; the stubborn white men ready to sacrifice all for some bewildering idea of sovereignty yet not unaware that the game was hardly worth the candle — brave adventurers, perhaps, striving for a secular Holy Grail, or subconscious victims of the lust for empire.

Parke observed that the Zanzibaris could display remarkable callousness towards one another. On 15 January 'a skeleton named Tofik' stumbled into Ipoto, a famished Zanzibari straggler who had managed to follow Kilonga Longa's caravan. He was on his last legs but his comrades did not want him near them at the fire or in their huts, the only possible excuse for their unkindness being that the starving man emitted a strong odour 'like the worst gorganzola cheese'.[17]

Kilonga Longa employed a craftsman to mend guns, another to make ivory-handled knifes. There was a Manyuema 'doctor' whose methods inter-ested Parke, who saw that he had a prominent position and was greatly respected. He used herbal medicines, drew red and white stripes on the bodies of the sick and built a little house beside the dwelling of a man going on an ivory raid to ensure his safety. A form of massage was available to pull, rub and squeeze the limbs, and the people had faith in his treatments.

The river from which they got their drinking-water was heavily polluted with human excrement swept into it by rain-water seeping down from the village where the Manyuema squatted at random, thinking 'that the calls of nature have a prior claim to decency'.[18] They washed periodically in the stream and following the Arabic custom cleansed themselves with water after evacuation.

Parke and Nelson were now walking a little but their larder was emptier than ever since the arrival of Kilonga Longa's 400 followers. Sometimes they subsisted on rice gruel; on better days the officers and Umari shared a cup of rice for breakfast and had corn for luncheon and a little maggoty meat for dinner.

The plight of the Zanzibaris, some of whom died from starvation, was even worse, for the Manyuema refused to feed them believing that Stanley would not honour his debts. They offered themselves as slaves and the officers suggested that they could be 'boarded out' in nearby villages. Such a course would not be without danger, for cannibalism was widespread in the forest. 'Last night [Parke wrote] one of the slaves went to the river about 200 yards from the Village to draw water. On the way he was attacked by his Comrades and eaten there and then.'[19]

Throughout those dismal days Parke continued to express the conviction that Stanley would eventually relieve them, but Nelson was less sanguine.

Notes

1 *Diary*, 28 October.
2 Ibid.
3 Jephson's *Diary*, p. 169.
4 *Diary*, 3 November.
5 *IDA*, I, p. 238.
6 Jephson's *Diary*, p. 181–2.
7 *Diary*, 11 Nov.
8 *Diary*, 22 Nov.
9 *Diary*, 28 Nov.
10 *IDA*, I, p. 256.
11 *Diary*, 5 December.
12 *Diary*, 6 Dec.
13 *Diary*, 7 Dec.
14 J. Charles Shee, 'Report from Darkest Africa', *Medical History*, 1966; 10: 27.
15 *Diary*, 1 January 1888.
16 *Diary*, 10 Jan.

17   *Diary*, 15 Jan.
18   *Diary*, 24 Jan.
19   Ibid.

7   Fort Bodo

The moon over Stanley's camp at Fort Bodo was still in its first quarter
when, on 18 January, Lieutenant Stairs was given final orders for his departure next day to Ipoto with a hundred rifles. The well-provisioned party,
familiar with the territory, covered the seventy-nine mile journey rapidly.
Parke was in his tent on 25 January repairing a broken rifle for Kilonga Longa
when Ismailia came to say that a caravan headed by a white man was
approaching. Drums were beaten and there were shouts of greeting.

We could scarcely speak with joy as we anticipated our relief was near. After a few
minutes Stairs arrived at the head of a column of the finest looking fat muscular men
with glossy skins I ever saw, the same men who left the camp just 3 months ago all
but 2 days. They cheered and we cheered. They fired a volley and Nelson and myself
fired off every chamber of our revolvers as a salute. The men kissed our hands and
were conscious that they were doing a good work in relieving us. When here before
they were serfs to the Manyuema but now they paraded about with a manly pride of
themselves.[1]

Stairs had come to take the invalids, the boat and as many loads as
possible to Fort Bodo where Stanley had established his headquarters. There
was an early *shauri* with the chiefs who were hardly surprised when the
officers repudiated any question of payment. The Manyuema had not respected their contract and so did not merit further reward. Nelson had
already given them kit worth £100, a rifle, a watch and various odds and
ends. The chiefs did not venture active remonstrance in the presence of
Stairs' strongly-armed force, especially as most of their own men were out
raiding.

Some of the wretched men who were with us [Parke continued] came dropping in as
the news spread and their awful skinny appearance was like a nightmare beside
Stairs' men. Many of our men were away at native villages and many had died from
the treatment of the Manyuema, many from starvation and disease, some I have
good reason to believe were eaten, if the remains of a fire and a few bones is
circumstantial evidence.

We did some packing and rearranging of loads and selecting of boxes last night and finished this morning.

Uledi set off to the Ituri River for the dismantled *Advance* and the rest of the day was devoted to preparing to leave Ipoto. The officers decided to kill the fatted calf (actually the milch goat) and they feasted on food brought by Stairs. It was one of the happiest evenings of Parke's life and they sat up late yarning with Stairs. He told them all that had happened on the way to the grass-lands; how they had found food in abundance in Ibwiri and emerging on the plain with less than half the men regained their strength; how, defying repeated attacks, they proceeded to the lake but had no news of Emin Pasha. Lack of food and the natives' hostility underlay Stanley's decision to withdraw to bountiful Ibwiri and build Fort Bodo (the Peaceful Fort) in a forest clearing where Chief Boryo's model village had stood prior to their arrival.

Rain delayed their departure next morning until eleven o'clock. There was a further *shauri* with the chiefs who begged for this and that. Stairs presented Kilonga Longa with two rifles and ammunition and they parted ostensibly on good terms though Parke would gladly have crucified the Manyuema, being painfully aware that his men were nightmare-like shadows beside their now well-nurtured comrades. Only sixteen of the thirty-nine entrusted to his care at ill-starred Ipoto were starting the journey to Fort Bodo. Nelson was still very shaky on his legs and both he and Parke had diarrhoea which they attributed to over-lavish helpings of goat-flesh. The Zanzibaris invalids, broken by privation, moved with the utmost difficulty and when three miles were completed they made camp.

The distances covered gradually increased but three men died on the road and within days they were back on starvation rations, foraging for plantains. Uledi joined them with the boat but the bulky sections slowed their progress through the bush.

Friday, 3 February – Marched 5 miles. Stairs gave me letters to Stanley and Jephson, as Nelson, myself and all the men except those carrying the boat should go on to Fort Bodo and not delay for the boat as food was scarce, and Stairs would follow on with the boat. We shall arrive on 7th or 8th, Stairs on 10th or 11th. Got another return of Erysipelas. I am to leave a letter for Stairs at Kilamani on the right hand side of the door of a certain hut saying if the natives attacked us and how we are getting on [this letter was afterwards found by Stairs].

From elevated ground at Kilimani on 5 February they could see all about them with a freedom they had not experienced since leaving Stanley Pool. The view extended over the top of the forest for more than twenty miles in all directions; there was nothing to see but an endless ocean of dense, blackish-green foliage, magnificent but dispiriting. Here and there were deserted clearings where elephants were destroying the plantations.

They passed a burned village on 7 February and dug holes in the ground to obtain drinking-water. Next morning at eleven they saluted Fort Bodo with a few rounds of rifle-fire as they straggled into camp behind the flag-bearer. Parke with the vanguard was welcomed warmly by Stanley and Jephson — 'Stanley was quite cheery for the first time.'[2] Nelson, bent and wan, stumbled after him an hour or so later looking like an octogenarian.[3]

Fort Bodo at Ibwiri, where there was an excellent water-supply and an abundance of plantains, was designed and rapidly built by Stanley to provide an area safe from attack where the expedition could rest permitting smaller parties to reconnoitre at the lake and others to return to Ugarrowa's or if necessary to Yambuya. It had a stockade, three 16 foot high watch towers and huts for Stanley, the white officers and the headmen. These had thick walls built with mud on a framework of interlaced saplings and given stability by strong poles at the corners, the sloping roofs thatched with leaves. There was a granary filled with Indian corn; latrines were provided and a trench was being dug. Roads led in and out of the the fort — the Manyuema Avenue and the Nyanza Avenue — and the Egyptian flag was flying over it. Close by some acres were cleared for the cultivation of beans and Indian corn. Milk was provided by three cows and twenty goats. The disadvantages included rats, fleas, mosquitoes and armies of red ants; snakes were disturbed when the bush was cleared and in the forest there were hostile natives and pygmy tribes with poisoned arrows who plundered the plantain groves.

Stanley drove men to their limits. Despite Parke's recent ordeal at Ipoto he was asked on the day after his arrival at the fort to supervise a party of axemen (they worked from 7 am to 6 pm, resting from eleven to twelve-thirty) extending the Nyanza Avenue. Jephson was required to leave with a foraging party within fifteen minutes of being given the order. His men looted neighbouring villages and, escaping from his control, inflicted violence on men, women and children:

I found one little boy speared to death in a hut. Of course if I see cruelty going on I put a stop to it at once, but it is impossible when the men are out of my sight. They captured five or six women, this I don't mind as the women always get away after a few days and from them the Zanzibaris are able to pick up a few words of the language which is useful.[4]

Stairs arrived with the boat on 12 February and left four days later to collect men and loads from Ugarrowa's 200 miles away and to despatch couriers to contact Barttelot and the rear-column.

Stanley himself planned a second journey to the Albert Nyanza with Jephson and the boat, leaving the doctor and Nelson at Fort Bodo. Nelson undoubtedly was not fit to travel but the prospect of a further long sojourn in camp displeased Parke, bitterly disappointed at the thought of missing the meeting with Emin Pasha, the dearly-bought consummation of their efforts. He ventured to ask the leader to bring him along and Stanley had agreed to do so when the ill-luck that had dogged the expedition again intervened. Stanley became aware of an increasingly painful arm with enlarged axillary glands which Parke expected to suppurate and form an abscess. But this was only the prelude to an illness briefly referred to in *In Darkest Africa* where the recovered patient compliments his physician: 'Dr. Parke has been most assiduous in his application to my needs, and gentle as a woman in his ministrations.'[5]

Called to Stanley's bedside at 3 am on 18 February, the doctor found the greatly alarmed leader afflicted by severe upper-abdominal pain, and tender over the liver and gall-bladder, experiencing, he believed, a recurrence of an old complaint which had nearly killed him on three occasions, the last attack in his chambers in Bond Street lasting three months. Parke's treatment was based on a principle which saw virtue in evacuations of the bowel even in the most dire circumstances. He gave Stanley a strong purgative (*Pilula Calomel podophylum et Colocynth*) and administered a castor-oil enema.

I put him on milk diet exclusively mixed with almost equal parts of water given in small amounts always cold. Pain over stomach very acute, vomiting very distressing very much darker in colour than ordinary bile. Great flatulence and belching, no sleep. I applied turpentine stupes and gave drops 40 of laudanum internally and $1/2$ gr morphia hypodermically at bedtime which gave great ease. I sat up all day and night with him. His tongue was coated with a thick white fur. Continued vomiting at short intervals all day and night. Bathed in profuse perspiration. Circulation and respiration rapid and he has now an attack of intermittent fever. This form always attacks when one is down from any cause. I gave quinine per rectum. Applied Indian corn poultices sprinkled with laudanum. His boy Saleh washes his feet and calves of legs and it has greater power to make him sleep than medicine.[6]

Parke deployed all the therapeutic resources at his disposal. When a castor-oil enema yielded no result on 20 February it was repeated in the afternoon with added turpentine and there was a satisfactory response. Opiates were repeated to ease pain. Urinary retention required catheterisation — 'he was astonished when I used the large catheter instead of a small one.'[7]

I have sat up with him two nights in succession and Jephson last night. Feels a little better but I am greatly alarmed about him. First I thought it was gall stones but now I am convinced it is subacute gastritis with congestion of liver.[8] Cannot sleep without morphia and Saleh rubbing his feet. I always have two boys sleeping in the room or at the door to be ready for this work and also to get what may be required but during the night they sleep and snore to such an extent that I have to rouse them every few minutes.[9]

As the diet of cold milk and water in equal parts in small amounts was beneficial, Parke began to worry about the health of the few animals yielding milk — 'if they die, Stanley dies also, for our European provisions have disappeared months ago, except for tea and coffee'. At times the patient was irascible and struck out at his servant, William Hoffmann, with his stick. When feeling livelier his thanks to Jephson was to contrast with what he called the latter's 'overweening pride — pride of birth & pride of self' with Stanley's own virtues. This caused Jephson silently to reflect on his leader's faults, impatience, ill-temper and untruthfulness.

I have now run short of my supply of castor oil [Parke wrote on 20 February] but the castor oil tree is found all across Africa and the natives make oil for rubbing on their bodies and especially where there is any pain. I collected quantities of the seeds and made oil which was just as good and effectual as what I brought with me excepting not so clear in colour. I used it on the men's ulcers, gave it as a purge and also encouraged them to annoint themselves as it made the unhealthy skins become glossy and fat probably absorbed as it undoubtedly makes them cool when exposed to the sun for it is the custom of the natives to smear themselves with oil or fat. Even our Zanzibaris say it cools them.

The seeds were toasted in a pan, pounded to a pulp in a large wooden mortar and boiled. When oil floated it was poured off. Dissatisfied with the dark oil, Parke had the husks of the toasted seeds removed and pounded only the white kernels. Oil made in this way 'is exactly like what is bought in a druggist's shop in England'.

Parke and Jephson sat up alternately until 27 February when the abdominal pain diminished and Stanley began to take beef-tea as well as milk. Eucalyptus inhalations eased bronchitis and the painful arm was painted with Tincture of Iodine. By early March Stanley was taking sago and chicken-tea, but soon he was again pyrexial. 'High Fever, gave Enema of $1^1/_2$ pints of Gruel soap and oil. At 2 pm gave 25 grains of Quinine.'

Parke suspected William Hoffmann of drinking Stanley's milk and he was infuriated by the servant's objectionable flatulence which caused his master to say 'Get out of the room you dirty beast.'[10]

Friday, 2 March – Gave Stanley 25 grains of Quinine as a prophylactic against fever. I sat up last night for the third night in succession. Like most people he is very irritable when ill. He made Uledi give William thirty-five this morning.

Meanwhile the abscess (probably a major cause of the septic fever) had ripened as Parke predicted. The doctor lanced it on 6 March using cocaine as a local anaesthetic and obtained two teacupsful of pus. Next day Parke noted 'he is hectic this morning and sweats a good deal.'[11] Jephson, too, had come down with fever and Nelson was ill and using a native medicine made from plantain stalks to allay itching.

The abscess continued to drain and within a few days the patient was allowed to walk a little in the fresh-air; he enjoyed roast chicken, felt stronger and constantly asked for food. He had only a 'confused recollection' of the first week of illness when he was delirious and slept under opiates but now he liked to be carried to the Nyanza Avenue where there was a splendid colonnade of trees. He read drowsily in an easy-chair and was delighted to watch the corn-fields and listen to the wind blowing over them. 'This is the music [he wrote] to which I listen devoutly, while my medical friend sits not far off on the watch, and sentries stand still at each end of the avenue on guard.'[12] He sat there until Parke helped him to his feet and supported him as he walked slowly to his hut with backward glances at the dancing corn.

A man was killed while foraging and another wounded. Stanley improved steadily and it was Parke's turn on 11 March to have a bout of fever following a wetting but he shrugged it off and set about preparing 'an Ambulance or Landau' for the leader. This consisted of a number of cowhides sewn to-gether permitting the convalescent to sit or lie fully protected from sun or rain by a roof and borne by two carriers. On 16 March the poultices were discontinued; Stanley could put his arm in a sling and he was taking a normal diet.

Two men, Sarmini and Kamwaiya, were fatally wounded by arrows shot at them from behind the perimeter of the forest clearing. Uledi captured a tiny, perfectly-built pygmy woman. The extended Nyanza Avenue in which Stanley took great pride was half-a-mile long but secretly Parke felt it was a waste of labour. Nelson, somewhat recovered, was to take command of forty-eight men remaining at Fort Bodo and Parke trained the boys to wash the invalids' ulcerated limbs with water and carbolic acid.

From 19 to 22 March – No sign of Stairs. Had a general parade of 141 men and 7 Muniparas (or chiefs); 41 and one officer remain to hold the Fort with 26 rifles. Stanley, Nelson, Jephson and myself had some target practice yesterday. On 19th and 20th [Stanley] remained with the workmen at the river during a shower of rain. The weather is in a very bad state. I offered to do the work and told him to go in as he might get a return of his illness but he refused. Tried an Indian remedy for Fever, Javi Hari, dose from 40 to 100 drops.

From 23 to 30 March – This is Good Friday and is the last day of work for the men as we leave on Monday for the Nyanza.

The advance-party of 125 including boys and officers mustered on 31 March.[13] Each man was given his load and Parke and Jephson decided to reduce weight by leaving their tent poles behind and cutting poles every night in the forest.

Notes

1 *Diary*, 25 January 1888.
2 *Diary*, 8 February.
3 *IDA*, I, p. 337.
4 Jephson's *Diary*, p. 226–7.
5 *Diary*, 19 Feb.
6 *Diary*, 21 Feb.
7 *Diary*, 20 Feb.
8 In terms of modern pathology this seems an unlikely diagnosis. Acute inflammation of the gall-bladder could explain the clinical picture but Stanley would have been fortunate to survive so many attacks of cholecystitis without further complications. A series of attacks of acute pancreatitis is a possible explanation.
9 *Diary*, 27 Feb.
10 *Diary*, 21 Feb.
11 *Diary*, 7 March.
12 *IDA*, I, p. 347.
13 Parke's figures do not always tally.

8   Meeting Emin Pasha

Leaving Fort Bodo at noon on 2 April after the cessation of heavy rain, Parke was buoyed-up by a sense of the renewal of an adventure. Soon the oppressive forest would close behind him and soon, God willing, they would establish contact at last with Emin Pasha, the elusive phantom for whom so many men's lives had already been sacrificed.

The dismantled boat was a hindrance along the forest tracks and as usual vigilance was needed to protect themselves against invaders. They made camp at 4 pm after completing eight miles. Parke was called to Stanley's tent where the latter was nursing a painful knee and fretful in case he was again developing fever. Next day, although he was carried, the pain persisted. Parke gave him quinine and said it was due either to rheumatism or exhaustion. Jephson's fever was combated by the doctor's favourite nostrum, *Pil. Pod. Cal. Col.*

The caravan stopped at 10.30 am on 6 April having arrived at a plantation where they found an ample supply of bananas and a number of vessels containing Pombi or banana wine. Stanley's knee finally responded to applications of St Jacob's oil.[1]

At the Ituri River the *Advance* was assembled on 10 April to ferry the party across. Shots were fired to clear natives away from the opposite bank and Parke was sent over to hold this bank until the transport was completed. The natives disappeared into the forest where they caused a commotion that reminded him of a pack of hounds in full cry. In the vacated huts there was a quantity of bark-cloth, an assortment of ornaments including bracelets made from human teeth, and ten pounds of salt, a welcome finding which for some time added greatly to the enjoyment of their meals.

'We marched to the open plain', Parke wrote on 14 April, his words inadequate to express his emotions. As they approached the grasslands the doctor, who by now had been enclosed in the steamy forest continuously for 289 days, was sent ahead to find the nearest point of emergence. An hour-and-a-half later he marched onto the plain 'after nearly 12 months in the bush.'[2] He exchanged a dark world of gloom and shadows for a realm of grass, brilliant sunshine and blue skies. Stanley smiled to see him 'quiver with delight. Deep draughts of champagne could not have painted his cheeks with a deeper hue than did this exhilarating prospect which now met him.'[3] A nearby village supplied material for celebration including native tobacco which Parke had cause to remember. 'Jephson and myself gorged over a real Alderman's dinner of Goat, Chicken & Beans. [We] got very pale and sick after smoking the Tobacco which was stronger than we expected.'[4]

At the next village they were surrounded by warlike natives. Fetteh, the only interpreter for the tribes of the plain was badly wounded in the chest by an arrow at the lower sternal margin. He vomited blood and collapsed. Rifle-power gained control and the sharp-shooters maintained it from high vantage points in the hills. The tall grass and brushwood was cleared from the immediate area and a boma was provided. 'One of the parties brought in the head of a blind native whom they had shot.'[5]

Fetteh (who was given nutrient enemas) changed places with Stanley in the ambulance chair and Parke was hampered a little by a knee sprained, he thought, when running after the retreating natives but possibly evidence of onchocerciasis, a filarial infection. The natives took up positions on the neighbouring hills and called to each other with voices distinctly audible for miles, a phenomenon Parke had noticed on the Nile during the Gordon relief expedition.

They camped on 14 April on an isolated hill and fired at natives in the vicinity. The latter showed less disposition than usual to take flight and before long some unarmed men were sent out with peace overtures. 'After a while the natives came in one by one.'[6] They crouched submissively before Stanley and explained that they had mistaken him for an agent of their enemy, Kabba Rega, King of Unyoro. They told him that a *Mazunga* (white man) had come in a canoe made of iron to the nearest end of the Albert Nyanza. Here at last were tidings of Emin Pasha! The natives called him *Malleju*, the bearded one; he was alive and not far off.

Remained all day in camp [Parke wrote on 15 April] and received visits from Mazamboni, who is the Chief of all the surrounding country and his satellites. To seal our friendship according to native custom we were obliged to perform blood-brotherhood. Jephson was the martyr. He and Mazamboni sat on the ground facing each other with their legs extended, Jephson's right leg on the top of Mazamboni's left leg and Mazamboni's right leg on the top of Jephson's left leg. Marabo, a Zanzibari who understands these things, got one of my lancets and made a small incision on the inner side of Jephson's left knee and Mazamboni's right knee. When the blood appeared some salt was rubbed into the cut, a few mysterious signs were made and Marabo repeated a few appropriate remarks and the ceremony was finished. And now we were all friends... The natives were very frightened of our rifles although they have been attacked by rifles before when invaded by the Warasura or sharpshooters of Kabba Rega, King of Unyoro.

Fetteh was well enough to interpret and they had heard of two white men on the lake, presumably Emin and his henchman, Captain Casati, who had come to Africa to survey the Bahr al Ghazal and later found work in Equatoria.[7] Mazamboni's guides led them in a triumphal procession to Gavira's where they camped on 16 April. They were given goats, a cow and some chickens and they were told that a packet from *Malleju* awaited Stanley at Kavalli's, a day's march away and close to the lake. When shown a mirror, Gavira and his elders were astonished and a little frightened. Were the men they saw members of a hostile tribe? It took a little time before they understood that they were looking at their own reflections.

Dr Emin's letter, enclosed in protective oil-cloth, was finally handed over to Stanley on 18 April. The governor had been apprised of the white men's arrival at the lake and he promised to come to meet Stanley on hearing from him. 'We are all in great ecstasy as the trick is finished', Parke enthused. He noticed, too, that the letter was wrapped in a page of *The Times* with news of the first spring meeting (1886) at Newmarket where the Two Thousand Guineas Trial Plate was won by Mr Manton's 'Prinstead' with F. Barrett up. Emin mentioned that Casati was expelled from Unyoro by Kabba Rega.

At Kavalli's, a village on a grassy plateau named for the chief of the Babiassi, owner of large herds, they were given a cow and a goat. Parke, recalling his father's cattle in County Roscommon, was concerned to see how the animals were tormented 'by a Bird the size of a Thrush' which pecked their backs while feeding on insects and caused sores. He was amused to see that attempts to shoo the bird away caused the ox-pecker to run down the opposite side of the beast where it was safe from interference.

Parke and Jephson were instructed on 20 April to take the *Advance* down to the lake from the tableland which fell in four great rocky terraces, each about 600 feet, to the shore. They were to launch the boat, and Jephson should then proceed to M'swa, Emin's station two days' distance on the south-west side of the nyanza. They were accompanied by fifty rifles and two native guides and, as they descended the steep slope, they were astonished to see, far-off, a snow-covered mountain.

On the march we distinctly saw snow on the top of an immense Mountain to the south west. As this was an unexpected sight we halted the Caravan to have a good view. Some of the Zanzibaris said this white appearance of the Mountain was salt but Jephson and myself were quite certain that it was snow.[8]

Jephson does not mention 'the Snow Mountain' in his diary for that date, recalling instead that he and Parke 'had a splendid dinner of some mutton, the first we tasted since we left the sea.'[9] Kavalli had given them a fat broad-tailed sheep which made a pleasant change from goat-meat. The natives on the plain were friendly but the mosquitoes were quite intolerable and the huts stank of goats. They spent the night in the open beside a bonfire, the smoke of which helped to keep the insects away.

They set out at daybreak and marched for five miles over parkland rich in game to the water where the boat was assembled and launched. Parke was astonished by the number of animals about, antelopes, hartebeests, buffaloes and elephants. He shot two antelopes which gave them a good meal with enough left over to provide Jephson and the boat crew with two days' eating. They shoved the *Advance* off on the quest for Emin and gave it three rousing cheers.

Parke had a few shots at the crocodiles and on the way back to the foot of the mountain he shot two more antelopes and a number of guinea-fowl. 'The men have gorged to such an extent that they are incapacitated for work.'[10] Back at Kavalli's Parke told Stanley about the 'Snow Mountain'.

The differences between the arrows used in the forest and the barbed iron arrow-heads used on the plain interested Parke, who also saw that the natives on the plain had a variety of musical instruments resembling harps, banjos or zithers.

The strings are made from gut. Whenever an animal is killed there is great demand amongst the Zanzibaris for the aponeurosis or fibrous tissue covering the muscles over the loins as they use them for thread to sew their garments. They also use grass and the leaves of a peculiar Palm which they tease out and use for thread. Their needle is made from Rattan Cane with an hole in one end for an eye. The Manyuema are very clever in making very durable material from grasses. It is very thin and beautifully woven. They make coats and clothes from this material.[11]

Now that a meeting with Emin was imminent the camp was moved down from Kavalli's on the watershed between the Congo and the Nile. From Bundi at the crest of the plateau Parke gazed at Unya-Kavalli and other distant hills, and with the wonderful mountain he had seen in mind, he asked Stanley if snow ever appeared on these. Stanley explained that none of these eminences was more than 5500 feet above sea-level and that in equatorial regions permanent snow does not occur below 15,000 feet. Descending, and goaded by the constant spur of hunger, they raided a village which had refused them food and appropriated provisions for five days. These were augmented by Parke, Saat Tato the hunter, and other marksmen.

Two parties were sent out [on 27 April], one about 5 miles off to the shore of the Lake to report if Emin Pasha's Steamer was in sight. I took another party out to shoot some game which we succeeded in finding and brought back to camp. Saat Tato shot one kudu and Wadi Mabruki brought down two.

A highpoint of excitement was reached on 29 April, for that evening the Pasha was expected. Just before sunset they camped close to the lake and vied with one another, like children, as to who would get first sight of the steamer. Having the advantage of binoculars, Stanley, perched on an ant-hill, was the first to announce its arrival. As the *Khedive* approached bonfires were lit, shots were fired and 'the Zanzibaris became wild with joy, now that they were certain of the existence of the white man whom they often disbelieved in during their terrible wanderings in the forest.'[12] The steamer anchored in the Bay of Nyamassi, about two miles away, and Parke waited by the lakeside to receive Emin Pasha, who came ashore with Jephson and Casati in the *Advance*. He was of slight build, about five feet seven inches in height and bearded; he wore an immaculate white suit, spectacles and a tarboosh and had impeccable manners.

Jephson took Emin Pasha's arm and Parke walked with Captain Casati (with whom he held an animated conversation though neither spoke the other's language) in a torchlight procession along a track two hundred yards long that brought them to Stanley's tent, The explorer greeted the governor warmly and Casati and the officers sat with him while Stanley disappeared, to return like a magician with five half-bottles of champagne, actually given to him by the agent at Stanley Pool and concealed in a pair of long stockings in his box of personal effects to await this very moment. They drank to the Pasha's health and to Casati's. The governor spoke English fluently while Parke and Jephson did their best to entertain Casati using a mixture of French, English, Swahili and Arabic. Emin said he could not thank the British sufficiently for sending relief, adding that he did not know if he could leave Equatoria after accomplishing so much there and with everything in such perfect order.

It was an hour of triumph and fulfilment for Stanley and his officers, not a group to speak aloud of heroism and daring, nor to grieve unduly over human losses. They had finally located Emin Pasha and though in terms of immediate material needs he seemed in a better position to relieve them, they could now gather-up the rear-column and withdraw from Africa. And yet, as by candle-light they savoured the wine, itself a gracious symbol of alien intrusion, Emin's uncertainty may have caused them, were they not ruled by pragmatism rather than by thought, to wonder why were they there at all. Why had they listened so eagerly to the clamant voice of patriotism, a voice with commercial undertones, urging them to set out recklessly on a hastily improvised expedition with faulty logistics? Why, in the name of common sense, had they not recognized its mendacity?

Such questions are unlikely to have adulterated their pleasure as they chatted in the dimly lit tent in the centre of Africa, dazed by their achievement and glad to leave further decisions till the morrow. But they were to find that Emin lacked the capacity to decide tomorrow, or the next day, or the next week, or the next month; the tragedy of his indecisiveness was to play havoc with the expedition.

Stanley, bound to have recalled another meeting by another lake when he poured champagne for Dr Livingstone, wished to have some days at leisure in Emin's company, so they moved to a more pleasant location at N'sabwé, a grassy spot fifty yards from the lake.

We marched the column on a few miles further to a good camping ground as we shall probably remain for 10 days or so. Stanley, the Pasha and Casati have gone up in the steamer to appoint our new camp. The Pasha has brought many cows, sheep and goats, a donkey, onions, durha flour, also cloth and a demijohn or large glass bottle of clear intoxicating liquor, not unlike Poteen, distilled from grain. The cloth is especially useful as all of us are in rags and look fearful brigands compared with the beautifully neat appearance of the Pasha.[13]

Passing the anchored *Khedive* they found a line of soldiers drawn up to salute them. The Pasha was dressed formally and his Soudanese in their trim uniforms were certainly a remarkable contrast to the tattered Zanzibaris.

Emin and Stanley held endless conferences but the latter found it impossible to decide how the governor's mind worked and was baffled by his way of tapping his knee, as if to say: 'We shall see.' The Khedive had instructed Emin to return with his officials to Cairo where they would be fully remunerated, but he had given him the option of staying on in his province, in which case he would no longer be paid. Other options which Stanley mentioned were that Equatoria might be controlled by Emin from the Congo, a possibility that had King Leopold's blessing; or that the Pasha should move to the Victoria Nyanza and work under the auspices of the East African Association. Emin's own suggestion to Sir John Kirk, Consul-General at Zanzibar, that Great Britain should take the province over, had little appeal for the Foreign Office which dismissed it as a useless possession.

On board the *Khedive*, or walking by the lake, or in Stanley's tent their interminable conversation was resumed, but in his heart Emin Pasha was unprepared to turn his back on 'his country of aromatic and transparent honey, scented grass, tamarisk and palm'.[14] An instinctive patriarch, a scientist and polyglot rather than a ruler, a man inclined to cajole his subordinates rather than to issue firm orders, the governor considered the matter minutely. How could he desert his subjects? 'If the people go, I go', he said, 'if they stay, I stay.'[15] The Soudanese had taken wives locally. How could they move their harems? 'We have a large number of women and children,' he explained, 'probably 10,000 people altogether. How can they all be brought out of here?'[16] The Egyptian officials, a relatively small group of low-class people, many of them banished from Egypt for petty crimes, were a different matter. These he would gladly be rid of and he would be indebted to Stanley if he repatriated them.

It had been long foreseen that Emin, like Livingstone, might not wish to be escorted to Europe, a dilemma commented on by *The Times*:

Whether the gallant Austrian [sic] will wish in person for Mr. Stanley's escort home none can determine. He probably could not come to a conclusion on the matter himself as yet. A final effacement of the traces of the brave stand Dr. Emin has made within a ring of rancorously hostile fire would be a subject of poignant regret.[17]

And yet it was accepted that it would be a blow to Stanley 'if a second time he had to return after hunting down his noble quarry without itself to show as the crowning evidence of his achievement.'[18]

Among the many scenarios that had presented to Stanley's imagination was a rapid downriver journey from Yambuya with Emin's officers 'and some thirty women and fifty children whose return to Egypt it was desired to effect.'

On the one side there was the river to float down and take these women and children straight to the Atlantic without any trouble, with the prospect of being hospitably received all the way. This would be one month's journey, or forty days at the utmost, to the sea. The other route would involve 1200 miles of march through combative tribes against whom women and children would have to be guarded.[19]

The impossibility of leading a large caravan including followers through the rainforests was by now perfectly clear to Stanley but his miscalculation was to result in the havoc of the rear-column.

Emin concealed his internal political insecurity from Stanley and asked for an officer to accompany him to Dufilé to speak to the troops there, as a representative of the Egyptian government. He requested that Dr Parke should be allowed to go with him to read the Kehdive's orders to the people but Stanley could not spare the doctor and nominated Jephson instead.

A boma was built at N'sabwé to shelter the cattle, sheep, fowls and grain provided by Emin who was given thirty-one cases of Remington ammunition and had many gifts for the officers including the highly intoxicating native spirit. Parke was given cotton cloth to make shirts and trousers with, and a less useful present, a pair of red Turkish slippers 'fit for a Harem Lady'.[20]

Despite the camp's pleasant location it had certain disadvantages — blustering winds and mimosa trees with strong thorns. Parke had several bouts of fever and being something of a iatro-mechanist he attributed them to the strong gusts and exposure to sun while out shooting. Admittedly, he was also concerned to improve the sanitary conditions.

At the height of the fever, on 3 May, he had to walk three miles in the sun to attend Mabruki ibn Hassim, gored by a wounded buffalo. 'I found his Perinaeum so lacerated that the Guts and Bladder were quite exposed.' Several ribs were broken and there was a head-injury. Parke dressed the appalling wounds and the unfortunate man was carried to the camp on a cowhide stretcher.

Our hunters have brought in some game [Parke wrote on 4 May] but there is no food of any sort within 2 or 3 days march from here. I am down with fever again today, 106 all day yesterday but better today...

Idleness added to hunger bred discontent at N'sabé. The Zanzibaris were too lazy to walk to the shore to carry provisions from the *Khedive* but were prepared to go looting. The monotony was broken when Stanley erupted furiously on learning that when seven Zanzibaris had raided a nearby village one man was killed, another captured. He called the garrison to attention and thrashed those who had lost their ammunition. He even fined Saat Tato for wasting ammunition while hunting buffalo, causing Parke to observe sourly, 'cartridges are more valuable than meat in these parts'.[21]

Sent out with forty-two rifles to seek the missing men and punish the natives, Parke found no trace of the prisoner in the hillside village. He set fire to about eighty huts and seized three goats, some chickens and a quantity of grain. Towards sunset he prepared to withdraw, an action misinterpreted by the natives.

The natives [Parke wrote] considered our retreat was due to fear and came down upon us in great force. They seemed to rise from every rock and swarmed out of the cornfields where they were concealed. However, a few rounds stopped them. They made a great noise shrieking to each other from the hill tops and the Zanzibaris understood the language sufficiently well to know what they were saying. Those on the hill were telling the natives in the hollow to go into the corn and intercept us on the path as we descended the hill.[22]

Parke wisely decided to halt for the night at a small village and burned about thirty huts to clear a space around the camp. They erected a boma to protect themselves against arrows and feasted on the goats. They set out at daybreak by a roundabout route and reached N'sabwé safely at noon whereupon there was a scene — 'Bula Matari in tantrums' — as Stanley flogged and scolded some men who left their loads in the long grass before entering the camp, intending to recover their loot later.[23]

All men fell in [on 12 May]. There were 2 men short. He sent me with 29 men to teach them skirmishing, the remainder he sent to build huts. Stanley's drilling was laughable in the extreme. The men have 3 days provisions now as I brought 9 cups of corn, beans etc to each man. But they deserve to be without food as they would not carry up the food from the Steamer and it had to return with its cargo. The men returning yesterday as usual hid much food in the grass but it was found by a party under Uledi and brought to camp.

The *Khedive* which plied between Emin's stations arrived on 14 May and brought a few milch cows and a supply of millet. The governor's repeated generosity proved that his state of 'distress' had been greatly exaggerated. Each officer was given fruit and honey. Stanley rejoiced to receive a pound of good tobacco and a pot of pickles. Parke's wardrobe was amplified with a singlet, a blue jersey and a pair of drawers. Fetteh had largely recovered and Mabruki ibn Hassim was doing surprisingly well. There were visits from Kavalli and other chiefs and the Zanzibaris and their former foes sang and danced late into the night.

The steamers *Khedive* and *Nyanza* arrived on 22 May with 180 reluctant Madi carriers and eighty Soudanese soldiers, loaned temporarily to the expedition by Emin Pasha. Tending to spell African names phonetically, Parke had difficulty in distinguishing between the Madi (local tribesmen) and the Mahdists, followers of 'the Expected One.' Next day the governor gave Parke beads to use as currency during his journey and also a strong donkey. 'He thinks of everything to make us happy and comfortable.' Emin also gave Stanley a donkey and ten gallons of spirit of his own distillation — 'it is of clear colour and almost as intoxicating as whiskey.'

Stanley and Parke left the lake to return to Fort Bodo on 24 May which, as the doctor noted, was the Queen's birthday. Jephson remained behind to accompany Emin Pasha to his northern stations. They moved off at 6 am in the direction of Badzwa, a village ten miles away at the foot of the plateau, and Emin went with them for a mile or so. Then his musicians played the Khedivial hymn as he drew his personal guard to attention in a formal farewell.

Stanley led the caravan and as he marched he meditated on recent events. The journey had been perhaps half completed when a boy drew his attention to 'a most beautiful silver cloud' in the distance to the south-east, thought to be a mountain covered with salt.

Following its form downward [Stanley wrote in *In Darkest Africa*], I became struck with the deep blue-black colour of its base, and wondered if it portended another tornado; then as the sight descended to the gap between the eastern and western plateaus, I became for the first time conscious that what I gazed on was not the image or semblance of a vast mountain, but the solid substance of a real one, with its summit covered with snow. I ordered a halt and examined it carefully with a field-glass, then took a compass bearing of the centre of it, and found it bear 215° magnetic, It now dawned upon me that this must be Ruwenzori ...[24]

Marching with the rearguard, Parke also recognized the 'Snow Mountain' but he was in no mood to enjoy the spectacle because twenty of the Madi tribesmen, pressed into service as carriers, had deserted. He had put the remainder under armed guard but there were streams to cross and dense bush to negotiate and, about eight miles from the Nyanza, the Madi rebelled. Parke, fearing the column was about to be attacked, shot one of them dead and wounded another but the majority escaped. Nineteen men were recaptured and taken on to Badzwa.

Parke then retraced his steps to the Nyanza in order to let Emin know what had happened. He dined with Jephson and the governor and they drank the Queen's health. During dinner a message came from M'swa that 120 errant carriers had arrived there. He also learned that Mabruki ibn Hassim had died.

The steamer set off immediately to bring back the runaways and Parke returned to Badzwa to await them. Eventually eighty-two carriers arrived under military escort and tied together by cowhide ropes. The march was resumed and Parke, with the rearguard, had difficulty in driving the animals, seven cows, six calves, twenty-six sheep and seven goats, up the steep path. A cow with a broken leg had to be shot. The carriers regained a measure of good humour on the plateau and despite their bonds they sang and danced.

Having been reliably informed by natives from Bundi that two warlike chiefs, Kadongo and the powerful Musiri, planned to ambush them on the march, Stanley struck pre-emptively at Kadongo's village by night with complete success. He then called on his new allies, Kavalli and Mazamboni, for support in dealing with Musiri. And so Parke found himself in command of sixty of his own company and 1500 tribesmen prepared to do battle with Musiri. 'We burned several hundred huts and destroyed acres of beans but the natives who must have been warned had disappeared with their families and cattle and food to the hills.'[25] He was on his feet from 4 am to 1 pm. The bloodless victory was celebrated on the afternoon of 29 May by a magnificent phalanx dance.

The phalanx stood still [Stanley wrote] with spears grounded until, at a signal from the drums, Katto's deep voice was heard breaking out into a wild triumphant song or chant, and at a particular uplift of note raised his spear, and at once rose a forest of spears high above their heads, and a mighty chorus of voices responded, and the phalanx was seen to move forward, and the earth around my chair, which was at a distance of fifty yards from the foremost line, shook as though there was an earthquake. I looked at the feet of the men and discovered that each man was forcefully stamping the ground, and taking forward steps not more than six inches long, and it was in this manner that the phalanx moved slowly but irresistibly. The voices rose and fell in sweeping waves of vocal sound... The thousand heads rose and dropped in unison... Right up to my chair the host of chanting natives advanced... It was certainly one of the best and most exciting exhibitions I had seen in Africa.[26]

They marched next day to their old camp at the end of a range of hills and Parke carried a calf on his donkey. Mazamboni and his chiefs disappointed him by failing to bring food, but promised to make amends on the morrow. The doctor had a tiff with William Hoffmann about the way he shared out the chickens. Parke complained that out of sixty fowls bought by Stanley on the plain, he and Jephson were given only six apiece. 'William dispossessed of them by saying that they have died, in reality he has eaten them.'[27]

After a day in bed with fever Parke took charge of the rearguard which did not reach camp until 4 pm. He had hardly sat down to a delayed luncheon when Stanley appeared from his tent.

'Doctor,' he asked sharply, 'have you seen the sick man?'

'No', replied Parke not having been told of any new patient. 'Is he a Zanzibari?'

'No, a native.'

Parke left his meal immediately, annoyed by the implication that he had neglected a patient, and he was glad to find the native's complaint trivial.

They reached the Ituri River on 3 June and having seized three canoes crossed it the next day, taking four-and-a-half hours to do so, the carriers roped in groups of three. The cattle swam across and when a speculative crocodile ventured too close Stanley shot it.

Parke gave his donkey to Fetteh, who was spitting blood, but the interpreter was too weak to cling on; his companions were prepared to leave him lying by the wayside until the doctor said he must be carried on a stretcher. They were attacked by hornets as they entered the forest and by now they were living off the land again and constantly at risk from hidden archers. The carriers were unroped and Parke secured three days' supply of bananas which lasted him until they reached Fort Bodo on 8 June.

Notes

1 A liniment to be applied locally or taken internally, the ingredients of St Jacob's oil included tincture of opium, chloral hydrate, chloroform, sulphurated ether, oil origanum, oil sassafras, alcohol.

2 *Diary*, 11 April 1888.

3 *IDA*, I, p. 354.

4 *Diary*, 11 April.

5 *Diary*, 12 April.

6 *Diary*, 14 April.

7 Signor Gaetano Casati (1838–92) was sent to Africa by the Milan Geographical Society in 1876 when Gessi, governor of the Bahr al Ghazal, asked for a surveyor for his province. Following Gessi's retirement and death, Casati moved to Monbuttu and was rescued in an impoverished state by Emin. He was sent as agent to the court of Kabba Rega in Unyoro but this employment ended when Kabba Rega drove him out and destroyed the specimens and observations he had collected. Jephson's impression was that he 'lived almost like an Oriental. He scarcely ever left his own house till the evening, when he used to go and gossip with the people of the station. He sat in his hut all day and smoked; he had no books and kept no journal; I never could understand how he managed to pass the time, but he was very helpful to Emin.' (Jephson, *Rebellion* p. 196).

8 *Diary*, 20 April.

9 Jephson's *Diary*, p. 242. After a fuller view of Ruwenzori on 2 April 1889, Jephson wrote (p. 341): 'Last year we only saw what seemed to be a large solitary snow-capped mountain, but from this view of it is one great chain of snow-capped peaks extending one over another in the far distance. It was a beautiful sight, the great expanse of snow, shining in the sun in the middle of central tropical Africa. As the sun sank it turned the snow a rosy colour.'

10 *Diary*, 21 April.

11 *Diary*, 22 April.

12 *Diary*, 9 April.

13 *Diary*, 30 April.

14 A.J.A. Symons, *Emin Governor of Equatoria*, 2nd edn (London 1928) p. 47.

15 *IDA*, I, p. 381.

16 Ibid, p. 279.

17 *The Times*, 14 January 1887.

18 Ibid.

19 Ibid.

20 *Diary*, 2 May.

21 *Diary*, 10 May.

22 *Diary*, 10 May.
23 Ibid.
24 *IDA*, I, p. 405.
25 *Diary*, 28 May.
26 *IDA*, I, p. 413.
27 *Diary*, 1 June.

9   At the Fort in the Forest

After the customary rifle-shots of salutation and welcome, the inhabitants streamed out of Fort Bodo. Parke was greeted warmly by Nelson and Stairs who looked well — 'pasty' according to Stanley. The Zanzibaris, 'joy sparkling in their eyes', made no attempt to conceal their labile emotions.[1] The cattle, sheep and goats were driven to a boma prepared for them.

There was an immediate interchange of news: Stanley and Parke related the occurrences at the Albert Nyanza. Stairs described his fever-ridden journey to Ugarrowa's. Fifty-six men had been left there in September 1887; twenty-six died, one went down-river and three were out raiding; twenty-six accompanied Stairs of whom ten died on the road, one deserted and one, unable to proceed, was left at Ipoto. Only fourteen had reached Fort Bodo alive.

Parke found many ulcer cases but otherwise all was well at the fort in the forest where he was destined to remain for many months. There was Indian corn in the granary; the banana plantation with abundant fruit was raided constantly by pygmies from the neighbouring Wambuti villages and damaged now and then by elephants. Stanley's forty-sixth birthday on 10 June coincided with the end of Ramadan and the Zanzibaris sang and danced outside his tent.

The successful meeting with Emin Pasha boded well for the expedition's fulfilment but Parke knew that at least one Herculean labour remained: to unite the rear-column with the advance-party. 'It is a terrible thing to think of going back all the way for Barttelot', Parke wrote on 8 May but now Stanley had decided to undertake that challenging labour personally. It seemed apparent that Tippu Tib had broken his contract failing to bring 600 carriers to Yambuya. But where were Barttelot, Jameson and the rest of the rear-column? Were they still at Yambuya or were they striving towards the higher reaches of the Ituri? Was the rear-column still intact or had Barttelot's 'rashness and inexperience', allied to his inclination to punish indiscriminately, led to mass desertions to Stanley Pool?[2] Parke wrote the following letter to be taken to the Major by Rashid, Stanley's *maniapara*.

Fort Bodo,
Central Africa,
15 June 1888

Dear old Barttelot,

How are you and all the other fellows getting on? Stanley leaves here tomorrow ...
and he ought to be in Yambuya in 2 $^1/_2$ months at the most. He goes by himself and
takes no white men except his servant William, who you will have to watch closely
or he will steal your European provisions as he did ours. Stairs, Nelson and myself
remain here with 57 invalids and after a couple of months Emin Pasha comes here
with porters for the boxes and we all go with him to the Nyanza... Stanley says he
has nearly 600 loads at Yambuya so that I suppose you are still there as you have so
few men. When you do start, keep a good reserve of banana flour as you will find
yourself deuced hard up for food between the native settlements...

As you must be all hard up for Quinine, Stanley is bringing down a lb box which I
got from the doctor at Stanley Pool; it is all there is as far as I know, 5 grains a few
times a week is the best way to take it. It is no good whatever when you get the fever
unless the fever remains high for over 8 or 10 hours. Like a good fellow, tell whoever
looks after the medicines to look carefully after them, particularly the Hypodermic
injections as I have very little remaining and I give none to the Zanzibaris unless the
case is very bad...

Emin Pasha seems a real good sort, his people make everything except fezes, but
their boots wear out after two or three days' marching in the forest. Stick to your
boots by all means and try and pick up some from the Nubians for you will want
them and Stanley intends to get every pair he can.

Stairs and myself have sent letters to Jameson by Stanley... If your donkeys are
alive you should shoot them as they are a great trouble and no use in the forest and
Emin Pasha will give you any number. All our donkeys are dead. We ate Stanley's
and mine was shot. I scarcely know what to tell you as Stanley will give you all the
news. It is a good thing that we got Emin and the only thing [needed] to make us
happy is to have your Column up and all the white men alive and well. All of us had
sickness more or less, it was touch and go with Stanley last Feb. but now every one
of us are [sic] Fit and Strong. If you have time just take a note of what European
provisions Stanley takes for us. By all means keep some arrowroot and sago for
sickness.

Best wishes to yourself and the others,
Believe me,
Yours very sincerely,
T.H. Parke[3]

Stanley assembled a corps of 113 Zanzibaris volunteers and 95 conscripted
Madi carriers. He was to be accompanied by Parke (chosen at the last moment to replace Nelson, who was again unfit) as far as Ipoto to carry back the

103

loads left with the Manyuema. The garrison cheered them as they set off at 6.30 am on 16 June.

Parke's journey with thirteen men over relatively familiar territory was to take eight days. Heavy rain was encountered at Kilimani, their target for 17 June. Fifteen women were captured but there was little in the way of edibles to be picked up along the way. Parke became sick of eating a coarse porridge three times a day and looked forward to buying a chicken, beans and rice at Ipoto.

Stanley told me his greatest anxiety will be about us at the Fort [and I said I] hoped he would find us at the Lake. He said he would go to Yambuya for Barttelot's column and not further, even if the steamers had not come up, as Troup and Ward have had time to come up with their men in canoes. He will bring the Ammunition – 24 boxes, several Winchesters and Maxims – and cross Africa with them. If Emin Pasha says he cannot go as there is too little Ammunition, then Stanley's crossing will be proof that Emin could get out.[4]

He buried a basket of corn in a hut in an old clearing on 20 June knowing that it would be useful on the return journey. Two days later four of the captive women escaped. A Madi carrier consulted Parke about a white worm protruding from his hand.

'I treated it [Parke wrote] by twirling it on a stick and got out 2 feet when it broke. It is a Guinea worm and very common among the Madi men. It feels like a cord under the skin.'[5] Arriving at Ipoto with the rearguard on 23 June, Parke found Stanley already installed on the verandah of Kilonga-Longa's hut where some of the chiefs were sitting. They all stood up when the doctor appeared and made their salaams. Food was generously supplied.

An important *shauri* was held to discuss the ill-treatment of Parke, Nelson and their men. There was 'a profusion of lying' but eventually Kilonga-Longa apologized for the niggardly behaviour of the Manyuema in his absence and asked that the Sultan of Zanzibar should not be made aware of it. He produced nineteen Remingtons out of at least thirty known to be in their possession and a minute fraction of the stolen ammunition. Stanley finally returned eight rifles as a pledge for ninety doti of cloth and received back his watch and chain which he later presented to Parke.[6]

The invalided Zanzibaris left at Ipoto had died, but an old patient of Parke's, treated for an arrow wound, promised to give him a pygmy woman to carry his personal belongings. Needing a servant, Parke accepted the gift with alacrity but when he sent for her the donor had changed his mind. Before leaving Ipoto on 24 June to return to the fort Parke bought a Monbuttu pygmy woman for a handful of beans, twelve cups of rice and six cups of corn. With the assistance of

Manyuema slaves they carried forty-eight loads, rifles, ammunition, a box of Stanley's curios, a saddle and a tent and poles.

They camped on 26 June near a banana plantation to stock up with fruit. Two women were taken captive but they escaped in the night and stole some corn. Next day a Zanzibari was missing and two others who had searched for him perfunctorily were sent out again to look more thoroughly. They failed to return that night but next morning Parke found them strolling casually in the vicinity.

Now that they were running out of food Parke was glad to avail of the *mohindi* (corn) providently hidden on the outward journey and he was able to give two cupfuls to each man. When a Zanzibari broke down Parke carried his load of three rifles but called to Wadi Osmini, some distance ahead, for assistance. The order was ignored, an intolerable breach of discipline — 'on reaching camp I used some gentle pressure with my fist and he did his work well afterwards.'[7]

Parke arrived at Kilimani with all his loads intact. He had lost one man and classified many others as 'perfect goee-goees' — lazy, worthless persons. The two Madi carriers transferred to him by Stanley had guinea-worm. 'The Monbutti woman is worth any four.'[8]

When ordered to fall in on 3 July there were muttered grumbles and the men insisted that they could not start. Lacking a headman to rally them, Parke felt obliged to allow them a free day to forage, even though half of them stayed in their huts. The pigmy woman, tied by a rope to the door-post, amused herself 'by picking and eating lice off a child's head just like a monkey.' A careless forager returned with a nasty arrow-wound.

Arriving at Fort Bodo on 6 July with the loads still intact, Parke handed the stores over to Stairs who, despite his junior rank, had been placed in command because of his superior physical condition. Stanley had left explicit instructions: hoeing should start on 1 July, corn to be planted two weeks later; the banana plantation must be patrolled regularly. Jephson and Emin Pasha might be expected to arrive at Fort Bodo towards mid-August and if Jephson had brought sufficient carriers with him the fort should be evacuated to a camp near the Nyanza.

Two goats were killed, one of which was given to the men to celebrate Parke's return. The seeds presented to the doctor by Emin Pasha had germinated; he intended to sow a rice crop with seeds obtained from Kilonga-Longa but was confined to bed for two days with fever.

When Sudibelosi, the forager wounded at Kilimani on 3 July, died on 14 July, Parke performed an autopsy. The arrow-head, imbedded in the diaphragm, had not penetrated the lung but this was collapsed by a large collection of red, clotted fluid — 'a haemothorax'. The doctor was relieved to know that no procedure within his capacity could have saved his patient.

There was a scare in the Fort [on 15 July] as 2 shots were fired in quick succession close by and many wild natives were shouting in the bush just round the Fort. All our men were away getting Bananas with the exception of 5 or 6 skeletons. The Fort is always deserted on Sundays as we give the men a holiday. We thought it possible that the natives meditated an attack so we manned the Fort ourselves with our boys and a few sick men who were in camp, but the noise soon stopped and after half an hour one of our men returned and said he had shot at 3 natives close by and missed them all.

When the crops were sown, Parke took seven men on a punitive expedition against local natives who were pillaging the plantation.

Having gone towards the south-west I came on some Dwarfs stealing Bananas but could not get a shot. I tracked them to their Village a long way off in the bush and fired at them but did not knock one over; however, I certainly winged a couple, there was so much blood about. I captured one woman and 3 children and brought them to camp but they were subsequently released having their ears partially cut off. One mother ran away leaving her sucking child with us.[9]

They came upon the first of what appeared to be a series of pygmy villages and Parke, acutely aware that there were hundreds of cannibals about, accepted that discretion was the better part of valour. As he withdrew his platoon through the bush they were followed by natives who endeavoured unsuccessfully to surround them and managed to inflict a wound, fortunately superficial, on Ali Jumba.

This *ruga ruga* [foraging or raiding] work is absolutely necessary for protecting our Banana plantation so that we may be able to exist until Stanley's return. It is most dangerous work, for going over tops of logs the aborigines throw a poisoned arrow into one as fast as lightning, and if it enters deeply not all the powers of man can save one. Our men all wear leather Buffalo shields which were brought from the Plain but the officers have not worn one yet as it looks like cowardice yet it might be the salvation of one. The Dwarfs are very cunning and do everything to put us off their track. They walk along a beaten path and suddenly disappear into the thick bush where they again unite to go on to their village. Before going into the bush they send men on to go backwards on the path so as to make it appear that the party had gone in the opposite direction.[10]

Stairs, carrying the responsibility of command, was tormented by a nagging thought — 'What if Jephson is *too late!*' — and he was pestered by blacks who wanted to march on and invariably felt 'that the "there" is better than the "here".' He slept badly wondering where Emin, Stanley and Jephson were, and worrying himself about the safety of the ammunition until he was nearly crazy and obliged finally to get up and smoke.[11]

Knowing that a native woman had been captured by Fatheldi Wadi Hadi, the officers were uncertain as to what should be done with her. If allowed to stay and learn what a small force defended the fort she would tell her people when she escaped, as she was bound to do. Ordered to hand her over, Fatheldi delayed, presumably intending to reserve her for his carnal pleasure. Enraged by the indiscipline, Stairs went to his hut and hit him with his fist between the eyes. Having released the captor he struck the unfortunate man on the right shoulder with a stick which broke, causing an iron spike to penetrate the flesh.

A rumour circulated that Stairs had used a spear and on the following day when rations of corn were being handed out a mutinous remark led the Lieutenant to strike another man. His actions increased the air of restlessness and discontent pervading the fort, as the men wished to march to the plain where there was food in plenty; Parke ventured to warn him that he should give the men a hearing and he agreed to do so. 'I can see that mutiny is rife [Parke wrote] and unless the men are properly handled we 3 white men will be left alone to look after the boxes.'[12]

Elephants were a threat to the food supply. During the still night of 4 August a great beast trampled the Indian corn and could be heard 'tearing down trees and breaking big branches under its immense feet'.[13] Shots were fired at it and an ivory war-horn blown. Parke began to wonder would Jephson and Emin arrive before the food ran out. They killed a sheep a fortnight but only two remained. He shot two doves and made a trap with which to catch birds for the table.

By mid-August the peas and pumpkins were flowering but food was increasingly scarce and rats were eating the blankets having already feasted on the officers' home-made boots. Parke made constant attempts to improve the fort's sanitary condition but the Zanzibaris had careless and disgusting habits. They were also capable of extreme brutality, hanging-up a little girl by the arms and letting her die because she stole a fish. Another child who annoyed them was buried up to her neck.

'Waiting, waiting, it is terrible,' Stairs wrote: 'cooped up in a place of this sort, the tendency is to become cantankerous and narrow. It requires every-thing good in one to meet the daily work patiently and cheerfully; there is very little left in one by nightfall.' He was impressed by the attention Parke gave to his patients:

Parke has hard work with the ulcers now. The gales have cut down our crops, and there is less food for the men, and ulcers will break out as the result of weakness. Morning and evening every man gets his medicine, and has his limbs washed. Carbolic acid and potassium permanganate are our chief ulcer medicines now. We detected a man today, with Arab medicine (dawa) on his sores. He had a small bit of paper bearing texts from the Khoran [*sic*] neatly written by Morgan Morgarewa, our scribe, tied over his sores. I see now why he borrowed the paper.[14]

The morning sick-list included almost half the camp. A shortage of dressings forced the doctor to improvise, using powder from the cartridges as an application for the ulcers. The invalids were treated daily but most of them were obliged to take a turn at sentry duty. 'Out of 55 men and boys in camp about 30 have ulcers and 3 are simply rotting away.'[15] It was mandatory to move the ash-pit further away from the camp and to hoe the ground around the huts after cleaning them inside. Tape-worm infestation was also common and Parke prescribed 'Santonin' for Stairs when the latter passed a round-worm.

At 1.30 am this morning [9 August] Stairs came and woke me up to go out to the sentry box and listen to some noise in the tobacco which is planted only 15 yds from the Boma and just outside the Stockade. We could hear the stalks of tobacco being broken but we were uncertain if it was done by natives or by Buffalo or Elephant. One of the men coughed and all the noises ceased. This morning we went out to see the cause and found the foot marks of about 12 natives. This is very serious as they will take our corn when it's ripe. We visited the other sentries and found them asleep which is the usual condition of a Zanzibari when on the watch.

Awakened on 16 August by a recurrence of 'erysipelas', Parke dosed himself with quinine as his temperature soared. Nelson took the sick-parade but he directed any very ill patients to Parke to be seen personally by the medical officer.

A Washenzie (native) raiding-party was disturbed in the act of stealing tobacco and the highly-valued sweet potatoes. Two natives were shot dead and others wounded. 'The heads of the slain we had cut off and placed on the paths traversed by the Washenzie.'

Wednesday, 22 August – Anniversary of Nelson's birthday, about 35 years. He is very seedy today. All the huts were thoroughly swept out. The Zanzibaris are most abominably dirty in their huts; 23 sick this morning out of a total of 54. Unfit to work, 11; fit for light work, 19; officers, boys, 6; balance in poor condition, 18.

Towards the end of the month Parke had to lie down with a painful right leg. Hanamri, a Zanzibari who had the largest ulcer the doctor had seen, was a fatalist — 'he simply thought and emphatically declared that he would die and he did die.'[16] Bin Shumari, caught stealing beans and corn was given thirty with the rod. The last sheep was killed on 26 August. The meat did not last long and they hoped that Emin and Jephson would arrive soon for now they must rely on 'boga', a porridge (*mbuga*) made from the leaves of trees, herbs and the tops of bushes. A severe tornado swept the area on 30 August followed by torrential rain with hailstones as large as pebbles. Many huts lost their roofs, and trees were blown down by the furious storm which flattened the growing corn and damaged the crops.

Some days later the men held a *shauri*. Their representative, Ali Juma, told Stairs they wished to move on to the plains. He suggested either evacuating the fort completely or sending fifteen of the strongest men to the edge of the forest with an officer. If the natives were friendly they should proceed to the lake and enlist carriers for the loads. Stairs consulted with his colleagues and it was agreed that neither plan was feasible; if such a weak group ventured to travel, the Washenzie would spear the lot and cut their throats.

On 7 September Parke ventured a considerable distance into the forest but he failed to get game. Then Mohammed Zebir, a Nubian sergeant, went in search of food accompanied by a boy. When they failed to return a party of ten men with rifles also went to look for them unavailingly. A few days later Parke wrote; 'The men seem to think it a good joke that Mohammed Zebir has been lost. The natives will about have their last hash today.'[17] It was some consolation that the pumpkins were ripening and should soon be edible.

I had high fever again last night [Parke wrote on 21 September] heavy rainfalls nearly every day from 4.30 pm till 5.30. Stanley is about 14 days on his return journey, therefore if Jephson does not come soon Stanley will be here first. I wish that we all could get a month or two on the Plains with Emin so as to get strong for the march to Zanzibar. The men here are in a wretchedly weak state and ³/₄ are unfit for work as they cannot procure sufficient food to make them strong, as the Elephants, Washenzie and ourselves have been eating the Bananas for several months. Yesterday 5 men went out and brought back what would scarcely give them enough for the day. We have not had meat of any kind for over a month and we have no Arrowroot or anything except Indian Corn and Bananas in case of sickness nor has there been any for over 12 months. I am afraid we shall have to kill the donkeys the Pasha gave us.

The officers enjoyed sitting outside their tents at night under a sky brilliant with stars. The Southern Cross was clearly visible and Venus was frequently seen between the horns of the moon, making 'the Crescent and the Star.' They fretted over Jephson's failure to arrive which was delaying their march to the plains. 'The last day of September and no sign of Jephson or Emin...', Parke wrote in his diary, and reflected that 'hope deferred maketh the heart sick.'[18]

The white officers had fever singly and together and 'were like 3 Bears with sore heads'.[19] For twenty consecutive days in October Parke's temperature soared. Stairs moved him into a hut intended for Emin. 'Parke has bad nights, he is frightfully yellow; quinine does him no good.' He felt too ill to eat even when a donkey was shot and the tongue, a consummate delicacy, was reserved for him. He remained deeply yellow ('as yellow as a guinea') and passed claret-coloured urine. He managed, nevertheless, to totter to the men's quarters to open an abscess and carefully examined a Zanzibari with a recent arrow-wound. This was sucked by one of the man's comrades, instructed by Parke, but within a short space of time the victim became agitated, had a convulsion and died.

Got up early this morning [Parke wrote on 16 October] and saw the sick. There are only 12 now as compared to 25 a week or two ago. Since Stanley left we have lost 7 and one just going. I feel better this morning as the vomiting has ceased and am not so jaundiced but far from well. Nelson and Stairs had a tiff this morning. The latter was rather rude. He said to the Chief Maniapara 'why don't you ask me for things? Don't ask Capt Nelson but come to me' ignoring Nelson's position, which is very wrong and shows great want of tact and experience... Nelson then accused Stairs of giving our Onions to the men. Stairs admitted to giving two. This is bad taste as he should have asked Nelson and myself as we have very few.

Towards the end of the month the doctor was feeling dreadfully weak, no longer able to keep his diary and beginning to wonder if he was going to die. The expedition was turning out to be 'nothing but fatigues, famine and farming'.[20] But a change of medication from quinine to arsenic seemed beneficial; on 28 October his temperature fell to normal and his appetite revived.

The rains are getting much less [he wrote]. I cannot keep my mind off Restaurants, sausage-shops, fish-shops, butter, groceries and beer. We three come together every evening after dark in my house to chat and, before 5 minutes pass, food is sure to be the topic. When I come on a job like this again the Pigs will begin to fly. It is far the most severe and killing time I have ever spent.[21]

Stairs, the youngest of the trio, had 'a digestion like an ostrich's' and was least affected by illness. But the Lieutenant still had an arrow-head imbedded in his chest and this worried Parke. He planned to cut it out with the assistance of Nelson who would give the chloroform, and the pygmy woman to hold the bandages. Perhaps it was as well that a final attempt to remove the offending foreign-body by manipulation succeeded, making the anaesthetic unnecessary.

They continued to condemn Jephson's absence:

Jephson is very much to blame if he is [in] anyway the cause of the delay in coming for us to bring us to the Lake, for he knows that the white men cannot live for more than six months on grasses and Mohindi. Also the men are full of going to the Lake ... and they are nearly ready to desert us at any time but fortunately so many of them are laid up from ulcers that the healthy ones are not strong enough to fight their way.[22]

The Zanzibaris' culinary methods were primitive. They wrapped whatever was to be cooked in a banana leaf and put it in the fire. Parke fashioned useful grid-irons from the metal bangles which natives favoured as ornaments.

Parke's boy Muftah, a slave owned by Mohammed ibn Said of Zanzibar, told him that he was obliged to give the pay awarded him at Zanzibar (about £5) to his master, with the exception of six rupees. He was a chronic liar and something of a rascal meriting the stick. A pretty little girl, a ten-year-old native, was given to the doctor by one of the headmen. She was useful and looked after his fire at night but deserted after a few weeks much to his disappointment; he had, indeed, intended to take her home with him as a present for his sister. The Monbuttu pygmy woman had become his most devoted servant. Her cooking skills were considerable; he enjoyed the dish of fried locusts she prepared but could not bring himself to eat the smoked snake-meat she offered him. She knew which roots, leaves, fungi and insects were edible and collected them for him. She herself had a partiality for snakes' eggs which he did not share.

Arrow wounds were feared particularly because the arrow-heads were so frequently smeared with poison the identity of which Parke attempted to establish by discussions with his pygmy servant. He accompanied her into the forest to gather the herbs, barks, etc, that went into its composition. It was harmless, she assured him, if taken by mouth and if not fresh it merely caused local swelling and itching. He was determined to carry out an experiment using a pariah dog that Stairs had acquired. The pygmy pounded the ingredients — 'the large leaves, the bark, the pink thorny stem and the scrapings of the sticks' — and smeared the paste on to the arrows which she then dried in the sun.

Next day Parke made a deep incision in the dog's back about half-an-inch long and rubbed in the poison to be tested. The animal flinched a little but showed no immediate distress other than an objection to muzzling. Within thirty hours it had died. According to the pygmy there was an antidote which was applied beneath the skin.

Parke and Stairs often inspected the crops together and talked about home. They agreed that a good ham sandwich or a thick beef-steak would be delicious and resolved to patronize 'eating-houses' rather than café's in the future. Parke predicted that Jephson and Emin would come in the next ten days. Sometimes if the sentries were alerted at night by a suspicious sound the officers sneaked into the tower and standing absolutely silent listened for evidence of intruders in the plantations beyond which in impenetrable darkness lay the forest, black unending and deadly.

Their clothes required repeated patching, their boots were homemade, and smelled horribly. Parke was the best cobbler of the three white men and Stairs admired his meticulous stitching. Swahili was becoming their vernacular and expressions such as 'By the beard of the Prophet!' and 'By the shade of your grandfather's brother!' came naturally to their lips. They were forgetting, on the other hand, familiar English tunes. None of them could hum the 'airs' from Gilbert and Sullivan's *Patience* and the only music they readily recalled were old waltzes and songs like 'Bonnie Dundee'.[23]

Rain delayed harvesting the ripe corn but by 2 November it had all been picked off the big four-acre field, a poor crop, yielding only seventy baskets of 100 heads. The men foraged for bananas and fished successfully, but shooting at a monkey Parke missed. Using a sharpened arrow-head as a razor, Parke shaved his head and felt he looked like a convict.

Not until mid-November does it appear to have occurred to him that Jephson's 'unaccountable delay'[24] might have been caused by reasons beyond his control. Just then, in fact, Emin Pasha and Jephson were forcibly detained by rebels at Dufilé.

The weekly foraging parties tended to hide the better fruit and hand over the smaller bananas to the officers. The old corn was filled with weevils so it was decided to prepare meal from the newly-harvested crop. Stairs, whose arrow-wound had healed, calculated that they had enough corn to last three-and-a-half months. The new peas were ripe and a fresh crop was about to be planted. A large stork-like bird shot for the pot was the greatest treat.

'Just one month until Christmas,' Parke wrote on 24 November, 'a bright look-out as it will be another starvation one...' Three days later, on his thirty-first birthday, the Monbuttu woman agreed to take him into the forest again to identify the secret ingredients of the arrow-poison and its antidote. They are described in detail in *My Personal Experiences in Equatorial Africa*.

Parke's Hippocratic mission as a doctor did not, as we have seen, deter him from carrying out military duties in which capacity he claimed his right to wound and slay as readily as any infantry-man in that time of barbarity on the African continent. Early in December he commanded a platoon of nine who went to police the plantations and encountered a little group of Washenzie raiders who lay in ambush to attack them with arrows.

One woman was shot through the left thigh which was broken by Ali Jumba ... but as she was not killed and would have been certain to have died in agony, I ordered one of the men to give her the *coup-de-grâce* through the head. The native men escaped as is always the case. They are so active and once they get a yard or two into the bush it is impossible to see them for the amount of foliage. We left the children there so that the natives might come back for them.[25]

He went into the forest on 5 December with the Monbutti to make traps for ants which when collected in bulk and pounded into a paste made an excellent condiment to add taste to a stodgy 'boga'. Muftah, Parke's boy, went missing for some days before coming penitently to crouch embarrassingly at his master's feet, explaining that he was afraid to return.

I shall cure him [Parke decided] of being afraid of me by putting him down, having him held and breaking a few saplings on him. This is the third time he has run away from me and I have made the same vow but have never carried it out. I believe he would be much a better boy if I was a little more severe with him. Sometimes he is at the summit of my admiration and sometimes at zero. Today is 101 days since we have eaten meat. Stairs has increased 8 lbs since October 2nd, Nelson decreased 2, Parke the same exactly — Stairs 151 lbs, Nelson 138 lbs, Parke 148 lbs. Muftah came back this afternoon ... so I sent for one of the men and gave him 60 with a cane as their hides are very thick.[26]

Parke improvised a draughts-board and draughts with which to while away his leisure-time. The first cutting of the rice was finished on 7 December and an acre of ground gave a satisfactory yield. In contrast to this peaceful husbandry, a *ruga-ruga* party under Stairs' command shot two natives and wounded another, returning with 'a little loot'.[27]

The doctor prescribed anti-pyrine for Stairs' fever while he himself enjoyed a luncheon of locusts and rice. By common consent he was now 'Head Gardener' but had few vegetables worth growing and was concerned because after four rainless days the scorching sun was burning the cornfields. A portion of the unhusked rice was divided, 28 $^1/_2$ peêchis, each peêchi containing fourteen cups or between five and six cups when husked. Two cups represented a day's allowance when there was little else to eat and they proposed to give about 100 cups from each of their shares to be distributed among the men. Three peckfuls were reserved for seed and twenty cups were put aside for Jephson and Emin Pasha.

Stairs and Parke both had fever on 14 December for which the latter blamed a 'miasma' which followed the hoeing of the plantations. Next day Parke was well enough to go with the men to light fires to scare off the troublesome elephants. He wore homemade boots, resembling Veldtschoon, with soles and uppers of rhinoceros hide and cowhide respectively.

A full moon sailed over Fort Bodo. It was now six months since Stanley had set out for Yambuya and his return might be expected soon. Jephson's absence, on the other hand, was unexplainable, 'unless he had been taken prisoner', or perhaps Emin was afraid to trust his men with Stanley's ammunition. It was unlikely that there would be sufficient carriers and they would have to leave their collections of curios behind.

The great heat [Parke wrote] and want of rain is turning our corn from a beautiful dark green to a lighter colour with streaks of white which is a positive sign of its failure. *Ruga-ruga* are away again today after elephants. We get along very well with the men on the whole and rarely have any punishments. Stairs is a splendid man to manage them. He visits the sentries twice every night. We have a greater variety of food now, as the Monbutti and our boys have discovered many new kinds of leaves, bulbs, and pods which we bruise up together as a Boga [*Mbuga*].[28]

Prompted by Tennyson's *Amphion* in which he read 'And I must work through months of toil/And years of cultivation', Stairs offered a parody:

> With hail-storms wild and native gangs,
> With elephants twelve feet high,
> A chronic state of dreadful pangs
> Proclaims that we should die.
> A thousand rations scooped up clean,
> More 'grazing' for us all;
> We plant again with hopes to glean
> Perchance again next fall.[29]

But, just as Virgil has written — 'Sometime the memory of these things shall be a joy to you' — they were to remember the ordeals at the fort in the forest with a degree of satisfaction as, in due course, they sat around the camp-fires in the open country.

On 20 December a sentry on the Nyanza Avenue expressed the pessimistic opinion, which Parke was about to contradict, that Stanley would not return for another two-and-a-half months; but just then rifle fire was heard and from the watch-tower he had mounted, Stairs shouted that Stanley had arrived.

The latter who was preceded by a dozen sharp-shooters bearing the Egyptian flag has described the welcome he was accorded:

114

We approached the end of our broad western military road, and at the turning met some Zanzibari patrols who were as much astonished as we were ourselves at the sudden encounter. Volley after volley soon rang through the silence of the clearing. The fort soon responded, and a stream of frantic men, wild with joy, advanced by leaps and bounds to meet us; and among the first was my dear friend the Doctor, who announced, with eyes dancing with pleasure, 'All is well at Fort Bodo'.[30]

Notes

1 *IDA*, I, p. 428.
2 Ibid, p. 438.
3 *Diary*, Vol. 4.
4 *Diary*, 17 June 1888.
5 *Diary*, 22 June.
6 Now in the possession of the RCSI the watch bears the inscription: 'To Surgeon T.H. Parke, as a souvenir of Fort Bodo and Ipoto, 1887 and 1888 from his friend, Henry M. Stanley.'
7 *Diary*, 20 June.
8 *Diary*, 2 July.
9 *Diary*, 19 July.
10 *Diary*, 19 July.
11 W.G. Stairs, 'Shut Up in the African Forest', *Nineteenth Century*, 1891; 29: 57.
12 *Diary*, 21 July.
13 *Diary*, 4 August.
14 Stairs, *op. cit.*, p. 56.
15 *Diary*, 18 Aug.
16 *Diary*, 25 Aug.
17 *Diary*, 13 Sept.
18 *Diary*, 4 October (*Proverbs*, 13: 12).
19 *Diary*, 28 Sept.
20 *Diary*, 27 Oct.
21 *Diary*, 28 Oct.
22 *Diary*, 24 Oct.
23 Stairs, *op. cit.*, p. 53.
24 *Diary*, 12 November.
25 *Diary*, 4 December.
26 *Diary*, 6 Dec.
27 *Diary*, 9 Dec.
28 *Diary*, 19 Dec.
29 Stairs, *op.cit.*, p. 61.
30 *IDA*, II, p. 66.

10   The Camp at Kandekoré

To Stanley, fresh from the horrors of starvation in the Ituri rainforest, Fort Bodo was a welcome haven. His impression of its sumptuousness as described so cheerfully in *In Darkest Africa* ('prosperous fields of corn on either hand, and goodly crops everywhere; fenced squares, a neat village, clean streets, and everyone I met — white and black — in perfect health, except a few incurables'[1]) does not, however, altogether accord with Parke's account of damaged crops, short rations and deplorable sanitation. Be that as it may, he was obliged to tell his officers the dismal, unvarnished story of the rear-column as he had heard it at Banalya from William Bonny, who now accompanied him.

Having waited impatiently at Yambuya for the 600 carriers promised by Tippu Tib, Barttelot and Jameson visited Stanley Falls in turn, but unavailingly. Then after an unconscionable delay and further journeys they were sent 430 carriers and moved belatedly to Banalya — Troup having earlier been invalided home, and Ward (who had quarrelled with Barttelot) ordered to stay at Bangala on his return there from the cable-station on the coast. The men, meanwhile, were sickening from disease and uncooked manioc, and there was a series of deaths culminating in the shooting of Barttelot by a Manyuema on 19 June 1888. The Major, having forbidden a native woman to disturb him by beating a drum and singing in the early morning, seemed about to strike her, or to have actualy done so, when her husband shot him through a loop-hole in his hut. Jameson had gone down-river in an attempt to communicate with the agent at Stanley Pool, which to Stanley (then unaware that Jameson died from blackwater fever at Bangala on 17 August) amounted to severance from the expedition. The officers, Stanley alleged, repeating the words used by him in his report to Mackinnon, were guilty of irresolution, indifference towards their written orders and neglect of their promises.

Parke thought Stanley looked 'careworn and ragged to an extreme'.[2] For a day or two his starving men straggled into camp, weak and exhausted. They were attended by Parke who was appalled by their condition.

The men were really in a terrible state [Parke wrote] from debility and hunger. I never witnessed such a disgusting sight as the unfortunate ulcerated people came dropping in. The stench from the putrid flesh and dirty scraps of bandages was sickening and filled the air all round the Fort. Most of the ulcers were on the lower extremities, great gangrenous sloughing surfaces, some of them a foot long and as large as a soup plate with a foot of the bone exposed and in some cases the tarsal, metatarsal [bones] and phalanges entirely gone from disease. Great pieces of putrid flesh hanging in strings and the stink was simply awful.[3]

The return journey from Banalya had been agonizingly eventful.[4] The least of Stanley's troubles were two women among the Manyuema followers said to be possessed by the devil and given to singing and howling in the night. Smallpox, endemic among the Manyuema, spread to the Madi carriers, sparing the Zanzibaris vaccinated by Parke. There were forty-four deaths in the first fifty days; several unofficial and unprotected foragers were killed and eaten by cannibals; other members of the caravan attacked by tribesmen or pygmies were speared or sustained poisoned arrow-wounds, to which some rapidly succumbed though Stanley claimed to have saved lives by injecting wounds with ammonium chloride. As with all such claims alternative cures were offered: a Zanzibaris headman said the green tobacco leaves covering the wounds were an effective antidote.

Canoes capsized; red ants, bees and hornets penetrated their securest defences and hunger was a constant reminder of starvation, the abiding threat which claimed numerous victims. Between Amiri Falls and Avatiko in late October they had marched for seven days through country that offered no food whatever, relying on the sparse rations they could carry.

They reached Andaki on 1 November. This clearing was well supplied with plantains but on leaving it they encountered a bewildering tangle of bush, fallen trees, branches and matted creepers through which, day after day, they cut their way with billhooks and axes — 'a hungry column of men was behind, a wilderness before us'.[5] Miserable days of existence on weak gruel alternating with opportunities to feed greedily on bananas and plantains, debauches ending in digestive upsets.

After bridging a river a muster was held showing that thirty-four of the rear-column had died and sixteen were critically ill. At Ngwetza on 4 December they feasted and everybody in the caravan was given five days' rations. A few days later, seeing a young fellow stagger, Stanley enquired as to the cause. To his astonishment the explanation was hunger. But where were his rations? He was outraged to hear that having been told by a pygmy captive that 'the biggest plantains in the world' lay a day's march ahead the lad hadn't burdened himself with rations. Worse still, at least 150 others were guilty of similar folly.

Too worried to be angry, Stanley felt the nadir had been reached. He decided that all the able-bodied men must go back to Ngwetza for a fresh supply of food while invalids, women and pygmies remained in camp on iron rations. Six days later the inmates of the camp were reduced to foraging for fruits and berries while Stanley, desperately anxious, awaited the return of 200 men expected days earlier with food from Ngwetza. What had become of them? Had the entire column perished? Finally, on 15 December, impatience mastered him and he decided to go in search of the absentees.

He admitted subsequently to Parke that he went back to look for the missing men in such despair that he took poison and a revolver with him determined to destroy himself if he failed to find them, never having been in such an extremity before. He had set off at 1 pm with a party of sixty-five men and twelve women. They marched until they were exhausted, falling down with no fires to light, no food to cook. They resumed their search in the bleak light of dawn and an hour later met the column carrying the vital piles of plantains.

*

At the muster in Fort Bodo on 22 December the roll-call included 209 Zanzibaris, 17 Soudanese, 1 Somali, 151 Manyuema and followers, 26 Madis and followers, 2 Lados, 6 whites: total 412.[6] Stanley planned to make double journeys between the fort and the Ituri River and cross the latter to camp at Kandekoré, a clearing at the edge of the forest. Parke and Stairs would stay with the invalids while he went on with Nelson and Bonny in the direction of the Nyanza, hoping to establish the whereabouts of Jephson and Emin Pasha. Volunteers for double duty would receive extra pay in cloth.

Parke packed his medicines into two loads to be ready for the reunited expedition's departure. That evening as he sat with Nelson and Stairs the main topic of conversation was the unfathomable destruction of the rear-column, the ill-feeling between the Europeans and their men, the loss of stores and ammunition and the slaying of Barttelot. They would be glad to resume their trek and return to the lake.

Next day, with Stanley and Stairs in the vanguard, Parke marched out of the fort, leaving the corn still standing and the peas looking well. They marched ten miles to their first camp, from which Stairs returned to the fort with fifty men to assist Nelson. 'There were some men, unable to walk from debility, disease and ulcers, that were abandoned.'[7]

Nelson, who had regained his 'former martial tread and manly bearing',[8] supervised the final stages of the evacuation. Before leaving on 24 December he buried a large glass demijohn that some future traveller might unearth, containing a letter and a few tokens of their stay, and then set fire to Fort Bodo.

On Christmas Day Parke's gift from Stanley was four yards of blue serge, the makings of a pair of trousers; the box containing the reserve supply of clothing was lost on the journey from Yambuya. The festive dinner consisted of rice and beans with coffee contributed by Bonny and a glass of brandy to toast friends and relations at home. The fate of the rear-column which inevitably was discussed remained an insoluble source of amazement to Parke. 'Bonny tells us [he wrote] that Barttelot was mad and certainly from the description he has given us of the detailed events which have occurred at Yambuya we all consider that this is the kindest construction that can be put on his actions.'

Stairs, who had gone out with a foraging party earlier in the day, sent back a messenger to say that he could not return that night. He was unable to get the men together as they had scattered widely over the plantations and the neighbouring villages in search of such desirable luxuries as goats and fowls.

William Bonny had come up by steamer from Bolobo to Yambuya and brought the most recent mail (June, July 1887) with him. There were four letters for Parke: one from his mother saying all were well at home; one from a Miss Butterworth of Kensington; a wedding invitation from a mess-mate and a bill for £1.7.6 from the British Medical Association. Parke found Bonny 'a great drone', inclined to garrulity on the sad subject of the rear-column and Barttelot's tyranny, with emphasis on how his own advice was ignored, and obviously rather enjoyed telling his stories — 'He shows a great spleen to all the officers there although he pretends not to.' The MO listened intently, nevertheless, to the eye-witness's account of the tragedy[9] which Troup and Ward amplified later in their books.[10]

★

Herbert Ward, Bonny and John Rose Troup had reached Yambuya on 14 August 1887 with 131 men and many loads. They got off to a bad start with Barttelot who refused them their share of the European provisions saying he had no instructions from Stanley to open the boxes but eventually under pressure gave them three months' supply instead of the six they expected. Next day a party of Tippu Tib's ivory-hunters arrived and Jameson went with them to Stanley Falls. He hoped to collect 600 carriers but the Arab leader was away settling a dispute on the Lumani River. The carriers were promised by the end of September and when none arrived Barttelot and Troup went again to Stanley Falls, where Tippu Tib admitted his difficulty in gathering them together, which was partly due to Stanley's failure to supply ammunition.

On a typical day at Yambuya, 'first drum' sounded at daybreak, 'second drum' at 6 am followed by a general muster when tasks for the day were assigned and Bonny took a sick parade. The officers' breakfast at 6.30 consisted of a cup of tea, plain boiled rice and fried plantains. Work continued until 11.30 and, after luncheon (rice and fried plantains), was resumed at 2 pm ending at 5.30. Dinner at 7 pm was a repetition of the earlier meals and their spirits rose precipitately if fish was available. Time passed slowly and, as the months slipped tediously by, uncertainty sapped their self-confidence while the sequence of deaths in the camp continued. Where was Stanley? Had the advance party encountered disaster and perhaps death in the forest or was it just that the journey was longer than expected?

They tried to make the best of an appalling situation. Bonny kept himself busy attending the sick or smoking and chatting with Troup. The Major paced about restlessly. Ward spent two or three hours a day improving his Swahili. He painted, sketched and made pen-and-ink drawings. He botanized with Jameson and read the latter's copy of Stanley's *Through the Dark Continent*.

Barttelot was on terms of enmity with Selim bin Mohammed, chief of the neighbouring Arab camp. Ward, on the other hand, got on well with Selim and they exchanged gifts and talked together. From time to time Arabs passed by with valuable consignments of ivory and strings of slaves roped together. Selim said he had commonly seen local natives 'kill a slave and eat the flesh in front of him'.[11]

None of them escaped illness. Ward was laid up with dysentery for five weeks 'suffering the horrors of the damned'[12] before he could crawl from his bed into the open, more dead than alive. At Christmas they managed to lift themselves above the slough of despond. Jameson and Ward sat up at night making Christmas cards and on Christmas Day some dainty morsels were produced for dinner from their scanty stores, a tinned ham, pickles, a bottle of sauce. Barttelot shared what was left of the bottle of brandy given to him by Stanley, and Bonny was called on to sing. Their chief toast was 'Absent Friends' — this was drunk in silence as they thought not only of those at home but of the comrades who were somewhere ahead in the forest.[13]

The improvised feast was inevitably followed at New Year by an emotional reaction: 'Death is about... Thirty-nine graves now in our little God's Acre and six months gone! Good God! Will these porters never come? Must all of us lie down and rot and die?'[14]

Barttelot and Jameson went to Stanley Falls once more in February 1888 and Jameson agreed to follow Tippu Tib to Kassongo several hundred miles up-river, accompanied by Assad Farran the Syrian interpreter, who was in due course to add his glosses to the reports on what had happened to the rear-column. He was an unfortunate choice of companion ('Assad gets dirtier and more lazy than ever'[15]) whom, at least once, Jameson threatened to shoot. Resenting this the interpreter did not hesitate to blacken Jameson's character when the opportunity presented. They returned to Yambuya early in June with 430 carriers, many of them slaves. Meanwhile Barttelot had sent Ward to the cable station at St Paul de Loanda on the coast with despatches for the committee and Troup was invalided home on 9 June.[16]

Ward (sometimes called 'Mayala Mbemba', Eagle Wings) accepted without demur Barttelot's order to proceed to the coast and cable for instructions.[17] Although knowing that he must pass through populous districts he decided that 'we shall have to make them smell powder, or else be cooked and eaten.'[18] As he left Yambuya, he was given a letter[19] by Barttelot which he found grossly offensive leaving no interpretation other than that the Major suspected him of theft.[20]

Had the time and energy expended on these long treks, Bonny argued, been devoted instead to short double journeys along the path travelled by Stanley, steady progress might have been achieved. As it was, the monotony of camp life, bad food and want of exercise had fostered sickness and ill-temper. The officers were at logger-heads with their men and with one another. There were floggings and an execution; deserters, if recovered, were chained and he hinted at further brutalities. There was a horrid rumour, too, of gruesome sketches made by Jameson at the cannibal feast he is said to have attended at Riba-Riba on 11 May.

Only 139 of the original 271 left at Yambuya survived, but the caravan which finally set out eastwards on 11 June 1888 included the Manyuema carriers and their followers. Having suffered many desertions and followed a number of wrong paths it reached Banalya, a well-appointed Manyuema village, on 15 July, after more than a month in the bush.

Bonny said that Barttelot was universally hated. At Banalya on 18 July he had a dispute over carriers with Abdulla, a resident chief. He rebuked the Manyuema repeatedly, but probably not unreasonably, for their wasteful and dangerous habit of firing their rifles without reason. He was irritated to a degree by the way the women sang at all hours and and forbade them to do so. This had led to his murder by Sanga whose wife he threatened for her disobedience. The bullet struck him in the chest, killing him instantly. Bonny arrived on the spot a moment later to find him lying prone in a pool of blood with a revolver in his hand.

Bonny had sent immediately for Jameson who had gone back through the bush for some extra loads. He arrived on 22 July and found that many of the carriers had scattered, taking their loads with them or dropping them in the forest. Most of these boxes were retrieved by Bonny before Jameson set off for Stanley Falls. His intention was to seek justice for Barttelot's murder[21] and to proceed then to Bangala to communicate with the committee. After doing so Jameson hoped to return to Banalya with fresh carriers and to continue the march.

Listening to Bonny's dismal story, Parke felt comment on the disaster to be unnecessary. There had been a heavy loss of trade-goods and the effect on the expedition was profoundly depressing. He was, indeed, inclined to marvel that Stanley had had the resilience to carry on. He could have been pardoned had he, on 'finding the rear-column so completely wrecked', gone down the Congo and home to avoid 'facing that awful forest again'. Parke's respect for his leader was increasing steadily.[22]

*

Stairs brought back chickens and goats which were handed over to Nelson, generally agreed to be the best cook. The flesh was greatly enjoyed and they also dipped into the allowances of European provisions stored with the rear-column.

Nelson and Stairs went ahead with 100 rifles to establish a bridgehead at the Ituri River and send back fifty-five men to complete a double journey thus compensating for the lack of porters. Parke whiled away the time at 'Cross Roads Camp' tailoring, mending his tent and welcoming the New Year.

Happy New Year to all at home [he wrote] and a sincere wish that I should never spend another in this blessed country. I am not at all tired of the Expedition but I do detest this constant going backwards and forwards in the forest and sitting down to farm for weeks and months. I would like to be always on the move and doing something as it is more healthy and not so demoralising and doleful. I went off for about 6 miles with a lot of men and women for food, we had about 50 shots driving away the natives who attacked us. The last year has been eventful to all of us. Out of 13 Europeans 6 are present here, 1 is with the Pasha, 1 has been murdered, 4 have returned down the Congo, 1 is at Bangala about 600 miles off and, of the 2 Syrian

122

interpreters, one is dead and the other has been sent home.[23]

On 3 January an unwary Soudanese was badly wounded quite close to the camp. With great difficulty the doctor removed the four arrows deeply imbedded in his spine using a scalpel and a pair of strong forceps. Resuming the march they were obliged to leave 'many behind to die as they were unable to crawl from enormous ulcers. They stink like a dirty abattoir...'[24] Kibbo-bora, a Manyuema chief, stayed by the roadside to comfort his dying brother. A distance of eight miles was achieved on 6 January.

I was late getting to camp as I was on rearguard and delayed by the sick, one of whom I was obliged to have carried. I wonder some plague does not break out amongst us for the awful stink emanating from the huge gangrenous ulcers is simply awful; the smell hangs in the forest so that you could track a huge ulcer like a drag hunt. How these wretched beings can move along with dead bone protruding and half the foot rotted off... It is a wonder that they do not commit suicide for they can always procure a rifle and a bullet from their comrades.[25]

The Manyuema women carried heavy loads as ably as the men. Parke thought some of them were 'extremely handsome especially Mrs Kibbo-bora Number 1'.

They were of light brown colour with small hands and feet and walk very upright. Pretty brown eyes, thin nose and lips, small ears, short curly hair and high forehead. The general outline of their figure is extremely good. They are of a very cheery and good-natured disposition and are superior to the men. Their dress is now reduced to a fringe or veil. Some of them have a handkerchief which they wear round their head twisted into a circle to prevent their load from pressing on to their skull, and a few have a handkerchief or two thrown over their shoulders. Our carriers never place their load directly touching the head, they always make a small circular pad with a hole in it from bark cloth or grass which they place between their head and the box. We marched early as I was on rear-guard again. I was obliged to go very slowly as the rear of the column had just enough life and not enough energy to push themselves on.[26]

Bonny went back for Kibbo-bora and his loads; Stairs reported favourably on the situation ahead and they crossed the Ituri River in canoes on 9 January to camp at Kandekoré, a village on a hill at the forest's edge within sight of open country. Bananas were plentiful and it was hoped that some goats and fowls would be available. Next day the men were mustered to segregate the unfit. 'So this is to be a Convalescent Home, 87 Zanzibaris, 9 Soudanese, 20 Manyuema, 20 Madis, Stairs and myself, also Nelson who has an ulcer and cannot march although he is anxious to go.'[27]

Stanley called the officers to his tent and gave them what Parke called 'a long lecture'.[28] He impressed upon Stairs the importance of obeying every order without swerving an iota from the agreed programme. He delivered himself of some moral apophthegms — 'the path of duty was the way to glory'[29], and 'There is a tide in the affairs of men which if taken at the flood leads on to fortune'[30] — before turning to Parke:

Now, Doctor, I particularly address myself to you. Stairs will perform all that is required as Superintendent and Governor of the camp, but I look to you mostly. These 124 men on the sick list, some are but slightly indisposed, and some are in a dreadful state. But they all require attention, and you must give it devotedly. You must see that your worst cases are fed regularly. Three times a day see that their food is prepared, and that it is given to them; trust no man's word, see to it yourself in person; for we want these men to reach home. I warn you solemnly that your 'flood-tide of opportunity' has come. Are you ambitious of distinction? Here is your chance; seize it. Your task is clear before you, you are required to save these men, who will be the means of taking you home, and of your receiving the esteem of all who shall hear of your deeds.[31]

It irked Parke to have to stay behind again. 'I am always left at these standing camps to look after the sick although I am quite fit and have never been carried since we started.'[32] Stanley's enjoinments may have amounted to a statement of the obvious but Parke was taken aback when Stanley said they were not going to bring Emin out with them. The prime object of their relief, Stanley maintained, was to supply the governor with ammunition. 'We have so few men left that we could barely drive through to Zanzibar by ourselves without the trouble or responsibility of looking after Emin and his people. We have only 219 Zanzibaris alive and many of these are sick.'[33]

Stanley moved eastwards on 11 January intending to visit his new allies, Mazamboni, Gavira and Kavalli, on his way to the lake. Parke got down to business at once at Kandekoré.

Our Camp, or really a large Hospital, is called Kandekoré and Stairs is in Command. Almost every man gets treatment and some of the worst cases have to be fed on their backs as they are too weak to sit up. They are simply reduced to skin and bone from starvation, a very sickening sight. As long as the gluteal region retains its rotundity there is no danger but it is remarkable that once a man's gluteal region goes and he gets flat, immediately he breaks down. This is the site of an old village where we found an enormous quantity of tobacco ready to smoke. We shall have to fortify the place as we are to be here for a month. There are plenty of bananas and perhaps an occasional goat or chicken. It is very tough being obliged to remain here with so many unable to walk.[34]

Nelson was again hampered by ulcers but Stairs, an energetic engineer, set about providing a boma, huts, two watch-towers and latrines. Parke offered his patients a choice of medicines, 'red, green, black or any other colour they chose' but potassium permanganate and water was the most popular application.

Last night I had a Goat killed for the sick and although the officers should have some, yet we gave all to the sick. I gave the worst cases soup and meat last night and twice again today. I have hard work with these men and some are sure to die. Uledi, who was sent back with a party for the sick men who were left in the road, returned on Thursday last [10 January] without any. I believe he never went back further than the last camp. However, if his story is true, the 4 Zanzibaris and 8 Manyuema must have been killed by natives as I saw some wild natives and had a flying shot at them as they ran into the bush.[35]

He sometimes shared his scanty stock of European provisions with his patients but quite often the officers' sense of fair play seems to have been overborne by the urges of self-preservation and the consciousness that they were the expedition's fragile corner-stones. When a goat was killed they usually took at least half of it, making soup for the invalids with the remainder. A Zanzibari ventured once to complain to Stanley on this account: 'The white men had meat of goat, and fowls, and fish; we have had nothing but manioc and therefore died.'[36] Not to be put down, Stanley had blamed the uncooked manioc for all their problems.

Parke managed successfully to hide his true feelings about distressing sights and nauseating odours from his patients, confiding only to his diary his disgust and his concern with the demoralizing effect of the ulcers on the afflicted men. 'They get as filthy as pigs and are great liars...' All their wrong-doings were attributed to their illness and there was an incessant demand for sympathy. 'If a man has been sick for a long time he invariably develops into a Goee-Goee which means a good-for-nothing grumbler.'[37] Ali bin Said, a patient who had been fed regularly, stole a goat and, despite his illness, was given twenty with a rod. There were a number of cases of dysentery which responded well to treatment with a lead-and-opium mixture.

The approved treatments for ulcers were potassium permanganate, carbolic acid, silver nitrate and general cleanliness. The African traditional remedies included rubbing a copper ring on a stone and transferring the dislodged copper to the ulcer by means of a wet rag. By reducing granulations it favoured healing. For small ulcers a herbal paste was applied which hardened and acted as a shield, preventing further injury by twigs and grass. For headaches and a variety of pains a method of 'cupping' was applied using a hollow horn to create a vacuum.

Monday, 14 January – Had another small goat killed today and gave it all to the sick, as both Stairs and Nelson and myself fully realize the value of keeping these men alive as we have barely enough Zanzibaris with us to reach Zanzibar, for we can never face the forest again. By mixing a few cups of Indian meal in with a stewed goat makes a more substantial feed for the sick. Four of the biggest goats would not supply all the sick with more than half a cup of soup. Nelson is still on his back with 6 ulcers on his feet and legs.

For some days in mid-January Parke was stricken by fever. He felt 'like a Bear on a hot grid-iron' and was too ill to see his patients, who were dealt with by Nelson and Stairs. He moved to a recently completed hut, larger and cooler than his own.

These huts are really beautiful to lie in, made of beautifully green leaves and boughs and creepers hanging about in careless extravagance and the bed made of leaves, grasses and tops of bushes which surpasses any spring bed. My feverish symptoms are now much aggravated, my body feels as if broken across and every limb aches, most of the pain is concentrated in lumbar and sacral regions. Nothing gives relief. Temperature 104 and day and night continuous vomiting and diarrhoea. Little black ecchymosed specks under the skin on the trunk, great tenderness over the left lobe of the liver and stomach, also over the right lobe but not so severe.[38]

He crawled to see patients then retired to bed feeling that death would be a relief. His medication was quinine and Warburg's tincture, his diagnosis 'bilious remittent fever', his temperature settled gradually leaving him dizzy and confused in his convalescence. He returned to full duty on 24 January and was glad to see most of the men putting on flesh. Nonetheless, seven died at Kandekoré.

My chief Hari calls out 'dawa, dawa', both morning and evening when the sick crowd round me where I sit upon a chair and dole out Burrows & Wellcome's tabloids which are superior to any form of medicine both for efficiency and to minimise transport. A heavy shower fell last night. Hassan-Sadalla, a Zanzibari, died today from an acute attack of Diarrhoea caused by eating rotten meat or surfeiting on ripe Bananas. A half a goat was given to the sick today.[39]

Despite its horrors, the forest had had the advantage of shade which the large clearing at Kandekoré lacked. Parke thought it an unhealthy place and his Monbutu woman had two attacks of fever. He told her she might remain in the forest but she preferred to stay with her master. There were no regular duties to keep the men active so it was arranged, as a form of occupational therapy, to make a road to the river. Nelson's ulcer recurred and Parke thought him in poor condition to cross Africa having had the same complaint intermittently since August 1887. Stairs tried the Maxim gun which failed to function properly. This did not surprise Parke, sceptical of machine-guns, which he thought better in theory than in practice. He could recall an incident at the Battle of Abu Klea where, when he was MO with the Naval Brigade, the Gardner-gun jammed at the critical moment of attack as the Arabs rushed the square.

Monday, 28 January – The *ruga-ruga* returned early today. They told a long story how they went in the exact direction they were told. This was all stoutly verified by the Chief who went in charge of the party. Suspecting that they were lying, Stairs cross-examined them and found that they had gone in the very direction they were told not to go in as they crossed the river close by. They were all fallen in and Stairs told them how they had broken faith and that if Stanley were here they would have behaved differently. They must have eaten about 40 goats as Stairs could account for 26 and they only brought back 3 and a kid, although they know that we have given goat meat to the sick on occasions when we have denied it to ourselves.

The penitent men confessed to Stairs that they had, indeed, disobeyed orders and fell at his feet, a gesture of humiliation that failed to impress the doctor.

Parke was puzzled by Stanley's interpretation of the purpose of the relief mission and could not understand why now he seemed 'so particularly anxious not to bring the Pasha away with him, but to simply hand him over the ammunition.'[40] The expedition's diminished number increased the risk of attacks and the addition of Emin's party, even if composed largely of women and children, would make a more imposing caravan.

Thursday, 7 February – One Manyuema died today from chronic dysentery. His comrades always say [when a man is ill] 'Oh, he's well.' They are more unkind to the sick than the Zanzibaris are and don't seem to think more about dying than eating. Yesterday a *ruga-ruga* party of about 30 left camp to return tomorrow; however 4 or 5 returned this evening bringing 10 or 12 fowls and a goat. The remainder of the party went down for more food.

Parke rather hoped they would not stir from Kandekoré for a month or so as many men were still unfit. He was not displeased, however, when, on 10 February, Rashid, Stanley's headman, arrived with forty Zanzibaris and 100 of Mazamboni's carriers, to move them to the expedition's new quarters at Kavalli's. He marvelled at the respect Stanley now commanded in the area and his ability to enlist the help of tribes which fought him so fiercely on the first trip to the Albert Nyanza. Rashid confirmed that Jephson and Emin, prisoners of a rebel faction at Dufilé, were released when the Mahdists came up the Nile in steamers and took Rejaf. Jephson had arrived at Kavalli's on 6 February; the Pasha was expected any day. The latter's circumstances were totally altered by the rebellion of his soldiers and the Mahdists' threat, a combination that was forcing him to leave Equatoria.

Rashid brought food but no meat. He was accompanied by Mazamboni's brother, Catto, and another chief whose men put on a spectacular performance to mark the departure from Kandekoré. They sang and danced ('their dance is of a wriggling licentious character') to the beating of three drums.[41]

Two men unable to march were left behind on 12 February when they set off early to camp at noon, still availing of the shade of the forest but with a full view of the open plain. Next day on the grasslands they marched unprotected from the sun and, lacking firewood, had to burn grass. They camped in the early afternoon at Malonga's and two days later reached Mazamboni's, which reminded Parke of an enormous fair-green with crowds of natives glad to sell chickens and sweet-potatoes in return for cowries. A letter from Stanley informed them that Emin Pasha had arrived at Kavalli's with the first batch of his people, having finally decided to travel with them to Zanzibar.

After feasting on a roasted ox, Indian meal and sugar-cane, their march continued along a well-watered valley where large herds of humped cattle grazed on an undulating, grassy plain sprinkled with flowers. Mazamboni's carriers spoke the language of Unyoro, the kingdom of Kabba Rega, their inveterate enemy. They appeared to hold themselves in the highest regard and Parke was struck by how the sheen of their brown glossy skins contrasted, to their advantage, with the sickly complexions of the white men.

They reached Kavalli's at about 11.30 am on 18 February and Stanley's perceptive glance took in the condition of the recovered invalids immediately. 'As Surgeon Parke came in, I mentally blessed him, for to this fine display of convalescents he had largely contributed by his devotion.'[42] Jephson's appraisal was more critical. 'Most of them looked very well, but some of them were perfect skeletons... Poor devils, how I pitied them as they marched along in a stolid painful manner & looked up at one with a doglike pitiful look which went to one's heart. Stairs, Nelson & Parke all looked very well. Of course we were very glad to meet again after being separated so long... '[43]

Notes

1   *IDA*, II, p. 102.
2   *Diary*, 20 December 1888.
3   *Diary* 21 Dec.
4   *IDA*, II, pp. 20–65.

5 Ibid, p. 46.

6 These are Stanley's figures (Ibid, p. 105) which differ a little from Parke's — Zanzibaris 205, Nubians 15, Somali 1, and Manyuema.

7 *Diary*, 23 Dec.

8 *IDA*, II, p. 102.

9 *Diary*, 31 Dec.

10 Troup, *Rear Column*; Herbert Ward, *My Life With Stanley's Rear Guard* (London 1891).

11 Ward, *op. cit.*, p 71.

12 Ibid, p. 46.

13 The Christmas menu: Goat soup à l'Africaine; Grilled goat-steak à la Yambuya; Roly-poly pudding à la Ward. Wine list: Tea *noir*, Cognac *une liqueur à chacun* (Troup, *op. cit.*, p. 191).

14 Ward, *op. cit.*, p. 59.

15 Jameson, *Story of Rear Column*, p. 282.

16 Troup, *op. cit.*, p. 274. Conveyed by steamer to Stanley Pool, Troup rested with friends before facing the ordeal of being carried in a hammock to Matadi. He caught the Portuguese mail-steamer at Banana Point on 17 August and from Lisbon travelled by rail via Paris to Dover. On the channel steamer he eagerly bought an English newspaper. 'On opening it the first thing that caught my eye was the heading of the telegram announcing the murder of Major Barttelot.' Naturally he was stunned: 'Though I had feared such an event, it was a terrible shock to me to read the fact in print... It was too terrible, alas! to think of it now that it had really happened! The long anticipation of it had not after all prepared me for it...'

17 The Committee's instructions were that Stanley's orders were to be followed and that Barttelot should not recruit a detachment of fighting men to follow in Stanley's wake.

18 Ward, *op. cit.*, p. 96.

19 Ibid, p. 101 — 'I am sending this [Barttelot wrote] to warn you to be very careful in the manner you behave below — I mean as regards pecuniary matters. I shall require at your hands a receipted bill for everything you spend, and, should you be unable to purchase the champagne and the watch, you will not draw that 20 *l*. The slightest attempt at any nonsense I shall be down upon you.'

20 Ward completed the voyage to the coast without major incident and returning up-river in the *En Avant* encountered the *Stanley* with Troup on board, invalided home. He was given Barttelot's instructions to stay at Bangala thus cutting him off from the expedition — 'the unkindest act which has been done to me'. He was still at Bangala on 16 August when a canoe arrived containing a white man, 'a deathlike figure lying back in the men's arms, insensible'. It was Jameson who responded just a little to Madeira and chicken soup. 'Oh, in-fi-nitely better', he whispered, but he died at 7.32 pm on 17 August and was buried next day by Ward who wrapped a Union Jack around his body and another around his varnished coffin.

Thoroughly distressed, Ward then set off to the coast to apprise the Committee of Jameson's death and await orders. He was instructed to go to Stanley Falls, leave the ammunition there and sell the remaining goods to the State — 'If help wanted, engage and take back Casement.' Barttelot's and Jameson's effects should be collected.

With a party of fourteen (himself, six fit Zanzibaris, four invalids and three boys), Ward finally left Stanley Falls on 10 March 1889 travelling in canoes (provided by Tippu Tib) and overland for fifteen days. There was a death *en route* and one man stayed at a mission station. Eventually they reached Banana Point and embarked in the *Afrikan* bound for Rotterdam. They crossed to England on 4 July and a few days later Ward's black companions took ship for Zanzibar. Ward received an honorarium of £330 from the Committee.

21 Sanga was tried at Stanley Falls, found guilty, sentenced to death and hanged.
22 *Diary*, 27 January 1889.
23 *Diary*, 1 Jan.
24 *Diary*, 4 Jan.
25 *Diary*, 6 Jan. There were in fact a number of suicides.
26 *Diary*, 7 Jan.
27 *Diary*, 13 Jan.
28 *Diary*, 10 Jan.
29 Tennyson, 'Ode on the Death of the Duke of Wellington'.
30 Shakespeare, *Julius Caesar*.
31 *IDA*, II, p. 107. On this occasion Stanley also spoke scathingly of Bonny who had annoyed him by seeking permission to do some private exploring. 'He seemed as if wakened out of a dream when I told him that to escort refugees to their homes was a far nobler task than any number of discoveries.'
32 *Diary*, 10 Jan. Parke's boast that he was never carried is contradicted by an entry in Bartellot's diary 31 March (*Life*, p. 78): 'I started at 7 am, and got a message from Stanley to send Parke on, as he was ill. He had to be carried in a hammock from the Lufu River to camp as he was in a fright about himself.'
33 *Diary*, 10 Jan.
34 *Diary*, 11 Jan.
35 *Diary*, 12 Jan.
36 *IDA*, II, p. 8. The well-being of the white men was obviously in Troup's mind when having purchased twelve goats at Stanley Falls he managed to deliver his flock success-fully to Yambuya. 'It was with satisfaction that we all gathered around the goats and made mental calculations whether the dozen of them could be made to last us five officers through the next four months', *Rear Column*, p. 173.
37 *Diary*, 15 Jan.
38 *Diary*, 19 Jan.
39 *Diary*, 24 Jan.
40 *Diary*, 31 Jan.
41 *Diary*, 10 February.
42 *IDA*, II, p. 141.
43 Jephson's *Diary*, p. 336.

Parke's Castle, Dromahair, County Leitrim
(Photo by author)

Clogher House, Kilmore, County Roscommon (Photo by author)

William Parke, JP, in Masonic dress
(Courtesy the Secretary, Masonic Lodge,
Mohill, County Leitrim)

Thomas Heazle Parke, 'Bwana Doctari'
(From *My Personal Experiences of
Equatorial Africa*)

Interior view of T.H. Parke Masonic Hall,
Carrick-on-Shannon, with portrait of Parke
over mantlepiece (Courtesy the Secretary,
Masonic Lodge, Mohill, County Leitrim)

Statue of Surgeon-Major Parke by Percy
Woods (Photo by Patrick Nolan)

Surgeon T.H. Parke
(Courtesy RCSI, Stoker Donation)

Henry Morton Stanley

Ward

Barttelot

Jameson

Jephson

Nelson

Stairs

Emin Pasha
(Sketch by Dr R.F. Felkin)

Dr Parke with his pygmy servant (From
My Personal Experiences of Equatorial Africa)

'The Execution' (From *The Graphic*)

The Mountains of the Moon
(Sketch by Lt Stairs, *The Illustrated London News*)

Farewell to Africa: Stanley and his officers leaving Mombasa in the steam-ship *Katoria*, with Parke on *chaise-longue* (From *The Illustrated London News*)

'Rescued!' (From *Punch, or The London Charivari*, December 14, 1889)

'Between the Quick and the Dead' (From *Punch, or The London Charivari*, November 22, 1890)

Menu of dinner in Royal College of Surgeons in Ireland
(Courtesy RCSI)

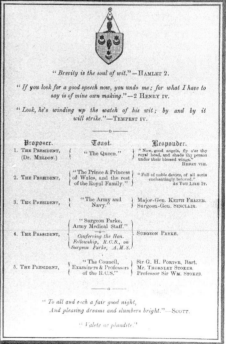

11   The Road to Zanzibar

Emin Pasha and his officers were dressed in spotless white with brass buttons decorated with a star and crescent. Parke was particularly impressed by the massive figure of Selim Bey, the governor of Laboré, a coal-black six-footer weighing more than twenty stone, a Soudanese whose indolent good nature appealed to Stanley. 'There is a man to eat, to sleep, and snore, and play the sluggard in bed, to dawdle slip-shod in the bed chamber, to call for coffee fifty times a day, and native beer by the gallon...'[1] Not until later was there a suspicion that Selim Bey was involved in a conspiracy to seize the expedition's arms.

The camp adjoined Kavalli's village and was situated about eighteen miles from the lake and 2000 feet above it on the plateau in open country. Kavalli, chief of the Wahuma, a handsome man, was attired in a beautifully prepared antelope skin; he had thin lips, an aquiline nose and Parke was struck by his fine brown eyes and 'constant rather cunning blarney smile'.[2] The Wahuma were herdsmen and despised the tillers of the soil. They favoured ivory and iron bangles on wrists and ankles, carried long sticks and were followed by pariah dogs.

Parke found Jephson in good form and something of an 'Eminist', given to saying ''pon my word, I can't help but sympathise with the Pasha, he's such a dear good man.'[3] The doctor soon pieced together an outline of what Jephson later described fully in *The Rebellion at the Equator*. Initially, as already mentioned, Emin had asked Parke to go with him to speak to the people in his stations but Stanley selected Jephson as spokesman.

★

Jephson's journey started as an idyll, the *Khedive* steaming northwards to visit Emin's lakeside stations and those on the Nile. The mountains rose sheer from the water, towering above the lake to a height of some 3000 feet; the waves slapped against the massive wall to be thrown back in showers of spray. Where the cliff-face was broken by slopes and gullies, trees adorned the crevices. Baboons, chimps and monkeys leaped and frolicked; the king-fishers' flights intertwined in twisting skeins of colour across the sky. Here and there where streams of clear, cold water fell, deltas had formed, flat plains, some amounting to several acres in extent with established settlements. Jephson had watched natives smoking their pipes, tending their goats and chickens or fishing in little one-man canoes. The women talked and laughed as they prepared fish for curing in the sun. It seemed to him to be an Arcadian existence.[4]

They left for M'swa on 28 May proceeding to Tunguru and thence overland, after some delay, to Wadelai on the Nile, Jephson riding an Abyssinian mule. The stations were clean and well-designed with compounds and sturdy bamboo houses where he availed of the almost forgotten luxury of soap and warm sponge baths. There was a formal reception at every station and when Emin Pasha had addressed his people Jephson called on the clerk of the station to read letters in Arabic from the Khedive and Nubar Pasha; he then read Stanley's proclamation to the soldiers, assuming responsibility for those who opted to travel to Cairo.

Whether Jephson talked with the stations' chiefs and officials or with the soldiers of the 2nd Battalion he was given the same answer: 'If the Pasha stays we stay; if the Pasha goes we go.' Behind this passivity and apparent willingness to leave the decision to the Mudir he sensed a lack of enthusiasm for settling in Egypt. From Emin himself he learned with disquiet that the soldiers of the 1st Battalion, stationed at Rejaf, had long ago rebelled and he could not fathom how this important news had been concealed from Stanley. Actually the leader had at least an inkling of what was going on. The European conception of Emin's situation was of a governor threatened from outside and supported internally by devoted followers, but Stanley had learned something of Emin's insecurity from the governor of M'swa, Shukri Aga, and from Selim Bey, both of whom visited him at N'sabwé. His own arrival would make matters worse. It was feared that the English wished to force an evacuation of the province. Their ragged appearance was viewed with astonishment casting doubt on their authenticity. A conspiracy to sell the soldiers into slavery was suspected with Emin playing the role of traitor to the Khedive.[5]

The *Khedive's* engine was unreliable; the Pasha dallied over the affairs of the Province; Jephson had fever and when Dufilé was not reached until July he was already conscious that before long he would be expected at Fort Bodo. He landed at Dufilé to the sound of the Khedivial Hymn and when the soldiers cut the throat of a bullock, as an expression of welcome, their guest duly stepped over the stream of blood. He was accommodated in a cool, thick-walled house with high ceilings and dined lavishly with the chief of the station, Hawish Effendi, the main dish being a goat roasted whole and stuffed with ground-nuts, onions and beans. They discussed the state of the Province and Hawish Effendi warned Jephson strongly not to go down to Rejaf where the 1st Battalion held control. Next day the Pasha made light of this warning but did agree not to go further north than Kirri where they would await a deputation from disaffected Rejaf.

They encountered a strong spirit of insurgency at Kirri and withdrew to Muggi and Laboré but they were openly heckled at the latter station and Jephson's version of the expedition was challenged. A massive Soudanese stepped out of the ranks to say that they were being lied to and that the Khedive's letter was a forgery — had it come from Effendina (the Khedive) he would have *commanded* them to return to Egypt and not have allowed them to do as they pleased. The only road to Egypt that he knew of lay through Khartoum. They would travel by that road or remain in the Province.

Incensed by the breach of discipline, Emin sprang forward to seize the soldier's gun. He demanded his arrest but a struggle ensued and Emin and Jephson were surrounded. The Mudir drew his sword to face a threatening mob but just then a raid on the magazine was reported and the soldiers rushed off to investigate taking their insolent comrade with them. Emin held his ground and Jephson followed the insubordinate men and spoke to them, trusting correctly that his unarmed presence would have a calming effect. After a long parley he persuaded them to reconsider what he had said about the expedition.

They retreated next day to Chor Ayer where they intended to spend the three-day festival, Id el Kebir, and while there received very bad news. The two chief mutineers of the 1st Battalion had arrived at Rejaf and a rebellion of the 2nd Battalion had broken out at Dufilé.

Approaching Dufilé, which it was not possible to circumvent, on 20 August, they wondered how they would be received. The absence of shots of salutation was ominous and the customary line of soldiers drawn up to welcome the Mudir was missing. Drunkenness and an excited atmosphere were evident, and, as they passed through the postern gate, Egyptian officers with detachments of soldiers stepped in front of and behind them. The people pointed at them in scorn and derision, the only exception to this universal expression of contempt being the action of a little Circassian tailor who broke weeping from the crowd to seize Emin's and Jephson's hands and kiss them.

They were subjected to a loose form of house-arrest: Jephson was free to go about the station and to visit Emin but he was followed wherever he went. The mutineers sent for rebel officers from the 1st Battalion to join them and they planned to pack the steamers with soldiers and attack the expedition when Stanley returned to the lake. By now Jephson was overdue at Fort Bodo which increased his feeling of restriction as he paced a small yard between a noisy school and the compound of an Egyptian officer whose wives and slaves cried and shrieked in response to incessant beatings. Jephson's idyllic adventure had turned into a nightmare which seemed likely to have a bloody ending.[6]

The rebel leaders from Rejaf arrived at Dufilé on 31 August with flags flying and trumpets sounding. A series of councils followed which charged Stanley with being an adventurer, declaring the documents forgeries and the expedition a ploy to lead their families into slavery. Called before a motley collection of disaffected clerks and officers, Jephson chose attack as the best method of defence and denounced their breach of the Islamic laws of hospitality. He insisted that there was no point in their going to the lower end of the lake to interview Stanley, who was rumoured to have arrived there, unless he himself was taken with them. They agreed to take him, surprisingly, and although he was suffering from fever most of the time, he accompanied them in the *Khedive* to Wadelai and Tunguru, where it became clear that the news of Stanley's presence at the lake was unfounded. Jephson was still under guard when they reached Dufilé again on 21 September.

The council was re-convened and Emin was forced to sign an acknowledgement of his deposition. Hawish Effendi was dismissed, forfeiting his possessions; his women were flogged until they divulged where his treasures were hidden. The rising tide of revolutionary violence, fortunately, was reversed by the unexpected arrival at Lado of steamers crammed with Mahdist forces, the terrible Donagla.[7] The Mahdists' envoys soon arrived in Dufilé, a bizarre trio who were dubbed 'the Peacock Dervishes' because of their many-coloured robes. They were thrown into prison, tortured and beaten to death, accepting their martyrdom with great serenity.

It was no longer possible for the rebels to send Emin to Rejaf which was taken by the Mahdists on 19 October. Fugitives from the northern stations arrived in Dufilé adding to the confusion existing there since the rebels had made it a centre for drinking and debauchery. The insurgents, uncertain as to how to handle the latest threats, sought Emin's advice, giving him the sardonic satisfaction of pointing out that he was no longer their Mudir. Jameson was amazed by the time wasted making silver bullets from silver dollars as the Mahdists were 'known' to be impervious to ordinary bullets.

Public opinion began to favour Emin. The common soldiers protested to their leaders that their troubles began with his imprisonment; they clamoured for his release and this was granted on 17 November. Accompanied by Jephson, he was escorted to the landing-place between two lines of soldiers. At 7.30 am they steamed away from Dufilé, the Mudir's flag, a crescent and three stars, flying as usual at the stem. When Emin came ashore at Wadelai he was warmly welcomed and as he entered his compound his old servant, Hadji Fatma, exclaimed loudly, 'Allah be praised!'

Somewhat in the manner of a gentler Nero fiddling while Rome burned, Emin went over his collections of birds and began to pack them to await his eventual departure. He received the neighbouring chiefs with his customary cordiality and went here and there to deal with an epidemic of fever. On 1 December the approach of the Donagla was rumoured. They were thought to be within a few days' march of Wadelai but, even so, not until three days' later, when it was reported that Dufilé had fallen and the Donagla were searching for Emin and 'the white Christian' (Jephson), was it agreed to evacuate the station.

Given their allowances of ammunition on 5 December, the soldiers refused to follow Emin saying they now intended to return to their own countries. The caravan left with its military force depleted to twenty guns and the women and children moved with great difficulty until the steamer picked them up next day and transported them to Tunguru.

Having put some distance between himself and the Donagla, Emin decided to stay at Tunguru to avoid giving the impression that he wanted to escape. And this despite the latest news that Dufilé had been re-taken and the anti-Eminists were again in the ascendant.[8] Jephson shot a Nile goose which was the *pièce de résistance* at the Christmas dinner, held, following the German custom, on Christmas Eve and attended by Emin's friends, Casati and Marco (a Greek merchant).

Dufilé was evacuated on 5 January and anti-Eminists then dominated the council at Wadelai. Emin was reported to have been sentenced to hanging; Jephson and Casati were to suffer a similar sentence for aiding and abetting his flight to Tunguru. Finally, on 26 January, there were letters from Stanley in which Jephson learned of the decimation of the rear-column. 'Are the Pasha, Casati and yourself to share the same fate?' asked Stanley who ordered his officer to start at once for Kavalli's 'and bring me the final decision of Emin Pasha, and Signor Casati, respecting their personal intentions'.[9]

Under the spur of his leader's instructions, Jephson went by steamer to

M'swa and by canoe to N'sabwé and Nyamassi Island. With difficulty he recruited carriers for the overland journey to Kavalli's where he arrived on 6 February. 'Stanley received me in his usual calm manner, tempered, however, by a smile; I think he was pleased to see me again, I know I was glad to see him.'[10] The relief of escaping assuaged the anger caused by Stanley's letter of rebuke — 'Eight months have elapsed & not one single promise has been performed'[11] — which to Jephson's mind was 'greatly lacking in common sense & I think the way he speaks about the officers of the rearguard is not very pleasant.'[12]

★

It was learned on 13 February that Emin Pasha had moved to Weré, south of N'sabe, accompanied by his close associates — Casati, Marco, Vita Hassan, a Tunisian apothecary, Selim Bey and others. The news evoked delight among the Zanzibaris; they sang and danced late into the night and next day Jephson was sent with 120 carriers to offer assistance. For weeks after Parke's arrival at Kavalli's a shuttle service of porters operated between the camp and the lake but the Egyptian officials and their friends had endless expectations. Vast piles of luggage awaited transport up the steep, stony slope to the plateau. Marco, escorted by Bonny, brought with them beds for himself and his harem, ox-hide mats, Persian carpets, baskets, pigeons and other superfluities, more than 150 loads.

A rumour that Kabba Rega had taken a lakeside village brought Emin Pasha down from the plateau, accompanied by Nelson and a contingent of armed Zanibaris. The information proved to be groundless and the Mudir was back at Kavalli's on 25 February with sixty loads including an old Saratoga trunk requiring two men to carry it. He also brought with him his little daughter, Ferida, whose Abyssinian mother was dead. This pretty child was eight years old; her complexion was olive-coloured and she had lovely dark-brown eyes.

With a degree of cynicism, Stanley agreed to an appeal that 'ex-rebels' from Wadelai could go with them to Cairo provided they arranged transport for their followers and goods, did not burden themselves with unnecessary articles, and were ready to travel on the date appointed. He established a 'confederacy' on the plateau to include the area between the Ituri River and the Albert Nyanza, guaranteeing protection to the tribes against the raids of Kabba Rega and the Balega of the mountains in return for contributions of grain and cattle. An attack by an ally of Kabba Rega was a convenient pretext for retaliatory action by which he acquired a herd of 125 cattle.[13]

136

Slow to praise a man to his face, Stanley's writing inclined towards fulsomeness and he eulogized Parke generously:

No country in Europe can produce his equal in my opinion. There may be many more learned perhaps, more skilful, older, or younger, as the case may be, but the best of them have something to learn from our doctor. He is such a combination of sweetness and simplicity. So unostentatious, so genuinely unobtrusive. We are all bound to him with cords of love. We have seen him do so much out of pure love for his 'cases', that human nature becomes ennobled by this gem. He is tenderness itself. He has saved many lives by his devoted nursing. We see him each day at 8 am and 5 pm with his selected circle of 'sick' around him. None with tender stomach dare approach it. He sits in the centre as though it were a rare perfume. The sloughing ulcers are exposed to view, some fearful to behold, and presenting a spectacle of horror. The doctor smiles and sweetly sniffs the scented air, handles the swollen limbs, cleanses them from impurity, pours the soothing lotion, cheers the sufferers, binds up the painful wounds, and sends the patient away with a hopeful and gratified look. May the kindly angels record this nobleness and obliterate all else... At Abu-Klea our doctor was great; the wounded had cause to bless him; on the green sward of Kavalli, daily ministering to these suffering blacks, unknowing and unheeding whether any regarded him, our doctor was greater still.[14]

When not carrying loads the men built huts to be ready for the newcomers. One of the Pasha's soldiers at Kavalli's was overheard asking a Soudanese how he thought the Zanzibaris would respond if the Egyptians were to seize the expedition's boxes. Down at the lake five soldiers deserted and Parke became increasingly aware that the Pasha's people could be 'a great source of trouble and danger to us'.[15] Already 600 loads had been brought up from the Nyanza.

Aware of the demanding nature of the doctor's work, Stanley, wishing to give him a 'holiday', sent him to the lake on 7 March with a party of seventy men. The descent was easy apart from the blistering heat of the stony slope underfoot and the mimosa thorns on the plain. They rested in the shade of great tamarind trees before proceeding to an encampment on the shore. Next morning Parke's problem was to convince the Egyptians and Soudanese that there was a limit to what could be carried. 'Even the servants had several loads to be transported for them.'[16]

Parke reached the foot of the plateau at 10 am but some of the men with sore feet failed to arrive until afternoon. They rested until 3 pm and were half-way up by nightfall; 'we simply lay down on the grass alongside the cool and crystal stream which zigzagged down the slope.'[17] On his return to Kavalli's, Parke said the change had been agreeable but it was hard work. Even the best men found that climb difficult and there was a lot of grumbling. He hinted broadly to Stanley that they were undertaking a lot of unnecessary labour but the latter said he felt obliged to treat the Pasha's people as his guests.

This liberality, Parke realized, was exercised at the expense of those who man-handled loads of rubbish, including heavy grinding-stones, from the lake to the plateau. The inevitable protest came on 10 March when carriers refused to go to the Nyanza. Stanley acted swiftly. He knit his brow, buckled on his revolver and blew his whistle, ordering all companies to fall in and immediately disarming the 'mutineers'. The ring-leaders were flogged with the kurbash and a reorganized detachment of porters set off meekly to collect the loads.

Parke disliked most of Emin Pasha's officers instinctively. They drank heavily and he regarded them as 'bloated, congested and overfed masses'.[18] With the Pasha himself, however, he was soon on the best of terms and they sometimes dined together. Emin invariably offered three or four courses though personally he ate sparingly; his table was sure to be covered by a tablecloth, clean though worn. He was an entertaining conversationalist but sensitive to criticism of his people or province. He told Parke he was the son of a merchant. His parents had died when he was young and he was brought up by friends, living on practically nothing in his university days. He said he had served as a medical officer in the Turkish army but was forced to leave Constantinople for political reasons after writing radical articles for newspapers.[19]

Accompanied by Jephson, Stanley took a long walk in the neighbourhood of the camp. They noticed that the bed of a stream had been dammed up to make washing places for the Zanzibaris and that drinking water was drawn from the stream. An order was posted that water for cooking and drinking must be drawn from further up-stream. 'I shall write in my notebook', Stanley teased Parke, 'that if I die here you have palpably poisoned me.'[20]

Cartridges were distributed to the men. Kites are very common here. They are always about when any meat is killed and swoop down and actually take the meat out of the men's hands. All the women I have seen in this neighbourhood have holes in their upper lips and some of them with large circular pieces of wood a couple of inches in diameter forced into the hole project out from the face which prevent them from kissing even if they wanted to. The Pasha is a very keen collector. He has already got many birds, bugs, fish and insects. He will have great difficulty in carrying out his collection as carriers are scarce.[21]

Nelson, Stairs, Jephson and Parke went with the Pasha to the Baregga Hills for a picnic and to collect still more specimens. Parke felt sorry for Emin who remained unhappy about returning to Europe and had not yet quite accepted that to go back to a province where soldiers had rebelled would be a fatal step. Emin appeared to derive comfort from the assurance that he could have done nothing more for his people and, after a conference with Stanley and his officers on 26 March, he finally contracted to accompany the expedition which now was scheduled to leave for Zanzibar, come what may, on 10 April. Osman Latif Effendi, Lieutenant-Governor of Equatoria, and Awash Effendi would come with them.

When representatives of the rebellious officers and clerks, repenting their actions, sought permission to come out with the expedition it seemed that they could constitute a problem — 'The soldiers alone will number about 800 or more as as they are all polygamists with their wives and children they will number a huge force compared with our 200 Wangwana and 21 Nubians.'[22] The Pasha interceded on their behalf 'to an unreasonable and self-abnegating extent' while accepting that their presence would constitute a threat. Stanley eventually agreed to accept them provided they were ready by 10 April and they laid down their arms before entering his camp. At the very first sign of disorder they would be shot at.

Wednesday, 27 March – This morning the Pasha came to my tent and told me he had received a long letter from all his clerks asking for some advancement and reward as he had rewarded the soldiers. This communication is specially impertinent and unreasonable at this time as the Pasha has done what he could to get these people and their families away out of the clutches of the rebels. Also it must not be forgotten that many of them are criminals and all are bad characters having been connected with Arabi's rebellion or been convicted of crime in Egypt and were then transported to penal servitude to the Equatorial Province for punishment. Certainly they looked like a party of midnight assassins.

The news from Mazamboni's on 27 March that a white man had arrived there was most exciting. Perhaps it was Jameson? Parke sincerely hoped so. He would be glad to hear his friend challenge some of Bonny's nasty innuendoes and repudiate an ugly story concerning the cannibals' revels at Riba-Riba. But the party sent to verify the rumour found it to be untrue.

The doctor disliked Bonny and also had it in for Stanley's servant, William Hoffmann, whom he had found to be a liar and a thief — 'the most dirty man in the camp'.[23] Much to Parke's surprise he noticed a change in Jephson's attitude towards Emin Pasha. He was rude to him, needling him for having to flee for his life and reminding him that his orders had been disobeyed.[24] The Pasha's extreme politeness invariably prevented him from arguing with the younger man, but when Parke ventured to mention the Mudir's debt to

Stanley, Emin said quietly that he had been reminded of it repeatedly by Jephson.

Whenever Parke dropped in on Emin he was given a cup of coffee and a cigarette. Emin referred to Gordon's chain-smoking and said he had developed the habit of taking opium. He had observed this when he noticed 'a fulness and sweetness' of Gordon's voice after taking the drug which may have been responsible for some of his eccentricities. He might box a man's ears, for instance, or give him a few lashes of the kurbash and immediately afterwards hand the delinquent two or three dollars.[25]

An epidemic of diarrhoea was attributed by the MO to an excess of sesame oil in the food but he remained concerned by repeated contamination of the water supply. Sentries were posted at a stream half-a-mile from the camp to ensure that its water remained potable.

M'Bremer, driven to despair by a syphilitic ulcer, shot himself in his hut after drinking pombe. A Manyuema died in delirium from typhoid fever. Cases of severe itching (probably scabies) were treated after a thorough washing of the affected areas with a mixture of gunpowder and oil. The Pasha's 'yellow bellies' had their enlarged spleens rubbed with Tartar Emetic and Oil of Rosemary. The Egyptians and Soudanese consulted Parke 'in swarms' for complaints real and imagined. There were several septuagenarians and some cases of syphilis. Emin told Parke that the Monbuttu people had a method of inoculation to convey a form of syphilis milder than the sexually-acquired disease.

To Parke's delight his Snow Mountain was clearly visible on 30 March:

Today the Snow Mountain which Jephson and myself saw in April last year and afterwards seen by Mr Stanley and myself on 24 May following stands out very clear but not so distinct as when I saw it first. We all took sketches of it, the Pasha, Casati, Stanley, Stairs, Jephson, myself and all the men could see it. The peaks were covered with snow, the mountain range ran for a long way to the east, and, a continuation of Mazamboni's peak cuts off the view to the west.[26]

His pygmy woman, quick to pick up Swahili, told him that her tribe rarely ate human flesh and were ashamed of doing so.

The dwarfs live by game which they kill in the forest. Whenever possible they sell the meat for corn to the Wasongora or a larger native who occupy clearings in the forest and who are much ... darker in colour. The dwarfs are great thieves and get into trouble by taking the bananas from the plantations of the Wasongora. They are itinerants and don't seem to live in any one camp for longer than a month. They catch their game by means of nets which are beautifully made from bark or grass twine and the meshes, diamond shaped, about five inches long by three in depth, very like in strength and shape to salmon drawing-nets. They are about 100 yds in length and nearly five feet in height. When not set for catching the game they are kept in the huts coiled round a long pole.[27]

They set the nets in a semi-circle, drove the game towards it and killed with their poisoned arrows. They also used pits to trap animals and heavy, spiked beams suspended over game tracks and set to fall when the animal breaks a vine stretched across the path. Elephants were killed by this method, the broken spikes striking a great beast at the back of the neck.

Rumours that the Pasha's people were not solidly behind him continued to circulate. The suspicion that his soldiers were planning a *coup* necessitated the posting of night patrols, for rifles had been stolen. By the beginning of April Emin's people had all come up from the lake and with Major Awash Effendi, Rushti Effendi and a few other Egyptians, Stairs set up an advance camp at Mazamboni's with about eighty Zanzibaris and some 200 native bearers.[28]

Finally, to end the uncertainty about Emin's support, Stanley mustered his own men on 5 April and directed Emin to sound the assembly in the Egyptian camp. When they were slow to obey, Number 1 Company hurried them up with clubs and sticks, regardless of rank. All who proposed to follow Emin were instructed to fall in on one side, those not wishing to go to Egypt on the other.

When no defectors declared themselves Stanley ordered Emin's soldiers to lay down their arms. The few who refused to do so were seized and punished. The Pasha's personal servants had not yet appeared and Jephson was sent to roust them out. Arriving on the square and asked if they intended to follow Emin all replied in the affirmative with the exception of Serour whom Emin named as the chief conspirator. He was placed under guard with three others suspected of disloyalty. The Pasha's followers numbered 182 men, 264 women, 105 children: total 551. Having established Emin's now undivided support, Stanley made it clear that henceforth he himself commanded the entire party. It amounted to more than a thousand souls including 380 women and children.

Parke, though well disposed towards Emin, was annoyed by his vacillation and realized that even now the Pasha wished to stay on in Central Africa augmenting his collections, caring little about how he had delayed them.

He knows that he cannot remain here alone with his people as his life would be as uncertain as if he returned to his own Rebels in the Province; therefore he sees that he has no other option but to come out with us. He has often told me that he would like to remain on in his Province provided he could get his books and letters periodically as before through Unyoro and Uganda from Zanzibar. This, however, is impossible, owing to the insurrection in Uganda where the Arabs are fighting to place Karemma on the throne instead of Mwanga, the rightful heir, who has been christened by the French Priests... But even if the Pasha could receive his letters in this way he has nowhere to go as his own people are his worst enemies, for they would treat him as a prisoner or perhaps kill him and, even if his people did receive him back as their Governor, the ammunition which we brought for his relief would last only a couple of months against the invasion of the Mahdi's people. Already his own people have sacked his ammunition stores and taken everything, including the 33 boxes of ammunition which we handed over to him in April 1888.[29]

For two days before their departure there were celebrations at Kavalli's and eighty Wahuma women paid Stanley the compliment of dancing before his tent.

Their movements are clumsy like the Nauch dance with a peculiar characteristic voluptuous wriggle about the buttocks their great object to be obtained in the dance is to be able to shake the green banana leaves which are stuck in their belts both fore and aft from side to side. One large bunch is placed behind in the fissure of the buttocks, another smaller bunch in front. We all start tomorrow, thanks be to God, as our hearts are sick of the delay.[30]

A general muster was called for 6.30 am on 10 April. The carriers received their loads and were assisted by local volunteers. Number 1 Company moved off at 8 am bearing the Egyptian flag and leading Emin Pasha and his followers slowly and trustfully into the vast unknown that separated them from Zanzibar. The nearby hills were lined with well-wishers who waved their farewells.

A few donkeys were available for designated riders while little Ferida, Emin's daughter, was borne in a hammock like a princess. Most of the children walked or were carried by long-suffering parents and the extended, straggling caravan was protected by a substantial rearguard but delayed by the associated cattle drive. The lowing, bewildered beasts plunged and turned, wishing to regain familiar pastures, but were forced to accommodate themselves to the pace and direction of the human procession. And in the wake of the inchoate Odyssey lay an empty camp strewn with discarded oddments, tin baths, baskets, bedsteads, grinding-stones and an enormous copper pot, an unwieldy desolate flotsam, every item of which once held its familiar place among the lares and penates of a home in Equatoria.

The first night in improvised shelters was wet and windy. A number of tents, including Parke's, were blown down but despite the tempest a raiding-party was despatched to bring back food. Next day a meat ration was given to the entire caravan. By the third morning the local volunteers had tired of their self-imposed task. There were more loads now than carriers and, though fifty-four porters were recruited at Gavira's, it was necessary to discard all but the most essential burdens.

At Mazamboni's, which was reached by 3 pm, two adjoining camps were formed, 'the relief expedition in one and the relieved in the other'.[31] Parke's factotum, Hari, like a Muessin calling the faithful to evening prayer, exhorted the sick to assemble for medical treatment.

The caravan was already developing the slow rhythms of a complex, organic entity, a momentum likely to quicken. The sadness of the painful uprooting was partly eased by the assurance of a safe future in distant Egypt. The Pasha's people had escaped certain death at the hands of the Mahdists; despite their fluctuations they deserved a reward for their valour. Like an inert machine responding to a sluggish engine, or in the manner, perhaps, of some fabulous millipede accepting the obscure dictates of primitive ganglia, the caravan was stumbling along on its reluctant journey. It was most desirable, now, that it should continue to proceed with an increasing celerity; instead it was fated to be brought to an unexpected halt when Stanley fell ill like one of Virgil's heroes victimized by Juno's spiteful anger.

Notes

1 *IDA*, II, p. 138.
2 *Diary*, 18 February 1889.
3 *IDA*, II, p. 131.
4 Jephson, *Rebellion*, p. 8.
5 Smith, *Relief Expedition*, p. 209.
6 Jephson, *op. cit., passim*.
7 Smith, *op. cit.*, p. 236. This author sees both the rebellion at Dufilé and the Mahdists' attack as a direct outcome of the arrival of the expedition. The Mahdist force under Omar Saleh hoped to destroy all traces of the Khedive's rule in Equatoria and to capture Emin Pasha. They found Lado deserted.
8 When Dufilé was re-taken by Selim Bey, Omar Saleh retired to Rejaf to await reinforcements from Omdurman. Ivory, ammunition and documents were seized including papers from the Khedive and Nubar Pasha to Dr Emin. These were sent to Omdurman with a letter expressing Omar Saleh's assurance that Emin, the Christians with him and the steamers would be taken. Copies of these papers and of Omar Saleh's report to the Khalifa were sent to General Grenfell at Suakin and soon rumours circulated in England that the expedition had encountered disaster. There was a correspondence between Lord Salisbury and Sir Evelyn Baring regarding the possibility of ransoming them from the Khalifa (Smith, *op. cit.*, p. 243).
9 *IDA*, II, pp. 115–16.
10 Jephson, *op. cit.*, p. 441.
11 Letter Stanley/Jephson (Jephson's, *Diary*, p. 321).

12 Ibid, p. 329. Jephson, who had just heard of the fate of the rear-column, must have been astounded by Stanley's comments: 'But the officers were plunged in their own follies, the rear column was wrecked by indecision. Barttelot, Jameson & Ward reaped only what they had sown.' Letter Stanley/Jephson, Ibid, p. 322.

13 *IDA*, II, p. 145.

14 Ibid, p. 148.

15 *Diary*, 4 March.

16 *Diary*, 8 March.

17 Ibid.

18 *Diary*, 21 Feb.

19 *Diary*, 13 March. These confidences were not altogether accurate: Ludwig Schnitzer, Eduard's merchant father, died in 1845; the widow remarried; her son got on well with his stepfather and corresponded with his mother from the Ottoman Empire. While in Turkey, Hairoullah Effendi (as Dr Schnitzer was called) was sometimes entrusted with political missions which his command of languages facilitated; he wrote for the *Neue Freie Presse* of Vienna to the displeasure of the Austrian and French consuls at Scutari but his expulsion seems unlikely.

20 *Diary*, 16 March.

21 *Diary*, 20 March.

22 *Diary*, 25 March.

23 *Diary*, 3 March.

24 *Diary*, 5 March.

25 *Diary*, 24 March.

26 *Diary*, 30 March.

27 *Diary*, 3 April.

28 W.G. Stairs, 'From the Albert Nyanza to the Indian Ocean', *Nineteenth Century*, 1891; 29: 953.

29 *Diary*, 5 April.

30 *Diary*, 9 April.

31 *Diary*, 12 April.

12   The Mountains of the Moon

Called at 2 am to Stanley's tent, Parke found the ashen-faced leader sitting upright in bed, immobilized by intense upper abdominal pain. He admitted that he should have consulted the doctor days earlier but put it off because of the extra work. Now he was afraid of a recurrence of the attack that almost killed him at Fort Bodo.

I immediately gave him castor oil, one ounce and 40 minims of tincture of opium and applied a mildewed mustard leaf which had lost its strength after so many months of damp in the forest and applied stoups to an early hour in the morning. Gave a half a grain of Morphia and Atropine hypodermically at 4 am which slightly lessened the pain. At 7 am he commenced distressing and severe vomiting of undigested meat eaten 24 hours previously and with much bilious matter. Gave 3 tablets of Morphia of $^1/_6$ of a grain each hypodermically. He drank some milk which was quickly vomited as curds accompanied by bile. He drank a little tamarind water which he also vomited.[1]

A soap-and-water enema with castor oil and turpentine resulted in 'a great discharge from the bowel of scybalae and semi-fluid excrement'. There was fever, sweating, a slow pulse and a heavily coated tongue.

For many days Stanley's mind slipped from fevered dreams into delirium. He grappled anxiously with anticipated dangers. He fought running battles with Kabba Rega's spearmen, faced the long bows of the Wahuma, or the hostile Wasongora, or the fearsome Wanyankori. He rehearsed the desperate strata-gems necessary to avoid destruction at the foot of the Ruwenzori, crossed imaginary rivers and energetically created bomas urging every man and woman to assist him until his restlessness was eased by Parke's hypodermic needle.[2]

The doctor sat up with his patient for six consecutive nights. Catheteriza-tion was needed on a number of occasions and morphia was given repeat-edly to ease paroxysms of severe pain resembling gallstone colic. Dr Emin, when consulted, agreed with the overall management and advised an addi-tional camphor linament and tincture of opium to be rubbed in over the liver before the poultices were applied.

After a draught of chloral hydrate, Stanley slept well during the early part of the night of 16 April but required morphia at 3 am. He was now able to lie on his right side, a favourable development, and in the morning sat on a chair. He drank milk and took tabloids of peptone and sodium bicarbonate to relieve flatulence. A cough mixture of squills and ipecacuhana was administered on 19 April and the patient took chicken broth, milk and arrowroot. He sat up for a couple of hours, the pain greatly diminished.

And now it was the doctor's turn to be ill. 'This afternoon my temperature rose to 105, my urine became very bloody and was exactly the colour of stout.'[3] Bonny nursed Stanley and Parke retired to his tent.

I have been confined to my tent [he wrote six days later] with a pernicious form of bilious intermittent fever exactly the same as I had at Fort Bodo but much more severe. I am very much reduced in weight and feel very weak all over as I have lost much strength. Although I was florid yet in the last few days I have become quite pale from the amount of blood and bile passed in the urine. It was a very sharp attack but now I am right for recovery. Yesterday I went to Stanley's tent about 20 yards off assisted by Muftah my gun bearer and a stick. The Pasha had asked me to go as Stanley was so unwell and wanted me to see him.[4]

Parke was alarmed to find that Stanley was medicating himself and taking generous doses of opiates — 'He has been taking very much morphia. When I asked him yesterday how he slept he said very well after those 2 grains of Opium.' He put his foot down at once and reassumed charge of prescriptions.

Bonny was the latest fever victim. Nelson and Jephson were also ill, the latter severely affected, 'only just able to crawl about'. During Jephson's illness, when his life was thought to be at risk, Parke — 'our priceless doctor' as Stanley called him[5] — rose from his own sick-bed and, with support, made his way to his collapsed colleague.

The Pasha has been very kind and comes over to see me every day, sometimes even 3 times. He is really very well up in his work as a medical man considering what he must have forgotten during the last 13 years in Africa. I feel him a great support even on account of his presence, for my work is now very responsible with all those white officers and over 1000 blacks. I only hope that the whites may live until they reach Zanzibar at least. I would also like that the blacks would live too but I know that a large number of them must die on the line of march from want, exposure, fatigue, disease etc.

Unwilling to allow his authority to slip into the hands of others, Stanley listened to daily rumours of sedition and dealt with reported atrocities. One of the Lieutenant-Governor's men who shot a friendly native was put in chains and ordered to carry a load. And when Rehan, a freed slave, stole a rifle and deserted with twenty-two of the Pasha's people, Stairs was sent to bring him back from the lake.

On 29 April Stanley rose, dressed and sat in a shelter specially made for him near his tent. All narcotics, to Parke's relief, were discontinued — 'he has evidently acquired a taste for opium and morphia; for the smallest ache he takes a full dose because he says the Doctors in London told him to do so.'[6] Parke said he ought never come to Africa again and Stanley expressed determination to get to Zanzibar and out of the country as quickly as possible.

On May Day, Parke was busy making candles:

We have now got a couple of hundred head of cattle and several goats so we are rich in meat for the march. I have just made a supply of candles ... simply by making a wick of thread or linen put it through a cane mould and pour in bullock's melted fat mixed with a little bees wax, place the mould in cold water for a moment and the candle is easily removed. It has the same appearance as a halfpenny dip.

When Stairs returned from the Albert Nyanza on 2 May with the deserters, the ring-leader, Rehan, who had stolen a rifle, was tied and placed under guard pending his trial. Stanley appointed his officers, with two of Emin's, to form a court of justice which found him guilty of inciting the Pasha's soldiers to desert, and of stealing a rifle. The immediate decision was that Rehan's life should be spared if one of the headmen would be responsible for his custody, and obliged him to carry a load to the coast, or see that he was chained with other prisoners.

The impracticability of their clement verdict was soon apparent. Rehan was cunning and would be clever at releasing himself. Who would look after him in camp? 'We all agreed that he would be neglected and perhaps die or escape, therefore we agreed that he should be hanged forthwith.'[7]

Stanley, weak from his illness, read the charges, the evidence and the verdict with considerable vigour, tumbling to the ground as he did so. 'It was a very exciting moment', Parke wrote in his diary, but macabre would have been a more apposite term. Not only was the amended verdict crazily illogical but the execution was botched when the rope broke and had to be mended. 'He was pulled up again to a height of 14 feet from the ground where he remained for the night. The Pasha's people also came out in numbers to witness the sight.'[8] Rehan's detachment throughout the awful procedure amazed Parke who as Medical Officer spoke to the Soudanese after the rope broke and he fell to the ground. Jephson, too, registered his astonishment in his diary: 'I never saw a man go to his death with such complete sang-froid, he did not utter a word nor did his face change in any way; he just walked quietly to the tree & waited until the noose was fixed.'[9]

A plan to delay the expedition was uncovered on 3 May when through a mix-up a letter from one of Emin's captains, Ibrahim Effendi Elham, intended for Selim Bey in Tunguru, was delivered to Stanley who opened it and read it. Captain Elham, he was astonished to learn, was urging his friend to send fifty soldiers immediately and to follow on speedily with 200 more. This would enable them 'to obtain all you and I wish'.[10] Forewarned, Stanley planned to disarm Selim Bey the moment he appeared but apart from a letter of complaint that Soudanese soldiers were being used as beasts of burden, and another asking for more time to join the caravan, nothing more was heard of him.[11]

Their journey was resumed on 8 May after some days' preparation and a lively night of singing and dancing. The untidy caravan assembled early and to the shouts of last-minute instructions shrugged itself to a start, the van-guard stepping off smartly guided by Stanley carried in a hammock behind the flag-bearers. Emin Pasha's people, young and old, came next, a long faltering line urged to form the semblance of a disciplined file and followed by the expedition's companies and a rearguard, and escorted by Chief Mazamboni and 300 carriers.

They did not aim to cover more than a modest distance to allow the unaccustomed walkers to acquire the rhythm of the march. They had not yet achieved the co-operation necessary if a large body of people is to move without hindrance, each person or family-group as yet vying to get ahead or lagging behind in a manner that impeded their neighbours. The worst cul-prits were the Egyptian and Coptic clerks, the best marchers the black people from the Makraka and Dinka countries.[12]

For some days confusion reigned. Crossing a ravine, for instance, each person seemed to think only of himself or herself, their dependants and their possessions. They pushed, shoved and jostled to gain a few yards, at the risk of losing their precious mats and cooking-pots and to the annoyance of others. Orders were disregarded as each endeavoured, come what may, to get through the rocky bottle-neck as fast as possible but only succeeding in creating a struggling mass in which mothers protected their screaming chil-dren and hulking men cursed those whom they accused of obstructing them.

They camped at Bundegunda and moved next day to Bunyambiri, villages protected from the cold winds off the lake and prodigiously fertile. Being still accompanied by Mazamboni they could enjoy the local produce without stint and feasted on yams, sweet potatoes, beans and bananas but three of the Pasha's soldiers deserted.

The rough path they followed wound and undulated at the base of mountains inhabited by the Balegga, while some miles away to their right stretched the dark mass of the forest which fortunately they did not have to enter. Within days, Parke saw the southern-most end of Lake Albert tapering into a mirage-like plain in the centre of which he gained a distant view of the shining Semliki River which they had yet to cross. On the horizon were the snow-capped mountains close to which they planned to travel.

Parke was pleased to know that Stanley had had chicken and a glass of milk for breakfast but now he was concerned by Jephson who was 'very feverish and hysterical'.[13] Falling ill towards the end of April, Jephson now had a serious relapse and was afraid the fever would kill him.

I was up twice last night to see Jephson who seems to me to be in a perilous condition. He does not sleep at all. I gave him $^1/_2$ a grain of Morphia at 11 pm and at 3 am I gave him a very large dose of hydrate of Chloral. His temperature commences to rise about 8.30 or 9 so that I give him about 20 grs of Quinine about 5.30 every morning. Neverthless his temperature at 11.30 is 103 and at 4.45 pm 104.2. He took one ounce of castor oil at 3 pm today. I have also given him $^1/_{25}$ of a grain of Arsenic 3 times a day for the last week.[14]

Medication with quinine was continued but on 13 May the temperature registered 103.4°F. 'I gave him a tepid bath and two grs of Opium afterwards.' During the following week Jephson's temperature remained high and Parke gave him half a bottle of Madame de Warburg's tincture and arsenic.[15] Stairs also was ill with fever.

Tuesday, 14 May – Marched to the east for about 6 miles on the lowlands, halted about 10.30 amongst plenty of Bananas. Jephson slept a little while last night ... Stanley complains of constipation and pain in his bowels so I ordered him at 6 o'c an enema... Stairs was normal this morning... Nelson went with his company to the river...

A broad plain stretched for miles to the south-west of the Albert Nyanza and at times looked as if it were covered with water enabling Parke to understand why Sir Samuel Baker spoke of Lake Albert 'stretching illimitably to the South'. The low swampy plains of the Semliki Valley were uninviting but ahead Parke could see the Ruwenzori range 'which is covered with snow and called the mountains of the moon by Ptolemy and Herodotus and other ancient writers who thought the Nile took its origin or source from these mountains'.[16] The caravan was most imposing and even when moving in close file extended over about two and a half miles.

Nelson had benefitted greatly from the nourishing food at Kavalli's and

Mazamboni's and was restored to health. He led a party to the Semliki River to find a suitable crossing-place. He reported that it was sixty to eighty yards wide; there were no canoes and the natives would oppose them.

The caravan reached the river on 17 May after an eight-mile march under a burning sun. Three canoes were discovered and commandeered under fire by Uledi and Saat Tato. The latter received an arrow-wound requiring Parke's attention. The political climate improved when Parke went through a ceremony of blood-brotherhood with the local chief, Bakamuggar.

The ceremony consisted in sitting down on the ground facing each other with legs extended, my right over his left and his right over my left. Marabo then made 2 small incisions over my heart and 2 over my stomach and afterwards put a little salt into the wounds and then took a leaf and put a little of the native's blood on my wound and vice versa. He muttered several mysterious sayings and made signs like a conjuror. He said such things as may all your children, goats and fowls die of a bad disease if ever the vow of friendship be broken.[17]

With fifty rifles, Bonny established a bridgehead on the opposite side and the crossing of the Semliki River was supervised by Parke and Nelson, taking two days to accomplish. Their figures accounted for 1168 souls and 610 loads. The oxen were driven across. The operation was interrupted by a party of Kabba Rega's Warasura but they were put to flight by Nelson's company of Zanzibaris.

Sent to reconnoitre, Parke found a reasonably good road to the south-east but the sole came off one of his boots and he felt he would give £200 for decent foot-wear. Stanley consoled him with the gift of a pair of scarlet breeches. He was relieved also to find that Jephson's and Stair's temperatures had fallen. They stayed in camp on 21 May: Jephson's temperature was still normal but each day brought its own medical problem — 'Casati has a big spleen and the Pasha has a colic.'[18]

The rain ceased at 5.30 am and the caravan started at six proceeding through bush and forest clearings in the direction of Ruwenzori. Ten cows were sacrificed to give a meat ration to the entire caravan on the Queen's birthday — 'long may she live!' Next day they followed a good path through the forest, resting on reaching swampy ground by mid-morning. Beyond this, after crossing hilly country, they found enormous banana plantations with an inexhaustible supply of fruit.

They rested in camp on 27 May:

There is a beautiful view [Parke wrote] of the snow-capped mountain from here. The range runs from N.E. to S.W. and terminates about 10 miles from here to the south. For about 10,000 feet it is covered with verdure and is creased all over by ravines with a good many trees and bushes in places. The summit is nearly always covered with a cloud excepting in the early morning about 6.30 am before the sun gets strong and the moisture begins to rise from the earth. It is a very foggy country about the foot of the mountain.

Tottering now with the aid of a stick, Jephson resumed keeping his diary, after a blank interval in which he could just recall being carried from camp to camp, lying awake at night hardly caring whether he lived or died and accepting that death might be the easiest solution. 'Parke who has been, as he always is, most untiring in his efforts to get one well blames me terribly for the ways I have fallen into of looking at it all & will not allow me to speak about it, though he admits I nearly passed the threshold of life & death.'[19] And Stairs, by now the most robust of the officers, woke the doctor during the night of 2 June seeking relief from an earache.

Skirmishes with natives led to fatalities on both sides. Four of the expedition's men were wounded and Parke dealt effectively with a severely wounded elbow, almost full function being regained. A shortage forced him to boil the bandages and reuse them but by application of Listerian principles and potassium permanganate his patients' wounds healed with normal temperatures and little suppuration.

They passed through recently deserted villages, their occupants driven out by fear of Manyuema ivory-raiders, a hundred of whom visited the expedition's camp early in June keen to barter rice and chickens for beads and cloth. They encountered a length of road with steep declivities followed by almost perpendicular ascents that necessitated the discarding of further luggage.

They marched at daybreak on 6 June and halted after five miles to avail of the proximity of large fields of Indian corn and a banana plantation. Urged by Stanley, Stairs volunteered to climb the mountain accompanied by forty Zanzibaris and by the Pasha, who had to turn back after a thousand feet.[20] 'Halted in camp [Parke wrote next day]. Stairs went up the mountain to explore and report. The Pasha gone bug hunting but returned in the evening. Jephson's temperature went up to 106 last night. I am anxious about him.'[21]

Stairs and his men spent the night on the mountain, hoping to reach the snow when the climb was resumed, but in the morning the lieutenant realized that before reaching the snowline he must cross several deep ravines. Prudently he withdrew, having reached 10,677 feet, taking a number of botanical specimens down with him for identification by Emin Pasha.

'I feel deuced bad today', the doctor admitted on 8 June, his temperature

105° F. The recurring fever which affected him was aggravated by a palmer abscess which prevented him from keeping his diary until Nelson lanced it. As the caravan emerged from the bush it marched at the foot of the mountain onto the freedom of the open plain. At sunset there was a view of Ruwenzori in its full magnificence — the mist suddenly lifted to reveal peak after snowy peak, a spectacle that drew all eyes, 'a perfect picture of beautiful majestic desolateness...'[22]

On 14 June the caravan descended again onto grassy plains and entered Muhamba in Usongora. Next day they were back in the hills and a friendly herdsman showed them where to find the cattle of Rukara, an enemy warlord. A herd of twenty-five fine beasts was thus quietly added to the expedition's herd of a hundred animals and they proceeded to rest at the zeriba of Ruessé from where through a misty haze the waters of the Albert Edward Nyanza (Muta Nzigé) were visible.

They travelled from Rusessé to Katwé crossing a silent plain that fell in terraces of spiky grass towards the Nyama-gazani River. Here they had a farewell view of Ruwenzori which in Stanley's words, 'suddenly cast its cloudy garments aside to gratify us once more'.[23] Katwé, the headquarters of Rukara, had been hurriedly vacated forfeiting a supply of Indian corn.

Pleased with the flight of the Warasura, the indigenous natives were friendly and supplied the expedition with food and guides. They were additionally grateful when Stanley burned their enemy's village. Inevitably there were clashes with Kabba Rega's allies but the expedition's superior rifle-power scattered them. Parke's boy, Muftah, angered his master by leaving his best stockings behind when striking camp and disappointed him by deserting him during episodes of fever, returning when health was restored, unprepared to put up with the evil temper that inevitably accompanied the illness. The doctor reported the youth to Stanley who ordered thirty strokes of the rod.

There was a not altogether unexpected row between Stanley and Emin who in many ways were incompatible. Entering Usongora they had agreed that all the young, able-bodied men should form a united defence corps. When this was accomplished the Pasha realized that his guards and orderlies were no longer freely available. He demanded that his people be restored to him and reacted temperamentally when Stanley commented on the futility of his behaviour.

'You had better leave me where I am,' the Pasha said.

'You can do as you like, Pasha,' Stanley retorted. 'You are a thankless, ungrateful man.'[24]

Parke went with Bonny and the Pasha to see two salt-lakes in the vicinity which attracted natives from all over the region. Next day they marched eighteen-and-a-half miles, following the path of the defeated Warasura and halted close to some mud huts with coloured paintings on the walls, reds, blues and browns, the first attempt at frescos Parke had seen in Central Africa. They were attacked on 22 June when traversing a rocky pass, the brunt of the musket volley being taken by the Wahuma guides who were leading. Parke then went ahead with Number 1 company driving the attackers into the hills.

They saw a few giraffes, many herons, sacred flamingos and herds of antelope. There were extensive plantations at Buruli where they halted for forty-eight hours with instructions to gather food supplies for six days. Nelson took a party of riflemen to search for the Warasura but the latter, having learned their lesson, kept their distance. Saadi Mpsa of Number 2 company died of pneumonia.

Having completed a fourteen-mile march through terrain rich with wild date palms bearing small yellow fruits, and crossed five rivers on 25 June, they were obliged to camp in the bush where the coffee-coloured drinking-water came from stagnant pools. A few days later more than 200 persons were suddenly prostrated by illness which Stanley, one of the victims, said had 'raged like a pest through all ranks, regardless of age, colour or sex.'[25] Parke and Jephson were among the affected but despite the severe toxicity there were no deaths. Yusuf Effendi, an Egyptian officer, died from liver disease, the sixth death in the Egyptian camp. A few of Emin's people were also speared on the road.

They had skirted the north and east sides of the Albert Edward Nyanza and when they camped close to it on 1 July they had, for once, a splendid view of water usually wrapped in 'an impenetrable and loveless mist'.[26] The Pasha's muster-roll for the month accounted for 555 souls: 44 officers and clerks; 90 married women and concubines; 107 children; 223 soldiers, guards and servants; 91 followers.

They stayed in camp next day because of the large number of fever cases and then moved six miles to the south to a camp at the lakeside. Parke filled the quinine bottles of the expedition's officers from his dwindling supply so that they could medicate themselves if separated from him for a couple of days.

Notes

1   *Diary*, 13 April.
2   *IDA*, II, p. 194.

3   *Diary*, 20 April.
4   *Diary*, 26 April.
5   *IDA*, II, p. 198.
6   *Diary*, 29 April.
7   *Diary*, 2 May.
8   Ibid.
9   Jephson's *Diary*, p. 349. Ward, also, was oppressed at Yambuya by this puzzling fatalism: 'Poor devils! they do not seem to care about death; in fact they seem apparently to look forward to it as a relief to their suffering' (*My Life*, p. 77).
10 *IDA*, II, p. 199.
11 It did transpire later that Selim Bey's intention to join Stanley was genuine but failing to make up lost ground he settled near Kavalli's. He was still there in 1891 when Major F.D. Lugard (later Lord) Lugard arrived from the East Coast with Shukri Aga and seventy Soudanese soldiers who had been to Cairo and received their pay.

     Selim had about 600 men with their slaves and followers including a number of attractive-looking girls in slave-sticks, the restrictive device used to shackle recent captives. Remaining loyal to the Khedive he declined an engagement with Emin under the German flag but agreed reluctantly to serve with Lugard in Uganda on the understanding that his appointment was ratified by the Khedive. Moving eastwards with his men and their followers, stealing cattle and enslaving local women, his caravan grew until it numbered over 6000 persons. After Lugard's departure in 1892, Selim Bey was embroiled in civil strife supporting the Islamic claim for more territory. He was arrested and sentenced to be deported but died on his way to the coast. See Nicholas Harman, *Bwana Stokesi and his African Conquests* (London 1986), p. 168; Pakenham, *Scramble*, p. 444; Smith, *Relief Expedition*, p. 424.
12 Stairs, 'Albert Nyanza to the Indian Ocean', p. 956.
13 *Diary*, 10 May.
14 *Diary*, 12 May.
15 Jephson's intense suffering is described in his *Diary*, p. 377. 'Fever, Fever that strikes one down like a sledge hammer & burns into one's very vitals leaving one as nerveless & weak as a child. My God, am I not brought low enough yet? Must I die by slow degrees? A quiet death is so much easier. I am reduced to mere skin and bone & I am an object to look at, my arms & legs are mere skin & bone with the muscles standing out like cords — a study for an anatomist.'
16 *Diary*, 14 May.
17 *Diary*, 17 May.
18 *Diary*, 21 May.
19 Jephson's *Diary*, p. 355.
20 William Hoffmann, *With Stanley in Africa* (London 1938) p. 142.
21 *Diary*, 7 June.
22 *IDA*, II, p. 264.
23 Ibid, p. 311.
24 *Diary*, 16 June.
25 *IDA*, II, p. 325.
26 Ibid, p. 329.

13   The March to Mackay's

What route should they take now? Stanley held a conference to discuss this vital question on 3 July. The shortest way to the east coast lay through Uganda, crossing the Victoria Nyanza to Kavirondo, but the king and the Waganda were likely to be hostile. The path through Ruanda to Lake Tanganyika had undeniable attractions but a proverb warned that it was easier to get into Ruanda than to get out of it. Many caravans had disappeared there. On balance, then, the best way was through Ankori and Karawagé which would also enable them to visit the Rev. A.M. Mackay, the most famous African missionary since Livingstone and one of those who had been in correspondence with Emin, among the first to draw attention to his isolation.

They set out next day carrying five days' provisions and marched over a plain leading to steep hills, difficult territory for many ill and feverish persons, 'groaning and wriggling about like primiparae'.[1] Parke's unfeeling remark is forgivable when one realizes that the doctor himself was also in the grip of fever. Stanley issued strict warnings against foraging or looting when they camped at Kitété having climbed a thousand feet and gained a full view of the south-east end of Lake Albert Edward.

A local chief forbade further advance through Ankori until the king's permission was obtained. Antari, the 27-year-old monarch, was away but his mother sent messages of welcome and freedom to proceed, promising goats and guides. The caravan continued its ascent for some days in mountainous country attaining an altitude of 6160 feet at the summit of Kinyamagra before descending an eastern slope. The news of their victories over the hated Warasura had gone ahead and the natives, the Wanyankori, were friendly and offered food and assistance. 'Ankori is your own country in future,' they were told and half-nude women bustled about fetching water for them and performing their chores.[2]

Tuesday, 9 July – Marched until 11 am and halted where there were a few huts and some bananas. Shortly after our Arrival some 6 or 8 men speaking Swahili arrived. They were very respectable looking, well clad and could read their prayers in

Swahili. They said that a year and a half ago the Waganda deposed Wanga [Mwanga] and placed his brother Karema on the throne and killed the Katakiro (or prime minister). Wanga is at present on an island in the Victoria Nyanza and he is principally supported by the Christians and a large number of the Waganda. He is the lawful heir to the throne being the eldest son of M'tesa. His morals are said to be not very good and also that he dislikes the Arabs. The entire Arab traders support Karema. All missionaries and traders had to fly from Uganda owing to the rebellion. About 2000 came to Ankora and these men who have visited us were refugees and had formerly been pupils of Mackay of the Church Missionary Society and they know how to write very well the Swahili language.

Samuel and Zachariah, the spokesmen for the Christians, explained to Stanley that Mwanga, now a Christian, still possessed a large flotilla of canoes and retained control of the islands in Lake Victoria. His efforts to regain his throne were already supported by Bwana Stokesi[3] — an Irish caravan-leader and ex-missionary — and they vainly attempted to enlist Stanley's sympathy but he politely avoided involvement in this dangerous quarrel.[4]

Parke ignored differences of upbringing, education and nutrition when he argued that black people bore fever with less resolve than the superior Europeans. The former, he found, were generally prostrated by the intolerable malaise. They literally lay down under it and wished to die — they were sometimes speared on the roadside — while the stoical white men struggled on in their misery. He could by now easily recognize the prodromal talkativeness, the dishevelled hair, bad temper and glassy-eyed appearance that ushered in a bout of fever.

Mahommed Hari, one of the Pasha's people, died and two men tormented by ulcers decided to remain in Ankori with their harems and servants. Bacteriology being still in its infancy, Parke blamed the environment for the high prevalence of fever. The sickly papyrus swamps into which twenty-six cows and several goats sank and perished exhaled a damp miasma. The rocky valleys out of which the caravan climbed, sweating with exertion under a blazing sun, led to gusty hilltops which chilled fatigued bodies to the bone. He attributed to sunstroke some subtle illnesses which modern medical investigation might have identified more fully.

One of these cases ('he has got Partial paralysis of his limbs, extremely high temperature and is now losing his speech'[5]) may have died, Shee suggests, from polioencephalitis.[6] Songora Baracka ('has now got Ptosis and partial loss of speech, in fact Bell's palsy'[7]), a Zanzibari who became ill a few days after a dental extraction, may have had a brain-abscess — 'he became completely paralysed and the muscles of respiration in their turn failed'.[8]

156

The Egyptians' greatly enlarged spleens due to *schistosoma mansoni* infection[9] resulted in protruberant abdomens, hence the derisive nickname, 'yellow bellies'. Parke despised their indolence. The 'scoundrels' smoked, talked or told their beads while black servants saw to their comfort. There were also a few Coptic women whose loose morals had attracted notoriety in Khartoum among the Islamic fundamentalists.

The Zanzibaris' carelessness led to the theft of two rifles which Parke recovered. Large herds of hump-backed cattle grazed on the plateau but milk and butter were not offered to the expedition, or even available for sale. A long march led to a chain of barren hills beyond which they camped at a large settlement well supplied with grain and fruit. They stayed there for two days to collect a week's food in preparation for the crossing of the Alexandra Nile (Kagera River). Having repossessed more stolen guns they marched (on 17 July) over high hills and through deep valleys and on reaching camp were brought goats, fowls and sweet potatoes by the natives who demanded cloth but they had none to give them. Parke managed to barter two spoonfuls of beads for two chickens.

Sunday, 21 July – On leaving camp this morning three of the Pasha's people preferred to remain where they were as they were suffering from ulcers and would not move — we had camped amongst bananas. As the rear-column marched out of the camp some children who were left behind by the Pasha's people were immediately seized by the natives, not for cannibalism as these people are not cannibals, but a sort of adoption sometimes called slavery, which simply means they are to work for their food.

The young Prince of Ankori visited the camp next day and was united in blood-brotherhood with Stanley. Shots were fired and the Maxim gun was displayed to celebrate the event. Parke reflected that by now Stanley must have very good blood in his veins being linked with innumerable kings, princes and sultans. Their sleep was disturbed by fleas and other pests and in the morning they emerged from their infested huts like boiled lobsters.

What Parke called 'ophthalmia' (possibly trachoma) was prevalent among the men while he himself was 'perfectly blind' in his right eye, the result Shee suggests,[10] of onchocerciasis contracted in the Congo. Excellent coffee grown locally was available but it was dear and besides most of the officers were too feverish really to enjoy it. 'Bonny as usual has more complaints than Jenner could master; from the crown of his head to any other part of his body, alike, he has a complaint.'[11]

Some of the carriers pressed into service by the raids made from Mazamboni's and M'pinga's remained veritable slaves. They had been handed over to the Egyptians 'who tied them together in threes & fours and gave them outrageously heavy loads & drove them along the road'. Jephson was horrified by the cruelty meted out to them and Stairs reported that two women prisoners were beaten to death by the Pasha's people 'who had simply crushed their heads in the most barbarously brutal manner'. Jephson was amazed by his own complicity. He should have refused to have had any part in capturing them — 'it is a thing I shall always feel remorse for'.[12]

They reached the Alexandra Nile on 25 July. This river was as broad as the Semliki but swifter, drawing its waters from Ruanda and Mporo to the west, Uhha, Urundi and Kishakka to the north-east; it ran north before turning finally eastward to debouch eventually into the Victoria Nyanza. Three canoes were lent to them and it took two days to ferry the caravan across. Parke's Manyuema tent-bearer went back to fetch his wife, who was ill, and they were both speared by natives and left dead on the wayside.

Entering Karagwé, a barren dried-up country, they were still faced by rocky hills and stony ravines and were obliged to take their drinking-water from stagnant swamps. Parke's defective eyesight made him feel most insecure. 'Stanley bought a goat today [28 July] the first provisions bought by him for the expedition since we left Zanzibar except for a few chickens and a couple of goats which were bought on the Congo.' Stanley, Stairs, Bonny and three other men too weak to walk were carried and three loads for which there were no porters had to be thrown into the river.

The thermal springs at Matagata where they arrived on 29 July attracted visitors from long distances to drink their medicinal waters and bathe in the hot pools where they lay for hours at a time. Parke had a bath and enjoyed it.

The death of one of Kibbo-bora's wives from dysentery did not surprise the doctor as he had warned days earlier that without treatment she would die. He had given her medicine but when she improved she stopped attending. Her husband then gave her a load to carry and so was to some extent responsible for her death which neverthless he lamented immoderately. Parke was appealed to for cloth with which to wrap the remains. They gave him a little girl in exchange for two doti of calico and, in order to gain the child's freedom, he borrowed the cloth from Marco the Greek, whom he promised to repay twice the amount at the mission station.

Tuesday, 30 July – Some natives were here today using the waters as they were suffering from syphhilis. There is a constant supply of water running through the baths and a large discharge of water which keeps them fairly clean. The baths vary in size from 20 ft by 6 by 3 and 3 feet deep with a gravel or clay bottom. The water has a temperature of 111 Farenheit in the hottest spring, the others are very little colder but close to the large or northerly bath there is a spring of cold water. The hot water is not unpleasant to drink and is extremely good to make tea... The baths occupy the south-west end of a ravine with precipitous hills closing in all round except on the east side. There are Rhinoceros in this country.

Stanley said that Parke accorded the same courtesy to African women that he would have shown to ladies in a London drawing-room. We have seen that he recoiled from the spectacle of close human nudity but he rather admired the lovely Manyuema. 'Some of the women are undeniably handsome with thin noses, thin lips and high foreheads and beautiful necks and shoulders.'[13]

At the beginning of August his pygmy servant was severely stricken with fever which had attacked her repeatedly since she emerged from the dark forest. She struggled on despite increasing weakness until she could no longer bear the direct rays of the sun even when using the umbrella Parke made for her. Finally he decided to leave her in the care of friendly natives. Their parting was very pathetic and she presented him with her ivory ankle-bracelet.

She was always faithful and hardworking [he wrote] and never the least trouble. Her morals were above suspicion and it is she I have to thank for the comparatively good health which I enjoyed in the forest especially during the starvation period when she procured tubers, roots, leaves, fungi and insects to eat which no one knew of but the natives of the forest.[14]

On the following night, Parke was called after midnight to see Stanley and a hypodermic injection of morphia was needed to relieve severe pains in the legs. Kafuro, a former Arab settlement now in ruins, was reached on 3 August and Kiengo, an old man who had been one of Speke's and Grant's guides, came to see Stanley. He sought Parke's professional advice and gave him a sheep as a fee.

The march continued over rough, gravely ground and up precipitous hills on a gloomy wet morning against a chilling wind. The cold was intense and among the Pasha's people several children died. A guide refused to go on with them. He asked to be paid off but had underestimated Stanley who had him tied and taken to the next camp in ropes before paying him what he was owed.

Arriving at a well-stocked banana plantation fires were lit and ten cows were killed to feed the caravan. Next day the officers formed a committee to discuss certain unspecified misdemeanours of which William Hoffmann stood accused. That evening when Stanley invited the officers to his tent they found him in unusually good form — he attributed his feeling of well-being to two aperient pills which the doctor had given him.

They passed from Karagwé into Ihangiro where they could no longer depend on native bounty and must buy their food with acceptable currency. Allowances of beads, cowries and cloth were handed around to enable this to be done. From Kavari they could see Lake Urigi, a long narrow stretch of water. When they camped beside the lake the fish they bought there was condemned by Parke as inedible and infested with guinea-worm.

The 'twelfth' of August used to be a golden day in Ireland for a man of Parke's upbringing. 'Grouse shooting begins at home but this is a very tragic day with us ...'[15] The column halted at Mutara, a native village, which thieves from the caravan raided. When the villagers protested one of Emin's Nubian soldiers, Fath-al-Mullah, 'fired at a native and killed him on the spot'. The outraged villagers pursued the looters into the camp and Stanley had to hand the murderer over for condign punishment. Parke watched him 'dragged off to the doom that awaited him at his captors' hands.' He was speared to death by a decree that demanded 'blood for blood' an example of rough justice (that McLynn rather unfairly debits to Stanley's 'sadism'[16]). Throughout his diary, Parke displays a distinct propensity to make the physiognomy fit the crime. On this occasion he wrote 'the prisoner has a diabolical face, was an awful scoundrel and earned his sentence.'

Wednesday, 14 August – Remained in camp today so as to rest the Pasha's people and also make the first distribution of money for to purchase rations. Thirty-two cowries were given to each person for 4 days rations of food. Each white man [had] 6 times that amount, but the Zanzibaris spoilt the market before long as a fowl could be bought for 5 cowries in the morning and in the evening the wily natives asked 100.

After a long march through picturesque country they came to Uzinja where they were held up for an hour or so awaiting the king's permission to proceed. This annoyed Parke who thought Stanley had too much patience with these petty 'Kings and Queens and Princes' — 'for halting an entire Caravan of nearly 1000 people is no trifle.'[17] A local chief consulted Parke privately in an empty hut and gave him two bunches of bananas and two pots of banana wine. The Victoria Nyanza was visible on 16 August and to the Europeans the sight of it symbolized meaningful progress. It carried with it a cheering prospect of receiving letters and Parke was prepared to admit that he was now 'quite sick of the job and 4½ months before us to the coast. I feel thoroughly worn out.' Soon, too, it would be time to send letters to the coast, to friends and to those in charge of funds: 'We must have funds to meet us at Zanzibar for there we shall have to put on decent clothes and afterwards find our way home, perhaps via Cairo. I am fairly puzzled what to do as I came into Africa a beggar and I leave it a greater beggar.'[18]

Consulted again by the old chief, Parke gave him pills and answered his questions with extreme care.

Yesterday his people asked me if a chicken should be killed — but I said not — for the Sorcerer would have to name someone (generally someone he disliked) who had given the evil to the King. The chicken is killed and the liver etc. taken out and through this means the Sorcerer is able to tell what man gave the King the diseases. Also they wanted me to say decidedly if the Devil (Shitan, Swahili) was in his head. I said no for otherwise someone who had put it there would have to be killed according to their custom. The Sorcerer has many opportunities of doing away with his enemies by this means.[19]

They camped in a plantain grove on the shores of the Victoria Nyanza where Parke found the water 'much fresher, nicer and better than either the Albert or Muta Nyzigé — Albert Edward'.[20]

Aware of the increased strength of their limbs and their hardened soles the marchers, disciplined now and well able to keep a long, unbroken line, achieved increasing distances. When Stanley urged them to complete the journey to Mackay's, about 110 miles, in ten camps they responded cheerfully to the challenge — 'Aywallah Bwana, Inshallah' ('Yes, Master, please God we shall do it').[21]

Monday, 19 August – Left camp at 6.10 am and marched until noon when we struck the Victoria again and camped in the opening in a burning hot plain. We are now out of Kajumba's country and into another. The Kingdoms are becoming more numerous. The King of Usui has conquered all down to the lake shore so we shall have to encounter him tomorrow or after although we have come somewhat out of our way to escape his mercenary demands on strangers. We may have a brush with him but it will be over in a few shots...

Passing into Usimba they saw a zebra that a lion or a leopard had killed and Parke cut off its mane as a souvenir. Local opposition to their presence was expected for the caravan had paid no tax but the natives were too wary to interfere with them. Bonny, attacked by fever, asserted that lack of appetite was an advantage in a region where there was no food to eat but the doctor listened to him sceptically. 'He is fond of greasy stodge cake and as he is the man in charge of the provision animals he certainly helps himself to the best joints.'[22]

They had not seen running water since the Alexandra Nile and for some days they were obliged to camp in low scrub where the natives had only tobacco to offer them. They arrived eventually at a deserted mission station elegantly built from simple materials by the White Fathers who had left it because of the fractiousness of the Wanyamweizi and the scarcity of water.

'The chapel was extremely well built, with a cross in it and other paraphernalia connected with such a place.'[23] Their next march took them closer to the south end of Lake Victoria where on 28 August they were welcomed to the Church Missionary Society's Station at Usambiro by the Rev. A.M. Mackay and his colleague, the Rev. Mr Deeks.

Notes

1 *Diary*, 4 July 1889. *Primipara*: woman in first pregnancy.
2 *IDA*, II, p. 335.
3 See Nicholas Harman's account (1986) of the colourful career of Bwana Stokesi (1852–95) who may have lent something to the creation of Allan Quatermain in Sir Henry Rider Haggard's *King Solomon's Mines*.
4 Mwanga, Kabaka of Bugunda (successor in October 1884 to Metesa) was 'a large, oafish-looking young man, who laughed too easily and had frequent fits of temper, provoked by smoking hashish' (Pakenham, *Scramble*, p. 298). He faced threats from those who coveted his throne; he was suspicious of the 'Turks' to the north and in conflict with Kabba-Rega of Unyoro; he was aware that the real motive of the visiting *Mazungu* (Europeans) was 'to eat the country' (Smith, *Relief Expedition, passim*). In his darker moods he suspected he would be the last of his line.

   A conflict of mores existed at Mwanga's court where a variety of factions competed for his good-will. The rival groups, the English Protestants and their followers (Waingerezi), French Catholics (Wafranzi) and Muslims (Waislami) differed doctrinally but combined to oppose the Futabanghi, the marijuana smokers, with their tradition of a semi-divine Kabaka.

   This unhappy situation was aggravated by the murder of Bishop Hannington at Busoga in October 1885, and the further anti-Christian outrage in the following June when twenty-six royal pages were burned alive for refusing to renounce their faith. These boys and young men, having learned from their mentors to abominate homosexuality, had become critical of the *lukiko*, the Kabaka's council (Harman, *op.cit.*, pp. 94–108).

   Mwanga was deposed and replaced by a pretender on 10 September 1888. He took refuge at Magu at the southern end of Lake Victoria and later with the White Fathers at Bukumbi. By now the tripartite force that deposed Mwanga had split. The Waislami stood apart from the Christians who protected the chastened Kabaka and planned to reinstate him with the assistance of Charles Stokes, who, in March 1889, arrived at the lake with the sections of a large sailing boat which was assembled and named the *Limi* to honour the Irishman's Wanyamwesi wife.

   The armed flotilla's first attacks failed but left Mwanga in safety on an offshore island and it was in this situation that Stanley's help was sought and refused. A further onslaught was launched on 5 October 1889. The combined Christian force burned the capital, massacred the Arabs and restored Mwanga temporarily to his throne. The Waislami re-grouped to drive Mwanga back to the islands but Stokes returned with fresh ammunition and the Kabaka was reinstated on 11 February 1890. (Harman, *op. cit.*, pp. 104–7).

   The 'Martyrs of Uganda' were solemnly beatified by Pope Benedict XV in 1920 and canonized by Pope Paul VI on 18 October 1964.
5 *Diary*, 13 July.
6 See 'Report from Africa' (*Medical History*, 1966, 10, p. 34) by J. Charles Shee whose knowledge of tropical medicine was gained at first hand in Africa.

7 *Diary*, 10 July.
8 *Diary*, 12 July.
9 Shee, *op. cit.*, p. 33.
10 Ibid, p. 34. Onchocerciasis, a filarial infection due to transmission of *Onchocerca volvulus* by black-flies causes a variety of lesions including 'river-blindness'.
11 *Diary*, 24 July.
12 Jephson's *Diary*, pp. 382–3.
13 *Diary*, 31 July.
14 *Diary*, 1 August.
15 *Diary*, 12 Aug.
16 McLynn, *Hearts of Darkness* (London 1992), p. 358. See also Jephson's *Diary* p. 393: 'The guides tell us the natives will all collect tonight from the villages round & have a feast & drink quantities of pombe, they will have the prisoner bound in their midst & the women will all insult & beat him & when the men have drunk sufficient pombe to madden them, they will rush on him in a body & hew him to pieces. That is their custom.'
17 *Diary*, 15 Aug.
18 *Diary*, 16 Aug.
19 *Diary*, 17 Aug.
20 *Diary*, 18 Aug.
21 Stairs, *op. cit.*, p. 965.
22 *Diary*, 26 Aug.
23 *Diary*, 27 Aug.

14 Emin Pasha's Accident

A small man with a rich brown beard, Alex Mackay wore a white linen suit and a grey Tyrolean hat. Born to the manse at Rhynie, Aberdeenshire, in 1849, he had worked in Edinburgh and Germany as a draughtsman and engineer before responding to the call of the mission-fields in 1876. A practical Christian, he now opened his stores to the expedition and saw that all were fed. From Mackay they learned with sad hearts that Jameson died from blackwater fever at Bangala on 17 August 1888. Old newspapers provided them with less tragic material and Parke's first question to his host was 'Is the Queen alive?' He then asked about the Prince and Princess of Wales and heard without dismay that two German emperors had died and Wilhelm II was reigning. Stanley and Stairs received two letters each and it was thought that mail for others may have been taken by Arab raiders attacking German caravans.

The doctor literally stepped into dead men's shoes (and clothes), those of Bishop Hannington and the other murdered missionaries. He was supplied with trousers and given a pair of socks by Mackay, to be paid for on reaching Zanzibar. He was also given boots, handkerchiefs and forgotten luxuries such as a sponge, pyjamas, soap and twenty candles. He badly needed to replenish his dwindling supply of medicines and Mackay provided quinine sulphate, potassium permanganate, carbolic acid, calomel and Warburg's tincture.[1]

The expedition stayed at Mackay's for three weeks to enable the older and weaker members to regain their strength but Stanley felt excluded and suspicious when Emin and Mackay talked together in German. The mission station, though sited unattractively in a dried-up wasteland with burned grass and withered trees, was impressively built but shamefully short of staff; it had a strong boma and a large workshop equipped with a wide range of tools and machinery. Mackay's house had many bookshelves from which books overflowed into the drawing-room, the bedrooms and even into the church. Every evening the missionaries invited about twenty children into a room where they sang hymns and prayed.

They were not wholly dependent for supplies on Mackay for two hundred loads belonging to the expedition had been brought for them from the coast by Bwana Stokesi who had just left for Uganda with his Wanyamweizi carriers. Charles Stokes, an Irishman from Enniskillen, a tall bearded figure impressively attired in Arab robes, was the most reliable caravan-leader in East Africa with a remunerative side-line in selling guns for ivory.[2] The stores included beads, cloth and preserved provisions. They also had fourteen pack-donkeys and a few riding asses.

A further attempt by Emin and others to interest Stanley in going to the relief of Mwanga was unsuccessful and on 16 September, the eve of the departure, they were fêted by Mackay, and the officers of both camps enjoyed a sumptuous dinner of beef and chicken washed down by medicinal wines. Stanley proposed a toast to Emin Pasha and Mackay (destined to die from malaria at Usambiro on 8 February 1890) toasted Stanley. Emin acknowledged that everything he could have hoped for, or that his friends might have asked for, had been done in good measure.[3]

Their path now led to the south-east along the established trade-route across the plain to Zanzibar. Stanley's reluctance to pay adequate 'hongo', the tax customarily levied on caravans as they passed through each successive district, may have been responsible for the harassment they encountered, but here and there the scar-faced Soudanese were accused of cannibalism. An Egyptian follower was robbed of his possessions and sustained an arrow-wound and a lacerated forehead.

Approaching Bwana Stokesi's station at Malissa's, where they had intended to buy European provisions, they came into conflict with a phalanx of. Malissa's warriors and a few men were killed before they managed to withdraw. Next day in a further tussle with Malissa's men, seven natives were shot before the caravan could proceed. Their way took them by villages on either side and they were followed by a column of threatening warriors. From time to time the natives used their muskets but a volley of rifle-fire would set them running. On one occasion, only, were they provoked sufficiently to use the machine-gun to frighten off the attackers.[4]

Afflicted by 'ophthalmia', Parke was no longer keeping a diary but Jephson did not follow Stanley's habit of euphemizing actions taken by the expedition's men when freed from restraint.

Stairs was sent out in one direction & I with my company in another to drive off the natives & to burn their villages. One regretted having to burn the villages because they were so pretty & fresh looking... We drove away the natives & burnt the villages all round, and the men got an immense amount of loot. Towards evening the natives began to mass together in the open, about three quarters of a mile from camp, so the Maxim was directed against them, one man was killed & the natives, in terror of the unusual sound, fled right & left pursued by a party of Zanzibaris who were so infuriated with the natives that they cut the dead man up & slung pieces of him on their guns.[5]

On 4 October they reached Stokes's boma at Mittinginya's and, hoping to recruit carriers to aid the Egyptians, passed on into what Stanley called a 'hornet's nest of angry tribes'.[6] Unfortunately Stokes was still away and a group of wild Masai hired by the chief took four of their donkeys but were forced diplomatically to return them. Using persuasion rather than compulsion they eventually succeeded in engaging twenty porters. The caravan was overtaken on 17 October by two ailing French missionaries, Pères Girault and Schysne, who decided to join them.

Parke tended to highlight the ordeals of the march, the reluctant *wangwana*, slow to approach their loads, the heat or torrential rain, the fatigue and debilitating fever. There were, however, more attractive features, the drummers, the shanty-singers along the route, colourful evenings typified by those recalled by Grant: 'Nothing can exceed the noise and jollity of an African camp at night. We ... were often unable to hear ourselves talk for the merry song and laughter, the rattle of drums, jingling of bells, beating of old iron, and discordant talk going on round our tents.'[7] To this cacophony Jephson added more alien sounds: 'A lion was roaring all night & troops of great apes paraded the rocks. One could easily hear the patriarch ape laying down the law to the rest of his people, his words being sometimes received with rounds of applause at another time with howls of derision.'[8]

At Mackay's mission station there had been rumours of Germans fighting with Arabs at the coast and as they moved east they encountered increasing evidence of a German presence. A caravan travelling in the opposite direction greeted them with cries of 'Guten Morgen!', parodies of German salutes and scraps of pidgin-German. A native carrier shouted to Emin, 'Arab Bagamoyo kaputt!'[9]

While in Ugogo, Emin received a letter from Major Wissmann who styled himself 'Imperial German Commissioner for East Africa'. He promised hospitality at Bagamoyo and reminded him 'that whatever the English have done for you, we, the Germans, are your countrymen.'[10] A German garrison commanded by Lieutenant Rochus Schmidt held Mgwapa which the expedition reached on 10 November. Schmidt offered them champagne, brandy and cigars; he decided to escort them for the remainder of their journey and treated Emin with a degree of respect that the latter knew he could never expect from Stanley. On 24 November, Lieutenant Schmidt introduced Emin to the priests of the French Mission of Saint Esprit who, a little to the Pasha's surprise, had never heard of him.[11]

They were halted at Mgwapa when the Baron von Gravenreuth arrived with 100 soldiers. A German caravan accompanied by two newspapermen brought them many cases of provisions presented by Wissmann and by Gordon Bennett through his correspondent. The reporters, one of whom was far from sober, sent off three messengers to the coast with bulky letters already written for the press by Stanley, Parke surmised.[12]

Just at the end of November a column sent by the Imperial British East Africa Company brought them 170 loads of rice, twenty-five cases of European provisions and a supply of boots and clothing. At about eight in the evening on 3 December they heard the 'boom' of the Sultan's gun at Zanzibar calling believers to prayer. The almost-forgotten sound evoked cries of unrestrained joy, and with a tremendous outburst of cheering, the men left their fires and pressed around Stanley's tent to sing his praises. There was no doubt now that homes and friends were near.[13] They were met the next day at the ferry of the Kingani River by Major Wissmann with horses for Stanley and Emin, who went ahead with him and Lieutenant Schmidt, leaving Stairs in command.

Entering Bagamoyo the Zanzibaris were overjoyed to see the sun sparkling on the water. Ships of the German and British navies were anchored in the roads dressed with flags and bunting. A German military band played 'God Save the Queen' and Europeans from Zanzibar and its neighbourhood had assembled to meet them. Stores purchased by the relief committee were produced and tattered garments were exchanged for bright-coloured finery. There was a holiday atmosphere and a feeling of achievement.[14]

Major Wissmann and the German officers held a banquet that evening in the Pasha's honour and Jephson recalled that after making an excellent speech Emin had come round to talk with each of them individually — 'he was transformed by happiness and content.'[15] It was one of those unique occasions when the dictates of conviviality are permitted to rule; political and personal differences are set aside and eternal friendships are pledged. Then, as if in response to a mutability that presides over human affairs, the laughter stopped abruptly. Conversations ceased, anecdotes were interrupted, and each man asked his neighbour if what they had heard could be true. The Pasha was dead! He had fallen from the balcony.

Overcome by wine, perhaps, Emin had wandered from the festive hall into a corridor leading to a balcony from which, due to his shortsightedness, or being unaccustomed to two-storey buildings, he had tumbled into the street, his fall partly broken by the zinc roof of a 14-foot high shed. Parke rushed down to find Emin lying prone on the ground, bleeding from the ears, unconscious but still breathing. The comatose figure was taken to the German Hospital with Parke in attendance. A cold compress was applied to a swollen eye.

Next day the doctor's report was favourable; Emin had shown signs of returning consciousness just before dawn. Parke attributed the aural bleeding to local damage and said the skull was not fractured. Two German doctors disagreed: they said the base of the skull was fractured and warned that only 20 per cent of such cases recovered. Their diagnosis was correct but Parke's prognosis was quite accurate.

When the expedition embarked for Zanzibar on 6 December Parke said Emin was unfit to sail with them. Stanley went to say good-bye to the Pasha and assured him that the doctor would stay with him for as long as necessary. Parke was glad to do so and he accepted in good part the fractiousness and abuse that can be expected from a patient with a contused brain, and some unpleasantness from the German staff. For several days Emin felt sore all over having fractured some ribs and sustained many bruises. Both eyes were swollen and the bloody discharge from the ears continued for three weeks, compelling evidence of the skull fracture. On 8 December 'catarrh of the lungs' was evident. Parke regarded his patient as dangerously ill and gave morphia and an enema.

Much to the Pasha's annoyance the German officers had opened his belongings. He asked Parke to collect the boxes, five in all, apart from some other loads and, for safety, they were placed under his bed. 'He seemed furious [Parke wrote] at his boxes being opened and said that the Germans should have asked his leave or spoken to me first, as I was his companion on the march.'[16]

On 11 December Parke called Drs Brehme and Lotsche of the German Navy in consultation and he remained at his patient's bedside throughout the night. Soon after this T.H. Parke himself became the victim of blackwater fever and was removed to the French Hospital in Zanzibar under the care of the French nursing sisters and Dr Francis Charlesworth who, on one dreadful evening called his friends to the bedside, despairing of his survival. For days, Parke took nothing except iced champagne and he insisted later that his sense of taste was never so benumbed as to prevent him from appreciating it. 'After so much wandering, drinking bad and half tepid water for 3 long years I never tasted such delicious nectar.'[17]

168

The refugees, released from restraint, misbehaved in Zanzibar, drinking and rioting, and the Consul-General decided to move them on to Mombasa pending the arrival of a steamer to take them to Suez. Once more Emin Pasha was not well enough to join them nor did he wish to do so, even had the German doctors permitted it.

As the day finally approached for Stanley and his officers to leave Zanzibar, Parke, still in hospital, urged Jameson to go over to Bagamoyo to see the Pasha and to encourage him to accompany them. Jephson did so on 28 December and spent many hours at the German Hospital. 'I told him that Parke had said if he could be carried on board the mail steamer, and accompany us, he would be well before we got to Suez.'[18] Emin seemed pleased to see Jephson but the latter was struck by 'the inexpressible sadness of his tone' as he refused to be reassured or to be cajoled into joining the British group which left next day for Mombasa in a warship, Parke carried on board by a detachment of blue-jackets. Hoffmann stayed in Mombasa to work for a year with the British East Africa Company and the others embarked in the SS *Katoria* on New Year's Day bound for Suez which they reached at 4.40 pm on 13 January ready to bring down the curtain on a drama that was in effect ending as 'Hamlet without the Prince'.

Would the story have ended differently had Parke not fallen ill? The Irish doctor certainly thought so:

When leaving Emin said he would certainly follow in the next steamer in about one week to Cairo and fully intended to do so and was quite fit to do so. In fact if I had not gone sick he would have come home with us, of this I am quite convinced, for amongst other things he was anxious to have the cataracts removed from his eyes as his left eye was almost blind and we had arranged that I should assist at the operation.[19]

Be that as it may, at Suez they were rapturously received: the Khedive's aide-de-camp, the governor of Suez, the British and American consuls, and nearly the entire population of the town turned out to welcome them. The *Times* correspondent thought they looked well with the exception of Parke who 'is much pulled down'.[20] They stayed overnight at the British India Agency. Bonny, who had kicked over the traces in Zanzibar, drinking and brawling in the Grand Hotel, was expected to continue on in disgrace to England but he insisted on joining them although cold-shouldered by the officers. Next morning they took a special train to Cairo, where the exceptional precipitation was far heavier than anything they had experienced in the rainforests. Planks were laid from their carriages to the top step at the entrance door of Shepheard's Hotel to avoid the flooding. They were met by

Sir Evelyn Baring, Lady Baring and other dignitaries and a banquet, attended by Nubar Pasha, was held that evening.[21]

Stanley drove to the Palace where during half an hour's conversation with the Khedive he spoke highly of Emin's administrative ability, 'his one defect as a ruler being his unwillingness to countenance harsh measures even when necessary and just.' He referred with pride to his officers, praising Stairs' 'ready apprehension of orders, Dr Parke's absolute devotion, Mr Jephson's passion for work, and Captain Nelson's thorough manliness.'[22] A State banquet was held on 20 January, and then the Khedive's ball, attended by more than 1000 guests, on the following evening.

Parke was still convalescent and his eyes seemed to stare from a wasted anaemic face but with remarkable resilience he had reported for duty at the Citadel Hospital within a few days of his arrival, and he proceeded on 22 January to Alexandria where he was welcomed by a fellow-Irishman, Brigade-Surgeon Gore, FRCSI, Senior Medical Officer of the Alexandria garrison.[23] He was entertained to a dinner presided over by Sir Charles A. Cookson who said that Parke's adventures 'surpassed the wildest imaginings of romancers'.[24] Responding to the toast of his health, Parke gave a short account of the difficulties encountered by the expedition praising Stanley's energy and determination.[25]

Bonny — unreliable, mistrusted and ostracized — left for home on 25 January and by the time that Parke returned to Cairo his other companions, too, had departed. Stanley was now writing his book and he refused to be disturbed when the doctor offered to take him for a drive.[26] But on 3 April when the Khedivial Geographical Society gave Stanley an elegant Egyptian casket containing a beautifully illuminated diploma written in Arabic, Parke attended the presentation ceremony.[27]

By now it was known that after initial set-backs, a recurrence of the ear discharge and a partial paralysis of the tongue, Emin Pasha had recovered and crossed to Zanzibar as the Sultan's guest.[28] He was expected to go on to see the Khedive but instead returned to Bagamoyo and entered the German service with a salary reputed to be £1000 a year. According to an indignant *Times* correspondent he was due to lead a large caravan in mid-April to the Victoria Nyanza: 'Within four months of his reaching the coast he returns as a paid subordinate officer of a German company to the very latitude where he so recently lived as the heroic Governor of an immense province amid world-wide admiration.'[29] His name became a byword in England for incompetence and ingratitude, for few knew enough about the man to recognize him as the tragic victim of circumstance.

At the outset of his travels, Emin Pasha wrote to Parke from East Africa acknowledging the Irishman's letter:

Many many thanks for all kind words you give me. I always considered you as the only *friend* I made during our long and weary trip and if circumstances have pushed me in a very different direction from what I fondly hoped, I always flatter myself with the idea that such things should not influence our mutual relations and that you will stick to me. You are quite right in supposing me affected by several relapses after my first recovery ... but I escaped and now seem mending. Besides some slight difficulties of deglutition and a slight deafness of the right ear, I am well and work heartily.

He realized that Parke must wonder why in such precarious health he should return to the interior instead of heading for Egypt.

Well you know the disparaging manner Stanley assumed as my protector, you know that my hopes have not been fulfilled, and that from the beginning of my residence in Bagamoyo I was asked to work for Germany. Stanley repeatedly told me I might look to Mackinnon so I did, and when at last besides empty promises I got nothing, I was forced to look out for a bit of bread for my child. I undertook to lead this expedition firstly to show Stanley I was able to work without his help or tutorship, and secondly to get a hold on my own countrymen. Until this very day I do not know if the German Government will pay me or not. You see therefore I acted only under the stress of circumstances and I am not such a fool as it seems at first. I tell you these miseries [?] at the risk to annoy you. I always wished to clear myseslf from the name of apostate and to you, as friend, I trust I may tell things I studiously refrain from telling elsewhere. You will have observed how pointedly I abstained from writing a single word in relation to Stanley and the Expedition. I only fulfill what I promised. But if some day or other I am forced to reply then please do not think worse of me.[30]

Emin Pasha concluded his letter by thanking Parke for arranging for the latest work on entomology to be sent to him; by congratulating him on his recovery and asking for his photograph. 'If there was at Zanzibar such a thing as an able photographer I should have had mine.'

Parke also heard from Captain Casati who wrote to him from Cairo on 23 June 1890:

I will always remember with pleasure the worthy friendship tied between us, and I hope it will be everlasting in spite of the distance that separates us. My gratitude to you will never elapse, remembering the kind and eager cures that you had for me in my illness during our Journey.[31]

Notes

1 *Diary*, 29 August.
2 Harman, *Bwana Stokesi*, *passim*.
3 Jephson, *Rebellion*, p. 446.
4 Jones, *Relief Expedition*, p. 344.
5 Jephson's *Diary*, p. 403.
6 IDA, II, p. 405.
7 Cited by McLynn, *Hearts of Darkness*, p. 154.
8 Jephson's *Diary*, p. 408.
9 Jones, *Rescue*, p. 344.
10 Jephson, *Rebellion*, p. 467.
11 Jones, *op. cit.*, p. 337.
12 Ibid, p. 339.
13 Stairs, 'Albert Nyanza to Indian Ocean', p. 967.
14 Jephson, *Rebellion*, p. 472.
15 Ibid, p. 473.
16 *Diary*, Vol. 4.
17 *Diary*, Vol. 4.
18 Jephson, *op. cit.*, p. 477.
19 *Diary*, Vol. 4.
20 *The Times*, 14 January 1890.
21 Frank McLynn, *Stanley: Sorcerer's Apprentice* (London 1992), p. 316.
22 *The Times*, 15 Jan. 1890.
23 A prizeman at Queen's College, Cork, Albert Augustus Gore (b. Limerick, 1838) graduated MD, LKQCPI and LRCSI in 1860. Twice wounded in the Ashanti War, 1873–4, he served in Egypt and India. Author of *Medical History of Our West African Campaign* (1876); *The Story of Our Service Under the Crown*; *A Historical Sketch of the Army Medical Staff* (1879); articles in medical journals including 'How they went up the Nile. From Gemai to Korti, 1884', *Dublin J. Med. Sc.*, 1891; 91: 16–35, 121–132. He died at Whitechurch, Salop, 1901.
24 *The Lancet*, 1893, ii, 780.
25 *British Medical Journal*, 1890, i, 310.
26 McLynn, *op. cit.*, p. 318.
27 *The Times*, 4 April 1890.
28 A serious relapse was reported (Ibid, 16 Jan 1890): 'The copious discharge from the ear has begun again.' Doctors wished to transfer him to Zanzibar but were prevented by rough weather. Unfavourable bulletins were issued: 'He is depressed and fears are entertained that his brain is affected.' The recovery process then gained control and continued without interruption. On 30 January Emin Pasha despatched a telegram to the Khedive: 'Convalescence progressing. Thanks to my kind master.'
29 Ibid, 2 April 1890.
30 *Diary*, Vol. 4.
31 *Diary*, Vol. 4.

Part Two

15   The Honorary Fellow

Parke left Egypt on 7 April taking ship with Stanley who, with extraordinary energy, had already completed *In Darkest Africa*. They were accompanied by Stanley's private secretary, Mr Wilson, when they boarded the SS *Hydaspes* at Alexandria. Quite a flotilla of boats bearing consuls, geographers and journalists advanced to escort the vessel into port as it approached Brindisi. They were received by the Sub-Prefect, the Mayor of Brindisi and two members of the Italian Geographical Society who presented Stanley with the gold medal of the Society.[1]

From Naples they went to Rome by rail, proceeding via Genoa and Nice to Cannes where on their arrival on 13 April shortly before noon they were met by Sir William Mackinnon and by Jephson, who had come over from Hyères where he was recuperating. They were also met by a number of Stanley's friends and by the usual crowd of onlookers and reporters.

A message from the Prince of Wales, who was briefly visiting Cannes, awaited them and they drove immediately to the Hôtel Prince de Galles where they were cordially received by his Royal Highness who was just about to leave the city. They then drove to the Hôtel Continental where they were Mackinnon's guests. Interviewed by journalists, Stanley spoke sourly of Emin Pasha, de Brazza and Dr Carl Peters. Parke said Emin's cataracts were incurable and, forgetting that prognosis is more difficult than diagnosis, predicted, incorrectly, that he would be blind within a year. Carried by the Paris papers the remark attracted wide attention and was misinterpreted by Emin's future biographer who believed that Parke intended 'to depreciate Emin's abilities in the eyes of the world'.[2]

A wonder he was not killed when he walked out of the hotel window, but he is a wiry little fellow, with a wonderful amount of reserve force, a brilliant conversationalist, amiable and charming when discussing scientific subjects, but by no means so easy to get along with, I should imagine, when dealing with business matters. All along the march to the coast he spent most of his time looking for bugs and beetles, and never ate a meal without having a cloth properly laid with knives and forks, and

175

as many of the equipments of a table as he could rake together. I devoted myself earnestly to him after his accident, and, I believe, saved him, but since he went over to the Germans we have not heard a word from him.[3]

The drenching rain they had encountered in Cairo visited them again as they went to the railway station on 17 April to catch a train for Paris and Brussels.[4] When they reached Quevy on the French frontier at noon on 19 April, they were met by Captain Prynton, aide-de-camp of the King of the Belgians, attended by Lieutenant Liebrechts who had seen service in the Congo and by the Burgomaster and aldermen of Brussels who welcomed them on behalf of the Belgian capital. Parke and Jephson, soon joined by Stairs and Nelson, were put up at the Grand Hôtel Britannique, while Stanley was accommodated in magnificent style in one of the princely State apartments at the Royal Palace and dined that evening with the King and Queen.

The Burgomaster's banquet was held in the spectacular Gothic Hall of the Hôtel de Ville on 20 April.[5] The other entertainments which Parke and his companions enjoyed included the Congo Exhibition; a performance of *Salammbô* at the Opera House; a fête at the Bourse attended by more than 3000 persons, the élite of Brussels; the Anti-Slavery Society's luncheon; a ball held in aid of the funds of the African Red Cross Association; and a royal garden party given by the King at Laeken. They visited Antwerp and were presented with the medals of the Royal Geographical Society before dining with the *Cercle Artistique et Littéraire*.

Ostend was *en fête* on 26 April, the ships in the harbour gaily dressed, when Stanley and his officers sailed in the *Prince Albert* for Dover where, amid flags and streamers, thousands milled about hoping to get a glimpse of them. Stanley had asked that their reception should be informal and the Mayor and Corporation fought their way through the throng to present an address of welcome that had the rare merit of brevity. The great man looked bored and miserable, avoiding interviewers so sedulously that the *Pall Mall Gazette's* special correspondent turned his attention elsewhere and observed 'Lieutenant Stairs, tall and taciturn; Mr Jephson short and smiling; Surgeon Parke, a regular young Apollo.'[6]

At London's Victoria Station, to which they travelled by a special train along a line enlivened by little groups who waved to them as they passed, they had to force their way through another welcoming crowd. That evening Parke went with Stanley, Sir William Mackinnon and Colonel Sir Francis de Winton to visit the Prince and Princess of Wales at Sandringham where the royal party included Prince George of Wales (the future George

V) and the Princesses Victoria and Maud. After dinner the explorer gave the first of his many talks in England on his experiences. They spent the night at Sandringham and attended divine service next morning. A dinner to honour Parke was held in London a few days later by the Army Medical Staff. The officers each received a gratuity of £400 from the Emin Relief Committee (Bonny, the NCO, was given £200) and the army authorities relented on their stipulation of unpaid leave.

The Emin Relief Committee's reception at St James's Hall, Piccadilly, on 2 May, presided over by the Prince of Wales, was a gala occasion at which full dress and decorations were worn. The band played 'Here the Conquering Hero Comes' when Stanley stepped on to the platform at 9 pm. A little later Parke listened to his leader's tribute to his own work which had increased when the Egyptian refugees joined the camp. 'Every afternoon he called his patients about him, and all forms of hateful diseases were treated with a remarkable consideration and sweet patience.'

The *Pall Mall Gazette's* reporter found Stanley's remarks on his medical officer's achievements particularly interesting:

The Doctor has to obey orders, it was clear, just like the Captain. 'Take those 130 invalids; halt them; and bring them round.' Those were Stanley's orders. It was not his business but Surgeon Parke's, to find the means for carrying them out. The Doctor succeeded. Therefore Stanley thought well of him. 'In a month's time Surgeon Parke had 80 out of 130 in prime condition.' The Doctor had delivered his human consignment up to time and sample. That is 'Stanley's way'.[7]

Then Stanley's softer side took over and he referred to the tender, personal care he had received in his own illness. When he sat down there were cheers and calls for 'Parke'.[8] Three days later the Royal Geographical Society honoured the travellers at the Albert Hall with Sir M.E. Grant-Duff, president of the Society, in the chair. The evening was a great success and Stanley's audience and his officers were stirred by the vivid descriptive passages in his address:

I have sat at my tent door watching the twilight deepen into a sepulchral gloom, knowing the elements were gathering for a war with the forest. I have heard the march of the storm advancing with the speed of a hurricane and the sullen roar of the forest, as with nerves collected it swung its millions of giant heads to wrestle with it, the roaring and rending and crashing. I have seen the mighty swaying and surging of a countless array of tree-tops and their leaves all quivering and rustling, and the undergrowth dancing as though in approval of the strength of its gray sires, and then I have heard the rain follow in a torrential downpour, hushing the storm and the strife, and descend in cascades from the drowning trees.[9]

After the address, the Prince of Wales presented medals to Stanley and his companions. Each of them was cheered in turn but *The Times* remarked 'it should be added that the demonstration in honour of Dr Parke was very emphatic.'

The crowd waiting to see Stanley blocked the approaches to the Guild Hall when on 13 May the Corporation of London held a reception to honour the explorer and his officers. They were met by the Lord Mayor and Lady Mayoress in the Library and proceeded to the hall where Stanley expressed some impatience with the English for their inability to show their best qualities until stimulated by competition and goaded by rivalry: 'Like growling camels they require sharp spurs to action, otherwise they would chew the cud for ever.'

Having recited a list of the great names of African exploration he prepared to add to the litany: 'the young gentlemen, Stairs, Jephson, Parke, Nelson, and Bonny, may write Congo, Nile, Ruwenzori and the triple Nyanzas after their names as clear signs of the splendid fortitude with which they bore privations that sicken us even now at the thought.'[10] He capped his remarks with lines from *Antony and Cleopatra*:

> Though daintily brought up, with patience more
> Than savages could suffer: they didst drink
> The stale of horses, and the gilded puddle
> Which beasts would cough at.

When called upon to speak, Parke was obviously nervous; Jephson was 'equal to the occasion' according to a reporter, but boring; and Bonny was determined not to be left out in the cold.

Next day, Parke appeared before the Royal Commission on Vaccination and his evidence was taken. He had seen some cases of smallpox during the Nile campaign but not many. Smallpox was endemic in Africa and caravan-leaders feared it greatly; vaccination was uncommon except with Egyptian troops in Nubia. He described his vaccination of about 550 men excluding those recently vaccinated or displaying healed smallpox pitting. The Soudanese had submitted to the procedure voluntarily. One European, Jephson, remained unvaccinated ('He did not like to be vaccinated; he objected to it') and Parke had not pressed it on him. He did not subsequently develop smallpox.[11]

The London Chamber of commerce and the American colony in London also entertained the travellers. At the latter occasion in the Portman Rooms, the guests included Mr (later Sir) Henry T. Wellcome whose pharmaceutical company's tabloids had been so useful. The toast of Stanley's chief officers was proposed by Mr P. Du Chaillu and Parke, responding, recalled how at a critical stage of his illness Stanley had said: 'Doctor, put up the Stars and Stripes and cheer me with something bright to look at, that I may at least die under the American flag.'[12]

Known widely as 'the man who saved Stanley's life', Parke was inundated with requests for lectures, and editors of English and American periodicals wanted articles from his pen. He continued to be a recipient of honours. The University of Durham gave him an honorary DCL but the first body to recognize his achievement had been his Alma Mater, the Royal College of Surgeons in Ireland, which elected him to its honorary Fellowship (FRCSI) on 11 December 1889.[13] Army surgeons of high position had been similarly honoured but the election of Dr Thomas J. Crean, a Boer War VC, was barely carried in 1902 by six votes to five. Nobody opposed Parke's election, but Sir George Porter, FRCSI, did object to the sum of £26.5. being voted towards entertaining the honorary Fellow, his father and other guests at the annual College dinner. 'I protest', he said, 'against money of the College being voted to pay for a dinner to any individual, no matter how distinguished.'[14]

The festive occasion on 31 May was attended by Surgeon-General Sinclair, Principal Medical Officer for Ireland, John Mulhall, private secretary to the Lord Lieutenant, Colonel Duncan, Deputy Adjutant-General, and presided over by Mr Austin Meldon, FRCSI, a man of such corpulence that a nineteenth-century wit asked 'What is more difficult than a camel entering the eye of a needle?' the unkind answer to his riddle being, 'Mr Meldon getting into a fly.'

The fare was lavish and many of the dishes on the menu were named for notabilities — 'Consommé à la Mulhall', 'Saumon à la Sinclair', 'Ris de veau à la Stanley', 'Côtelettes à la Parke', 'Poulet Printanier à la Frazer'. After the royal toasts, Mr Meldon delivered himself of the kind of mendacious utterances guaranteed to raise a laugh on formal occasions: 'We Irish are all fond of fighting, not from a sense of duty or even of glory, but simply for the fun of it.'[15] Surgeon-General Sinclair said that, of the army and navy's 800 medical officers, 429 possessed Irish medical qualification. Parke spoke of the risks and hardships his companions shared; he also acknowledged the sound practical training he had received in the College and at the City of Dublin Hospital which had enabled him to deal with medical problems encountered in most difficult circumstances. The toast of 'the Army and Navy' was responded to by General Frazer, Commandant of the Dublin District, who testified to the popularity of Irish army doctors. The other speakers included

179

Sir Thornley Stoker and Sir William Stokes, the latter destined to die from typhoid fever in the Boer War.

On the following morning Parke was affected by what *The Irish Times* described as 'a sudden faintness' while attending service at Baggotrath Church. He was taken by his father to Surgeon Wheeler of Merrion Square, with whom he was staying, and by evening he was well enough to go to Roscommon by train to see his family. This was probably an early example of seizures that continued to affect him infrequently and no doubt were an insidious and potentially lethal relic of his travels in Africa.

Referring to the College dinner an *Irish Times* leader-writer remarked that Parke was the only Irishman who had ever crossed Africa:

The unobtrusive and simple style of Surgeon Parke's references to what occurred during the three years' struggle, and his ready admission to a debt of gratitude to his Dublin teachers, drew from the audience the more cordial expression of their regard, and the welcome, as expressed, his countrymen everywhere will repeat and endorse. In the history of the College of Surgeons there is no more memorable record...[16]

The attendance at that dinner included the inveterate diner-out, Sir Charles Cameron, who was present on 7 June 1893 when the Savage Club entertained Stanley. Sir Charles found the explorer difficult to talk to — 'but the moment I mentioned that I was a great friend of Surgeon Parke ... he became greatly animated, and we conversed about him for several minutes. "But for Parke," said Stanley, "I might not be alive."' Parke had brought a specimen of reddish-coloured water taken from Lake Albert Edward to Cameron's laboratory in 1890 and it was found to contain 'far more solid matter in solution than is present in the dense water of the Dead Sea in Palestine.'[15]

Parke was presented with a silver salver by the editor of *The Lancet* in the journal's office on 6 June 1890. That evening a banquet was held in his honour by the London medical profession at the Criterion Restaurant. Sir Andrew Clarke, president of the Royal College of Physicians of London, took the chair and the attendance included many leading physicians and surgeons. The qualities for which Parke had been praised were enumerated by Sir Andrew — 'his culture, his refinement, his acquirements, his modesty, his skill' — and it was remarked how unusual it was to find such diverse qualities in one person, all that went to the heroic in man and the loving in woman. On 1 July, Parke was entertained by the the Freemasons of North Connaught at a banquet held in the Town Hall of Carrick-on-Shannon presided over by Colonel Ffoliot, of Hollybrook, near Boyle.

Stanley's engagement to Dorothy Tennant, a London artist and socialite, was announced in June, their marriage to take place on 12 July. As this date approached illness intervened, a relapse of 'gastritis' or possibly a psychosomatic disturbance determined by Stanley's sexual ambivalence,[18] but Parke and Dr Ewart decided that the ceremony could proceed. At Westminister Abbey the nave and choir-stall were resplendent with red carpeting and Dr Livingstone's grave was marked by two magnificent wreaths, one presented by the bride and bridegroom, the other by the expedition's officers who acted as groomsmen. The best man was Comte d'Aroche, sent by the King of the Belgians.

At 2 pm, supported by a stout stick, Stanley walked up the aisle and stood before the altar to claim his bride who came towards him on Sir John Millais' arm. He was obliged to rest before the reception which was held in two marquees at 2 Richmond Terrace, Mrs Tennant's residence. Then at 4.20 pm the couple left like royalty in an open carriage for Waterloo Station accompanied by Parke and Jephson. Dr Parke went on with them to Melchet Court, near Romsey, which had been lent to them by Lady Ashburton for their honeymoon. Next morning Stanley walked a little in the grounds but later retired feeling unwell. Parke told the reporters that the gastritis was serious but not dangerous.

The medical profession did Parke proud. He was less than satisfied, however, by the way the army authorities treated him. When Knott congratulated him on his appointment to the 2nd Life Guards he denied that it was a matter for congratulations and ventilated what was to become a chronic grievance.

I have received no thanks or recognition for my services that I have heard of. I have simply had my leave cancelled and gone back to ordinary duty to a most expensive station and, strange to say, my pay now is only £21 a month although I had £40 before I went on the Expedition. The Government have behaved most disgracefully I think and certainly I don't consider the medical staff worth living in and will leave as soon as I can get any other job.[19]

The Lancet took up the cudgels on his behalf by drawing attention again to the military authorities want of recognition for meritorious services rendered by army medical officers except during warfare. 'But we do not know of any more striking instance than that of Mr Parke, the companion of Mr Stanley, who has borne ample testimony to the very valuable services rendered by his medical colleagues during that remarkable expedition.' Why should not Parke be promoted immediately to the rank of Surgeon-Major?[20]

He visited his sister, Harriet (Henrietta), and her husband, George Henry

Stoker, in Cork in September and the local doctors quickly organized a celebratory dinner. When the Stanleys arrived back in England on 8 October from their second honeymoon (accompanied this time by Jephson), Parke met them at the station but found Stanley devoting his entire time to his mother-in-law.[21]

On 16 October he replied warmly to a letter from Emin Pasha (dated 15 May and already cited) being delighted to know that the ex-Governor was reasonably well again.

I am very sorry that you went back to Africa. Even if you settled down for a few months and wrote a book you would make thousands by it. Jephson has finished his, I believe, and Barttelot's and Jameson's diaries are to be published and Bonny also is writing one. I should like to compile one as there is so much money to be made...

As requested he sent Emin his photograph and brought him up to date regarding his companions and their leader. 'Stanley goes to America on the 29th to lecture. His wife is a very charming person and extremely clever. She is well known as a good painter and a great favourite.' He enquired for Emin's little daughter, Ferida, and expressed the hope that when Emin came to the coast again he would proceed to Europe.

I made a remark [he continued] which you may have often seen in the papers *viz* that your sight was going and that you were very shortsighted. Everything one says is printed and modified by the quoters. I made it because most people thought you fell out of the window because you had too much champagne at the Banquet, which idea I wished to show was incorrect.

I see by the papers that Wissman is not returning to Africa again. I hope Muftah [his boy] is making a better gun-bearer for you than he did for me. Pray write to me when you have time.[20]

Parke did not hear again from Emin Pasha and it may be added paren-thetically that the Pasha, partially deaf from the skull fracture, remained under commission to show the German flag in Central Africa and to make treaties that would pre-empt British occupation of areas between Lake Victoria and Lakes Edward and Albert. His march into the interior began on 26 April 1890, accompanied by Franz Stuhlmann, a zoologist, three German NCOs and a well-appointed caravan with some 600 porters. He raised the German flag at Tabora, an exercise not within his terms of reference, and his reports dealt with scientific rather than political matters. His apparent lack of a coherent immediate purpose led to an order on 4 April 1891 for his return to the coast. Ignoring this he evolved a plan to travel towards the Cameroons.

He passed through the Semliki Valley in July and from Mazamboni's contacted Selim Bey who indignantly refused to serve under the German flag. He left Mazamboni's in August, women and children forming a majority in his caravan, but was obliged to return there unable to traverse the rainforest.

Smallpox was the next misfortune and, hoping to avert an epidemic, Dr Emin ordered Stuhlmann to march ahead with the apparently unaffected, proceeding towards the East Coast. He himself was obliged to remain with an ailing remnant at Mazamboni's for six months. He then set off with a small group for the West Coast engrossed with the prospect of new places and further specimens. Now in poor health, and with swollen feet, he could still enthuse over the presence of a red-nosed rat.

Intending to accompany parties of ivory-traders, he sought the assistance of Ismailia, the Arab who had kept Parke and Nelson on short rations at Ipoto, and had gained his own station near Fort Bodo. With Ismailia as personal guide, Emin reached Ipoto on 18 June 1892 and then directed his steps towards Arab strongholds on the Congo. A letter written to Professor William Flower in this period explains that though Emin's collections are small 'they hail from the remotest corners of the Continent never before visited by a naturalist, and scarcely to be visited again for years to come.' He expected to be forced to stay in the region for some time but managed to persuade the locals to collect for him: 'I hope to be able to obtain many interesting objects, amongst which, first in line, I shall try for a White Chimpanzee.'[23]

The sands finally ran out for him at Kinena's where, having been given a dark and nasty hut to sleep in, he spent most of his time on the chief's veranda leisurely arranging his specimens. On 12 October, the eve of his projected departure — and at the suggestion of his host (who had orders from his superior, Kibonge, who was being harrassed by Congo State officials, to kill him) — he sent his men into the fields to collect provisions for the journey leaving their arms on the veranda.

Treacherously, Kinena kept his guest in conversation and gave the men time to reach the plantations. He then signalled to Ismailia and Mamba, another Arab, to seize Emin, and said, 'Pasha, you have got to die.' Shortly after this the unresisting Emin, who had asked that his younger daughter[24] be cared for, had his throat cut, dying instantly. His decapitated and naked body was thrown unceremoniously into the bush. His head and possessions were sent to Kibonge, the Arab chief who decreed that he should die. His men were forced into slavery.[25]

Notes

1 Parke, *My Personal Experiences of Equatorial Africa* (London 1891), p. 514; *The Times*, 8 and 11 April 1890.
2 Georg Schweitzer, *Emin Pasha: His Life and Work*, 2 Vols (London 1898), ii, p. 17.
3 *The Times*, 14 April.
4 Ibid, 18 April.
5 Ibid, 21 April.
6 *Pall Mall Gazette*, 28 April.
7 Ibid, 3 May.
8 B.L. Reid, *The Lives of Roger Casement* (New Haven 1976), p. 12. The immense audience included the tall young Irishman, Roger Casement, who had charmed the expedition at the Inkissi River in April 1887. Casement was accompanied by his sister, Nina. A pick-pocket stole his gold watch as he left the hall.
9 *The Times*, 6 May.
10 *Pall Mall Gazette*, 14 May.
11 The lymph used had been brought out from London. There were no ill-effects other than painful arms. There was no second case of smallpox on board but the captain (unvaccinated) developed the disease later. About half the vaccinations failed to take or showed only abortive vesicles, indicative, of an immune or partially immune state.

   Parke believed that the vaccination had protected his men and saved many lives. During an epidemic at Banalya there had been 'an immense difference' of susceptibility between the vaccinated Zanzibaris and the native carriers many of whom developed the confluent form of the disease. The natives in the interior were unaware of the potential benefits of vaccination.
12 *The Times*, 31 May.
13 He had thus become a member of a select group which included Robert Adair for whom the romantic song 'Robin Adair' was written; Percival Pott commemorated by 'Pott's fracture'; Louis Pasteur; T.H. Huxley and others accomplished in surgery and science.
14 Minutes of Council, RCSI, 24 May.
15 *The Irish Times*, 2 June.
16 Ibid, 2 June.
17 Sir Charles Cameron, *Reminiscences* (Dublin 1913), pp. 114–5. Cameron's guests at the Savage Club included his relative, Commander Verney Lovett Cameron, RN, CB, the first European to cross Africa from east to west, 1873–5.
18 McLynn, *Sorcerer's Apprentice*, pp. 394–6. 'He was simultaneously attracted to and repelled by the sexuality of women and eventually "solved" the problem by a platonic marriage to Dorothy Tennant.'
19 Letters, THP/JK, 23 August. Presumably the higher pay was for service abroad and active service.
20 *The Lancet*, 1890, ii, 412.
21 McLynn, *op. cit.*, p. 235.
22 Parke papers, RCSI. Stoker donation.
23 Schweitzer, *Emin Pasha*, 1, p. xiii.
24 A two-year-old, she was born to a copper-coloured native of Equatoria, Emin's compan-ion since leaving the East Coast. It was expected that she would be educated in a mission school at the expense of the Congo Free State.
25 Emin predicted correctly in the few moments he spent attempting to reason with Kinena

that he would be avenged. Kibonge was court-martialled and shot in 1893; Ismailia and Mamba were hanged at Kasongo in April 1894 (Roger Jones, *Rescue*, pp. 381–8).

16   The Battle of the Books

Messrs Samson Low gave a dinner at the Holborn Hotel to celebrate the publication of *In Darkest Africa*, a two-volume work written with remarkable speed at the Hotel Villa Victoria in Cairo. The guests included Thomas Hardy who is said to have whispered to his fellow-novelist, William Blackmore, that truth pays nearly as well as fiction.[1] On 28 June the *Pall Mall Gazette* remarked 'The book of the year is out today — workmanlike, complete, and up to time, as all Mr. Stanley's performances are.' The first English edition had 20,000 copies and there were ten foreign editions. Eight miles of binding cloth were used and seven-and-a-half tons of paper; 7000 persons had worked on its production and 268 presses were employed to print it.

This was the first complete account of the expedition. Other books, as already mentioned, were being prepared and apart from their intrinsic value as records, true or otherwise, there was money to be made. Stanley's advance was reputed to have been in five figures. Jephson was promised a sum approaching £1000 for *Emin Pasha and the Rebellion at the Equator*. But an injunction was granted against Troup who attempted to publish *With Stanley's Rear Column* in 1889 in contravention of his contract.[2]

Deciding to throw his cap into the ring, Parke wrote to his brilliant friend, John Knott, from Hyde Park Barracks on 17 September: 'I want a little advice from you. I have a fairly good-sized diary of my African experiences and I want to compile a book to come out as soon as I can write it. There is plenty of information in diary form but it wants polishing up into better literature. Would you give me a hand with it as you promised?' Stanley and others, he explained, had urged him to do so and he intended the book to be of general interest rather than strictly medical. 'If you think that you had time and would assist me but not appear as the author in any way I would be very glad to come to any arrangement which you consider fair and consistent.'[3]

Knott's academic success has already been referred to.[4] Educated at a National School in County Roscommon, he had private lessons in Greek and Latin from the Protestant Dean of Boyle and taught himself to read French,

German and Spanish. Obliged to run the family farm due to the failing eyesight of his elderly father (who had been treated unsuccessfully for cataract by Sir William Wilde), he read widely and after working in the fields in the daytime applied himself to Gray's textbook of anatomy in the evenings. He married in 1873 and his courageous young wife, Elizabeth Shera, had agreed to supervise the farming with the assistance of local labourers, enabling him to study at the Royal College of Surgeons in Ireland where he excelled as an anatomist.

After graduation, Knott visited medical centres abroad and then set up in practice at 34 York Street, Dublin, close to the College where, while waiting for patients, he established himself as a crammer. His selfless spouse did not live to enjoy his new status. She died in 1879 but her husband's determination was unshaken. He increased his academic standing by becoming FRCSI (1880) and MKQCPI (1881) and took the MA and MD of Dublin University. Domestic felicity was regained by his marriage in 1881 to Phillipa Balcome, daughter of a retired army colonel, with whom he had two children, a boy and a girl.

Knott's literary bent is evident in an unpublished journal, a record of a farmer's year, which he kept through 1874, and in a trickle of articles, later to become a flood, which began to appear in the 1890s. As a student he was awarded the Pathological Society's gold medal for *An Essay on the Pathology of the Oesophagus*, a monograph published in 1878. He presented the fruits of anatomical research to learned societies, orthodox work which was published by the Royal Irish Academy.[5] An early excursion by Knott into the field of medical history led to an article on female circumcision published by the *Medical Press and Circular* in July 1890. When Parke sought his aid, just two months later, he did so at a psychological moment when, having failed to obtain a chair in anatomy, Knott was turning his attention to broader cultural interests. The opportunity to be associated with a popular publishing venture, albeit in an anonymous capacity, was irresistible and money earned by writing would have amplified his insecure income.

Returning from cavalry manoeuvres at Berkshire on 24 September, Parke acknowledged Knott's encouraging reply (Knott's letters have not survived) and affirmed that he had not spoken to any publisher but had Marston of Samson Low, Marston, Searle & Rivington in mind. Marston was Stanley's and Jephson's publisher. He had given Jephson £800 for his book so Parke could probably expect £1000 for his. 'I will gladly give you £200 for preparing the book for me which I doubt if you can finish before Xmas as I would like it to be a respectable size.' He offered to send Knott a cheque for £100 and the diary for 1887 immediately. 'The rest I would send very soon as I must rewrite some parts, for the writing etc. has been so damaged by wet and abuse.' He would ask Knott to undertake not to use the material for any purpose other than compiling the book 'and also I don't wish you to let anyone know that you are doing the work for me as I want it to appear my own work entirely.'

Next day he placed £100 to Knott's credit and sent the diary as promised. Writing on 29 September he warned his collaborator to disregard the numerous cutting remarks regarding Stanley:

I want on the whole to show that there is pleasure in following a man who does not seek private or public opinion, who tells the truth bluntly, has great resource, takes all the responsibility, is not afraid of the initiative, no red tape and will sacrifice anything to carry out his object so unlike English Generals. I have never heard him once give unqualified praise while he was in Africa. I do not want to make him out an angel because I disliked him for the first year or so and then was compelled to admire him when I saw what he could do as a leader.[6]

Like all prospective authors he began to visualize his finished book. 'Would you give me an idea of the size?' he asked Knott. 'As I must soon talk to a publisher about advertising.' He told Knott that when he met Stanley, who had been in Brussels, the great man's first question was, 'Are you writing your book?' Mrs Stanley promised to do some drawings for it but Stanley said later that the book should be a textbook on Africa's climate, diseases and their treatment as there was no point in writing about what he, Stanley, had already described. Parke felt, neverthless, that more could be said about Ipoto and Fort Bodo. Sir James Paget, too, he explained to Knott, had suggested 'making a sort of textbook of it'. Jephson, whose book was expected to be published on 25 October, had advised him to write the book before consulting any publisher and Parke warned Knott against 'padding it up with much Natural History as the other fellows know that I am not very well up in this line.' Names should be mentioned whenever possible 'and the small personal incidents' were desirable.[7] He continued to make a fair copy of the diary and promised to send it in a few weeks.

He had speaking engagements in Leeds and Newcastle-on-Tyne and the honorary degree DCL of Durham University was conferred on him on 21 October. Next day he presented medals and certificates to the South Shields St John Ambulance Brigade and on 23 October he dined with Mr Butler, Vice-Chancellor of Cambridge University which had given Stanley an honorary LL D.

*

The Life of Edmund Musgrave Barttelot, edited by Walter Barttelot, was published on 23 October and a letter from Mrs Jameson in *The Times* announced that her late husband's diaries were in the press. Stanley's failure to write personally to the Barttelots had angered the family and they were infuriated to learn that in a letter to Sir William Mackinnon he referred to the rear-column as 'wrecked by the irresolution of its officers, neglect of their promises and indifference to their written orders.' When eventually he wrote to Sir Walter Barttelot from Cairo in April 1890 the sympathy that a grieving father might have expected was lacking. Even the words of praise were nicely balanced to expose the officer's character defects: 'Ardent, impetuous, outspoken, prompt as tinder to utter the thoughtless word, but generous, zealous, brave, the *beau idéal* of a jockey of Mars — '[8]

Walter G. Barttelot replied to the libel on his father's behalf charging Stanley with doing his brother and his companions 'a cruel injustice'. Point by point he answered Stanley. 'The true history of your Expedition', he wrote, 'is a very sad one, and not the least regrettable fact is that when arrangements made by yourself are not successful, the unfortunate result is always attributed by you to the fault of your officers.'[9]

Major Barttelot's diaries and letters provided material for a biography designed to discredit Stanley and present the young man as a knight errant — 'For honour Edmund Barttelot had gone out to the relief of Gordon ... for honour he had come out to the relief of Emin Pasha, Gordon's lieutenant' — but without attempting to conceal the ill-temper that obtruded so obviously. He was acting in self-defence, admittedly, in the Soudan when he shot dead a Somali water-carrier who struck him with his weighted stick, but at Yambuya Barttelot's violent streak was never far from the surface and is typified by his own diary note:

Friday, May 11 – The Belgians left this morning at 5 am for Stanley Falls; and in the evening the natives were insolent to me, and one man tried to knock me off the path as I was walking up and down our promenade. I knocked him flat with my stick — wrong on my part, perhaps, but almost unavoidable.[10]

The Africans called him *Kapeppo* (whirlwind) and *Mikalee* (him of the strong mind) and he imposed an iron discipline, a 'veritable martinet' (the words are Troup's[11]) who attempted to exact from untrained men the standard of obedience expected of the flower of the British army.

When Barttelot's *Life* was published *The Times* predicted that 'a very distressing controversy must inevitably arise.'[12] The anonymous reviewer accepted that there was much for Stanley to explain but felt that Walter Barttelot had not presented his case skilfully — 'he too often mistakes for proof what is at best only presumption...' The book challenged Stanley's disinterestedness, accused him of wishing to secure Emin's ivory and alleged that Sanga was, in modern parlance, Tippu Tib's 'hit-man'.

Stanley wrote briefly to *The Times* on 26 October saying that the 'attacks, accusations and insinuations can be very easily disposed of'; he had so far avoided giving 'the *whole* history of the Rear Column' in his book out of consideration for the feelings of others. But Troup and Bonny had yet to speak; if the truth was withheld he might be obliged to publish 'the official documents' in his possession but was reluctant to do so.[13] Interviewed by *The New York Herald*'s London correspondent before his departure for the USA he hinted at a hidden reason for Barttelot's death and said that the Major was killed rather than murdered.[14] Pressed to clarify the distinction Stanley avoided a direct answer, his innuendoes leaving no other explanation than his belief that Barttelot was killed for taking Sanga's wife as a concubine, an accusation surely without foundation.[15] There is nothing other than Assad Farran's embittered and unsubstantiated allegation to suggest that any of the expedition's white officers established liaisons with native women. Parke, as we have seen, found the proximity of sparsely clothed black females repulsive but he did register admiration for some of them later. Jephson, too, had an eye for a pretty girl,[16] Ward spoke of 'the dusky beauties of the village whose artistic *toilettes* consisted only of a necklace and a smile'[17] and young William Hoffmann was heard to say that a particular group was 'the 'ansomest as I 'as ever seen.'[18]

Troup, interviewed at Boston, Massachussets, maintained that he could not have made a written protest against Barttelot's leadership without risking a charge of mutiny. The coldness between himself and the Major resulted from the latter's failure to visit Troup when laid up for weeks with fever. Asked had he any comment to make against Stanley's character, Troup said: 'No! People will discover his right character soon enough'.[19]

Jephson's *Emin Pasha and the Rebellion at the Equator* published on 1 November was described in *The Times* as 'a melancholy and in some respects a repulsive story' but told 'with excellent temper and taste'.[20] Emin Pasha emerged as 'a sort of Hamlet incapable either by temperament or through the circumstances of his life of summoning up resolution to set right times which are out of joint'. Jephson's recollections of Barttelot were those of happier times — 'full of life and go, and spirits, with all his gaiety and brightness and deserved popularity. And this was the end of it all!'

Troup's *With Stanley's Rear Column* was reviewed on 7 November by *The Times* which described it as 'in the main a polemic against Mr Stanley'; it repudiated many of Walter Barttelot's specific charges and acknowledged that Major Barttelot was ill-suited for command — 'he had an intense hatred for anything in the shape of a black man ... [and] frequently mentioned the fact.' The reviewer cited a letter from Stanley to the author: 'I hear of many things which had better never be mentioned — and what I see dare not be described... What is the use of enumerating any thing of what strikes me dumb with horror and aghast with wretchedness?'

Stanley's arrival in New York on 6 November in the *Teutonic* was reported by *The Times* and naturally he was questioned about the rear-column controversy. The first version of Troup's book, held up by the Relief Committee's injunction, was, he said, 'a wholesale condemnation of Major Barttelot'. At Zanzibar Stanley had received a long letter from Troup 'violently abusing Major Barttelot and vindicating me'. He couldn't comment further without reading Troup's recent publication, but the log-book, as yet unpublished, contained vital evidence and Bonny's story hadn't yet appeared.

Barttelot's distress of mind was referred to by Troup: the Major had high words with Selim bin Mohammed and Bonny had felt they might be obliged to shoot the Arab who threatened to kill troublesome Zanzibaris. There was a furious row between Barttelot and Tippu Tib when the former accused the ivory-dealer of not keeping his word.

Troup was legitimately incensed that the subordinate officers should be blamed for decisions taken by Barttelot who was in supreme command. He claimed that he himself had 'fulfilled the explicit instructions' given to him by Stanley.[21] He insisted that Stanley's orders related to certain contingencies and that if the lack of porters necessitated discarding too many loads they should stay and await his return. 'Twist the paragraph any way you like, I cannot see what other meaning they could convey to any one... '[22]

He had been taken aback to find that the Belgian officers whom he talked to on board the *Stanley* after leaving Yambuya were well informed concerning 'the condition of affairs' in the camp. They had been gossiping with Assad Farran and learned 'many circumstances of which I was totally ignorant'. They questioned Troup closely but he refused to answer them — 'and would not express my opinion on the probability of their truth'.[23] Nor does he disclose the nature of their accusations.

Parke, writing to Knott, regretted 'that this scandal has occurred between the Barttelots and Stanley' — it could surely have been avoided by private discussion. It was Parke's belief that the young officer's rapid promotion was a mistake, and misled Stanley into expecting exceptional qualities. Barttelot was certainly courageous and energetic — '99 out of 100 are brave in my experience' — but coolness, commonsense and an even temper were far more valuable qualities.[24] He was disinclined to credit the suggestion that Stanley had an eye on the ivory. 'Troup is all wrong' for even if Tippu Tib's carriers had arrived and carried ivory to the coast it would have gone to pay for the expedition's expenses and any balance given to the Egyptian government. Parke discredits Troup's entire involvement. 'Troup was sent home sick and did no work and he is jealous. I have never seen him.'[25]

Walter Barttelot, as Bonny was to show, suppressed the most glaring instances of his brother's brutality but the disciplinary measures he mentioned are sufficient to confirm that Stanley left the wrong man in command. 'Twice Major Barttelot had to make examples, and use the death penalty; in one case it was unfortunately remitted at the request of the officers, and the man [John Henry] was flogged instead; and he eventually died.' Even little Sudi, a ten-year-old servant whom the Major described quite tenderly — 'the queerest little mite you ever saw, and when he has his long clothes on, looks like a baby in its night-dress'[26] — did not escape his wrath. 'I punished my boy Sudi for idiocy in the morning and when I returned towards evening found he had deserted'.

Bad blood existed between the rear-column's men and those in the nearby Arab camp. During Barttelot's absence at Stanley Falls there were unsavoury incidents. 'While I was at the Falls there was a woman palaver here at Yambuya. The Manyuema complained that our men molested their women whenever they went away.' And the Soudanese and the Zanzibaris chaffed their neighbours for eating human flesh.[27]

From the beginning, it seems, Barttelot had bickered with Stanley who responded by threatening to destroy his service career, and as the Major brooded at Yambuya he began to detest his leader with a pathological fervour. He also disliked Selim bin Mohammed, chief of the Arab camp. He appears to have got on well enough with Bonny who was given to pettty gossip; they walked together in the evenings and the ex-NCO told him with unpleasant candour how he was hated by Stanley and by Tippu Tib. Not surprisingly the young officer felt the fates were conspiring against him. 'Perhaps my days are numbered', he reflected as his mood became paranoid.[28]

Tippu Tib, as already mentioned, had eventually supplied 400 men, commanded by Muni Somai, who was to be paid £1000, guaranteed personally by Barttelot and Jameson. After a palaver, Tippu Tib gave them thirty more men. They would carry reduced loads and the excess stores were to be sent down-river to Bangala by steamer for storage. The rear-column left Yambuya on 11 July but within four marches there were twenty-two deserters. Barttelot then made a forced march to Stanley Falls and returned with chains to shackle the fractious Zanzibaris. He reached Banalya on 17 July and two days later was shot by Sanga.

The controversy was fanned by *The Times'* remark that Stanley's latest revelations to its New York correspondent must 'send a thrill of horror throughout the civilised world'. But these were based on what William Bonny had already told him, information to be made available to *The Times'* readers by Bonny himself on 10 November. In this article he made disclosures never before offered to anybody other than Stanley, Walter Barttelot and Mrs Jameson who earlier had demanded the whole truth from him. These facts had forced him to conclude that Barttelot was not in his right mind. 'I believe now, and I believed then that he was insane...'

Barttelot had suspected Stanley of being 'a Palmer' (i.e. a poisoner) and he himself seriously considered poisoning Selim bin Mohammed. He asked Bonny (who was in charge of the medicines) for any tasteless poisons and when asked why he wanted them, admitted what he had in mind. Bonny's response was to remove all the dangerous drugs from the medicine chest but Barttelot found a bottle of potassium cyanide Jameson kept for killing insects. He added a little to a measure of water and tasting it with his tongue found it too salty.

He developed a habit of standing before the natives 'showing his teeth and trying to frighten them by grinning at them like a fiend.' His violent actions included stabbing Chief Ungunga gratuitously in the shoulder with a pocket-knife, striking little Sudi 'a terrific blow on the forehead with a stick' and later kicking the boy, inflicting a leg wound that resulted in fatal gangrene. John Henry, a mission boy who spoke several languages and functioned as an interpreter, was condemned to be shot for alleged desertion but his sentence was commuted at the insistence of the entire garrison. 'Then, by God! I'll give him 300 lashes', declared Barttelot in a rage.

On the following morning at daylight John Henry was marched out and tied to a post. Four big Soudanese in our party, not one of them under 6 ft in height, were selected to administer the punishment. Each man was to deliver 75 lashes. John Henry never uttered a sound after the first 30 lashes, as he became insensible to the pain. This scene was the most horrible I ever saw. Mortification set in, the man's flesh fell off in pieces on the ground, and his body swelled to twice its ordinary size. Within 24 hours John Henry died.[29]

Whereupon, Barttelot had written in his diary, 'I am certain he must have been shot or hung, sooner or later, for he was a monstrous bad character.'[30]

On his return from Stanley Falls with the chains, Barttelot was in a maniacal fury. He demanded sixty slaves from Abdulla Karonga, the head-man at Banalya, and threatened to destroy the village if they were not provided. Suspecting a Manyuema of firing into his hut, he prodded him with his steel-pointed staff 'and finished up by beating the man's brains out before the eyes of all in the village'. Most bizarre of all, he seized a woman and sank his teeth in her cheek.[31]

Bonny then had a horrifying tale to tell, incriminating Jameson, who, he claimed, had attended a cannibal feast and sketched its various stages. It seems unlikely that, as alleged by *The Times*, Jameson knowingly 'purchased' a girl to be sacrificed and watched as she was tied, killed, dismembered and eaten, but the story of his attendance at the cannibals' meal was authentic and had been told by his servant to the entire camp. Jameson himself had related it to his colleagues. The story had circulated, too, at private parties in England but people had felt it better not to speak about it. Several of them had seen the sketches which Troup mentioned to Ward during their brief down-river meeting in the *Stanley*.

According to Assad Farran's lurid account of Jameson's notorious sketches, the naturalist was wholly to blame for the gruesome event on which they were based. When he expressed a wish at Riba-Riba to see a man killed and eaten, the Arabs put their heads together and told Jameson to buy a slave to give to the cannibals. The price would be six handkerchiefs which Jameson agreed to pay and having done so a young girl was led forward, killed and dismembered.

The natives cut the child to pieces — 'one was cutting the leg, another the head and breast, and another took inner portions of the belly. After the meat was divided, some took it to the river to wash it, others went straight to their huts'. Meanwhile, as Assad Farran recounted it, Jameson 'had his book and pencil in his hand, and was making rough sketches of the scene'. When the feast ended Jameson went to his house to complete six neat sketches with water-colours which were shown later to the chief and the officials. Captain Vangèle, skipper of the *Stanley*, expressed surprise that Jameson watched such a hideous scene. It may have gradually dawned on him that his draw-ings were reprehensible. His story as told to persons at Yambuya began to vary and the incident outraged the Congo State authorities.[32]

Assad Farran also described Barttelot's unsuccessful attempts to procure edibles by capturing women and children and holding them for ransom. His demands, unfortunately, were too high — 'five goats and twenty fowls for each woman'. One man did ransom his wife for a goat and some fish but the others escaped. (The interpreter added that Bonny captured seven women and kept them in the camp for weeks. 'This time they were tied by a rope round their necks and in the night they were taken to the officers' quarters.'[33])

A flood of letters reached *The Times*.[34] The Barttelots, understandably, supported the Major's integrity. Herbert Ward said he had seen nothing in Barttelot's behaviour 'derogatory to his reputation as an officer'. Troup supported Bonny's allegations: 'Major Barttelot was cruel, terribly cruel — there is no doubt of that...' Sir Henry Rider Haggard had come to know Jameson on board ship when the latter was on his way to Egypt: 'a more gentle, kindly, good-hearted gentleman I never met.'[35] Mrs Ethel Jameson insisted that the facts had been grossly distorted: 'My husband did see an act of cannibalism, he did not make sketches at the time, he did not give handkerchiefs to procure a victim — of this there is authoritative and attested evidence.'[36] The horror of cannibalism was so great that the letter-writers overlooked or avoided the sexual implications of the interpreter's revelations.

Parke expressed himself privately to Knott:

This is very unpleasant about Stanley, Barttelot etc. Stanley told me he could prove everything he said. I'm afraid Barttelot played the fool by publishing his book. I have kept out of the Controversy so far but I expect will be drawn in and certainly shall stick up for Stanley for although I disliked him for the first year yet I acquired a very high opinion of him as he is reliable, sure to succeed and shares hardships. No dozen Generals in the British Army could have pulled the Expedition through.[37]

He thought it absurd for people to say that Stanley should not have selected Barttelot for the expedition — 'he had the best recommendations of any of us' — but his rapid promotion only went to show 'how much fairness and value can be put on the opinion of the Authorities of the Army while many deserving men are not thanked'.

Two days later, Mrs Jameson published a version of the 'cannibal story' given by her late husband to the Emin Relief Committee. She also included a graphic account of the awful incident on 11 May 1888 in *The Story of the Rear Column*. It appears to have occurred as the consummation of a spell of abandoned singing and dancing by a group of Wacusu cannibals, and Jameson was involved almost innocently as he listened with disbelief to Tippu Tib's attempt to clarify local customs.

The natives were heavily painted with white clay and some carried spears and branches of leaves as they danced in and out of the reception house, adopting grotesque postures and putting their bodies through quite extraordinary contortions. There were four drummers with pedestal-shaped side drums. Some people carried chickens with their throats cut. They had been two months in the bush, Tippu Tib explained, undergoing a self-imposed period of isolation as many of the tribe had been dying. Now having finished their 'medicine-making' they were celebrating their return and on such occasions it was common to have a cannibal feast.

I told him [Jameson wrote] that people at home generally believed that these were only 'travellers' tales', as they are called in our country, or, in other words, lies. He then said something to an Arab called Ali, seated next him, who turned round to me and said, 'Give me a bit of cloth and see.' I sent my boy for six handkerchiefs, thinking it all a joke, and that they were not in earnest, but presently a man appeared, leading a young girl of about ten years old by the hand, and then I witnessed the most horribly sickening sight I am ever likely to see in my life. He plunged a knife quickly into her breast twice, and she fell on her face, turning over on her side. Three men then ran forward, and began to cut up the body of the girl; finally her head was cut off, and not a particle remained, each man taking his piece down to the river to wash it. The most extraordinary thing was that the girl never uttered a sound, nor struggled until she fell. Until the last moment, I could not believe that they were in earnest. I have heard many stories of this kind since I have been in this country, but I never could believe them, and I never would have been such a beast as to witness this, but I could not bring myself to believe that it was anything save a ruse to get money out of me, until the last moment.[38]

When he went back to his hut, Jameson made 'some small sketches' of the gruesome scene but detractors insisted that whatever he might say, he wanted it to happen and produced the cloth to facilitate it. His six sketches depicting the tied girl, the knife-thrust, the spurting blood, the dismemberment, the natives scrambling for the pieces and running away to cook them, were universally deplored. Bonny capped the story with the suggestion that Barttelot, realizing what a wide circulation it would achieve, feared he would lose his commission (as Jameson's commanding officer) and was tipped into insanity. This hardly seems likely but one might ask was fever relevant in Barttelot's case? 'Any perceptible deterioration of temper [according to Parke] among the members of Mr Stanley's staff made his companions at once suspect a commencing attack of African fever.'[39]

Bonny also recalled seeing the head and neck of a native in a glass case in Mrs Jameson's London home — her husband bought it and sent it to London to be embalmed. Mrs Jameson had actually drawn Bonny's attention to it, asking, 'Do you know this gentleman?' 'Yes,' he replied. 'I know him well. I have shaken hands with him many times.' The glib answer was actually untrue — the head was that of an unknown warrior slain by the Arabs.

A Visit to Stanley's Rear Guard (1889), written by J.R. Werner, a Congo Free

State engineer serving in the river-steamer *AIA* which visited Yambuya between 8 and 11 May, described how the author 'saw the Major just inside the door of one of the huts; going in [I] found Mr Troup lying on a camp-bed looking as if he had not a week to live.'[40] Werner mentioned the 'esplanade' where Barttelot and his companions took their constitutionals and the road leading to the cemetery 'where the graves of nearly eighty of Major Barttelot's men ... made one pause and reflect on the uncertainty of human life.'[41] Werner met Jameson, whose personality captivated him — 'Jameson's stock of yarns seemed endless ... he never lost his temper, and always had a song or a joke ready for dull moments.' Werner did not refer to Tippu Tib's row with Barttelot but described his own leave-taking in the latter's hut. 'The Major was sitting on some boxes, his face buried in his hands, and his elbows on his knees; he seemed more depressed than I had ever seen him before.'[42]

Parke expected the controversy to die down and blamed Walter Barttelot for publishing 'his absurd Book' which had compelled Stanley to speak out and consequently 'his brother's memory is greatly dirtied' and the Jameson 'affair' was brought to light.[43] The doctor took no active part in this furious 'battle of the books' but was drawn in indirectly when a Belgian correspondent published the report of an interview with Parke from the *Indépendence Belge* strongly favouring Stanley:

Je ne parle pas que pour moi. Tout ceux qui ont accompagné Stanley dans cette traversée mémorable vous diront qu'ils ont appris non seulement à admirer sa vaillance, sa promptitude, sa rectitude de coup d'œil, et son implacable volonté, mais à aimer en lui la bienveillance, l'esprit de fraternité, la générosité que l'on trouve à fleur de sa dure écorce. Nous le suivrons de nouveau avec joie, quand il voudra, jusqu'au bout du monde. Quant aux noirs, la foi qu'il a dans leur perfectibilité et sa compassion pour leur misère semblent même parfois poussées à l'exagération.[44]

Saleh bin Osman, Stanley's servant, issued a lengthy statement, based largely on hearsay evidence, on happenings within the rear-column. He described how when Barttelot was being carried across a boggy stream the unfortunate porter on whose shoulders he rode stumbled and the officer was drenched. Arriving at the opposite bank, Barttelot flogged the man and threatened to shoot him. On the evening of Barttelot's death, according to Saleh, the Zanzibaris and the Soudanese danced and sang. 'They burned down the wooden triangle on which they had been so often lashed and flogged, and they played drums where the whipping-place had once stood.'[45]

This obviously contrived account infuriated Ward and evoked an angry reply: 'Let Mr. Stanley give up publishing affidavits from his negro valet as to the demerits of dead men and answer for himself whether he should not bear some responsibility for the disasters of the rearguard.'[46]

Andrew Jameson wrote to *The Times* from Dublin to defend his brother from tales gathered 'from every coloured horror-monger on the Congo'.[47] The publication at Christmas of Jameson's melancholy *Story of the Rear Column* led a *Times'* reviewer to say that no one 'could acquit Mr Jameson of grievous blame' but those who read the diary will not believe him capable of the cold-blooded ferocity of which he was accused. *The Times*, on the whole, was sympathetic towards Jameson describing him as 'a competent and sagacious man, worthy of the part to which he had been appointed, and of the praise of which his commander has most selfishly and ungenerously sought to rob him'.[48] A cartoon in *Punch* depicted Justice, stern-faced, confronting Stanley at Barttelot's and Jameson's gravesides.[49]

Roger Jones dismissed as otiose the selection by Jerry Allen (1965) of Barttelot as the model for Kurtz, the Company's agent with a penumbra of evil, in Conrad's *Heart of Darkness*.[50] Ms Allen's theory is interesting, neverthless, for it is probable that when Conrad visited Stanley Falls in September 1890 the fate of the rear-column was still a talking point among the Belgian officials and others. But Barttelot's fury and 'sensationally demonic actions'[51] lack the mystery attached to Kurtz's 'unspeakable rites' whereas the authentic story of a white man mixed up with cannibalism was truly abominable, while, on the other hand, the most arresting person Conrad encountered on the river was Roger Casement. He had 'a touch of conquistador in him'.[52] Conrad's fictional creation, Kurtz, may well be derivative of Yambuya, a composite character embodying Barttelot's anger, Casement's intelligence and imagination and Jameson's unmerited notoriety.

Herbert Ward did justice to the naturalist whom he had never heard utter a bitter word. Ward described him as 'one of nature's noblemen' and at Yambuya had found him invariably bright and pleasant, able to rough it with the best, laughing at the inconveniences he met and making a joke of his sufferings.[53]

*

By mid-November, Knott was asking for more material and Parke explained that he had not yet copied the diary — 'I shall send you the rest immediately if you like, but as I have to write some more in it I would like to finish it before sending it, if you will allow me a week longer.' The second volume of the diary was sent by registered post on 21 November but soon after this the 'author' annoyed the ghost-writer by asking to see some pages of the manuscript.

Parke hastened to mollify his friend and denied trying to hurry him: 'I assure you that there is no one alive in whom I have more confidence or whose advice I would rather have than your own and I know that you could not do more than you have done and are doing for my book.' His reason for asking to see the manuscript was in case that reading it might jog his memory and recall forgotten incidents. On second thoughts he realized that 'it would only cause delay to scatter the manuscript' and busied himself with the fair copy of the original diary which was in a very dilapidated condition and almost illegible. He was held up by conjunctivitis but posted the fourth volume of his manuscript on 29 December.

'You now have everything worth having', he told Knott. Then despite the earlier rebuff he asked Knott again if he should read over 'any you may have finished'. He wondered when they might give the book to a publisher and looked forward to the opportunity of offering articles to journals.

'Stairs, Nelson and myself are all for Stanley', Parke insisted, still fretting over the unpleasant controversy. They had experienced his ability to inspire confidence and his ability to overcome difficulties. With regard to the rear-column, Jameson was an amiable, good-hearted fellow — 'the least of us likely to have committed the horrible offences yet his own representation of the cannibal story exonerates him from wilfully causing a murder but leaves his memory under an indelible stain.'[54] Barttelot was exceedingly bad-tempered but Parke had found him good company if one had no official dealings with him. Bonny was vain and sensitive.

When Herbert Ward published *My Life With Stanley's Rear Guard* in 1891 he admitted that he and Barttelot failed to hit it off from the beginning. The latter with 'the autocratic manner of a British officer' was restless, narrow in outlook and driven by suspicion and yet he had a better side, being an excellent raconteur with a wealth of humour and an unbounded affection for his father:

... the man would have been a cold spirit indeed who would have failed to respond with an admiring thought, as he rang the pleasant changes of reference to the 'dear old Guv'nor'. He was British, too, to the fingertips in the matter of his tastes. He dearly loved a horse, and it was amusing to note sometimes how horseflesh was such a frequent standard of reference, in the discussion of human ills and remedies. His talk was a breath from country lanes and pleasant fields; his stories constantly were those of the hunting field; and as one's recollections travel in sorrow to that lonely grave in the primaeval forest, one cannot help the saddening thought, that better far would it have been if the glories of the chase he loved so well had held him fast; rather than the unhappy influence which drew him on to death at the hands of the assassin's rifle, and a grave in an African desert.[55]

He agreed that Barttelot 'was very heavily handicapped by a violent temper, and an utter lack of sympathy with the black character.' But there was no irresolution, no neglect, no indifference. Stanley's *amour-propre* was wounded by the comic sketch Ward had made of him and he had resented the fact that Jameson's relatives were informed of evidence against him in the naturalist's diary which Stanley seized and refused to give up until threatened with legal proceedings. Ward insisted that there had been no 'immorality' at Yambuya and contradicted Assad Farran flatly: 'I know of no instance in which the native women, who were captured, were brought to white officers' quarters, as he states.'[56]

Parke's short, sanitized account of the rear-column in his own book, suggested, without thorough consideration of what was involved, that Barttelot should have moved on from Yambuya in August. 'This delay was, obviously, a great error of judgement …'[57] Stanley might incur blame for not keeping the entire expedition together but haste was vital. The parallel Parke and Stanley liked to remember was Wilson's unfortunate delay at the Nile to which, rightly or wrongly, they attributed the loss of Gordon at Khartoum. Parke's loyalty to Stanley was now fully engaged. He was not prepared to highlight his leader's faulty logistics nor did he venture to assert his own medical authority as to the unfitness of the unaided rear column — 'the scum of the expedition'[58]— to bear loads through the dense rainforest. Accordingly it was left to Herbert Ward to pose an unanswerable question: 'When Tippoo Tib furnished 400 carriers, only one third of the loads was transported, and everything went smash as the result. Now, if such disaster resulted when two-thirds of the porters carried one third of the loads, what would have happened if without any porters we attempted to carry all the loads?'[59]

H.R. Fox Bourne, an official of the Aborigines Protection Society, strung together descriptions of a series of violent events and discreditable incidents culled from the books of Stanley's critics and published them as *The Other Side of the Emin Pasha Expedition*. He hoped that by finding fault with the expedition and by exposing its blunders and brutal excesses 'something may perhaps be done to deter civilized Englishmen from ever again sanctioning or applauding such proceedings as make up its history.'[60]

The 'Battle of the Books' did not end in 1891. Peter Forbath used a novelist's licence in *The Last Hero* (1989) to present a lurid account of the impossibly handsome Barttelot's erotic encounter with a lovely odalisque when stupified from hashish at Stanley Falls, and of his death under the beautiful Circassian's dagger.[61] Forbath's libellous depiction of Parke characterizes the doctor as a drunk-sodden, simian poltroon: 'There was something monkeyish about him — his bandy legs, his hairy face, the way he stood with his arms hanging loosely at his sides and his head thrust forward on his scrawny neck.'[62]

Notes

1 *Pall Mall Gazette*, 27 June 1890.
2 As mentioned (Chapter 1) the officers' contracts forbade the publication of accounts of the expedition until six months after the issue of the offical report. Troop's intention to publish *With Stanley's Rear Column* in 1889 led the Relief Expediton's committe to seek an injunction against publication. This was granted but Troup made a counter-claim against Stanley for not fulfilling his contract to the letter. A compromise was reached in Stanley v. Troup on 20 May 1890. The plaintiff withdrew his action and paid the costs leaving Troup (and the other officers) free to publish after 15 October 1890.
3 Letters, RCSI.
4 For a full account of Knott's career see Lyons, *'What Did I Die Of?'* (Dublin 1991).
5 The Library of the Royal Irish Academy, of which he was a member, possesses three bound volumes of pamphlets, off-prints, etc, presented by Knott, his contributions to medicine and allied sciences, 1903–13.
6 Letters, RCSI.
7 Letters, 10 October.
8 Bartellot, *Life*, p. 367
9 Ibid, p. 382.
10 Ibid, p. 236.
11 *The Times*, 29 Oct.
12 Ibid, 23 Oct.
13 Ibid, 26 Oct.
14 McLynn, *Sorcerer's Apprentice*, p. 348.
15 Paul Du Chaillu, the French discoverer of pygmies and gorillas, ridiculed the allegation, explaining that Africans did not kill to preserve female chastity, on the contrary they would offer their women's favours openly (McLynn, *op. cit.*, p. 349).
16 Jephson considered the women at Mazamboni's 'nice & pleasant looking, especially the Wahuma of whom there are a good many' (Jephson's *Diary*, p. 349). Arriving at a village on 11 July 1889: 'The women here are rather fine looking & quite covered with skins, nicely dressed & bark cloth' (Ibid, p. 379). Elsewhere on 20 July: 'the women as a rule are very fat & not nice looking' (Ibid, p. 381).
17 Ward, *Five Years*, p. 238.
18 Parke, *Experiences*, p. 84.
19 *The Times*, 1 November.
20 Ibid, 1 Nov.
21 Troup, *Rear Column*, p. 280.
22 Ibid, p. 284.
23 Ibid, p. 264.
24 Letters, RCSI, 8 Nov.

Surgeon-Major Parke's African Journey 1887–89

25 Ibid.

26 Barttelot, *op. cit.*, p. 292.

27 Ibid, p. 222.

28 Ibid, p. 223.

29 *The Times*, 10 Nov.

30 Barttelot, *op. cit.*, p. 231.

31 'This was one of the occasions upon which I saved the life of Major Barttelot, for he would have died with his teeth in the woman's face had I not beaten off the crowd of enraged natives who started to attack the Major with their cudgels'. (Bonny, *The Times*, 10 Nov.).

32 Assad Farran, whom Troup called 'an inveterate liar', felt obliged later to change ground but his retraction (copied by *The Times*, 15 November 1890) was less convincing than his original version: 'The story is entirely untrue, and such a charge against Mr Jameson I declare to be unfounded. The six handkerchiefs given by Mr Jameson were a present...'

33 Assad Farran's affidavit sworn before Stanley in Cairo was printed in *The Times*, 14 November 1890.

34 Two Belgian officers attested to having seen the sketches in a notebook to which Jameson had appended the title 'Drama in Six Sketches'. R. Bosworth Smith wrote from Harrow-on-the-Hill to say that when he was in Egypt in the winter of 1888 he met many of Major Barttelot's personal acquaintances who did not doubt that he had been justly slain; R. Holden, a captain in the 4th Worcestershire Regiment who had served with Barttelot in Cyprus remembered him as 'an honest, frank, kind-hearted, generous, fearless and out-spoken young Englishman — a true friend with a love of adventure' (Ibid, 12 Nov.); Barttelot's previous commander, Colonel R. Fowler-Butler, said that in his experience Barttelot 'was hasty, nothing more' (Ibid, 18 Nov.).

35 Sir Henry Rider Haggard, ibid, 10 Nov.

36 Ethel Jameson, ibid, 13 Nov.

37 Letters, RCSI, 13 Nov.

38 J.S. Jameson, *Story of the Rear Column*, p. 291.

39 *The Lancet*, 1892, i, 1177.

40 J.R. Werner, *A Visit to Stanley's Rear Guard* (London 1889), p. 225.

41 Ibid, p. 228.

42 Ibid, p. 273.

43 Letters, RCSI, 21 Nov.

44 *The Times*, 19 Nov.

45 Ibid, 17 Nov.

46 Ibid, 19 Nov.

47 Andrew Jameson, ibid, 22 Nov.

48 Ibid, 24 December.

49 *Punch*, 1890; 99: 247.

50 Jones, *Rescue*, p. 445.

51 Jerry Allen, *The Sea Years of Joseph Conrad* (New York 1965), p. 275.

52 From Joseph Conrad's letter to R.B. Cunninghame-Graham — cited by B.L. Reid, *Lives of Casement*, p. 14.

53 Ward, *My Life*, 1891, p. 33. I find Jeffrey Meyers's indentification of Emin Pasha as 'an important model' for Kurtz inconvincing (Jeffrey Meyers, *Joseph Conrad* [London 1991], p. 195).

54 Letters, RCSI, 29 Dec.

55 Ward, *op. cit.*, p 32.

56 Ibid, pp. 157–62.
57 Parke, *Experiences*, p. 363.
58 Troup, *The Times*, 1 Nov.
59 Ward, *op. cit.*, p. 163.
60 H.R. Fox Bourne, *The Other Side of the Emin Pasha Expedition* (London 1891), p. vi.
61 Peter Forbath, *The Last Hero* (London 1989), p. 549.
62 Ibid, p. 325.

17 'My Experiences of Equatorial Africa'

Stationed with the Life Guards in central London, Parke became involved in the social whirl and was invited to country houses. 'I had a long talk with the Prince of Wales a few days ago', he told Knott without enlightening him as to their topics of conversation. 'I shall see old Gladstone today', he wrote. 'Last night I dined with Hartington, Goschen, Mathews etc, etc, at the Duke of St Albans', so you see I am getting on.'[1]

He was conscious of his lack of political knowledge but felt he made up for this 'in African news which curiously enough interests them greatly.' The comment was rather naive. They were avid for every scrap of news of Africa and had for years manipulated strings affecting that unfortunate continent. On an occasion when he was more at ease, the Duchess of St Albans introduced him to Bram Stoker, related by marriage to John Knott, at the Lyceum Theatre where he was Henry Irving's manager.[2] He was invited to a private house to meet HRH the Duke of Clarence (the dissolute Prince Eddy[3]) and was the Duke of Cleveland's guest at Battle Abbey.

He visited Lord Salisbury[4] at Hatfield and the possibility of an appointment as a Commissioner abroad was ventilated. There were further discussions at the Foreign Office but eventually he told Knott, 'I have refused the Oil Rivers billet as it is not good enough'. (Roger Casement accepted this post or a similar one in 1892).[5] Another possible assignment was to accompany Lord Randolph Churchill to South Africa for nine months but the War Office refused to grant him leave. A false report in the newspapers that he was going abroad brought him a shoal of letters from creditors and others.

Parke regularly deplored what he saw as a lack of opportunity in Dublin for Dr Knott to develop his literary talents. 'I wish you could get an appointment in London,' he wrote, 'you are simply lost over there. He spoke to Sir James Paget, surgeon to St Bartholomew's Hospital, and others in the hope that they would give Knott 'a lift'. 'I lunched with Quain on Sunday and told him all about you and how you are lost in Dublin and he suggests getting on the staff of one of the medical journals... Mapother ought to be of service to you.'[6] Parke mentioned Knott's erudition to the editor of *The Lancet*.

The death of Mr John Marshall, FRCS, FRS, professor of anatomy at the Royal Academy of Arts and consulting surgeon to University College Hospital, created a vacancy which Parke decided ingenuously would suit Knott well. 'I don't know if it would be worth your while to apply for it or where you could apply for it — '[7] He called on Sir Frederick Leighton to canvass on Knott's behalf but the President of the Royal Academy was out and a recurrence of 'African fever' prevented Parke from returning next day. He also canvassed Professor Flower, Director of the National History Museum, on his friend's behalf. The latter promised to do his best for him but warned that even in London there were insufficient opportunities for scientific men. Flower then looked up Knott's entry in the *Medical Directory* and, impressed by what he saw there, said he should certainly apply, but again warned that many good men were interested in the post.

So many magazines had asked for articles that Parke was anxious to avail of the market which would be less valuable before long. 'I heard from Stanley and Jephson and both urge me to publish whatever I have got as soon as I can, for the African craze is on the decline.' The less said about the rear-column the better, he indicated to Knott, for it threw a cloud on the whole expedition. Troup, whom Parke had never met, and Ward whom he met just once, could hardly be said to have known the expedition at all and Parke preferred to say as little as possible about them — 'for they only make capital out of it'.[8]

Parke's chapter in a new edition of *The Book of Climates* was dictated by him to its author, D.H. Cullimore, who visited Hyde Park Barracks for the purpose. Parke recalled the varying conditions he had experienced in Egypt — Alexandria was damp and oppressive with cool nights: 'This is no place for the consumptive, asthmatic or rheumatic to linger; he should push on at once to Cairo, where he will find a warm dry climate, good hotels and pleasant society.'[9] He praised Cairo's pure, warm air and 'deliciously cool and limpid evenings'. It was a large city, over-crowded and dirty in parts — 'though great sanitary improvements have taken place since the British occupation'[10] — and the invalid's health should improve all the quicker 'for the knowledge that forty centuries of civilization' surround him.

He recommended a voyage in a *dahabya*, a Nile boat, as 'most restorative and invigorating'. The cost of a steamer to tow it from Cairo to Aswan was about £20. 'A steamer is not, of course, absolutely necessary, but it greatly conduces to comfort and convenience. During these trips the evenings are generally damp and all invalids should go below at nightfall.'

Egypt, he warned, was expensive and not a place for the man of scanty means. The greatest health hazard was 'Nile boil' whereas Zanzibar was 'exceedingly feverish and unhealthy'. The Congo, which he referred to briefly, is not capable of the first degree of colonization — 'which enables white men to work in the fields and on the farms' — but could be lived in by employing natives to do the work, an arrangement that would have had Parke's full approval. Syphilis was common here and all over Africa although promiscuity was no greater than in most other lands.

Of all these countries 'the most famous, most fertile, and most powerful' was Uganda and it possessed the most beautiful climate. South of Lake Victoria, Usukuma is 'a fair, fertile, and healthy district'.[11]

Leaving this district [he continued] of the Albert Nyanza, and the Mountains of the Moon, whose snowy summits and cool declivities will in future times afford many cool and healthy retreats for the European residents of these regions, we descended southward to the district round Lake Muta Nzige. This country ... may be described as a land of fogs and hills, of high and strong winds, and much fever, which is generally due to draughts of cold air.[12]

As they had 'lived on heaps of stinks and mountains of smells and dirt' at Ipoto, Parke thought it might be appropriate for Knott to introduce a sketch of their 'nightmares of Bacteriology, with monas, vibrios etc, these sort of things around us, as the public would read of them with wonder'. He wished to make the book 'as much WE as possible'[13] so as not to be seen as an egotist. He received the first and second instalments of the manuscript towards the end of January 1891 and was now arranging for illustrations. Dorothy Stanley provided two decorative drawings of *putti*: the first, embossed in gilt on the front cover, depicts a white child showing his little black friend the River Congo on an outline map of Africa; on the title-page a black pair attempt to 'improve' their complexions with white paint.

I have not had much time lately [Parke wrote] so that I have not yet finished F. Bodo. I like it immensely, it makes me quite emotional. You have put it wonderfully well together, considering the very indifferent notes[14] I gave you. I read it with the greatest interest and I'm sure it will take. I have just written a word or a line where I think fit which you won't mind I hope, and also modified a little, for instance where the woman's ears were slit, I put pierced, and even this I thought too strong following the Jameson affair.[15]

Having completed the reading he wrote again to Knott:

I think it wonderful how you have been able to make so much of it, how you have grasped the very feelings which we felt and got it into such order. The real test is that it interests me so much. It is like a tale which I knew every detail of but had fresh interest given it in every line.[16]

He proposed to write to Marston to ask what he would give for it but would also consult other publishers — 'as old Marston is a screw'[17] — and give it to the highest bidder. Marston replied by asking how the book would compare in size with Jephson's, calculating that eighty sheets of manuscript would make 100 printed pages. He agreed that little should be said about the rear-column and liked the idea of using medical data. A few days later, Marston indicated that the manuscript should be cut — 'it is too much for the public taste' — and Parke wrote in turn to Knott: 'I write this immediately so that you need not be so anxious in writing for the sake of padding etc.' but he felt disinclined to make reductions — 'it may not bring in more money but it is greater satisfction to have a creditable book'.[18] Scribners had declined to bring out another book on Africa.[19]

During his American tour Stanley wrote to Parke warning the doctor that unless there was 'high literary style' to recommend it and Fayrer's[20] scientific knowledge to make it desirable he should reduce it to a single volume of 450 pages, allowing Marston's reader to cut it if not prepared to do so himself.

What the public wants from you now is a popular book relating to your Medical Experiences in Africa. Your name is sufficiently popular to sell such a book, but two would not sell at all, and you would be fearfully disappointed...

Of course I can undertstand a young author's ambition, but never mind that, think rather of recommending yourself to the public by modesty, and give the people and your profession only what they wish to know.

Supposing for instance we — Stairs, Jephson, Nelson, Bonny and I — got your book in hand. What do you think we should care about your geography and other things out of your sphere? Would we not all think we knew these matters better than you do? Would we not all hasten to look for your Medical Experiences, your Medical Observations, your advice and so on? Well just in the same way the public will, unless you had the pen of Stevenson to brighten the pages, and give us sketches of things which would go right to the heart.[21]

Parke offered 'Sunlight & Shadow in Africa' as a title and mentioned that he was to be a guest at the Booksellers, Publishers and Journalists Annual Dinner, with Marston in the chair, and would respond for the guests. 'Don't say much at home [he warned] about hearing from me as they will smell a rat, as they know I have spoken to them of your ability etc. and will say that I couldn't have written a book when going about so much.'

Parke and E.M. Holmes, curator of the Pharmaceutical Society's museum, read a joint paper to the Society on the arrow poison of the pygmies on 8 April. Parke enumerated the ingredients and described how they were collected in the forest and prepared as a paste freshly smeared on the arrows and allowed to dry. His co-speaker had identified the bark without hesitation as that of *Erythroploeum Guineense* (*Don.*), popularly called sassy bark; the green leaves were those of a non-poisonous commelynaceous plant; identification of the thorny creeper had been difficult but it was assigned to the genus *Combretum* ; the green stem was that of a species of *Strychnos*. The two active ingredients, then, were erythrophloein, a muscle relaxant, and strychnine, the dramatic effects of which had reminded Parke of tetanus. The supposed antidote proved to consist largely of wood ashes and the leaves of three plants which remained unidentified but this was of less importance for therapists would endeavour to counteract the specific poisons.[22]

As *The Lancet* had been so generous to him and presented him with a silver salver he wished to reciprocate and mentioned this to Knott: 'I wish you would write an article for me to send to *The Lancet* as I must send them something, but before you write it let me know if it will involve additional expense and how much, as I am stone broke living like a meteor in London.'[23]

The first roll of proofs reached Parke early in May and was duly forwarded to Knott who had generously agreed to write a paper for *The Lancet*. 'I would be obliged [Parke wrote] if you would carefully read remarks on vaccination so that I may not contradict myself as they will be particularly remarked.'[24] The title had not yet been decided on but Marston favoured 'Sunlight & Shadow in Africa'. ('I told him it was quite immaterial to me as long as I could make some money.'[25])

Stationed now at the Cavalry Barracks in Windsor which he preferred to London — 'as one has a good excuse for not going out to dinners and Balls etc. which are an infernal nuisance' — Parke enjoyed the springtime weather. 'After the first shower of rain the leaves and buds were out almost immediately.'[26]

Marston settled on 'Shadow & Sunshine' when Parke signed the contract and planned to publish in October. 'I have written him a very imploring letter asking him to change the title to "My Personal Experiences" etc. if not too late. I prefer it myself.' He arranged, too, at Knott's urging to demand a set of corrected proofs and expressed his enthusiasm to his co-author. 'The narrative is so good that I am more interested in reading it than any other narrative I know, quite independently of personal interest.'[27]

When the two title-pages were set up, 'My Personal Experiences' was preferred. Knott was then asked: 'Would you leave it as it stands or should I put all my degrees honorary and otherwise in a string after my name, *vide* enclosed?' Towards the end of May he was posted to the Royal Victoria Hospital at Netley, near Southampton. This delayed his proof-correcting a little but he assured Knott that his alterations would not harm the book. 'I have cut out about Vomiting, purges, passing catheter and diarrhoea which do not read quite the thing for the drawing-room, but it has not altered the text a bit.'[28]

After the freedom he had enjoyed in Egypt and Central Africa he found Netley restrictive.

I am getting more soured of the Service every day. This place Netley is all regulations and no real work. My work today consists in seeing if fish, vegetables and meat, etc. were rotten or not. I have only a dozen patients and I must ask the Senior Medical Officer for leave to do the smallest thing with them. Fancy I have not yet received the smallest thanks from the military or medical authorities of the Army.[29]

Knott appears to have protested about the deletions and Parke assured him that he should not feel uneasy.

I cut out some repetitions, also the frequent allusions to enemas, purges etc. also shortened the references with regard to stinks and ulcers which I am sure would disgust people by dwelling too much on them as I really felt sick myself when I read about them... I know that these infernal journalists would be down on me and particularly where I allude to shooting at the natives, as people over here cannot understand such treatment of natives. They won't understand our position and will only run me down in the same way they did Stanley.[30]

Work on the proofs which shuttled between Netley and Dublin continued.[31] Corrections began to be expensive, exceeding ten shillings a sheet, and Parke looked forward to going to Ireland in August but was uncertain that he would be granted leave. He felt he was 'shadowed' at Netley because while in London he had asked the Duke of Cambridge, the Commander-in-Chief of the British Army, for a court of inquiry into the conduct of some of the senior medical officers who, Parke alleged, had done their best to persecute him. 'However, HRH has exonerated me from all their serious imputations.'

Our worst enemies in the Medical Staff [Parke continued] are our Seniors. Up to this I have never had 'thank you' from either Military or Medical authorities, although they promoted Stairs who had no war service and about half my service, and allowed him leave to go to Africa which they have denied to me. I wish to heavens I could afford to leave the Medical Staff for it's not all gold that glitters.[32]

When the 'Introduction' was completed he felt satisfied that neither there nor elsewhere had he said anything 'that the Military Authorities can run me in for';[33] there was just enough to let them know what others thought of them — i.e. that the delay in sending steamers from Metammeh caused the failure of the Nile Expedition. It would also be appropriate to put in a few lines of tribute to Sir William Mackinnon and the other philanthropists who had contributed towards the expedition. 'And we did not bring out one lb of ivory.'[34]

Despite his misgivings, Parke was granted leave and went to Switzerland on 15 August. For several weeks he was out of touch with Knott but wrote to him in October asking that his notebooks should be returned. He had seen Jephson who told him he had made a lot of money by writing articles. He had also heard from Stairs who had returned to Africa — 'he can find no tidings of Emin from either Germans or anyone else. There is an epidemic disease amongst the cattle from the Red Sea to Tanganyika which has killed thousands and left the people very badly off and meat scarce'.[35]

My Experiences of Equatorial Africa was to be published on 2nd or 3rd November and Parke was pleased with the copy Marston sent him but did not think much of the engravings. 'You shall have a copy', he assured Knott, 'the moment they come out.' He wrote to his co-author again on 4 November: 'I suppose you read the reviews so far. I have no papers here except those belonging to the Mess or I should. have sent you *The Times, Standard, Daily Telegraph* and *Post* all of which I suppose you have seen; also yesterday's *Irish Times.*'

He was pleased with the reviews and astonished that *The Times* devoted two columns to his book which was seen to fill 'a distinct gap in the narrative of the expedition'. More could have been made of the pygmies but the inclusion of a chapter on bacteriology — 'which reads like a student's exercise' — was a mistake. The general reader would probably skip the botanical and chemical data, and the details of the experiment on Stairs' dog would shock the anti-vivisectionists. Neverthless the book was accepted as 'one of the most satisfactory literary results of an expedition which has had only too many unsatisfactory aspects'. Parke was praised for his modesty and for the 'cheerful and gently humorous tone' which made his book so attractive.[36]

'The story is now all told', *The Irish Times* reviewer remarked. 'Many are the gaps this narrative fills up.' It should be prized by the medical profession but is also 'a record of exploration and combat with adverse circumstances' that would match anything in the literature of travel. The chapter on bacteriology was praised highly; Parke's disbelief that Jameson was capable of deliberate cruelty was accorded mention. 'This is generous, and about all that can be said, but how much less than this was said by others.'[37]

The book was also noticed by *The Lancet* and the *British Medical Journal* on 7 November. Praising its vivacity, the former saw it 'as in some measure supplementary to Mr Stanley's volumes on "Darkest Africa"' and recommended it as 'one of the most interesting narratives of adventure that has appeared for many years.'[38] The *British Medical Journal* was fascinated by 'his reference to the unexpected and surprising practice of prophylactic inoculation of the syphilitic virus among the Bari and other tribes, and to the pre-European prevalence of syphilis'. Impressed by the author's 'characteristic modesty and reserve' it felt that Parke's name should be bracketed with Livingstone's.[39]

Towards the end of November, Parke heard from Marston and quickly conveyed his comments to Knott: 'The *Sale* has been fairly good — the *reviews* admirable. As yet *no* foreign house has made the venture of making a translation.'[40] The advance copy of *My Personal Experiences* sent to Australia for the Stanleys was acknowledged by Dorothy on 20 December. She had had it to herself as her husband was lecturing in Queensland. She had read it 'on and on' after its arrival, all that day and that evening and finished it the next morning, 'with a sigh that it *was* finished'. She believed it to be a most valuable work — 'without it the history of that Wonderful Expedition would have been incomplete and Science would have been the poorer'.

Having lavished as much praise as any author could decently hope for, Dorothy thanked him for doing justice 'to *my* Stanley, to *your* Stanley for he belongs in a way to you also.'

Dear splendid Bula Matari [she enthused] how little the world really knows him — I do not believe there is anybody to compare with him on earth — But I imitate Stanley and do not let him know quite all I think of him — because it might not be good for him (as *I* am the leader here you know).[41]

Marston spoke to Parke early in 1892 about the feasibility of reducing the size of the book and bringing out a cheap edition but by June the publisher had changed his mind. He had sold 1600 copies and could have sold 6000 if it had come out earlier but now most of the reprinted copies (250) remained unsold — 'The apathy of the public with regard to anything African is quite as remarkable as the excitement about it two years ago.'[42] Samson Low & Company paid Parke a total of £200 for his book whereas Jephson made £2000 from *The Rebellion at the Equator* which had been published a year earlier. The author found some consolation in the belief that it had been insufficiently advertised. And besides he had not lost financially and had certainly gained in reputation.[43]

211

My Personal Experiences is factual, conveying a faithful and unexaggerated impression of the rigours of the march, the hunger and external torments, the illnesses and injuries which he is called to deal with but Parke rarely reveals his inner thoughts nor does he succeed in depicting in any detail the extraordinary scenic background to his astonishing tale. Naturally it must be taken into account that the diary was usually written at the end of the day when its compiler was exhausted, drenched through perhaps and certainly not in meditative mood. The flashes of cynicism that enliven Jephson's diary are missing, however, nor can we expect to encounter the wealth of ornithological knowledge enhancing Jameson's pages.

Parke appreciated the hospitality he received from the missionaries and officials he met along the river but he neither praises the Christian endeavour nor condemns the outrages of the CFS. Jephson, on the other hand, has to laugh at the absurdity of white men 'teaching ignorant natives the mysteries of the Holy Trinity when the poor natives don't even know how to count three.'[44] The only apology for the expedition's rigid discipline is Wellington's saying invoked by Parke: 'Punishment is cruel — nothing so inhuman as impunity.'[45]

Admittedly, the nefarious commerce of the Congo had not yet introduced the full repertoire of abuses that became so notorious after Casement's report. The cash crops were ivory and wild rubber, the latter the more important but not in Parke's time when, indeed, the CFS officials were to be more critical of the behaviour of the expedition (and especially of the rear-column) than Stanley's officers could be of the Belgians.

My Personal Experiences must also be seen as a unit in a group of books written by Stanley's officers all from diverse viewpoints, one aspect of which has been considered in the previous chapter.

Jephson's interesting and reflective diary remained unpublished until long after his death. It offers many fine descriptive passages, for instance the arrival of the *Madura* at the Cape of Good Hope:

It is a grand bold headland standing far out into the sea from a black iron bound inhospitable looking coast and has a lighthouse on the top. There was a tremendous sea and the breakers were hurling themselves at the foot of the Cape and throwing up the spray against the face of the rock, which looked quite black in the bright sunshine.

The water all round was seething and boiling, the wind was piping loud and blowing the spray in sheets from the top of the waves, and huge breakers roared madly against the rocks whilst the Cape stood out grim and unmoved about the roar of the waters. It impressed me very much and made one feel small. Round the Cape on our way up to Cape Town the cliffs were splendid in the evening light.[46]

Jephson took to Stanley straightaway, attracted by his gift of word painting — 'he has, too, such a sense of the ridiculous which is nuts to an Irishman.' Before long, however, he was having second thoughts — 'it is very annoying that I should have toiled to do my part of the agreement & that Stanley should fail to do his.'[47] Then to his surprise Stanley wanted to make him pay for his donkey and saddle.

He was critical, too, of his surroundings: 'What a dreadful farce this Congo Free State is — one thing; it cannot last much longer, It must come to an end soon.'[48] He had an eye for flora and fauna but was more appreciative of the myriad of butterflies, the orchilla weed, the grey parrot and the huge hornbills, than of the local inhabitants. 'The natives here are hideous & they are so lacking in intelligent looks...'[49] He ventured to measure a village chief's exiguous beard but it 'was encrusted with palm oil & the dirt of ages & my hands were horrible after touching it'.[50] He did not confine his intolerance to blacks but was at odds with Captain Martin, the Danish master of the *Henry Reed*, who needed to be kept in his place.

Despite the antagonism separating them, Stanley and the officers of the advance party were eventually drawn together by the annealing agony of the long march. Jephson's 'conversion' occurred in a threatening situation on the plain above Lake Albert.

Stanley stepped out & taking a good steady aim with his Winchester Express fired at a native 550 yds distant & shot him through the head. The natives all rushed up to the body & were so utterly thunderstruck at the possibility of our being able to kill a man at such a distance that they took to their heels as fast as they could pelt & a body of our men pursued them till they were out of sight. Stanley had the dead native cut up, the Zanzibaris mutilated the body in a horrible way. He said it was the only way to put fear into the natives so that they would cease to attack us & and was the most merciful way for otherwise we should have to kill a great many before they would see it was best to let us alone. Of course it is horrid to our ideas to mutilate the dead, but I believe Stanley is right.[51]

Parke had softened towards Stanley when the latter returned to Fort Bodo, close to breaking-point, with the awful news of Barttelot's death and the decimation of the rear-column, and besides there was a doctor-patient relationship. No doubt both he and Jephson remained conscious of the great man's failings, which Jephson was reminded of whenever he heard Stanley speak of Ruwenzori. 'He says nothing of Parke & I having told him about it, but he makes it out to be his own discovery.'[52]

Professing to be 'a friend of Africa and the Africans', Jephson remained a realist refusing to be influenced by the 'flowery descriptions' of Burton and others who exalted African kings, their courtiers and palaces:

I only saw a dirtily clothed youth seated in the door of a small hut in which were a lot of black sluts, whilst some 250 natives squatted around upon the straw which had spread on the ground for their accommodation, all of them very dirty & had an exceedingly unpleasant smell & thought a great deal of themselves.[53]

Stairs' recollections of Fort Bodo and the march to the coast appeared in *The Nineteenth Century*. Nelson was exceptional in not committing himself to print. The remaining publications in this interesting group dealt with the rear-column. The primary purpose of Jameson's and Barttelot's relatives in editing their sombre letters and diaries was, as we have seen, to counter Stanley's notorious charges and to attack him. Troup and Ward conducted their own defences. They had all experienced the rough side of Stanley's tongue. His apparent lack of trust offended Jameson: 'It is impossible for anyone calling himself a gentleman, and an officer, to stand this sort of thing. The fact is, this is the first time Stanley has ever had gentlemen to deal with on an expedition of this kind.'[54]

The mere track linking Matadi and Leopoldville surprised Jameson: 'Such is the great road of the Congo Free State!'; more disappointing still the lack of opportunity to collect specimens — his time was occupied with the management of his reluctant carriers, a distasteful task. 'The work was truly sickening, as every twenty yards or so one had to stop to put a load on a man's head who had flung it down, and very likely give him a good dose of the stick as well before he would go on.'[55] Barttelot said he 'felt like a brute' as he flogged the men to keep them going.[56]

Above Stanley Pool it was possible to appreciate the full magnificence of the river, seeing the Congo as 'one grand unbroken stream, not enclosed by rocks as below, but flowing between beautifully wooded hills, their sides covered with tropical forests down to the water's edge'.[57] The wildlife, the orchids, the indigenous humanity were given Jameson's close attention, and particularly the cannibal Bangalas, their teeth filed into points. 'They told me that one of their chiefs, who was very rich, is now quite poor from buying nice, fat, young women to eat; this I know to be a fact.'[58]

A close friendship developed between Barttelot and Jameson when left together at Yambuya and the latter's most critical comment about the murdered Major is that he was 'quick-tempered rather than bad-tempered'. Jameson's book is, on the whole, a dismal record of an unhappy period during which things went from bad to worse to end in disaster. 'I am so thankful [he wrote] that I have a taste for collecting, etching, and things of that kind, for had I not, I don't know how I could possibly exist here.'[59]

The men, many of them in chains, were mutinous; floggings were almost a part of the daily routine, a necessary punishment for sentries who slept at their posts. And there were deaths — 'It is horrible to watch these men slowly dying before your face, and not be able to do anything for them'.[60] Jameson kept his diary in pencil during his journeys rewriting in ink on his return to camp. A large contingent of carriers were said to have been sent by Tippu Tib in August but they struck the river at the Upper Falls and seeing the blazings of the advance party concluded that the camp had been vacated and dispersed. On 26 September the Arab leader sent news that he was unable to muster the required men; they were scattered, fighting distant tribes and hunting for ivory. 'All our hopes of being able to go on after Stanley have been destroyed today'.

From the chiefs he spoke with, Jameson learned of Stanley's reputation for meanness; sometimes he failed to return gifts and he did not always keep his promises. Rumours (and they were nothing more) reached him from time to time concerning the advance party. 'It appears that one day they succeeded in capturing a large canoe, four men, a goat, and some women with babies. The women ran away, and left the babies in the camp, so they were drowned in the river.'[61]

When Barttelot, Jameson and Bonny finally managed to leave Yambuya, with the porters supplied belatedly by Tippu Tib, carrying loads reduced in weight and number, the headman, Muni Somai, specially engaged to lead the Manyuemas, proved incapable of his task. Then to Jameson's horror there was an outbreak of smallpox in the caravan. 'It is astonishing to see a man covered from head to foot with the sores of small-pox carrying a load.'[62]

Jameson's and Barttelot's accounts of the rear-column are complementary. The latter sent his dog, 'Satan', a Manchester terrier, home from Banana Point in the *Madura*, a tacit acknowledgement of the perils ahead. His initial ambivalence towards Stanley — 'He is a funny chap ... sometimes I like him fairly well and sometimes quite the reverse'[63] — hardened into hatred as he became convinced that Stanley, annoyed by the fractious Soudanese, blamed him for not keeping them in order and had spitefully decided to get rid of him in the rear-column. 'I feel very well at present [he wrote to his fiancée], but not always very bright, there are so many sad things happening all round; starvation, sickness and lingering death, which nothing can avert.'[64]

The only constant thing for Barttelot, month after month at Yambuya, was his friendship with Jameson, of whom he wrote: 'I have seldom met a man like him — sweet-tempered as a woman, courageous, honest and a friend of all.' The impossible position they faced in regard to transporting the stores is set out in a letter to Mackinnon:

215

It is apparent to all of us that the Manyuema men could not carry full loads, and that our *death-rate* up to March 27 is 67, and out of those left — 155 Zanzibaris and 29 Soudanese — 80 Zanzibaris only are fit to carry loads, and 30 of them are with Mr Ward; and our ammunition loads alone are 240, and others *absolutely necessary* (85), making a total of 325 full loads, or 650 half-loads. This would absorb all Tippu Tib's men and 50 of ours, leaving us only 30 Zanzibaris, should Ward's men have returned in time to come with us, for cutting roads, etc; and about 14 Soudanese as escort, for these are all the Soudanese who are fit.[65]

At Stanley Falls after Barttelot's death, Jameson found that Assad Farran had been traducing him with atrocious misrepresentations of his shooting at natives on the way to Kassongo and the cannibal incident at Riba-Riba. 'I am so anxious about everything [he wrote] that I lie awake for hours at night...' He tried in vain to persuade either Tippu Tib's son, Sefo, or his nephew, Rashid, to lead the Manyuema. Eventually Tippu Tib himself agreed to do so for £20,000. He would find Stanley, and relieve Emin Pasha but he proposed to travel via Kassongo, Tanganyika and Unyoro. Jameson knew that he could not adopt this route without the Committee's assent so he decided to go by canoe to Bangala and proceed from there to the cable station.

The most dramatic moments of the river journey occurred during the clear night of 11 August 1888 when, leaving an open reach, the canoes entered a dark narrow channel.

All at once it became lit up with dozens of fires on both sides, throwing a bright light back into the forest and across the water. We glided on without a sound from us but the zip-zip of the paddles, drums beating, horns blowing, shouts and cries on every side, the white loin-clothes of our men showing plainly who they were. Down this lane of fires and noise we went for nearly half a mile, when suddenly it opened out into a grand open reach of the river on our right, the fires, drums, &c., going on for more than a mile away down on our left.[66]

This vivid sketch is the last note pencilled into Jameson's diary and the noise and tumult remained with him as his mind clouded with fever. 'Ward! Ward! they're coming', he muttered in his delirium at Bangala. 'Listen! Yes they're coming — let's stand together.' He was buried at the foot of a giant cotton tree a thousand miles from the sea.[67]

Troup's book was a day-to-day account of Yambuya and his defence against Stanley's charges — 'He the leader of the Expedition, though absent, is more guilty — if guilt there is — than I, a subordinate, who was also absent.' Absent, first, when confined to his bed by fever and a back injury due to a heavy fall, while making his way over some slippery logs. Troup had had nothing to do with John Henry's awful punishment, the lethal flogging.

'From my hut [he wrote] I could hear what was going on, and I was much disturbed by this, as I did not approve of such severe punishment.'[68] Absent, finally, when invalided down-river in the *Stanley*. Tippu Tib, who came on board to say goodbye, was still shaking with rage. The Arab regretted giving any men to Barttelot after hearing a full account of what had gone on in Yambuya.[69]

Having written briefly on the misadventures of the rear-column in *Five Years with the Congo Cannibals*, Herbert Ward, in response to Stanley's challenge, published *My Life With Stanley's Rear Guard* (1901). Like Troup he protested that he 'was hundreds of miles away when some of the incidents which have most stirred the public mind are alleged to have happened.'[70] His inability to get on with Barttelot has already been mentioned — 'He [the Major] was a stranger to African manners and speech; with the ever-present suspicion of everyone and everything which this disadvantage must always excite.'[71] He dismissed the amazing charges of 'irresolution, neglect and indifference' as absurd and pointed out that Stanley conveniently overlooked his own failure to return to Yambuya by November as promised.

Jameson's diary tells how he happened to hear of the expedition by chance while visiting a friend one Sunday morning. 'It does seem [he wrote] as if one were guided by some hand or power.' He applied to join it because of an ambition 'to do some good in the world'.[72] Herbert Ward, like Parke, had never heard of Emin Pasha; he was quite unconcerned with the fate of the governor. 'For glory or profit I had no heed; but for sport and adventure I was keen and excited.' That Parke, too, was similarly motivated is indicated by the alacrity with which he acted on Barttelot's suggestion that he should join the quest for a man of whom he knew nothing. 'Life with Stanley [wrote Ward] promised new experiences, unthought of adventures, and all those things which from my early days had appeared to my sporting mind to make life worth living.'[73]

Had Parke wished to look critically at the expedition as a whole, he could have questioned the haste with which it was eventually formed. Suggestions for its sponsorship were made as early as 1885 but the final arrangements were concluded with extreme rapidity. Stanley offered his services early in 1886 but he was actually on a lecture tour in America in December when the Committee's cable reached him: 'Your plan and offer accepted. Business urgent. Come promptly.' He arrived in London just before Christmas. Even at this stage of his planning, Stanley envisaged a base camp on the Aurwimi River from which to take all of Emin's people who wished to withdraw. The final decision to travel through the Congo, nevertheless, was taken far too late

217

to stockpile food along the way and within a month of starting they lost fifty-seven men. Parke made no complaint of the haphazard logistics or of the haste that hampered planning.

Frank McLynn's *Hearts of Darkness* devotes an absorbing chapter to the psychology of explorers which he admits is 'as yet almost virgin territory'.[74] The explorers' own accounts of their motives are not always, he says, to be accepted at face value; their 'objective interest' may include aspirations to increased social status or involve idiosyncrasies and neuroses; likely to be most important of all are unconscious drives and impulses. In the latter context, McLynn's comment — here 'the Dark Continent becomes the perfect objective correlative for the dark side of the men who prised it open'[75] — surely presents a loaded and thoroughly unscientific apposition of adjectives. Further dubious methodology is introduced with the suggestion that the popular metaphor for the Nile as 'the cradle' of Africa indicates an unconscious wish to retrieve the pleasures of childhood.[76] It may be helpful, neverthless, to see if McLynn's scheme of interrogation can amplify our knowledge of Parke.

As a member of the Anglo-Irish gentry (albeit minor), Parke already enjoyed a secure social status and on his return from Africa he gained *entrée* to high places. He was, to all appearances, offered 'a rapid means of ascent of the greasy pole for the already privileged'[77] but no definite benefits emerged. This would explain the disillusion with his army career as he may have aspired, even in fancy, to advancement like that of Sir John Kirk, a Scots doctor who accompanied Dr Livingstone's second Zambezi expedition, becoming, later, British consul at Zanzibar.

Parke's personality was stable. He seems to have possessed the calm and mildness of speech that were such assets in Africa for Livingstone, whose apparent benignity could disarm potential foes.[78] 'How [asked a chief] could I give the sign to kill a man who smiled?' Parke was not a 'loner', or a man who was likely to find heart's ease in the wilderness; he moved comfortably in society and cannot be thought to have been influenced by a preference for the primitive over the cloying pleasures of civilization. An imperialist by upbringing — his maternal grandfather, General Holmes, was governor of St Helena, a paternal great-grandfather owned plantations in Ceylon — he was to become a propagandist for British colonization of Africa. We have insufficient knowledge of the man (or the child) to question him on the accommodating couch of psychoanalysis and, indeed, it is well to remember Sir Charles Sherrington's admonition on the limits of the interrogations of natural science: 'Mind, for anything perception can compass, goes therefore in our spatial world more ghostly than a ghost.'[79]

Whatever the *motivations* underlying a particular course of action, *opportunity* has a direct and more tangible function in determining the evolution of any career. Parke, Roger Casement and Charles Stokes are an unusual Irish trio to find on the move in Africa in the same decade. What had they in common save their Protestant ancestry[80] and the opportunity to leave 'the most distressful country that ever yet was seen'? Their personalities could hardly have been more different though more is known in that regard of the idealistic (and homosexual) Casement and the acquisitive (and heterosexual) Stokes. Parke found his gateway to Africa through the British army, the other pair through clerkships in shipping offices in the great port of Liverpool. Their disparities serve to illustrate the impossibility of supplying motivation with any degree of accuracy from the unconscious, for careers which ended so sadly: Parke swept away by a seizure in Scotland; Stokes bellowing like a bull as they killed him in the Congo, ostensibly for poaching ivory; Casement going to his death in Pentonville Prison with courage that impressed the hangman.

Notes

1 Letters, RCSI, 19 February 1891. Marquis of Hartington and eighth Duke of Devonshire (1833–1908) secretary of state for war (1882–5) opposed to Gladstone's Home Rule policy; known to his intimates as 'Harty Tarty' and conducted discreet affairs with 'Skittles', a famous courtesan, and with Louise, Duchess of Manchester.

   George J. Goschen (1831–1907), Chancellor of the Exchequer (1886–92) became first Viscount Goschen in 1900.

   The line of the St Albans took origin from Charles Beauclerk, the natural son of Charles II by Nell Gwynn and, linked by marriage to the family of the deVeres, had many Irish connections. The 10th Duke's mother was Elizabeth, youngest daughter of General Joseph Gubbins of Kilrush, County Limerick.

2 Stoker (1847–1912) had not yet written his most famous work, *Dracula* (1897). He was married to Florence Balcome (whose beauty attracted Oscar Wilde in early manhood); John Knott's wife was her sister.

3 See Christopher Hibbert, *Edward VII: A Portrait* (Harmondsworth 1982), p. 183–4. When Prince Eddy died from pneumonia on 14 January 1892 Parke wrote to Knott: 'The death of HRH the Duke of Clarence is terribly sad news.'

4 Lord Salisbury (1830–1903) granted a royal charter to the British East Africa Company in 1888.

5 Letters, 24 March. The term 'Oil Rivers' denoted the Niger delta and adjacent costal strip productive of palm-oil.

6 Richard Quain, MD, FRCP, an influential Harley Street physician, was born in Mallow, County Cork —'he would remember you if anything did turn up, although there were always so many after an appointment – but he is an Irishman and partial to his nationality'. Edward Dillon Mapother, MD, FRCSI, was of Roscommon stock. He held a chair of anatomy and physiology at RCSI (1867–89) before moving to London. His *Manual of*

Physiology was re-written by John Knott.

7   Letters, 3 January 1891.

8   Ibid, 14 Jan. When Ward visited Dublin in January, Knott attended his lecture and Parke was glad to hear that the audience applauded Stanley — 'for the Expedition could never have been carried through by any other man I ever met, and the press have been very down on him simply because he wrote all his letters for *The Times* only.'

9   *The Book of Climates*, 2nd ed. 1891, p. 261–70. Daniel Henry Cullimore, MD, MRCP London and Dublin, FRCSI, surg, HM Indian Army rtd. Late senior phys, North West London Hospital. Formerly cons phys to the King of Burmah. He read for his primary degrees in Dublin (LKQCPI, RCSI) and resided at Taghmon, County Wexford.

10   Ibid, p. 262.

11   Ibid, p. 269.

12   Ibid, p. 270.

13   Letters, 24 Jan.

14   'Many of the statistics in my diary are wrong but Stanley's book will correct them' (Letters, 13 Nov 1890). 'My notes are short, badly written and scattered too much but the difficulties of carrying on a journal were immense — you have the evidence.' (Letters, 21 January).

15   Letters, 27 Jan.

16   Letters, 29 Jan.

17   Letters, 7 February.

18   Letters, 9 Feb.

19   Evidently there was a change of mind for C. Scribner's Sons did publish *My Personal Experiences of Equatorial Africa* in New York (1891) and the *National Union Catalogue* lists a 3rd edition (London 1891). *The British Library Catalogue* lists a 2nd edition, imperfect wanting the map. The Commissioners of National Education included two extracts from Parke's book in their *Fifth Reading Book* (Dublin: Browne & Nolan 1897). *My Personal Experiences of Equatorial Africa* was reprinted in 1969 by the Negro Universities Press, New York.

20   The Surgeon-General, Sir Joseph Fayrer, MD, FRCP, FRCS, author of *Clinical Surgery in India*, etc.

21   Letter from HM Stanley to Parke, 20 February 1891, Kirkpatrick Collection, Royal College of Physicians of Ireland. Concluding his letter, Stanley wrote: 'Mrs Stanley has gone to Colorado and I am alone again, and free a while from feminine supervision. It is grand to be able to draw a free breath once in a while, When Mrs Dolly comes to my door and says 'Bula Matari! I want to speak to you,' I have to drop the cigar and the book, and look smug and complacent, and pretend that I am glad to have been relieved from the tedium of loneliness. Ah marriage is a great institution!'

22   *British Medical Journal*, 1891, i, 815–16.

23   Letters, 11 April.

24   Letters, 7 May.

25   Letters, 10 May.

26   Letters, 12 May.

27   Letters, 15 May.

28   Letters, 26 June.

29   Letters, 4 July.

30   Letters, 9 July. Stanley said he was obliged to defend himself vigorously against 'Quakerism, peace societies, protection combinations, anti-enterprise companies, and namby-pamby journalism...' It would not have been possible, he said, for men like Drake

or Raleigh to live in England in the 1890s.

31   The Library, RCSI, has a paper-bound copy of the page-proofs. This is stamped by the printers, William Clowes and Sons, on dates between 29 May and 25 July 1891. The corrections are in Knott's minuscule hand and concern style and punctuation. They are extensive — the margins bristle with commas, semi-colons and dashes — with here and there insertions pasted in by Parke.

In the following examples the unamended text from the proof-copy is given first in italics:

... taking skilful advantage of the planes of cleavage. p 61.

... taking skilful advantage of the direction of the planes of cleavage.

I gave small but repeated injections of a strong infusion of tobacco to the case of tetanus. p. 97.

I gave small but repeated enemas of a strong infusion of tobacco to the case of incipient tetanus.

— even when given by the dying. p. 97.

— even when offered by the dying.

There is also a latrine... p. 153.

A latrine is included...

Such woeful-looking people... p. 432.

Such perfect human rubbish...

On page 272 and elsewhere Knott has 'corrected' Madi to Mahdi failing to make the distinction between the tribe and the Dervishes.

32   Letters, 17 July.
33   Letters, 8 August.
34   Letters, 30 July.
35   Letters, 29 October.
36   *The Times*, 3 November.
37   *The Irish Times*, 3 Nov.
38   *The Lancet*, 1891, ii, 1044–5.
39   *British Medical Journal*, 1891, ii, 1001.
40   Letters, 23 Nov.
41   D. Stanley / THP, Letter, RCSI, 20 December.
42   Letters, 13 June 1892.
43   Letters, 5 March 1892.
44   Jephson's *Diary*, p. 401.
45   *Personal Experiences*, p 513.
46   Jephson's *Diary*, p. 77.
47   Ibid, p. 84.
48   Ibid, p. 70.
49   Ibid, p. 97.
50   Ibid, p. 98.
51   Ibid, p. 215.
52   Ibid, p. 256.
53   Ibid, p. 390.
54   J.S. Jameson, *Story of the Rear Column*, p. 32.
55   Ibid, p. 17.
56   Barttelot, *Life*, p. 79.
57   Jameson, *op. cit.*, p. 35.
58   Ibid, p. 31.
59   Ibid, p. 99.

60 Ibid, p. 95.
61 Ibid, p. 109.
62 Ibid, p. 325.
63 Barttelot, *Life*, p. 67.
64 Ibid, p. 89.
65 Ibid, p. 217.
66 Jameson, *op. cit.*, pp. 368–9.
67 Ibid, pp. 273–4.
68 Troup, *Rear Column*, p. 248.
69 Ibid, p. 256.
70 Ward, *My Life*, p. viii.
71 Ibid, p. 31.
72 Jameson, *op. cit.*, p. 264.
73 Ward, *op. cit.*, p. 3.
74 McLynn, *Hearts of Darkness*, p. 340.
75 Ibid, pp. 339–40.
76 Ibid, p. 350.
77 Ibid, p. 344.
78 David Livingstone had a manic-depressive temperament and like Stanley his personal relationships with his white officers were frequently strained. See Oliver Ransford, *David Livingstone* (London, 1978).
79 Sir Charles Sherrington, *Man on his Nature* (Harmondsworth 1955), p. 266.
80 Roger Casement's father was a member of the Church of Ireland; his mother (*née* Jephson), a convert to Catholicism, agreed that their children should be reared as Protestants. This decision was fulfilled but when on holidays in Wales without her husband Mrs Casement had her three sons baptised in the Catholic Church in Rhyl on 5 August 1868. Sir Roger Casement was 'reconciled' to Catholicism before his execution.

18   The Other Writings

Now that his book was out of the way Parke set his mind to exploiting other literary possibilities — 'I think *Harper*, the *Nineteenth Century*, *Fortnightly* etc. are the sort of Magazines to write for'[1] — and he appears to have had neither the least doubt that Knott was equally committed, nor any scruple about monopolizing his leisure time. 'So whatever subject you wish to select might be commenced as soon as convenient to you...' Knott had already supplied, gratis, an article on ulcers for *The Lancet* which was followed by a 'note on African Fever' of which Parke asked, 'Do you intend the note on "African Fever" as a grateful article or shall I take what he may wish to give for it?' He proposed to speak to Wakley again about a job on the staff of *The Lancet* for Knott but without divulging the existence of their literary partnership.[2]

'The Ulcer of the Emin Pasha Relief Expedition' by T.H. Parke was published in *The Lancet* on 5 March 1891 and described the development of rapidly-spreading ulcers initiated by minor trauma in the undernourished.

When the starvation was at its climax, the treatment of ulcerated surfaces went for little. The influence of antiseptics failed to keep pace with the decomposition of the dying tissues. Caustics merely laid bare a deeper stratum, which was rapidly attacked by the phagedaenic action, and it was disheartening to the last degree to watch them day by day — to feel so powerless in the presence of these gigantic opponents, famine and disease. Whole feet and legs were destroyed in a great many instances. A slight abrasion or accidental scratch established a solution of continuity of the cutaneous surface, perhaps a little above the ankle. From this starting-point the ulcerative process proceeded upwards, downwards, and laterally. The lower end of the tibia and fibula became exposed, the tarsal bones were in their turn laid bare, and as the disease progressed the destruction of the tissues became so complete as to sever the connexions of the latter, and also of the metatarsals, so that the bones of the foot, protruding in a necrotic condition, dropped out one by one on the line of march, or were, when almost quite detached, picked out and thrown aside by the unhappy owner after he had reached the camping ground.[3]

Parke's 'Note on African Fever' did not appear in *The Lancet* until 28 May

1892 but may be dealt with here. He stressed the value of quinine as a prophylactic to ward off 'the infection of African malaria' and described in detail the course of a bout of fever, the symptoms frequently precipitated by a wetting or by direct and prolonged exposure to the sun. He was surprised to find muscle function so little affected.

There was not one of the officers of the Relief Expedition who did not over and over again go through a hard day's work, including laborious marching over very difficult ground and constant attention to a number of worrying duties, while his temperature was all the time above 105° or 106°F. And such exertion did not appear to have any subsequent effect on the convalescence — indeed, all our worst cases of fever occurred while we occupied standing camps and were not constantly on the move.[4]

Since his return to England, Parke, with Knott's assistance, had brought himself up-to-date with research in malaria including the work of Alphonse Laveran, the French army-surgeon who described the parasites of malarial fever in 1881. Like many he was not fully convinced and, of course, he did not yet know that the disease was insect-borne, a fact established by Ronald Ross in 1897, which would have enabled him to understand why fever was so common at the lake.

When we had escaped from the depths of the primeval forest of Central Africa and emerged on the open plains towards the Albert Nyanza Lake, I had fondly hoped that the free and fresh air which we were allowed to breathe under a clear and open sky would carry with it comparative immunity from the previously persistent fever. But in this expectation I was bitterly disappointed. Malarial symptoms were even more prevalent and more continuous on the shores of the great Albert Lake than they had been in the untrodden pathways of the forest. Even Emin Pasha himself, who had but a few times suffered from intermittent fever during his thirteen years residence in Equatorial Africa, and who had come to regard his own physique as 'fever-proof', was over and over again attacked by fever (and severely too), during our prolonged sojourn on the lake shore.[5]

Much to his surprise his offer of an article on pygmies did not appeal to James Knowles, editor of *Nineteenth Century*, who explained that African travels 'have now been so much and for so long before the Public that the subject has, for the time, lost its attractions.'[6] He felt sure he could place it elsewhere — 'I think the Americans pay best' — and meanwhile another project was crystalizing in his mind. 'What would you say', he asked Knott, 'to my publishing a small book (like Porter's pocket-book on military surgery) as a guide to health in Africa? Also a list of Kit required etc — as the Country is opened up there will be a great demand for such a guide. I think it is a rather good idea. Something small.'[7]

The King of the Belgians was planning to offer a prize of £1000 for an essay on Africa but the regulations had not yet been announced so having discussed the 'Guide to Health' further, Parke expressed readiness to agree with whatever terms Knott might suggest — 'as I have such Confidence in your desire to make it a useful and permanent work.'[8] He was still hoping to go abroad, possibly in 1892, and was eager to get the new book started. He had a lot of useful information from his experiences in Egypt and the Congo and it should sell to colonists and Europeans working in Africa — 'a volume to sell for 5 or 6 shillings would be the thing, so that people going out would bring a copy to refer to on ailments, and practical hints, which would be of use and name the medicines so that they could treat themselves in the tabloid form.' He sent Knott a cheque for £20 ('the first instalment for the work') on 26 January and promised to send £10 on the first of each month until July.

A notice of *My Experiences in Equatorial Africa*, spread over six-and-a-half columns, appeared in *Nature* on 21 January. It provided so long a summary as to really make it almost unnecessary to read the book and settled then to enumerate its defects: the 'very second-rate account of bacteriology'; the 'coarse allusions to certain physiological and pathological phenomena'; the details not in good style 'except in a professional treatise'. The author's lack of knowledge of natural history was regretted and his reference to Emin's 'bug-hunting' derided. The illustrations ('if we except the two charming sketches by Mrs Stanley, and the view of Ruwenzori from a sketch by Stairs') were not up to the standard that might be expected of a serious travel-book.[9]

The Lancet proposed to establish an enquiry into 'African Fever' and Dr C.F. Harford Battersley of the Church Missionary Society, who had urged the Royal Geographical Society with the same end in mind, sought Parke's advice. Mrs M. French-Sheldon (author of *Sultan to Sultan*) wrote from America to offer her assistance to Parke by acting as a mediator with magazines.

The Royal Geographical Society invited him, early in March, to review the medical hints in one of its books. Parke agreed to do so but said it would be better to re-write the chapter. 'I would like to do this well for them [Parke informed Knott] and would like your valuable assistance to make it up to date. Please let me know what you would take to write it for me.'[10] Knott agreed to write the chapter for £15.

Referring to this chapter on 6 April, he suggested to Knott that it should be condensed and urged him to lay stress on the usefulness of opium in the treatment of malaria — 'for even here the fellows open their mouths when I prescribe opium at the onset of the fever' — it eased the dreadful pains and increased sweating. Opium was eaten in India as a prophylactic against fever and *bhang* was smoked throughout India and Africa for the same reason.

He was invited to speak daily at a three-day Masonic Bazaar to be held in Dublin in May in aid of the Masonic School and wondered if he should also offer to read a paper on the development of British Trade in Africa to the Dublin Chamber of Commerce and urge support for the building of a railway between Mombasa and Lake Victoria. He wished to have Knott's opinion. 'If you think this a good idea I would send you the material to put together for I have very little time.' He sent him '£20 in part payment which leaves £40 due and a Bill signed for that amount, which I hope to reduce shortly.'

The Principal Medical Officer at Netley refused, however, to give him leave to go to Dublin for the Masonic Bazaar — 'There is just a chance I may get over, but having to do with Senior Army Medical Officers one never can tell what they may do and anyhow there is a lot of work here now.'

His criticisms of the 'top brass' can hardly have failed to reach their ears. A letter to the *British Medical Journal* signed 'A.B.C.' was transparently Parke's.[11] It concerned Surgeon-Major Briggs, who, when posted back to India in 1890, felt honour bound to resign his commission to remain available to give evidence for Lady Connemara in her suit for divorce on charges of cruelty and adultery. When Connemara *v* Connemara was heard in November 1890 a decree nisi was pronounced, and *The Times* felt the details were 'unfit for publication in the columns of a newspaper'. Enough was told, however, to make it clear that on at least two occasions Lord Connemara had infected his wife with gonorrhoea and he had slept with her maid.

Briggs's application for reinstatement was sanctioned after the intervention of a member of parliament, on the understanding that he must lose pay and allowances from date of resignation to restoration, and other pecuniary penalties relating to pension rights. It was agreed that Briggs should be restored to full seniority without financial loss.

The *British Medical Journal* referred to the attitude of the Commander-in-Chief and his subordinates: 'Ought they to escape censure from the public opinion which they outraged?'[12] Parke's letter, appreciative of the journal's intervention, praised Briggs: 'a martyr since he was pressed out of the army by the despotic dictates of his seniors. His services on that memorable march across the Bayuda Desert are still fresh in the minds of many soldiers, and I can confidently say as an eye-witness that any success reflected on the medical arrangements was entirely due to Surgeon-Major Briggs.'[13]

*

Knott, *mirabile dictu*, had found time to publish under his own name two articles on Shakespeare's knowledge of medicine.[14] These impressed Parke who found them 'far more interesting than all the leading articles on Medicine, Surgery and Midwifery that I have ever read in the journals.' He drew Knott's attention to contributions by Wingate and Williams in the *United Service Magazine* and asked 'What are you doing with regard to the article on the Nile Expedition?'

Idealism had prompted Parke to join the expedition for the relief of General Gordon in 1884 and like many others he felt outraged by the Mahdi's victory. He now believed Stanley could have saved Gordon and referred somewhat unfairly to Sir Charles Wilson's 'apparently stupid indifference to the fate of Gordon'. Parallels and contrasts between the vast Nile Expedition and the smaller Emin Relief Expedition nagged at him, demanding expression: the enormous expense with total failure of the former and Stanley's success at a comparatively tiny financial cost; Sir Charles Wilson's cautious river trip to Khartoum and Jephson's brave venture on the lake in search of Emin in the unsupported *Advance*; Stanley's decisive departure from Yambuya, leaving the rear-column to look after itself, unlike Wilson's delay at the river-bank; the wrecked *Safieh* and *Talahawiyeh*, repaired by Arab mechanics, taking the Mahdists to Rejaf from where they had menaced Emin; Stanley's gloating to have evaded enemies who calculated on exhibiting them all in chains at Khartoum.

It annoyed Parke to think that Wilson had been thanked by the Queen. 'He is the only one to blame for the whole catastrophe; he also got a KCB. All Gordon's family hate him, except Gordon's sister who is more or less of the same temperament as her deceased brother.' Wolseley, the Commander in Chief, had cleverly avoided making a comment for or against his subordinate's report.

The involved interconnections between Gordon, Emin, Stanley and the fury of the Mahdi intrigued Parke and he conveyed his enthusiasm and material to the ever-willing Knott who elaborated 'Why General Gordon Was Really Lost' which was submitted to *The Nineteenth Century* in April 1892 and published in May. It offered 'the recollections of a non-combatant officer, who was present during the principal events of the campaign' and blamed the steamers' delayed departure for the expedition's failure.[15] 'I think we can prove all we have said if there is a discussion afterwards', Parke reflected in a letter to Knott. 'I only hope the military people won't think badly of it. However it is put in a very delicate and inoffensive way. I feel very eager to see how it reads in print.'[16]

An outline of Parke's journey with the Nile Expedition has been given in the first chapter but other details, not all praiseworthy or nowadays easy to understand, are disclosed in his correspondence with Knott. Marching with the rearguard from Gubat to the Nile, Parke had orders from Surgeon-Major Freddie Ferguson, another Irish graduate, to bring in all the enemy wounded he encountered but he felt impelled by their awful circumstances to employ a modicum of clinical judgement in interpreting this command. The small medical corps was already over-stretched by the needs of the British casualties.

'When I came to a native wounded who was not likely to recover', he explained, 'I would say to Beresford that it was absurd to carry him into camp as he would die.' And then Lord Charles Beresford would give an order to have the unfortunate man put out of torment with a bullet. Ferguson's directive, to Parke's mind, was 'an example of an inexperienced simple-minded doctor wanting to get kudos for his pretended kindness and gain favour with [the] authorities at the expense of his executive officers. Just like our Seniors!' Beresford, on the other hand, 'acted as any strong-minded man would have done', thus diminishing the total agony and avoiding filling the hospital with the enemy to a degree that prevented their own soldiers from getting proper treatment.

He praised the solid work of Surgeon-Major Briggs and dismissed Ferguson as 'a prig and tuft-hunter'. They had, of course, brought in quite a few wounded Arabs; some died, while others, inevitably, 'we deserted and left to die' when the British retreated from Gubat on 13 February 1885.

The article recalled how Gordon had voluntarily placed himself in a remote and perilous position, and the planning of a relief expedition. He alluded to the desert crossing during which they had to rely on leaky mussecks (water-skins) to alleviate the dreadful thirst as the Royal Engineers' pump was not in order. The jamming of the Gardner gun at a critical moment was something of a calamity and Sir Herbert Stewart's mortal wound a still greater disaster. 'Sir Charles Wilson, being next in seniority [an intelligence officer without combat experience], now succeeded to the command.'

During the attack on Metammeh (21 January), 'the exciting news was brought in that Gordon's steamers were in sight' and a contingent of Gordon's men reinforced their assault which, according to Parke's scathing account, was useless and faint:

he [Wilson] formed square and moved about until assisted by Gordon's men and guns who had arrived on the morning of the 21st; then Wilson retreated having lost many men and officers, he ordered the square several times to 'lie down' (an order I cannot find anywhere) when all fell prostrate in the prone position. When he retired after these useless manoeuvres, and our men exhausted, to some small mud huts where the wounded and remainder of our force was, he had the huts immediately put into a fortified Condition for defence as he thought the people of Metammeh, who were watching his antics and seeing his utterly useless attempt on Metammeh, would be inspired to come out and attack us.[17]

Two valuable days were spent in reconnoitring and collecting fuel, and Wilson's departure in the *Bordein* accompanied by the *Talahawiyeh* was delayed until 24 January.

Sir Charles Wilson's *From Korti to Khartum* describes how, having consulted with Lord Charles Beresford, he chose the two largest and best protected steamers. It was deemed prudent to spend 22 January reconnoitring down-river in case an enemy should be coming from the north. Beresford, who was unwell, had to be helped on board and rested in the cabin. A departure was planned for 23 January but fuel and rations had to be loaded and a lot of time was spent finding red coats for the twenty men of the Royal Sussex Regiment who accompanied them, a token force intended to strike fear into the Mahdi. 'So the hours slipped by, and we failed to make a start.'[18]

Nor were they ready at daybreak as scheduled; they did not finally get away until 8 am on 24 January. Beresford was not well enough to command the steamers as originally planned, which in one way was fortunate, for when the steamers struck rocks and foundered on the return voyage, Lord Charles performed an epic rescue operation in the *Safia* which had its boiler mended under enemy fire.

The *Bordein* carried 110 black troops apart from the crew; the *Talahawiyeh* had eighty black soldiers on board and towed a nugger (native boat) filled with dhura (maize) and carrying fifty additional soldiers. They were fitted with protective plating and had gun turrets in the bows and amidships. At the foot of the former was a cooking-place 'where all day long the slave-girls were baking dhura-cakes for the soldiers and sailors'.[19]

The steamers went aground in turn on sandbanks but were refloated. On 27 January they refused to believe a passing camel-man who told them Khartoum was taken and Gordon slain. Next day on reaching the junction of the two Niles there was no flag flying over the stricken city and hundreds of dervishes resisted a landing. Sir Charles Wilson 'gave the order to turn and run full speed down the river'.[20]

Parke questioned the need for the delay asserting that if even one steamer had been sent to Khartoum on 21 January with a contingent of British sailors and soldiers, the Gordon Relief Expedition would have been successful. He added a plea on behalf of Mr Gladstone who was so regularly blamed for the expedition being 'too late' when in fact the advance force was within a short distance of the city five days before its fall.

He was paid £15 which he divided with Knott: 'I am awfully pleased with *The Nineteenth Century* article and I have not had a word from the Authorities but they know that I have lots of proof.' He urged Mrs Stanley to send the magazine to Gladstone with whom she was friendly and eventually he sent a copy himself to the 'Grand Old Man' and wrote, perhaps tactlessly, to the Prime Minister expressing indignation 'at the way in which the loss of General Gordon's life has always been connected with your name by your opponents'.[21] The acronym GOM was, indeed, sometimes used to signify 'Gordon's old murderer'.

Major C.M. Watson replied to Parke's article in *Broad Arrow*, a naval and military gazette, maintaining that Wilson was blameless: his mission was neither to relieve General Gordon nor to end the siege. 'The duty of Sir Charles Wilson was that of a staff officer carrying a message.' The main assault could not have taken place until early in March. 'Had the steamers started from Gubat three days earlier, Khartum would have fallen three days earlier. That would have been all the difference.'[22]

Watson described Parke's accusation as 'unfounded and unjust' but as his tone was civil, Parke felt it would make the authorities uncomfortable if he were to answer him. The anonymous reply published by the *Speaker* was very different. Parke described it as 'a sickening, irritating, ridiculous re-view'[23] and with Knott's aid he set about preparing a 'Rejoinder'. A little later he learned that the *Speaker's* diatribe was also from the pen of Watson who, incidentally, was Irish (b. Dublin 1844) and a friend of Wilson, whose biography, in the fullness of time, he was to write.

Under the cloak of anonymity which the *Speaker* allowed, Watson excoriated Parke for turning his present prominence to pecuniary advantage and questioned his competence to write on matters of military strategy. 'His views upon the management of field hospitals, or the medical equipment of a field force, would doubtless have been valuable and interesting. Why is he, therefore, permitted to assume the *rôle* of a military critic of the operations on the Nile?' He believed that Parke had not studied the reports — 'His mistakes as to simple matters of fact are childish.' The 'considerable loss of officers and men at Metammeh', for instance, had actually consisted of two wounded. The steamers were not intended to bring up a relief force. The mussecks' leakage was expected and helped to keep the water cool.

Having disposed of the doctor, Watson turned his guns on a more substantial target, Lord Wolseley (hero of the Canadian Red River episode), who chose the Nile route condemned by many rather than the shorter approach from the Red Sea and wasted time building whale boats. Watson referred bluntly to the commander-in-chief 'far away at Korti' and to 'the carefully edited official despatch', concluding his polemic with a coruscating peroration: 'If in 1870, fifty able-bodied policemen had been substituted for the military expedition despatched with much pomp and circumstance to vainly pursue Riel and his handful of wretched half-breeds, Gordon might indeed "have been alive today".'

Parke felt sure that without resorting to rudeness he could 'squash' Watson, who had not been at Metammeh and depended wholly on hearsay. He still believed that had a steamer been sent up-river on 21 January it would have saved Gordon and Khartoum. Wilson had excused his delay by the need to supply fuel and and a crew, and because he had to ensure the safety of the force at Gubat, but Parke insisted that there were enough bluejackets to man a vessel; fuel could have been provided in two hours and others could have looked after the main force. The journey from Shendy to Khartoum, usually completed in four days, took Wilson five days. And why start at 8 am rather than 4 am as planned?

Watson said there were only two casualties at Metammeh but Parke recalled that he had had quite a few amputations to perform. 'The boots I wore in Africa belonged to a man whose leg I amputated at Mettameh.' He also remembered cutting a bullet from underneath the tongue of a man who was back on duty in eight days.

Parke's (and Knott's) 'Rejoinder' was sent to *The Nineteenth Century* towards the end of June but in the absence of James Knowles a sub-editor returned it explaining that 'So far as *The Nineteenth Century* is concerned there has been no reply to Doctor Parke's article' and it would be inappropriate to follow up a discussion initiated elsewhere. Parke consoled himself in the belief 'that the article has proved itself, and it would be weak to rise a further discussion' unless someone else brought it up.[24]

The editor, on his return, disagreed with his assistant and wired to Parke asking him to hold the 'Rejoinder' until they had an opportunity to talk about it. A meeting was arranged but was postponed when Knowles was suddenly taken ill. Parke urged Prothero, the sub-editor, to publish the article without further delay but when he eventually discussed the matter with Knowles he learned that both Wilson and Watson had been in touch with him — 'he refused the article written by the latter as it did not touch the central fact, and the former refused to write anything but told him that the blame should have been put upon *other shoulders*.'[25]

Parke avoided naming 'the other party', who, possibly, was Lord Charles Beresford whom he admired and who had become a VIP, a close friend of the Prince of Wales, an MP (1885–9) and fourth naval lord of the admiralty. If Beresford really were to blame for the delay the accusation would raise a blaze of publicity attracting undesirable notoriety to the 'Rejoinder'. Beresford's rescue-feat on the Nile under fire was applauded in the House of Commons; Lord Wolseley's despatch recognized his readiness, resource and ability. He was decidedly not a man to cross and Parke denied himself the satisfaction of replying to Watson.

Major F.R. Wingate, whose book *Mahdiism and the Egyptian Sudan* (1891) Parke had read, cited the evidence of an impeccable enemy source saying that after the British success at Abu Klea, the Mahdi was about to raise the siege until the totally unexpected delay at Gubat encouraged him to press his attack.[26] Lord Cromer, author of *Modern Egypt*, stated many years later, that 'after a careful examination of the facts' he believed that had the steamers left on the afternoon of 21 January, Khartoum would probably have been saved.[27] 'Appendix D' in Bernard A. Allen's *Gordon in the Sudan* (1932) deals specifically with 'The Delay of Sir Charles Wilson on the Nile'.

Allen has pointed out that in the original wording of his report to the Commander-in-Chief, Wilson stated his intention of proceeding 'at once' to Khartoum, and looks for an influence that led him to change his immediate purpose. Having studied the documents, Allen came to the opinion 'that it was probably Lord Charles Beresford's influence which induced Sir Charles Wilson to delay the departure of the steamers'. Confined to hospital with a septic saddle sore which had developed into what he called 'a horrid carbuncle', Beresford did not wish to absent himself from the adventure and may have urged the two-days' reconnaissance in the expectation, that shortly he would be ready to command the vessels.[28]

Allen believed that Wilson, as senior military officer, must bear the blame 'for a delay which was fraught with such tragic consequences', but he felt that Beresford should have shared the obloquy, a conclusion perfectly in accord with a suspicion gained from Parke's letter written after his interview with the editor of *The Nineteenth Century* who had spoken with both Wilson and Watson.

*

Earlier in the year Parke had resumed his efforts to secure an opening in London for Knott and the latter came to *The Lancet's* office for interview. Subsequently Wakley told Parke that he 'had swarms of men to review' but

Parke urged him to give Knott a chance to show his mettle — 'I was able to tell him what I knew of your literary and scientific work and about your prizes and essays while you were a student and that you were referred to by some of the best in Ireland to coach them on nice points in connection with legal investigations etc.' The editor asked if Knott would come to London for a trial period and wondered if he would make 'a Confidential member of his personal staff'. Parke suspected that Wakley had been making enquiries in Dublin and he was questioned specifically about how well Knott got on with local colleagues. He urged his friend not to sell himself cheaply — 'for like all Editors I expect he is a screw'.[29]

To Parke's disappointment, Wakley failed to write to Knott who, meanwhile, had set his sights on a vacancy for the post of assistant physician to Sir Patrick Dun's Hospital, although suspecting that 'the job is settled'. (In the event, Dr A.J. Parsons was appointed and earned a little footnote in the history of Anglo-Irish literature as physician to John Millington Synge, the playwright.) Parke, too, was job hunting and mentioned a possibility that he would go to Africa before the end of June. He was 'Joe' Chamberlain's guest for a short visit and found him a cheery host with a hospitable home.

Parke's letter to Knott on 12 May is evidence of their straitened circumstances: 'I received the enclosed yesterday, and as I thought it might lead to trouble if I did not pay up I therefore sent off to the Hibernian Bank direct a cheque for £40 which Cancels the Bill when added to the £20 I sent you. I hope this is right.'[30] He had recently passed an examination for promotion which would come in the ordinary course in February 1893.

On the eve of his return to Africa in 1891, with the permission of the War Office, to work for the recently established Katanga Company, Stairs had paid a spontaneous tribute to Parke in *The Lancet*, feeling sure that the extent of the doctor's commitment to his duties had never been fully realized. He had gone on to describe how at Fort Bodo, in the throes of fever and worn to a shadow, Parke 'crept out of his hut unawares to Nelson and myself, reached the hut of a black chief, Khamis Pari, and lanced for him a very large and painful abscess, cleansed and dressed a wound, and was found by Nelson and myself in an absolutely helpless condition, and carried back by us to his hut.' The reaction set in next day and Stairs and Nelson believed he had only a few hours to live. 'He has never spoken to any of us, or to anyone that I know, a single word of this.'[31]

Stairs sailed to Zanzibar in a familiar ship, the *Madura*. He was not long at Bagamoyo before encountering reminders of the previous expedition: the first, Emin Pasha's daughter, little Ferida, was 'very self-possessed and wearing an English sailor hat at a becoming angle'; Charles Stokes ('Bwana Stokesi') the Irish caravan leader was in celebratory mood after a journey to the Albert Nyanza and 'appeared undecided between pugilism and affection'; finally, Stairs met Tippu Tib on the way to attend the legal action taken against him fruitlessly for breach of contract by Stanley whose word, the Arab averred, was not to be trusted — he could say 'Yes' today and 'No' tomorrow.[32]

Leading 500 men, Stairs headed north-west accompanied by Captain Oskar Bodson, the Belgian officer who had tried Barttelot's assassin at Stanley Falls, Mr Robinson, an ex-Grenadier Guard, and the Marquis de Bonchamps. The medical officer was Joseph Moloney.[33] *En route*, Stairs pointed out to Dr Moloney the spot where Parke shot two of the Wahéhé, a tribe of professional brigands. They passed quickly through Ugogo and Unyanyembe to Karema crossing Lake Tanganyika and continuing their march to Bunkeia, capital of Misiri, King of mineral-rich Katanga. The expedition's purpose was to get Misiri to accept the protection of the Katanga Company and to fly the blue flag of the Congo Free State.

They reached their destination on 14 December 1891. Within a few days the palavers commenced and despite Misiri's unwillingness to submit, Stairs insisted on hoisting the flag he now served. Misiri fled to Munema, a nearby village, and next day Stairs sent Captain Bodson to arrest him. Bodson shot Misiri dead in the ensuing fight and was himself fatally wounded, dying after some hours of agony, consoled in the conviction that he had rid Africa of a tyrant.

Stairs erected a fort at Bunkeia but when men began to sicken and die — there were seventy-five deaths in January — he may have been reminded of Fort Bodo. On the outward journey he had been prostrated by malaria and relapsed severely early in January. Robinson and de Bonchamps were also ill and the doctor, accustomed to the milder epidemics of south London, was distracted. 'As I went about the camp [he wrote], I could hear Captain Stairs raving in one hut, Robinson moaning in another; while the Marquis de Bonchamps tottered about incapable of anything except dismal prophecies of burial far from the pleasant plains of France.'[34]

Dr Moloney despaired of his leader's recovery but Stairs rallied in February and began to prepare for the return journey to the coast via Lake Nyasa and the Shiré River. By mid-May, having recovered his strength and cheerfulness, Stairs was increasingly keen to get back to England but with no intention of staying there. ('Upon him the Dark Continent had long laid her spell with an absolutely imperious influence.'[35]) He wrote to Parke on 19 May while steaming through Lake Nyasa on the SS *Domera* and in a postscript remarked: 'Have a dose of Typhomalia [*sic*]. Almost died, twelve days unconscious. Well again now.'[36] He experienced yet another set-back while on the river and died on 9 June at Chindé within sound of the Indian Ocean.

'Isn't it sad about poor Stairs?' remarked Parke. 'I feel down in the very depths of sorrow. He was really one of the best fellows ever lived.' By a curious irony Parke and Sir Charles Wilson had been appointed by Stairs as joint-executors of his will. Knott's aid was solicited in preparing a note on Stairs for the *Royal Engineers Journal*.

Six months later, Nelson was to die of dysentery in Kenya while serving with the British East Africa Company; Bonny died in poverty in the Fulham Workhouse in the early 1900s. Troup and Ward survived well into the twentieth century: the latter (b. London 1863) lectured in America under the auspices of the J.B. Pond Lyceum Bureau and married Sarita Sanford, a wealthy American girl (unrelated to the proprietor of the Sanford Expedition) in 1890; they lived in London and Paris where he was a successful painter and sculptor — his statues of Africans are in the Palais de Luxembourg and the Smithsonian Gallery. The couple's third son was named Roger Casement Ward; Herbert Ward served in the Red Cross and the British Ambulance Committee in the Great War and died in 1919.[37]

Parke believed that 'the GOM' would win the 1892 general election which would be 'a great misfortune for Ireland'.[38] He viewed Stanley's prospects as Liberal-Unionist candidate for North Lambeth optimistically and canvassed for him but Stanley did not yet know how to handle the electorate and failed to win the seat which he was to be elected to in 1895.

In view of *The Lancet*'s failure to show further interest in Knott, Parke suggested that his friend should seek an appointment with the rival concern, the *British Medical Journal*. He also mentioned that the death of Sir William Aitken had created a vacancy for an examiner of candidates for admission to the Army Medical Staff. 'You would make your application through the Director General AMS. to the Secretary of State for War, War Office, London. I believe the pay is a few hundreds a year.'[39] Alternatively, Knott should apply for the chair of pathology at Netley which was to be given to a civilian. 'It is worth £800 a year and there is really little to do.' The Foreign Office asked Parke to serve on a Delimitation Commission in East Africa; the Royal Society offered him £100 to collect plants and the War Office agreed that he could go but stipulated *unpaid* leave which did not suit his impecunious state.

Meeting Mackinnon he was informed of the sorry state of the British East Africa Company's finances:

Old Sir William Mackinnon, Chairman of the Imperial British East Africa Company, told me yesterday that he wants the Government to take over the BEA territory as the Company has spent nearly all their Capital and it is really a business which should be under the management of the Government and not a private Company, and now there are Forts built all over the territory and the Company ought to receive assistance from whatever Government gets in.[40]

Commiserating with Knott on his failure to get an attachment to Dun's Hospital or any of the medical journals, Parke prophesied that everything comes to the man who can wait. 'In my own Case [he wrote with commendable insight] I find that the great danger is the tendency to grow into a Grumbling irritable Condition over such contemptible trifles, but now I never worry myself over other people's meanness.'[41] He wished he knew of some position he could ask Gladstone to nominate him to so as to get out of Netley — 'it is all red tape and fuss over the most trivial items.'[42]

By mid-August he had sent the desired manuscript to the Royal Geographical Society but an article 'Reminiscences of Africa' was turned down by *Blackwood's Magazine*. This was published later by the *United Service Magazine* which paid him £7.10.0. 'A Plea for a Railway to the Victoria Nyanza', rejected by the redoubtable Frank Harris's *Fortnightly Review* was also accepted by the *United Service Magazine*.

He spent an interesting day in Southampton with General Gordon's sister, Augusta. He was shown over the house and she questioned him about the allegation in his book that her brother was an opium-eater. 'I explained that Emin told me so, but that Emin was not always reliable and that Gordon's good name and ability could not be injured as his Conduct was unassailable.' He advised her take no notice of the remark and she admitted she had wondered if Stanley influenced him against her brother. She showed Parke a number of private letters and all of Gordon's journals and gave him a bust of the General. 'He certainly was a splendid man although in some ways he appeared to have a slate off.'[43]

Being attracted now to the history of the Parke family, he asked his sister Harriet (Henrietta) to consult on his behalf a Miss Hamilton, living at Douglas, Cork, and reputed to be 'a very great authority on the Subject of Genealogy.' He promised to send Harriet a copy of the history when completed.

The first Parke I can find is Capt. Robt Parke of Sligo and Leitrim who was one of the jurors in an inquisition held in Sligo 24th Sept 1627 and was the owner of large estates by purchase... It is believed that the first Parke came from Kent and came over with Sir Frederick Hamilton of Manor Hamilton.

He had missed Harrie's wedding to George Stoker of Cork on 21 April

1885 but was able to attend his youngest sister Emily's wedding with Herbert Malley, a Dublin solicitor, at Kilmore Church on 7 September 1892.

He was troubled by lack of money as his conduct over a bill from a Dublin bookseller, Hodges Figgis and Co, for £24.15 shows. He explained to Knott: 'I have sent him £12 as it is all I have at present. Don't you think you could get them to take back the books as secondhand even if they only gave half price, considering all he has received up to now.' He had already paid him nearly £40, a large sum for a man of slender means. When making the part payment he instructed the bookseller that he would write in future if he wanted to add to his library, thus inadvertently casting suspicion on the easy arrangement whereby Knott had obtained books and charged them to Parke's account. When this was pointed out by his irate friend his immediate instinct was to write to the bookseller and explain, but he saw that this might only make things worse.

The matter appears to have been resolved satisfactorily and an invitation to read a paper 'at Leeds or Birmingham' on Great Britain's interest in Uganda prompted a further demand on Knott — 'I would require it in a week' — for a paper giving the white man's chances, climatic, commercial and political, to occupy about an hour. The material was available in Stanley's and Frederick Lugard's recent letters to *The Times*. 'Do you think you could supply me with such a paper?'[44] The soldiers, he recalled, had gone sick in great numbers when Egypt was occupied in 1882 but attention to sanitary matters had made a difference. 'The Mountains of the Moon which is in the British sphere would make a perfect sanitorium for Europeans to pick up.'[45] Domestic slavery was not so very terrible; the dreadful thing was the seizing of villages, ransomed by ivory, and, when this was collected, the people were recaptured to carry it to the coast.

Parke's railway 'Plea' was published by the *United Service Magazine* in November 1892 and followed by 'Reminiscences of Africa' in December running on into the January and February issues. In the first of these he is pictured slogging between the Victoria Nyanza and the coast 'without serviceable shoes, with very elementary clothing' in the company of other 'half-clothed pilgrims' all of whom would have appreciated a railway capable of transforming a wearisome three months' journey to a matter of a few pleasurable days' travel. The commercial advantages were obvious; more important still the opportunity to abolish the slave-trade. He (or Knott) continues in plain, strongly welded prose to describe the terrain between Mombasa and Lake Victoria.

A great part of the route is undoubtedly through peaceful agricultural districts. The gradual ascent soon lands the traveller in the healthy highlands of the interior. The pestilential swamps of the coast are avoided. The unmanageable ranges of the adjacent German territory are also happily discounted. It penetrates a region which has well been described by Mr Stanley as the 'pearl of Africa', and which has been made holy ground by the devoted labours of Mackay and his assistants. So far as the eye of an unprejudiced observer can penetrate, everything seems to be in its favour. It intersects some of the most important slave routes, and could easily be made to influence many of the others. It would certainly be the best means of conveying the blessings of peace and civilisation to the troubled homes of the inhabitants of Uganda.[46]

The numerous products of a bountiful area are listed — animal, vegetable and mineral — the elephants, the coffee, the timber ('teak and ironwood'), the orchilla weed, the copper and the gold. What opportunities for the rising generation! What a field for the missionary! In which context it was appropriate again to recall the late Alex Mackay.

The neighbourhood of the southern extremity of the Victoria Nyanza has been consecrated by the heroic and devoted labours of a missionary of whom the English nation may well be proud. In the midst of the horrors of a barbarous persecution, 'Mackay of Uganda' lived his saintly life, and succeeded in leavening the savage natures around him by the example of his own daily conduct. The brightness and simplicity of his home at Usambiro is not likely to be forgotten by the survivors of the Emin Pasha Relief Expedition. When we arrived at his station without purse or scrip, and with very little to gird about our loins, the cordial and unaffected benevolence of his reception was such as to cheer up the most despondent.[47]

The danger of attacks during the laying of the railway line struck Parke as exaggerated. They would be temporary involving a fraction of the route:

everybody who has had much personal experience in the interior of the Dark Continent will, I think, agree with me in saying that after two or three years of fair dealing and honourable intercourse with the natives, there will be little to fear from any organised attack on the British railway. They will soon appreciate kind treatment when they have received it for a time, and the easy introduction of some home-made trinkets and a well-aimed distribution of scarlet cloth will, I can confidently venture to promise, soon soften the hearts of the chiefs and subordinate leaders of any African tribes with which I have come into contact.[48]

Labour problems were not insurmountable. If local workers were refractory, Indian coolies or Chinese labourers could be imported — or slaves could be purchased from their native masters. 'I am not sure that it would not be an excellent preliminary to their future emancipation.'

The economics were eminently justifiable in so rich a territory as

Uganda. The growth of natural products would be greatly increased by
cultivation and the delay in providing the railway was a reproach to British
enterprise.

Opening up, as it would, a large productive district, the ensuing commercial intercourse between the natives and British traders would soon be sufficient to defray the
expenses of the railway thus constructed. British emigrants would soon settle and
thrive in the country; they would carry the example of industry and civilisation with
them, and the fullest facilities for the extinction of the slave-trade would rapidly
develop with the facility of transit.⁴⁹

Parke's arguments are likely to strike modern readers as specious but represented to his contemporaries the acceptable face of imperialism which was to
be seen in a truer form with the annexation of Uganda in 1894.

The 'Reminiscences' opens with a geographical and ethnographical introduction continuing with much that would have been familiar to readers of
My Experiences in Equatorial Africa. The average elevation of the surface above
sea-level accounts for the cold nights — 'many of the children of Emin
Pasha's Egyptians were frozen to death in the arms of their careless mothers
as we were laboriously trying to tow them along in our wake to the eastern
coast.' The high humidity caused heavy mists over the great African lakes —
'and are suggestive of an endless supply of the malarial poison'.

A mini-essay on the Nile is offered and 'the Father of waters' which flows
through a country of rock and sand is contrasted with the more voluminous
Congo whose banks are rich in vegetation. Several pages are devoted to
pygmies and to bows and arrows, subjects permitting a characteristic display
of Knott's remarkable erudition with endless instances collected from ancient and modern literature, from Pliny to Dean Swift, from Assyria to
Nottingham Forest.

Parke believed that cannibalism was gradually dying out from the coast
inwards, the natives increasingly ashamed of the habit, indulging in it fur-
tively on private occasions. Nevertheless, he had often been stared at 'by the
bright dark eyes of females of beautiful features' whose looks seemed to say
that their carnal pleasure would be to cook him and eat him.

The talents of the African as a bargain-maker received special attention —
'Their buying and selling is accompanied by almost endless haggling: the
proverbial methods of the cattle-dealer at a remote Irish fair are entirely
thrown into the shade, and the generous luck-penny is never mentioned.'
The tribal healer 'combines the functions of wizard, of prophet, of prime
minister and medical adviser'. His special skill is his ability to reveal to the
distressed relatives of an ailing person the identity of whoever has intro-

duced the devil into the invalid. 'A cruel death is then doled out to the unhappy culprit, and his goods are confiscated.'[50]

The failure of the Nile Expedition and the consequent despondency are briefly mentioned — 'Officers and men, the healthy and the sick, the whole and the maimed — everyone was affected by the depressing tidings that the object of all our exertions had eluded our grasp; the glory which would have resulted from the rescue of one of the most remarkable men of the age, and the happy consciousness that we had performed a noble duty, had been irretrievably lost to us.'

The matter of female wearing-apparel (or lack of it) dealt with in Part II is brought up again in Part III in a faintly titillating way, reminiscent of some of Knott's later articles.

All along this portion of the great river [Congo] it was curious to observe the gradual diminution of quantity of material which went to make up the toilet of the native belle. At the coast, and for a considerable distance beyond, the body and limbs were pretty well secluded from the traveller's gaze. Little by little the dress diminished in longitude, till at Upoto, which we reached on the 6th of June, 1887, it reached the zero point, and the native beauty appeared in all the freshness and, we will hope, all the innocence with which Eve was ushered into the Garden of Eden.[51]

The religious ideas of the Congo natives, Parke had found to be as scanty as the ladies' dress. 'As we penetrated the depths of the Dark Continent the number of idols, of fetishes, and of ceremonies diminished progressively. In the primeval forest the native African, so far as I could ever see, appears to worship or reverence nothing — either in the heavens above, or in the earth beneath, or in the waters under the earth.' Uncertain, too, about marriage customs he noted somewhat clumsily: 'I think their matrimonial arrangements are arranged for them and the daughter is sold by the lb, for they have little love or affection.'[52]

He went to London in November to meet Captain Lugard who had returned to England in October to give an account of his stewardship in Uganda where, equipped with a Maxim machine-gun (the actual gun used on the Emin Relief Expedition), he imposed a British protectorate, and backed by Islamic soldiers had stirred up the deep animosity — partly sectarian, partly national — existing between the Catholic (French) and the Protestant (British) missionaries. Parke must have been impressed by Lugard, a small, blue-eyed abrasive man of his own age, whose propensity to order floggings and drastic correctives is just a little reminiscent of Barttelot. They had many mutual acquaintances: Lord Salisbury (now replaced by Lord Rosebery) at the Foreign Office; Sir William Mackinnon and Sir Francis de

Winton, chairman and chief executive respectively in the British East African Company; Shukri Aga, a former lieutenant of Emin Pasha's, whose Soudanese soldiers had been enlisted by Lugard; Selim Bey whose men also augmented his force. Lugard was in a position to do a good turn to an old Africa hand and he recognized Parke's enthusiasm as a propagandist for the retention of Uganda by the British even though the Company's coffers were empty. He enlisted him as a speaker and communicated with him in this connection:

Yesterday [Parke informed Knott] I received a long letter from Lugard asking me to assist him by going to a few meetings. If I can get leave I would like to read a paper at one or two places. Everyone is very Ugandary just now.[53]

Actually, the political crisis was ending: Rosebery, an Imperialist in Liberal robes, had threatened to resign if he was not given his way. It was therefore decided to send an Imperial Commissioner to Africa but as that worthy, Sir Gerald Portal, was an ardent imperialist, it was already clear that Uganda was to remain British.[54]

As the year drew to its close Knott faced a law-suit when a student threatened to sue him for 'breach of contract' and Parke agreed, if necessary, to appear as a witness for the defence: 'You are the last man I know who would do a dishonourable act as far as my experience goes. I have also known very many pupils of yours and certainly have never heard a word of any breach of contract on your part.'[55] He was also concerned by the delay in getting the *Guide to Health* out — 'I have raised money with a view to paying it back with what I may receive for the book.'[56]

Notes

1 Letters, RCSI, 23 November 1891.
2 Letters, 1 December.
3 Thos. Heazle Parke, 'The Ulcer of the Emin Pasha Relief Expedition', *The Lancet*, 1891; 2: 1270.
4 Thos. Heazle Parke, 'Note on African Fever', ibid, 1892; 1: 1177.
5 Ibid, 1177.
6 Letters, 2 Dec. James Knowles/THP.
7 Letters, 14 Dec.
8 Letters, 22 January 1892.
9 *Nature*, 1892; 45: 265–8.
10 Letters, 5 March.
11 *Brititish Medical Journal* 1892; 1: 737.
12 Ibid, 1892; 1: 674.
13 Ibid, 1892; 1: 737.
14 Knott's major article on Shakespeare and medicine was published later in the *Westminister Review*, 1903; 159: 436–44.

15 Thos. Heazle Parke, 'How General Gordon Was Really Lost', *Nineteenth Century*, 1892; 31: 789–94.
16 Letters, 18 April.
17 Letters, 27 March 1892.
18 Sir Charles Wilson, *From Korti to Khartum* (Edinburgh 1886), p. 127.
19 Wilson, *op. cit.*, p. 132.
20 Ibid, p. 174.
21 British Museum Additional Manuscript, 44514, 6.294.
22 C.M. Watson, *Broad Arrow*, 1892, p. 715.
23 Letters, 11 June.
24 Letters, 29 June.
25 Letters, 8 August.
26 F.R. Wingate, *Mahdiism and the Egyptian Sudan* (London 1891), p. 192.
27 Earl of Cromer, *Modern Egypt* (London 1908), Vol II, p. 8 fn.
28 Allen, *Gordon*, Appendix D.
29 Letters, 11 June. Thomas Henry Wakley, FRCS (1821–1907), eldest son of Thomas Wakley (1795–1862) founder of *The Lancet*, co-edited the journal with his own son, Thomas.
30 Letters, 12 May.
31 W.G. Stairs, *The Lancet*, 1891; 2: 1176.
32 Joseph A. Moloney, *With Captain Stairs in Katanga* (London 1893), pp. 28–35.
33 An Irish graduate, Joseph Augustus Moloney, LQKCPI (1886), practised at 7 Beresford Street, Walworth, London, SE. His travels up to this engagement consisted of a sporting trip to Morocco. He appears to have been conquered by the spell of Africa but his name disappears from the medical register after 1896 which may indicate his demise in that year.
34 Moloney, *op. cit.*, p. 213.
35 Ibid, p. 273.
36 *Jephson's Diary*, p. 416.
37 The Wards' eldest son, a captain in the Grenadier Guards, was killed at Neuvelle Chapelle in 1916; their second boy joined the Royal Flying Corps from Eton and was shot down, wounded and taken prisoner. The charges of treason against Roger Casement sundered a long friendship. Ward authenticated the so-called 'Black Diaries'; he changed his youngest son's name by deed-poll, declined to sign Sir Arthur Conan-Doyle's petition for clemency and refused to send a farewell message to Pentonville Prison.
      Awaiting his execution, Casement remembered the halcyon days along the river when his friendship with Ward was strong and warm and they were lugging with them the crankshaft of the *Florida* and avoiding the red ants. 'Oh! so long ago (February-March 1887 it was) and Africa has since been "opened up" (as if it were an oyster) and the Civilizers are now busy with hatred against me because I think their work is organized murder, far worse than anything the savages did before them' (Reid, *Lives of Casement*, p. 437).
38 Letters, 8 July.
39 Letters, 1 July.
40 Letters, 1 July.
41 Letters, 23 July.
42 Letters, 13 August.
43 Letters, 13 Aug.
44 Letters, 14 November.

45 Letters, 17 Nov.
46 T.H. Parke, 'A Plea for a Railway to the Victoria Nyanza', *United Service Magazine*, 1992; November: 204.
47 Ibid, p. 207.
48 Ibid, p. 210.
49 Ibid, p. 204.
50 Ibid; December: 333.
51 Ibid; 1893; February: 455.
52 *Diary*, Vol. 4.
53 Letters, 13 Nov.
54 Pakenham, *Scramble*, p. 433.
55 Letters, 18 December.
56 Letters, 7 Nov.

19   The Victorian Hero

Parke spent the Christmas season at Torquay where he stayed from 21 to 27 December and on 2 January 1893 he accounted to Knott for their meagre earnings. He had received £8 from an American magazine for an article on the African railway; £7.10 for 'Reminiscences of Africa'; £15.10 for two other articles — '£31 in all half of which is yours', but as Knott had agreed to share their expenses for books (£24.15) Parke deducted £12 'which leaves £3.10 to come to you up to date, will you tell me if this agrees with your calculation.'[1]

Sadly he could not get to Drumsna on 9 January 1893 for his father's funeral. William Parke of Clogher House died in his sleep on 6 January in his 75th year having appeared perfectly well on the previous evening.[2] The deceased parent's life was insured for £4000 but there were outstanding liabilities and it was feared that there would have to be a sale of property. Parke's mother's mental state, too, was in some doubt and writing to Knott on 13 February he mentioned his worries in this regard — 'the letters from home this morning describe her Condition as most dangerous to herself and all at home. No servant will remain in the house. If you know of any place for the treatment of such a Case please let me know.'[3]

His promotion on 5 February to the rank of Surgeon-Major obliged him to get a new kit, a costly business for a man who was chronically overdrawn.[4] An article based on his speech on Uganda was rejected by the *Fortnightly Review* and other journals but the unused pieces prepared for the Masonic bazaar appeared in an American magazine. He met Gladstone again at luncheon in Sir James Paget's and was introduced to Rudolf Virchow, a celebrated German pathologist and politician.

Marston paid an advance of £15 for the little book for African travellers ('which is not very promising', Parke remarked) and when the proofs arrived the author decided on 'Guide to Health in Africa with Notes on Country and Inhabitants' as a title. He also corrected his 'Hints for Health' for the Geographical Society's book and was asked to add some information for travellers on the treatment of horses and camels and to say how a poultice is made.

The question, as usual, was referred to his knowledgable friend hoping for a reply by return post. When for once Knott failed to oblige Parke told the Geographical Society that he could not undertake veterinary work.

He agreed with Knott, on second thoughts, that to add a list of Burroughs & Wellcome's tabloids would look too much like an advertisement. 'I should not think B & Wellcome have the smallest idea of ordering a single copy.'[5] Instructions for embalming should be given — 'I remember no one knew how to embalm the Prince Imperial.'[6]

Parke kept the proofs of the *Guide to Health* to pass on to Stanley who wrote a preface for it. Then while Marston was demanding an immediate return of the proofs, Parke was pressing Knott to write additional notes on Guinea-worm, embalming, disinfecting, transport, scurvy and haematuric fever. Next, Knott was laid up with bronchitis and naturally this explanation for the delay could not be given to the impatient publisher.

Writing as 'an old comrade' who had seen Parke's expertise, Stanley praised the text for its clarity and comprehensiveness: 'I am something of a "doctor" myself in regard to fevers and intestinal complaints — at least, I ought to be by this — and I feel assured that the advice herein given in regard to them is particularly wise and sound.'

When I think of the nine hundred and fifty Europeans at present in Congolese Africa, and the eight hundred whites in Nyassaland, German and British East and Central Africa, and of the army of pioneers advancing from the Cape towards the Zambezi, I wonder how many of them know how to distinguish between simple quotidian and the pernicious remittent fever, or between diarrhoea and dysentery, or bronchitis and pleurisy; how to ward off an attack of ague nine times out of ten; when to take quinine, and what quantity would be exactly sufficient to arrest a remittent during its treacherous remission. These are the 'little tricks' or tips which unfortunately, so few have survived to acquire experience of, so many have become discouraged and returned home, after only a brief stay, while others have lingered under the influence of the first attack, with liver, kidneys, and intestines terribly disordered, for want of the requisite knowledge.[7]

He regretted that Parke 'remained to this day so little appreciated by the Government he serves, and the Service which he adorns, as not to have received one word of thanks, or decoration or acknowledgement from either of them'.[8]

In mid-March Parke and Knott's precarious financial condition is again illustrated by the former's letter:

Your letter asking me to renew the Bill for the £60 has been delayed as I left Netley early on Monday morning ...

I have signed the renewal, although I have many times made a resolution never to sign a bill. My present finances are not in a flourishing condition. I gave my banker £100 and with this bill I shall be responsible for a little over £100 as I have had to assist a relative in the same way also, but I know it is all right.

Please send me the proofs with remarks on the other subjects I wrote to you about... There seems to be a regular panic over Home Rule in Ireland.[9]

This transaction had a curious aftermath and Parke described to Knott how 'a rather burly individual' brought him the Bill a few days later but he just wrote on a piece of paper and handed it to the presumed bailiff: 'As this has been settled in Dublin, I respectfully decline to pay.'[10]

By now Parke appears to have come to rely completely on his friend for even the slightest literary chore. When *The Lancet* asked him to review Mrs M. French-Sheldon's *Sultan to Sultan* (1893) he posted it off to Dublin — 'Send the book back when you finish it and don't mark it in any way. Give her a good review as it was a very plucky trip for her and she does it well. Besides she speaks well of me.'[11] The review of the lady doctor's book appeared in *The Lancet* on 29 April, praising *Bébé Bwana*, 'the heroine of East African exploration', mentioning that Parke and Stairs had supplied hints and directions.[12]

Politically a Unionist, Parke accepted that some concessions should be made to Ireland but he did not see that the people would benefit from the Home Rule Bill — 'they are *better* off as they are, if only the law was more strict and not so partial to the Land league teaching.'[13] He feared that the landowners would be reduced to a miserable condition. Marston sent the *Guide to Health* off to the printers saying that any further corrections must be held over until a second edition was needed. Parke had wished to add a few lines on the management of toothache and the extraction of teeth, always a problem for travellers.

Copies of the *Guide to Health* were available by mid-June and Parke posted one to Knott in York Street followed by what seems to have been his last letter to his friend; ironically it concluded with the remark, 'I suppose you'll tear up the old Bill'.[14] Stanley's preface was followed by chapters dealing with the geography, climate and meteorology of Africa, its natives, flora and fauna, the diseases likely to give trouble to travellers and rules for the preservation of health in the tropics. The wide range of quadrupeds is described in some detail, the hippopotamus and the enraged buffalo the most dangerous animals on the rivers and the plains respectively. The Tsetse-fly is recognized as a deadly menace to oxen, horses, camels, sheep and dogs. Locusts harm crops but Stanley's officers were glad to make a meal of them, 'after a slight toasting at the forest fire'.[15]

The early chapters owed much to reference works including books by Henry Drummond and Stanley. The latter supplied a description of the great forest. 'Imagine the whole of France and the Iberian peninsula closely packed with trees varying from twenty to 180 feet high, whose crowns of foliage intertwine and prevent any view of sky and sun, and each tree from a few inches to four feet in diameter.'[16] Parke who was at Dongola when the temperature registered 119° F in the shade used Drummond's account of the effect of the sun on those already down with fever. 'Then, indeed, the heat becomes maddening and insupportable; nor has the victim words to express his feelings towards the glittering ball, whose sailing march across the burnished and veilless zenith brings him untold agony.'[17] But, paradoxically, Parke claimed to have seen more cases of 'sunstroke' under a cloudless sky at Aldershot during the summer of 1881 than in Africa.[18]

Avoiding rigid anthropological schemes, the *Guide* confined its observations to Hottentots — 'lowest in the entire grade of human beings' — and Kafirs. It offered broad generalizations, propagandist and prejudiced rather than scientific: 'The mental characteristics of the negro are those of the primitive child. He is characterised by receptivity and spontaneity; yields immediately to all impulses; passes easily from foolish mirth to gloomy despair, and alternates continuously between fantastic hope and shrinking fear, the silliest prodigality and the shabbiest avarice.'

The legitimacy of British interest in establishing Africa's future industries is not questioned here or elsewhere in Parke's (and Knott's) writings. The *Guide to Health* assumes the appropriateness of England's interest in the unexploited mineral and vegetable wealth. The 'vast stores of unused water-power' validated a study of the continent's physical and meterological characters by the rising generation of Britons. Unlike Jephson whose sense of equity was disturbed by the behaviour of the European overlords, Parke accepted the apparently self-justifying benefits of colonial rule, despite the oppressive paternalism. Jephson had written to *The Times* to draw attention to a tendency 'to forget to speak of our faithful Zanzibaris, who were, at least, one of the most important factors in the success of the expedition.' He pointed out that when dwelling on the loss of *two* valuable European lives, it would certainly be proper to mention the hundreds of Zanzibari lives that were lost 'to say nothing of the many natives killed necessarily' while fighting their way through the hostile tribes that opposed them.

I have noticed, too, in this 'scramble for Africa' [Jephson continued] that European interests are always brought forward, whilst those of the natives, the lawful possessors of the country, are scarcely ever mentioned. It seems to me that the French saying, 'Quand on veut dessécher un marais on ne consulte pas les grenouilles' is the key-note of most European colonization in Africa.[19]

To which observation *The Times* leader-writer replied: 'Mr Jephson seems to presume a degree of native ownership of Africa by its negro population which is incompatible with the claims on the continent of any European State or society... In practice it is futile to assert for the negro a positive amount of sovereignty which would keep out white colonists. The soil, too, itself has rights ...'[20]

Dr Parke's 'modest but serviceable little hygienic handbook' was among *The Times*' 'Books of the Week' on 23 June following a brief notice of Moloney's *With Captain Stairs to Katanga*. Prompted by Stanley's preface, the reviewer remarked that the failure to reward the author's outstanding devotion was 'one of the anomalies, not to say scandals, of the public service'.[21]

As the new book offered an opportunity to ventilate the old obsession, Parke called on Ernest Hart and finding the editor of the *British Medical Journal* away, he wrote to his deputy:

If you intend to review my last book 'Guide to Health in Africa' etc etc I would like to explain the last paragraph of the preface written by Mr Stanley as none of the reviews so far has stated the central fact upon which the interest rests, viz that Lieut Stairs, *Royal Engineers,* and myself are the only army officers who crossed Africa with Mr Stanley on the Emin Pasha Relief Expedition 1887–89 — on our return to England, Stairs was promoted to be a Captain for his duty with the Expedition and also recd. a letter of thanks from the War Office.

Up to this I have recd. nothing whatever, not even thanks — ranked as a Captain.[22]

His service was longer than Stairs' and included the Egyptian campaign, the cholera epidemic and the Nile Expedition, 'He was an *Engineer* I was a *Doctor*. He gets promoted. I have not been recognized.' The slight was not merely to Parke as an individual but affected the Army Medical Staff generally.

Obligingly, the *British Medical Journal* pointed out that Parke's services had received no official recognition.

It may be gathered even from parts of the text that Dr Parke's path since his return has not been altogether free from official thorns, which may have recalled the physical pains of the underwood of the forest of Darkest Africa. But the same reticence and modest devotion to duty which he showed in the Dark Continent should stand him in good stead in threading the obscure labyrinth of British official-dom.[23]

It disagreed with his use of oil of male fern as a vermifuge in Egyptian chlorosis, for thymol was more effective; it drew attention to an error confusing bilharzia haematobia with filaria sanguinis.

The Lancet, without demur, accepted chill as the most fruitful cause of the development of African fever; it mentioned Sir Anthony Home's opposing view, after the Ashanti expedition, as to the value of quinine in prophylaxis; it offered hot tea as helpful for the cold stage of ague — 'but it must be as hot as can be borne.'[24] This reviewer, too, agreed with Stanley's comments. Decorations and awards, admittedly, were usually reserved for services rendered to the State but Surgeon-Major Parke's services were of an exceptional nature and there should be 'some distinction which could be given to such a man.'

Neither of the medical journal's reviewers scolded the little book's author for not explaining on the basis of the germ-theory how infections are actually caused. The praiseworthy intention of avoiding technicalities hardly excused his not revealing that typhoid (enteric) fever is caused by 'the Bacillus typhosus' of Eberth. The omission is surprising. Not only was Brigade-Surgeon Gore, Knott's superior officer, something of an authority on the disease but Knott had actually reviewed Dr (later Sir) John William Moore's *Text-Book of the Eruptive Fevers* (1892) in the columns of the *Medical Press and Circular*. Knott's review, it must be conceded, appears to have been more concerned with the pronunciation of the term 'angina' than with the scientific validity of an important treatise. John Knott's mind was more at ease in the past than on the frontiers of medical science and an element of mischief sometimes directed his pen, as in his suggestion that the polyglot author, John William Moore, 'was probably inspired by the Muse of Fever on the day of Pentecost'.[25]

★

Parke wrote a cheerful letter to Jephson on 7 August and asked 'when shall I see you again?' On leave in early September he stayed with Mrs Church Dixon at Oban until Thursday 7th when he moved south to visit the Duke and Duchess of St Albans whose yacht was lying at Ardrishaig, where they rented a house for their guests. The Duchess found him 'as bright and charming as he always is' when he came aboard, and after dinner at the guest house they attended Captain and Mrs Campbell's housewarming dance at which Parke was received as a celebrity.[26]

He took luncheon on the yacht next day, walked with the Duchess in the afternoon and that night there was another dance in the neighbourhood. The yacht steamed to Gourock on Saturday to pick up the Duke who had been in London, and on its return on Sunday morning Parke was at the landing attired in a dark blue yachting suit and yachting cap, ready to escort the Duchess and two of her children to church.

The day was lovely and they drove two and a half miles in a pony carriage arriving early and admiring the flowers and lime trees in the churchyard before service. The service had started about twenty minutes when Parke left the church abruptly. The Duchess heard some people running out after him so she followed and a neighbour said he had been taken by a seizure and was unconscious. He had been moved to a nearby house and two doctors were attending to him.

The Duchess went back to the church and after the service the groom said Dr Parke had recovered and was walking on towards the yacht. 'I followed', the Duchess told Stanley later, 'and to my intense pleasure found him a good way ahead on the road, with Dr Hunter, quite calm and collected.'

Parke felt irked by the experience and dawdled in the garden with Dr Hunter who subsequently advised the Duchess that the main precaution was to see that he did not tire himself. He was due to leave Ardrishaig on the Monday but to ensure that he rested the Duchess planned a yacht trip to Inverary and he agreed to stay until Tuesday. 'All Sunday afternoon', the Duchess told Stanley, 'we sat about in the garden by the loch and I felt so happy to see him so well.'

The guests, including a Dr Parsons, came aboard for dinner at 7.15 pm and Parke displayed no untoward symptoms other than that the fingers of his left hand looked bloodless and white. He displayed this (Raynaud's phenomenon) to the Duchess and Dr Parsons, saying that he had been subject to it since his return from Africa. 'He seemed quiet but in good spirits … and before he left I told him I hoped he and the House people who were coming to Inverary would be on board by 10 am.'

A cloudless morning dawned. The Duchess was looking forward to a pleasant outing, but her husband called out and placed a note from Dr Parsons in her hand. 'Dr Parke is most dangerously ill —', he said. He then added 'All is over!' Dr Parsons' note said Parke had been found dead when the servant went to call him.

The Duchess telegraphed the Parkes and the Stanleys before going to the guest house. 'I went upstairs', she told Stanley, 'to see his dear remains and there he lay on his bed dressed, with the exception of his coat and waistcoat and he was on one side the face terribly discolored, blood vessels, evidently having broken in the brain.' The footman had found him like that and Dr Parsons said 'he must have been dead hours and hours, probably immediately after he had gone to his room'. The Duchess asked the doctor to cut her a little of Parke's hair to give to those who loved him and when a neighbour brought flowers she put passion flowers round his head and myrtle near his hand. 'A purer angelic nature never lived', the Duchess assured Henrietta Parke in a letter of sympathy.[27]

The facial discolouration if unilateral may have been merely the post-mortem staining of dependent skin, or a convulsive seizure may have preceded death. J. Charles Shee has suggested that Parke had cysticercosis due to infestation with the pork tapeworm which had afflicted many members of the expedition.[28] It is said, however, that a postmortem examination revealed heart failure as the cause of death, but the extent of the autopsy is unclear.

Mrs Henrietta Parke, with her daughter, was visiting the Rev. Dr Clarke at Boyle Rectory when she received the dreadful news of her son's death. Bill Parke went at once to Scotland and accompanied the remains which were taken by steamer from Ardrishaig to Greenock and conveyed in the Laird Line's SS *Shamrock* to Dublin, where Benjamin Parke met the ship on its arrival at the North Wall at 10 am on Friday.

Surgeon-Major Parke was accorded military honours as his funeral passed through the city. By 2 pm when traffic was stopped on the quay a large crowd had assembled opposite the ship. There were many doctors present and most of the Army Medical Corps' officers. The Lord Mayor sent his official carriage and was represented by A.B. Shanks, his private secretary. The ships in the harbour lowered their flags as the coffin was brought ashore by men of the Army Medical Corps and fastened to a gun-carriage. This was preceded by 200 white-helmeted men of the Royal Sussex Regiment arrayed in scarlet — those symbolic coats, the search for which had delayed the departure of Sir Charles Wilson's Nile steamers in January 1885 — and accompanied by a band and drums.[29]

The military escort led the cortege along cobbled quays and through north city streets to the Broadstone Railway Station where the band sounded a formal farewell. At many stations along the line to the west groups had assembled to pay tribute to Parke, hoping, too, to see Stanley who, being in Ireland at the time, was expected at the funeral but did not actually attend. He wired to Mrs Parke from Ballywalter: 'Deeply regret cannot reach Drumsna in time today. Learned of it too late.'[30]

Relays of local men carried the coffin on their shoulders from Drumsna Station to Kilmore, a mile or so away, where the bereaved mother and sisters waited at Clogher House. Next day, after the wake, the coffin was placed in a hearse at 1.30 pm and they set off for Kilmore Church where the funeral service was conducted by the Rev. James Carey whose eulogy, with pardonable hyperbole, referred to 'the amazing variety of intellect' displayed by the deceased in the pursuit of scientific research and the alleviation of human suffering.

Proceeding to Drumsna, the hearse stopped near a tiny plot of ground in the interior of an old Presbyterian place of worship long considered unfit for religious services and used for burial by certain families — measuring seven yards by eighteen yards it is said to be Ireland's smallest cemetery. Local tenants carried the coffin to the graveyard gate and it was taken to the graveside by members of Masonic Lodge 651 to which the deceased had belonged. Several Masons in the regalia of their order were among the very large attendance which recalls W.B. Yeats's later memory of a Pollexfen funeral; 'And Masons drove from miles away / To scatter the Acacia spray'.[31] The Rev. Dr Clarke spoke suitably of Parke's career and achievements in Egypt and Africa referring to him as 'the holder of great dignity and great powers' — 'Roscommon today mourns his loss and England and the United Kingdom joins us in mourning.' The wreaths included those from the Duchess of St Albans; Dr Michael Cox ('With profound sympathy and distress'); Stanley Parke Stoker, nephew and godson and many others.[32]

*

Parke had an exceptionally attractive personality. His childhood neighbour, Dr Michael Cox, and his fellow-student, tutor and co-author, John Knott, hastened to honour him. Emin Pasha's first word on regaining consciousness after his fall was 'Parke'. Herbert Ward met him once and years later still remembered 'the resistless Irish cheerfulness that was his right by birth'.[33] Stanley came to regard Parke as possessing a heart 'of pure gold' and the best-fitted of his officers for African travel. Having seen him flounder in the forest yet perform a difficult operation in a hut in a clearing, the great explorer (not always totally reliable in his writings) captured the essence of his subordinate's character in an unmatched passage vibrant with truth.

With his unsophisticated simplicity, and amusing *naïveté*, it was impossible to bear a grudge against him. Outside of his profession, he was not so experienced as Stairs. When placed in charge of a company, his muster-book soon fell into confusion; but by erasures and re-arrangements it was evident that he did his best. Such men may blunder over and over again and receive absolution. He possessed a fund of genuine wit and humour; and the innocent pleasure he showed when he brought smiles to our faces, endeared him to me. This childlike *naïveté*, which distinguished him in Africa, as in London society, had a great deal to do with the affectionateness with which everyone regarded him. But he was super-excellent among the sick and suffering; then his every action became precise, firm, and masterful. There was no shade of doubt on his face, not a quiver of his nerves; his eyes grew luminous with his concentrated mind.[34]

His unique contribution to the expedition was the medical care bestowed unstintingly on slave and freeman alike. Even though he lacked specific remedies he probably did save Stanley's life. Jephson, tortured by fever, he secured from the ravages of despair. Stairs's death he prevented by sucking the arrow-poison into his own mouth. Nelson, dying from inanition, was drawn back slowly from the brink. Could the sick and wounded Zanzibaris have expressed their feelings they would have said Bwana Doctari 'was not a man but an angel'.[35]

Writing to *The Lancet* on 29 December 1831, William O'Shaughnessy (b. Limerick, 1809) drew attention to dehydration, salt depletion and acidosis as features of cholera, then epidemic in the United Kingdom, and pointed to the value of saline given intravenously.[36] Interest in this remedy lapsed when the epidemic was over. Not until the 1870s was intravenous saline reintroduced and it had not yet become a standard remedy when Parke tried it with partial success in the Cairo epidemic. His willingness to perform an autopsy under primitive conditions at Fort Bodo confirms the degree of his interest in medicine.

Fever and tropical ulcers, the major clinical problems which confronted him, were documented with Knott's aid in *The Lancet* and it is clear that Parke was resourceful in his attempts to heal the obstinate ulcers. His comments on *bhang* may indicate that he was unaware that Dr O'Shaughnessy, while working in India in the 1840s, had introduced cannabis to Western medicine.[37] On returning to England, Parke checked, as we have seen, the recent research in malaria but does not seem to have realized the importance of Laveran's *plasmodia* 'which he has found in the blood of malarial patients — sometimes free in the plasma, and sometimes enclosed in the red corpuscles'.[38] His favourite medicines were aperients and he did not fail to resort to Africa's classic remedy, the 'Livingstone rouser' — a pill containing rhubarb, jalap, calomel and quinine. Tape-worm infestation affected both Europeans and Africans. Parke attributed it to drinking water contaminated by antelopes but Shee blames eating the undercooked flesh of wild pigs.[39]

He had some interest in anthropology and joined Emin Pasha in measuring the pygmies at Kavalli's. They averaged 4 ft $3^2/_5$ inches and the length of their feet $8^1/_{10}$ inches. He made no comment of the disproportionately long feet, a characteristic, Shee points out, of mountain pygmies.[40] He surprised himself on 8 May 1888 by giving Emin's people a display of 'thought-reading' and an ability to detect hidden objects. 'I caused extraordinary excitement by finding an axe which Hawish Effendi ... had buried in the sand on the lake shore... This performance was looked upon as quite supernatural.' He does not attempt to explain this isolated visitation of extra-sensory perception.[41]

The priority of his sighting (with Jephson) of Ruwenzori went unrecorded by *In Darkest Africa* and the *Dictionary of National Biography*. Stanley has been accused of having 'robbed' Parke of this discovery, a charge not without substance, but the offence is mitigated by the acceptance that Stanley identified Parke's 'Snow Mountain' and named it Ruwenzori, the fabled *Lunae Montes,* and that Stairs was the first European to attempt an ascent. However incensed Parke may have been by the lack of recognition from the army authorities he never got hot under the collar over Ruwenzori which should really be seen as a corporate discovery — Parke and Jephson spotted it, Stanley identified it, Stairs stood on its slopes and later he wrote it was 'left to us to discover ... the snow-capped peaks of the "Mountains of the Moon".' It must be accepted, too, that Parke's description of 'snow on the top of a high mountain' was rather tentative when compared with Stanley's fuller representation[42] of the 'cloud-king' with its important function as a source of the Nile.[43]

Parke was almost exceptional among the members of the expedition in being obliged to return to a daily routine in England; most of the others managed to 'escape'. Stairs and Nelson, as we have seen, returned to Africa and to their deaths. Stanley lectured in America and Australia. William Hoffmann, after a spell in East Africa, went back to the Congo as an interpreter. Jephson lectured in California; later when asked by Moberly Bell, editor of *The Times*, to retrace the steps of Mungo Park he was obliged to turn down the assignment for health reasons.[44]

The conviction of his 'neglect' was a distinct chip on Parke's shoulder. The obsession is not easy to understand and may have been aggravated when Stanley and others continued to give it credence. It is difficult to see how he could have been honoured. Did he merely covet early promotion with its increased emoluments or was he a victim of the jealousy that abounds within the medical profession? A Parke family tradition holds that he was engaged to one of the Duke of St Albans' daughters, an unlikely alliance for an impoverished army doctor, and besides the girls were still teenagers. Furthermore, he appears to have spent more time in the company of the Duchess, an Osborne from County Tipperary, than in that of her daughters.

Count von Moltke said the men who crossed the Bayuda Desert and back were 'not soldiers but heroes'.[45] Parke had compounded his heroism in the Congo and the climate of his times demanded instant tokens of affirmation. His apotheosis is more understandable if one glances at the Irish cultural and political situation in 1893: it was a time of minor literary figures and rabid politicians. There was no Goldsmith, no Davis, no Moore; W.B. Yeats's verses were not yet stirring the national consciousness. Parnell had died in disgrace and Tim Healy, his most vociferous detractor, was horsewhipped outside the Law Library of the Four Courts for saying his widow was 'a proved British prostitute.'[46] An unhealthy decadence pervaded the fine arts of the *fin de siècle* decade and a man of action offered a highly acceptable alternative as a national hero.

Parke was the first Irishman to cross Africa. Many of his race had travelled more extensively and more fruitfully: Sir Francis Beaufort (1744–1857), for instance, gave his name to the scale of wind velocities; James Kingston Tuckey (1776–1816) was the author of *Narrative of an Expedition to Explore the River Zaire;* Sir Edward Sabine (1788–1883) was astronomer to Arctic expeditions; Francis Chesney (1789–1872) confirmed that a canal at Suez was a practicable proposition and published *Expedition for the Survey of the Euphrates and Tigris*. These worthies deserve to be better remembered in Irish annals, but evidently at a particular moment each lacked the support of an dedicated cadre determined on their elevation.

Many of Parke's supporters came from within the medical profession. The friend of his boyhood and former neighbour, Dr Michael Cox,[47] physician to St Vincent's Hospital, Dublin, was the first individual to articulate the need for a memorial, followed hotly by another Roscommon friend (and secret co-writer), Dr John Knott. Cox's open letter to *The Irish Times* expressed the hope that a call for a suitable memorial of Parke in the previous day's leader would be acted upon without delay.[48] 'His name is one to be remembered with pride and with affection, and his fame not unworthy of him who died at Zutphen.'

Knott's prolix reply accepted that a public memorial should be provided: 'But my accomplished friend Dr Cox is far too well read in the by-paths of history and fiction not to know that the story of self-sacrifice displayed by the hero of Zutphen in his dying hour was anticipated by Lucan's account of the passage of Cato across the Libyan desert'.[49] R.A. Duke of New Park, Ballymote, County Sligo, recommended a memorial in St Patrick's Cathedral.[50] The rector of Cloughjordan (previously of Carrick-on-Shannon) pointed out that a practical way to show appreciation of Parke, and help his family, was to buy his *Guide to Health in Africa*.[51]

A meeting held on 9 October at the Shelbourne Hotel, Dublin, presided over by Mr Edward Hamilton, president of the Royal College of Surgeons in Ireland, appointed ('independently of creed, class, profession or politics') the committee of the Parke Memorial Fund; its honorary secretaries were Herbert Malley, Parke's brother-in-law, and Dr Michael Cox. H.M. Stanley sent a cheque for £50; many smaller sums were given immediately and other donations were promised.

The form the memorial should take was discussed briefly. Surgeon-General William Collis favoured a statue in Dublin but to enable the Parke family and the committee to discuss the matter fully the question was left open.[52] Eventually Percy Wood, an artist of whom little is known, was commissioned to execute a full-length statue in bronze.[53] The work, judged to be of high quality, was completed in 1896 and unveiled on Leinster Lawn by Lord Roberts of Kandahar, the 'Bobs' of Kipling's verse, on Saturday 19 December.

Accompanied by his staff and an escort of jingling hussars, Lord Roberts rode to Merrion Street where a military band played martial airs and a section of Leinster Lawn was enclosed for the occasion. The awnings provided to give shelter were not needed the day remaining dry, the sun shining from a cold blue sky. The ceremony commenced at 2.30 pm with Surgeon-Major General Preston presiding. After Herbert Malley had dealt with the correspondence, Mr Wheeler, FRCSI, spoke on Parke's early years in medicine and 'Bobs' delivered an address on Parke's military career. He had not known Parke personally but was glad to honour a fellow-countryman.

The statue represented Parke, rifle in hand, dressed as he was in the Congo, standing in a very natural pose. On the pedestal another piece of bronze carving represents Parke sucking poison from his comrade's wound. The rope Lord Roberts used for the unveiling had performed, he said, a similar service for other statues by Percy Wood — a memorial to Crawford, a sailor who nailed the colours to the mast of the flagship at the battle of Camperdown in 1797; another erected by the Dominion of Canada to the Iroquois Confederacy; a third to commemorate the suppression of the North-West rebellion in Canada.

Unable to attend, H.M. Stanley wrote to explain his absence: 'I am pledged to leave London on the 19th in a different direction; but in spirit I will be with you, sharing the satisfaction ... of Parke's recognition as one of the greatest and worthiest soldiers of our age.' There were apologies, too, from the Duke and Duchess of St Albans, Lord Charles Beresford, Sir William and Lady Jenner, Sir William and Lady M'Cormac, the Director-General Army Medical Staff and others.[54]

Dr Michael Cox proposed a vote of thanks to Lord Roberts which was seconded by Dr Hawtrey Benson. Cox claimed that apart from Parke's family he was his oldest and earliest friend. 'It is not often', Cox said, 'that a medical man can pose as a hero. Very seldom, indeed, has a medical man been regarded as a hero, though not seldom have they acted as such. Not often, however, has the part of a hero been acted more notably than by the man we have met today to do honour.' It was generally agreed that the statue was an elegant and imposing addition to Leinster Lawn but some years later it became necessary to move it to its present less central site.

The Masons of Concord Lodge 854 had also planned ambitiously, and when the Parke Memorial Hall was opened in Carrick-on-Shannon on 8 June 1897 it contained a portrait of Parke painted during the subject's lifetime by Miss Ffoliot of 132 Sloane Street, London, daughter of the late Colonel Ffoliot, of Hollybrook, Sligo, a local notability.[55] The ill-fated Masonic Lodge was burned down by an anti-treaty group in the Civil War, on 16 April 1922.[56]

Four other memorials should be mentioned: a bust in marble executed by H. Barnes, presented to the President and Council of the Royal College of Surgeons in Ireland and exhibited to the Royal Hibernian Academy; the plaques erected at Kilmore Church by Stanley and Jephson, and at the Royal Victoria Hospital, Netley, by Parke's brother officers; and a memorial window in Ballybay where for a short time he was dispensary medical officer.

How readily today's general reader identifies 'the hero of Zutphen' (Sir Philip Sidney, 1554–86)[57] is conjectural and one suspects that to the average passer-by in Merrion Street the tall statue on Leinster Lawn outside the Natural History Museum either conveys no strong message or is, perhaps, mistakenly credited with the unmerited laurels of a biologist.[58]

The records of the Parke Memorial Fund's committee have not survived and it is not known when exactly or why a decision favoured the statue rather than some other, and perhaps more suitable, form of memorial. Busts and statues were, of course, very popular nineteenth-century urban adorn-ments, serving a dual purpose of commemoration and decoration. Gordon had his statue at the School of Military Engineering.[59] Dr Cox and his associates would have had many examples before them daily in the Royal Colleges of Physicians and Surgeons. A statue of Father Matthew, the temperance pioneer, was unveiled in Upper Sackville Street (now O'Connell Street) earlier in 1893;[60] the statue of Sir John Gray was erected in 1879. The former's crusade against drunkenness still captures the popular imagination whereas Sir John Gray, proprietor of the *Freeman's Journal* and instigator of the important Vartry water supply, is unknown to the average citizen. Parke, like Sir John, had a diminishing legend.

Apsley Cherry-Garrard, author of *The Worst Journey in the World*, defined polar exploration as 'the physical expression of the intellectual passion' and the doomed Captain Scott reflected that it had all been so much better 'than lounging in too great comfort at home'. Stanley and his companions, sweating and starving in the tropics, cannot be dismissed as mere masochists but in the retelling of Parke's story, the biographer is puzzled by certain disclosures — the 'mercy killings' at the Nile and in the rainforest and the unexpected presence of the ghost-writer.

The incontestable brutality of African exploration is hardly forgivable to twentieth-century readers but when Roger Casement ventured to ask Stanley whether a white man might not travel unarmed in Africa, the implied criticism escaped the explorer who laughed away the question. Travel among hostile natives necessarily begot violence, as it has done through the ages, and this placed those with guns at an advantage they were unlikely to discard. The white man in Africa, or Asia, or on the American plains retained his precious advantage in what was still personal combat of a type which, paradoxically, appears particularly repugnant to generations inured to mass killings from the air of 'foes' whose individual voices have never been raised against the aggressors.

The violence of the American frontier and the Indian wars gained tacit acceptance through a *genre* of romantic fiction typified by *The Virginian*. The horrors of the African wilderness, often related to the slave trade, were never similarly sanitized, but it may be argued that Parke and his companions, many of them soldiers, saw themselves committed to a military operation in which all who opposed them were enemies. They slayed without compunction and would have seen themselves as weaklings had they hesitated to apply the most rigorous disciplinary methods, including the kurbash and the noose.

When Parke led his company on a *ruga-ruga* he believed himself licensed to kill. Through his professional vocation he was primarily dedicated to healing and the relief of pain and it is in the latter context that one must look for possible excuses for his actions when dealing with the woman shot in the forest and the mortally wounded Mahdists at the Nile.

Agony is a dismaying spectacle. Present-day relief systems, helicopter ambulances, intravenous saline and transfusions of blood and plasma, potent analgesics and measures to combat shock, make it almost impossible for us to visualize what Parke was confronted with and obliged to make instant decisions — the appalling sight of badly wounded blacks, impossible to transport, almost certain to die, enraged and dehydrated under a blazing sun, still determined to kill and quite dangerous to approach. The desirable treatment was an injection of morphia: the practical alternative a bullet to the head. Parke's heroism must not be seen as stained by a callous action.

The promptness with which books on the expedition appeared has already been commented on. Stanley described how when he sat down in Cairo to write *In Darkest Africa* he hardly knew how to begin: 'My right hand had lost its cunning and the art of composition was lost by long disuse.' This was stretching the truth a little for he had kept journals and sent long despatches to the Relief Committee. Be that as it may, this practised author soon recovered his facility and his pen raced over the paper 'at the rate of nine folios an hour'.

Nothing is known of the composition of *Emin Pasha and the Rebellion at the Equator* by A.J. Mounteney Jephson other than the acknowledgment of assistance given by Stanley in its preparation. Jephson wrote other articles for periodicals, but his diary remained unpublished until edited for the Haklyut Society in 1969 by Dorothy Middleton who, in collaboration with the diarist's nephew, Brigadier Maurice Denham Jephson, supplied a well-written Preface, Prologue and Epilogue.

It is not uncommon for would-be authors lacking the flair or the time to write a book to produce it by proxy. The ghost-writer's well-established function is sometimes openly acknowledged but Parke was at pains to conceal his collaboration with Knott. And not content with a single publication by proxy, Dr Parke established a veritable partnership — with a silent partner. The result was not at all as financially rewarding for Parke as he had hoped, but it kept his name to the fore. 'I have not cleared a shilling so far [he told Knott] although of course I have benefited my reputation very much indeed.'[61]

One must concede an element of deceit in Parke's authorship — a deceit commonly practised by public figures who employ speech-writers — but it was his way of compensating for the failure of the army to confer some distinction upon him. What exactly he had hoped for is unclear, yet his failure to settle down after his return from Africa is evident, and he had strong feelings of resentment against the army establishment. Only to Knott did he unburden himself of 'the troubles and worries to which he was subjected by professional and official jealousy'.

The literary deceit was not of great magnitude. The only hint that the full authenticity of Parke's record was ever questioned is given by *The Times*' review on 3 November 1891. Drawing attention to a diary entry for 15 September 1887 which cited desertions as an argument for the Congo route

— 'for as even here among enemies they desert what would have happened if Mr Stanley had taken advice and gone from the East Coast? Simply this: we would not have had a man left by this time, as they would all have run back to Zanzibar' — the reviewer praised it as a remarkable passage 'if it were written on the date mentioned, as we are bound by Mr Parke's assurance to believe it was.' But he thought the passage in question (which does not appear in the manuscript diary and was added by Knott) had more force as evidence of Parke's loyalty to his chief than as an argument against the East Coast route.

Collation of the fair copy of Parke's diary with *My Personal Experiences* shows that Knott followed Parke's account faithfully in regard to chronology and major events, adding grace and life to the narrative. A sentence is added to the opening page to prepare us for Barttelot's evil fate: 'He is a hard worker, very energetic and always on the move; so that he should be a very effective officer, although hot-tempered and a rigid disciplinarian.'[62] Parke's reference to fatalism is rendered more fully by Knott: 'These people seem to look upon death with a philosopher's eye; they know of no appeal from the unalterable decrees of Almighty Fate.'[63]

A diary entry considering the probable fate of two missing persons — 'I expect that by this time the Washenzie have had a good feed off Mohammed A and the boy, as all the inhabitants of the bush are cannibals' — is extended in the book:

... their 'banquet' will not be as good in quantity as quality, I should say; as both missing individuals are poor in flesh.

I wonder what the Aborigines Protection Society would have done under the circumstances? Perhaps, after duly considering the surroundings, they would prefer to remain in their armchairs and pass resolutions. I'm quite sure these aborigines are quite as capable of protecting themselves as the members of the Society.[64]

Describing the confluence of the Nepoko and Aurwimi, Parke wrote, 'they formed a beautiful cascade 200 yards broad'. This is improved by Knott: 'They join at a right angle, and a beautiful cataract is formed at the line of confluence — the Nepoko dropping into the larger stream by a beautiful cascade.'[65]

Parke wrote, 'The forest is a complete wilderness, huge gloomy trees and dense thick bush beneath. Nothing can be shot in the forest... ' while Knott offered something more elaborate:

The forest is such an utter wilderness — huge gloomy trees and dense thick bush beneath — there is no chance of shooting anything in it... Of all the scenes of desolation for any human being to be left alone in! I could not have fancied it before

I came here. Snowed in at the North Pole, launched in a canoe in the middle of the Pacific Ocean, hardly either could compare with it.[66]

Parke: 'the camp as [we] marched away looked the picture of loneliness and death...'
Knott: 'the mingled picture — of scenic loveliness and ghastly human bereavement — which lay around us as we prepared to move, could hardly be overdrawn in the wildest flights of imagination.'

The comments of Herodotus on the source of the Nile are added by Knott, but elsewhere (*Diary*, 14 May 1889) Parke shows awareness of Ruwenzori's historical significance. Nelson's rule of thumb for cooking — 'His rule is a quarter of an hour per pound for either a "roast" or a "boil", or a "stew"' — was provided by Knott. He also found a suitable simile for the Manyuema women who were 'as nude and well-proportioned as their white sisters who are artistically represented on the walls of the Royal Academy'.[67]

Where Parke described the death from dysentery of one of Kibabora's wives, made to carry a load during her illness, he wrote: 'therefore her husband really killed her by neglect. As is the rule amongst the Manyuema when a death takes place they howl most horribly both day and night ... ' The same scene is pictured more effectively by Knott:

So her tender-hearted spouse really killed her, by his exercise of the two-fold office of neglect and cruelty. When she was dead, however, as is the custom with the Manyuema, he and his harem howled most piteously, night and day, for about twenty-four hours.[68]

Many other examples could be given of Knott's literary 'improvements' and of additions or omissions designed to show Parke always in the best light. For the latter's succinct diary entry: 'made my will, settled my accounts', Knott substitutes: 'In the early part of this day I settled my accounts and made my will, so that my earthly anxieties might be reduced to a minimum before facing the ordeal of the African forests and deserts.' Parke's admission that after a farewell luncheon held in his honour in Alexandria by the *Evening Telegraph* he was 'completely incapacitated from doing any more work during the day by this luxuriously sumptuous repast' is omitted by Knott, who then touches up the description of the farewell banquet with a sentence worthy of a novelist: 'Such a Babel of tongues, as the wine went round and conversation became more confidential!'

Parke kept his diary with commendable regularity, rarely missing an entry even when prostrated by fever. He may have made minor revisions when copying it for Knott's use and the latter's function appears to have been largely editorial, improving the style, ensuring a smoother narrative and contributing the set-pieces on bacteriology and the great water-tanks at Aden. He did not attempt to impose his own opinions; he retained the form in which Parke had described his trials and managed to preserve the spirit of the author's original account. Despite the knowledge of Knott's participation, the book remains Parke's authentic achievement with credit going to Knott for preparing it for publication. It would, of course, have been more honest had he allowed Knott a place on the title page.

Many of the changes are minor but interesting, neverthless: where Parke describes Tippu Tib as 'the slave dealer' Knott more diplomatically writes 'ex-slave dealer'; Emin Pasha's comment that 'the Congo is very badly managed' becomes 'the Congo State is so young' in Knott's version; Parke asks 'is the Queen alive?' but Knott puts it 'still alive?'. Referring to the threat of ants, Knott introduced the following sentence: 'We are obliged to strap our knickerbockers very tightly around the leg; petticoats would never do in this country.' Elsewhere the term 'Boycotting tactics!' is Knott's addition. Where Parke wrote 'this is the 73rd day of our march...' Knott added: 'it is slow, and tries one's patience: I wonder how Job would have got on here?' Parke's terse 'it is quite safe' is improved to 'and thus plays hide and seek with safety.'

Certain comments discreditable to Stanley are omitted. Knott softened Parke's own punitive activities substituting 'a dozen' where the diary reads: 'so I sent out for one of the men and gave him 60 with a Cane as their hides are very thick'; and again : '20 with a rod' (Parke), 'one dozen with a stout rod' (Knott). He dealt with his friend's conspicuously faulty spelling and occasionally corrected his anatomy.

Knott's apt quotations enlivened Parke's plain prose, his capacious store of general knowledge amplified it. The enormous relief of emerging from the primeval forest on 11 April 1888 required Knott's eloquence to express it adequately:

It *did* feel as a deliverance: I fancied that I could realise the feelings of Bonnivard when, after his six years of dungeon life in the Castle of Chillon, he was again able in freedom to look over his beautiful and beloved Lake of Geneva. I thought of Christian as his burden rolled down from his shoulders at the foot of the Cross...[69]

The dual authorship is of greater consequence, however, when the book is seen as a fully reliable source by biographers and others. Frank McLynn, for instance, quotes Parke's laudatory description of Stanley:

Mr Stanley looked careworn and ragged to an extreme degree — and I never felt so forcibly as now, how much this man was sacrificing in the carrying out of a terribly heavy duty which he had imposed upon himself. He might well have been living in luxury within the pale of the most advanced civilisation, housed in some of its most sumptuous mansions, and clothed with its choicest raiment, and — here he was. I had never before so fully believed in Stanley's unswerving sense of duty.[70]

The passage was actually the ghost-writer's; Parke's diary lacks this sympathetic tribute. It may, of course, be argued that Parke's letters to Knott and their conversations amended his earlier disparaging comments, justifying the encomium; it is certainly true that Stanley and his surgeon were ultimately united by mutual respect and amity. The following character sketch was softened by Knott with Parke's approval:

[Stanley] is very suspicious. Quite 2 years before he trusted us. Says what he means, in a very rough and unpolished way. No regulations or Code of Discipline could have made the men and officers regard him with greater respect... Never gives unqualified praise. Commands almost impossible tasks which must be undertaken at a moment's notice. Disliked him at first... He is neither tyrannical nor cruel, often beats his men as punishment; in most cases if he did not do so the expedition could be wrecked for want of discipline and control, the white men would have left their bones in Africa.[71]

Elsewhere Parke's praise was unequivocal:

Stanley gives me very valuable advice with regard to fevers etc. etc. and is very pliant and obedient to my suggestions on treatment, sanitation, etc. etc. and does his best to assist me under the circumstances, never blocking my work by despotic regulations and relentless red tape and furnishing signed, unservicable and bewildering documents as is so common in the Medical Department of the army.[72]

Iain R. Smith credited Parke's account of the expedition with 'especial value'.[73] Nicholas Harman's biography of Charles Stokes, the caravan leader, makes parenthetical reference to Parke in the context of the hanging of the Soudanese and the broken rope — 'The Irish doctor ... took the opportunity to study the feelings of a man facing his second execution: he found Rehan indifferent to his fate'[74]— which could convey an impression of callousness rather than concern and legitimate observation. But the biographer was not to know that he was reading a 'ghosted' account in which Parke's words had been significantly altered. Where Parke had written 'I had a conversation with him', Knott wrote 'I talked to him, as I was interested to observe what was his mental state in the wretched position in which he was then placed'.[75] And Parke's diary entry was made a day after the bungled hanging which possibly indicates that the matter was still troubling him. His questions were actually kindly and well-intentioned but overlooked the probability that the condemned man's senses were dulled with *bhang* and he left unconsidered his total incompetence to probe psychologically a man of different race:

> We shall not cross —
> dare not cross
> where the tide divides us
> skin from skin
> heart from heart.[76]

If the literary collaboration was greatly to Parke's advantage one wonders why Knott co-operated so fully. The £200 paid for 'ghosting' *My Personal Experiences* was certainly then a sizable sum of money and the work itself was a challenge, but in the later phase when Parke continued to direct minor literary chores to Dublin it was no longer a novelty and Knott might have been expected to circumvent the nuisance. It is possible, however, to discern an element of *cacoethes scribendi* in Knott's eccentric literary career in the course of which between 1890 and his death on 2 January 1921, this medical practitioner wrote more than 2000 articles and reviews. All was grist to his mill; he contributed to such Irish medical journals as then existed, sent unsigned articles to the *Freeman's Journal* and wrote regularly for the *Indian Medical Review*, the *Medical Record* (New York) and the *St Louis Medical Review*.

After Parke's death, Knott claimed to have lost 'the dearest friend of my life', the one man he could trust under all circumstances. Friendship may explain the unbroken partnership but Parke's continuing demands must have tested it sorely and one looks for additional factors behind Knott's amenability.[77] Their roots in County Roscommon would have drawn the two Protestant students together at the College of Surgeons in the 1870s where Parke, the elder of the pair, and a successful scholar may have been the more prominent figure. But Knott's career failed to blossom: the chair of anatomy he had set his heart on eluded him nor did he get the post of assistant surgeon at the Richmond Hospital that would have been an acceptable consolation prize.

The Parkes belonged to the landed gentry of County Roscommon and had always held a higher social position than the Knotts, an ascendancy typified by an event in 1837 when James Knott of Battlefield, then high sheriff of Sligo, refused to make the court-house available for the reception of the Lord-Lieutenant, Lord Mulgrave. William Parke, a member of the court-house committee with access to the key, opened the building in defiance of the sheriff and much to the gratification of the viceroy who directed

Mr Parke to kneel as they entered and knighted him: 'Arise! Sir William Parke.' John Knott's family farmed a mere 45 acres near Lough Gara at Kingsland and Tonroe, acting as bailiffs and rent-collectors to King-Harman the local landlord. And now Tom Parke was a public figure, bedecked with medals and moving in high society. These factors may help to explain the psychology of Knott's servitude to his former pupil, who, in his thoughtful way, had gone to great lengths to seek an opening for Knott in London, a city of opportunity.

An obscure scholar with a dawning literary ambition, Knott envied Parke's appeal for editors and seems to have been content to channel his writing under another's by-line while his friend managed curiously to extract satisfaction from vicarious authorship. The revelation 102 years after the publication of *My Personal Experiences* of John Knott's contribution hardly changes anything. It was not for literary prowess but for his actions on the Nile and in the Congo that Parke earned the recognition of the United Kingdom and a statue on Leinster Lawn. Lord Charles Beresford said he never met in the British Army or Navy a finer fellow than Tom Parke, while for Stanley he was 'the rarest doctor in the world'. What is important now are words written in *The Irish Times* in the days after his death — 'it would be to our shame if we failed to remember his history.'[78]

Notes

1 Letters, RCSI, 2 January 1893.
2 *The Roscommon Journal*, 7 Jan.
3 Letters, 13 February.
4 Letters, 15 March.
5 Actually, Burroughs & Wellcome placed three pages of advertisements for their 'Portable "Tabloid" Medicines for Travellers' in the book and included favourable quotes from *My Personal Experiences*.
6 Letters, 4 March.
7 H.M. Stanley, in T.H. Parke's *Guide to Health in Africa* (London 1891), pp. v–ix.
8 Ibid, p. ix.
9 Letters, 15 March.
10 Letters, 21 March.
11 Letters, 27 March.
12 *The Lancet*, 1893; 1: 1003. Mary French-Sheldon was exceptional among the African explorers in her longevity, 1847–1936.
13 Letters, 27 April.
14 Letters, 19 June.
15 Parke, *Guide to Health*, p. 59.
16 Ibid, p. 16.
17 Ibid, p. 19.
18 The soldiers who lose consciousness on the parade-ground every summer are felled by

'fainting-attacks' rather than sunstroke.

19 *The Times*, 10 April 1890.

20 Ibid, 11 April 1890. Complete consistency cannot be expected even from leader writers for to prove a point *The Times* had decreed on 21 January 1887 that the land through which the expedition would travel 'belongs to somebody or other'.

21 The review, incidentally, followed a notice of Dr Joseph A. Moloney's *With Captain Stairs to Katanga*.

22 Letter THP/Ernest Hart. Wellcome Library Ms 5423.

23 *British Medical Journal*, 1893, ii, 184.

24 *The Lancet*, 1893, ii, 33.

25 *Medical Press and Circular*, 1892; 105: 226–7. 'On page 9 we have to our inexpressible relief, for the first time found satisfactory answers to the queries of the *causes* of WASTING and of THIRST, by which, as anxious students of the febrile condition, we have for years been mentally tortured: "... micro-organisms, or microbes, consist largely of protoplasm. They are reproduced in vast numbers in the system during the course of the disease to which they give rise, and in their growth they consume a large quantity of *nitrogen* and of *water*." Typhus fever is nothing if not Irish in its predilections. Stimulants are notably beneficial in typhus. May not this happy effect be due to the notoriously powerful affinity of Hibernian protoplasm for the molecular constituents of its favourite beverage?'

26 The account of Parke's visit to Scotland and his death is taken from the Duchess of St Albans' letter to H.M. Stanley (RCSI).

27 Duchess of St Albans to Mrs Parke (RCSI).

28 Shee, *Medical History*, p. 36.

29 *The Irish Times*.

30 *Leitrim Advertiser*, September 1893. Stanley, accompanied by his wife, visited the West of Ireland later in the month. They arrived at Drumsna by the 10 am limited mail train and having visited Parke's grave and his relatives at Kilmore they left by the afternoon express.

31 W.B. Yeats, *Collected Poems* (London 1937), p. 176.

32 A presentation copy of *My Personal Experiences* was sent to Cork inscribed 'To my dearest Harrie and George, for Stanley Parke Stoker from yours affectionately "Bwana Doctari". Netley 6th November, 1891.' Young Stoker graduated in medicine from University College, Cork; he was awarded the MC during the First World War and settled in England in general medical practice.

33 H. Ward, *A Voice from the Congo* (London 1910), p. 212.

34 H.M. Stanley, *Autobiography* (London 1909), p. 381.

35 Ibid, p. 381.

36 Davis Coakley, *Masters of Irish Medicine* (Dublin 1992), p. 152.

37 Ibid, p. 154.

38 Parke, *Experiences*, p. 231.

39 Shee, *op. cit.*, p. 29.

40 Ibid, p. 33.

41 Parke, *Experiences*, p. 227.

42 IDA, II: '... on the 24th May, 1888, when scarcely two hours' march from the Lake beach, lo! a stupendous snowy mountain appeared, bearing 215° magnetic — an almost square-browed central mass — almost thirty miles in length, and quite covered with snow; situated between two great ridges of about 5000 feet less elevation, which extended to about thirty miles on either side of them. On that day it was visible for hours.'

43 See *The Way to the Mountains of the Moon* (1966) by Rennie Bere, district officer in the

Colonial Service and later Chief Warden of Uganda's National Parks, which describes Ruwenzori's flora and fauna and the history of its discovery. Aeschylus (525–456BC) held that Egypt and the Nile fountains were 'fed by distant snows'; Aristotle referred to a 'Mountain of Silver' south-west of the Nile; other ancient writers made similar references. Ptolemy's maps show the *Lunae Montes* as the source of the Nile. Edrisi, an Arab geographer depicted the great lakes and the Mountains of the Moon in a map, Al Rojari (AD 1154).

Nothing more was learned about the range until the late nineteenth century. A map by William Blaew (1660) placed the *Lunae Montes* well down in southern Africa. The 'enormous blue mass afar off' which in 1876 Stanley named Mount Gordon Bennett to honour the proprietor of the *New York Herald* may actually have been Ruwenzori but this lacks the certainty of the 'discovery' he made on 24 May 1888 having meanwhile paid scant attention to Parke's news about a 'Snow Mountain' seen by Jephson and himself.

Dr Franz Stuhlmann, travelling in an expedition led by Emin Pasha in 1891, went up to 13,326 feet on the western slopes and left his name in a bottle at a spot subsequent climbers called 'Camp of the Bottle'. G.F. Scott Elliot, a naturalist, studied the range's flora and fauna in 1894–5. Captain Claud Sitwell reached the snow in 1898. Harry Johnston compensated for overestimating the height of the range in 1900 (setting it at 20,000 ft) by discovering the Ruwenzori turaco, a lovely bird which Bere says, 'deserves to be known always by the resounding scientific name, *Ruwenzorornis johnstoni johnstoni*.

Rudolf Grauer, an Austrian alpinist, climbed 'Grauer Rock' on the summit ridge of Baker in 1906 in which year the Duke of Abruzzi's well-equipped party climbed most of the major peaks and clarified Ruwenzori's complicated topography. Dr Noel Humphreys made the first east-west crossing of the ridge in 1936 and climbed many peaks. Piloted by P.W. Lynch Bloss in a de Havilland Puss Moth, Humphreys made an aerial survey in 1931. He discovered twenty unrecorded lakes and described the range as 'an elliptical peneplain — deep cut valleys radiating from the centre'. Gordon Noel Humphreys was both a surveyor and a doctor, MA, Cantabury, 1910, LRCP Lond, MRCS, English, 1931.

44 Jephson failed to recover his health. His post as Queen's Messenger from 1895 to 1901 ended when he was found unconscious in charge of dispatches in a train on the continent; he worked briefly as an Usher at Court and as ADC to the governor of New Zealand.

Sir Henry Stanley died in May 1904 a few weeks before Jephson married Anna Head of San Francisco. The couple had met in 1891 but Anna's father, a hard-headed business man, was opposed to their marriage and had remained obdurate until he relented on his deathbed.

There was some talk of Jephson entering parliament but he died in 1908. His only child, an unmarried son, was killed in an Underground Railway accident in 1938.

45 C. Royle, *Egyptian Campaigns*, p. 393.
46 Frank Callanan, *The Parnell Split* (Cork 1992), pp. 187–8.
47 Born into an old Roscommon family at Kilmore, Drumsna, Michael F. Cox (1851–1926) graduated from the Catholic University Medical School in 1875 practising in Sligo before he joined the staff of St Vincent's Hospital in 1881. Parnell spoke from the balcony of his house. Physically imposing, a cultured sportsman and FQCPI he held the trust of Catholics and Protestants alike, being both a friend of John Redmond, the new leader of the Irish parliamentary party, and a member of the Privy Council.

Cox was author of *The County and Kindred of Oliver Goldsmith*, and *The Irish Horse*. His son, Arthur, was a leading Dublin solicitor.

48 *The Irish Times*, 14 September 1893.
49 Ibid, 15 Sept.

50 Ibid, 16 Sept.

51 Ibid, 20 Sept.

52 *The Lancet*, 1893, ii, 1039.

53 See Irish *Builder*, 1 May 1894; Anne Crookshank, p. 36 (O'Brien et al:, Dublin 1984).

54 *The Irish Times*, 21 December 1896.

55 Parke sat for the portrait in Agnes Ffoliot's London studio where on completion it was exhibited until Lt Col. Ffoliot handed it over to the Provincal Grand Lodge of Freemasons of North Connacht on 19 September 1893. Miss Agnes Ffoliot drowned herself in Lough Arrow in 1911.

56 It had been a week of violence in Sligo where on 16 April 1922 Arthur Griffith, addressing a public meeting, said, 'patriotic Irishmen have still a lot to learn, particularly the great lesson of mutual tolerance'. At the other end of the country Eamon de Valera was denouncing the treaty. During the night of 21 April the American Oil Company's stores were raided and a number of empty petrol tins were found in the ruined Masonic Hall where the regalia and the portrait of T.H. Parke were destroyed.

57 Sir Philip Sidney, poet, soldier and courtier was an important symbol for many generations: 'a spirit without spot' (Shelley, 'Adonais'); 'Our Sidney and our perfect man' (Yeats 'In Memory of Robert Gregory'). He died from a thigh wound sustained at Zutphen when fighting for the Dutch against the Spaniards, having refused to wear leg armour because a companion lacked it.

58 See N. Harman's *Bwana Stokesi*, p. 244: 'Parke's statue is still outside the National Gallery [*sic*] in Dublin but nobody there knows who he was.' The comment is unfair and the author must have spoken to the wrong person. The Natural History Museum has on display a tropical suit, cotton tunic and trousers, worn by Parke and donated by his sister, Miss Florence Parke.

59 This was unveiled by HRH the Prince of Wales on 19 May 1890. The work of Onslow Ford, ARA, it represented Gordon riding a camel and wearing the uniform of an Egyptian general. The bronze pedestal bears the single word, 'GORDON'.

60 This statue was unveiled by Lord Plunket, Protestant Archbishop of Ireland (soon to have his own statue in Kildare Place), his Catholic equivalent unable to be present. According to Sir Charles Cameron's *Reminiscences* 'an usually large number of inebriates were seen that day in Dublin'. Cameron gave a dinner party for the occasion. Though not himself a teetotaller he served non-alcoholic drinks labelling the containers in the style of vintage wines but supplying Madeira in a lemonade bottle for two elderly VIPs.

61 Letters, 23 July 1892.

62 Parke, *Experiences*, p. 2.

63 Ibid, p. 31.

64 Ibid, p. 268.

65 Ibid, p. 100.

66 Ibid, pp. 114–5.

67 Ibid, p. 344.

68 Ibid, p. 463.

69 Ibid, p. 210.

70 Ibid, p. 335.

71 *Diary*, Vol. 4. See *Experiences,* pp. 512–3 for modified version.

72 *Diary*, Vol. 4. Evidently he encountered nothing of the officious interference from Stanley that Dr R. Leslie feared. See Chapter One, fn. 5.

73 Iain R. Smith, *Relief Expedition*, p. 113, fn. 1.

74 Harman, *op. cit.*, p. 90.

75 Parke, *Experiences*, p. 419.
76 Lenrie Peters, *Selected Poetry* (London nd), p. 112.
77 A librarian who shared Knott's tastes described him as 'courteous and affable'; it was a delight to hear him discourse on his collection of rare books. Knott's interests ranged from the place of the strawberry in the history of therapeutics to the Bacon-Shakespeare controversy. He wrote on the medicine and surgery of the Homeric poems, the plague of London, Sir Walter Raleigh's 'Royal Cordial' etc, but was something of a trial to editors, to judge from George Milbry Gould's complaint that his eyes were aching from reading Knott's script: 'Your ink is poor and pale ... and you write so finely and condensed that deciphering is often straining.'

   A man of fixed habits and accustomed to reading in the Library of the RCSI, Knott set off for the College as usual on Easter Monday 1916 ignoring or unaware of the insurgents' activities in St Stephen's Green. The bedel answered his knock to tell him the College was closed but the Countess Markievicz (*née* Gore-Booth, with Parke blood in her veins) and two other 'rebels' seized the opportunity to occupy the building at pistol point.

   John Knott died from influenza and heart-failure on 2 January 1921.

78 An exhibition of 'Parkeana' was opened on 10 September 1993 at the RCSI in the presence of a number of T.H. Parke's relatives, some of whom had travelled from England, Canada and the USA. Two days later the centenary of Tom Parke's death was observed at St Brigid's Church, Dangan, Kilmore, County Roscommon, by 'An Ecumenical Service of Thanksgiving for the Life of Surgeon-Major Parke' arranged by Rev. Fr Laurence Cullen. An appreciative message from the President of Ireland, Her Excellency Mary Robinson, was read out and finally the Last Post was rendered close to the Victorian hero's birth-place.

Sources and Bibliography

Primary

Manuscripts:

Diary, four volumes. Mercer Library, Royal College of Surgeons in Ireland.
Letters: RCSI; British Library; Wellcome Historical Institute.

Printed:

'Report to the War Office on the Cholera Outbreak in Egypt', 1883.
'Empyema and its treatment', mentioned in *DNB* but not located.
'Evidence before the Vaccination Commission', 1890.
My Personal Experiences of Equatorial Africa, London: Samson Low, 1891.
Guide to Health in Africa, London: Samson Low, 1893.
'The Climate of Africa' in *The Book of Climates,* Daniel H. Cullimore, (ed.)
    2nd edn, London, 1891.
'The Ulcer of the Emin Pasha Relief Expedition', *The Lancet* 1891; 2:
    1270–1.
'Note on African Fever', ibid., 1892; 1176–8.
'How General Gordon Was Really Lost', *The Nineteenth Century,* 1892; 31:
    787–94.
'A Plea for a Railway to the Victoria Nyanza', *The United Service Magazine,*
    1892, November, 203–11.
'Reminiscences of Africa', ibid., 1892, December, 324–33; January 1893,
    344–55; February 1893, 447–56.

Secondary

Allen, Bernard, *Gordon and the Sudan*, London: Macmillan, 1931.
Barttelot, Walter G. (ed.), *The Life of Edmund Musgrave Barttelot*, London:
    Bentley, 1890.
[Bell, Moberly], *Khedives and Pashas*, London: Samson Low, 1884.
Bentley, W. Holman, *Life on the Congo*, London: Religious Tract Society, 1893.

Bere, Rennie, *The Way to the Mountains of the Moon*, London: Barker, 1966.

Beresford, Lord Charles, *The Memoirs of Lord Charles Beresford*, 2 vols, London: Methuen, 1914.

British Medical Journal, 1890; 1: 310.

Cameron, Sir Charles, *Reminiscences*, Dublin: Hodges Figgis, 1913.

Conrad, Joseph, *Heart of Darkness*, Harmondsworth: Penguin Books, 1989.

Cromer, Earl of, *Modern Egypt*, vol. 2, London: Macmillan, 1808.

Dictionary of National Biography.

Dolan, Arthur, 'Leitrim's Famed African Explorer', *Leitrim Observer Centenary Issue*, pp. 78–9.

Felkin, Robert W., 'The Position of Dr. Emin Bey', *Scottish Geographical Society Magazine*, 1886; 2: 705–17.

Forbath, Peter, *The Last Hero*, London: Heinemann, 1989.

Fox Bourne, H.R., *The Other Side of the Emin Pasha Expedition*, London: Chatto & Windus, 1891.

Harman, Nicholas, *Bwana Stokesi and his African Conquests*, London: Cape, 1986.

Hoffmann, William, *With Stanley in Africa*, London: Cassell, 1938.

Holt, P.M. and Daly, M.W., *A History of the Sudan*, 4th edn, London: Longman, 1988.

Irish Builder, 1894; 36: 110, 'The Parke Memorial, Dublin'.

Jameson, James S., *The Story of the Rear Column*, Mrs J.S. Jameson (ed.), London: R.H. Porter, 1890.

Jones, Roger, *The Rescue of Emin Pasha*, London: Allison & Busby, 1972.

Lancet, The, 1893; 2: 779–8.

Logan, P.J., 'Thomas Parke, Surgeon and Explorer', *Irish Sword*, 1964; 6: 248–51.

Longford, Elizabeth, *A Pilgrimage of Passion – the Life of Wilfrid Scawen Blunt*, London: Weidenfeld and Nicolson, 1979.

Lyons, J.B., 'A Forgotten Scholar: John Freeman Knott, 1853–1921' in *'What Did I Die of?'* Dublin: The Lilliput Press, 1991.

Mac Dermot, Betty, *O'Ruairc of Breifne*, Manorhamilton: Drumlin Publications, 1990.

Mc Lynn, Frank, *Stanley: the Making of an African Explorer*, Oxford University Press, 1891.

——, *Stanley: Sorcerer's Apprentice*, Oxford University Press, 1992.

——, *Hearts of Darkness*, London: Hutchinson, 1992.

Marlowe, John, *Mission to Khartum*, London: Gollancz, 1969.

Moloney, Joseph A.,*With Captain Stairs to Katanga*, London: 1893.

Mounteney-Jephson, A.J., *Emin Pasha and the Rebellion at the Equator*, London: Sampson Low, 1890.

——— , *Fortnightly Review*, 1891; 14–20.

——— , *The Diary of A. J. Mounteney Jephson*, Dorothy Middleton (ed.), Cambridge (Hakluyt Society) University Press, 1969.

Newspapers
The Broad Arrow and Naval and Military Gazette
The Graphic, 30 April 1890
The Illustrated London News, 3 March 1890
The Irish Times
The Leitrim Advertiser
The Pall Mall Gazette
The Roscommon Herald
The Roscommon Journal
The Times

O'Brien, Eoin, Crookshank, Anne, Wolstenholme, Gordon, *A Portrait of Irish Medicine*, Dublin: Ward River Press, 1984.

O'Conor, Abraham, *Concord Lodge, 854, Carrick-on-Shannon, 1787–1897*, Dublin, 1897.

O'Rorke, T., *History of Sligo: Town and Country*, 2 vols, facsimile edition, Sligo: Dodd's, 1986.

Pakenham, Thomas, *The Scramble for Africa*, London: Weidenfeld and Nicolson, 1991.

Ransford, Oliver, *David Livingstone*, London: John Murray, 1978.

Reid, B.L., *The Lives of Roger Casement*, New Haven: Yale University Press, 1976.

Royle, Charles, *The Egyptian Campaigns*, revised edn, London: Hurst and Blackett, 1900.

Ryan, Martin, Script of 'Into the Heart of Darkness', broadcast by Radio Eireann, 1987, produced by Tim Lehane.

Schweitzer, Georg, *Emin Pasha His Life and Death*, 2 vols, London: Constable, 1898.

Shee, J. Charles, 'Report from Darkest Africa 1887–1889', *Medical History*, 1966; 10: 23–37.

Smith, Des., '"The World's Rarest Doctor" Surgeon-Major T.H. Parke', *Roscommon Historical Journal*, 1992.

Smith, Iain R., *The Emin Pasha Relief Expedition 1886–1890*, Oxford: Clarendon Press, 1972.

Stanley, H.M., *In Darkest Africa,* 2 vols, London: Samson Low, 1890.

——— , *The Lancet* 1893; 2: 782–3.

——— , *The Times,* November 17, 1890.

Stairs, W.G., 'Shut Up in the African Forest', *The Nineteenth Century* 1891; 29: 45–63.

——— , 'From the Albert Nyanza to the Indian Ocean', ibid, 1891; 29:

Sundman, Per Olaf, *The Expedition,* transl. from Swedish by Mary Sandbach, London: Secker and Warburg, 1967.

Symons, A.J.A., *Emin Goveror of Equatoria,* 2nd edn, London: Falcon Press, 1950.

Troup, John R., *With Stanley's Rear Column,* London: Chapman and Hall, 1890.

Ward, Herbert, *Five Years With the Congo Cannibals,* London: Chatto & Windus, 1890.

——— , *My Life With Stanley's Rear Guard,* London: Chatto & Windus, 1891.

——— , *A Voice from the Congo,* London: Heinemann, 1910.

Werner, J.R., *A Visit to Stanley's Rear Guard,* London 1890.

Wilson, Sir Charles, *From Korti to Khartum,* Edinburgh: Blackwood, 1886.

Wingate, F.R., *Mahdiism and the Egyptian Sudan,* London: Macmillan, 1891.

Index

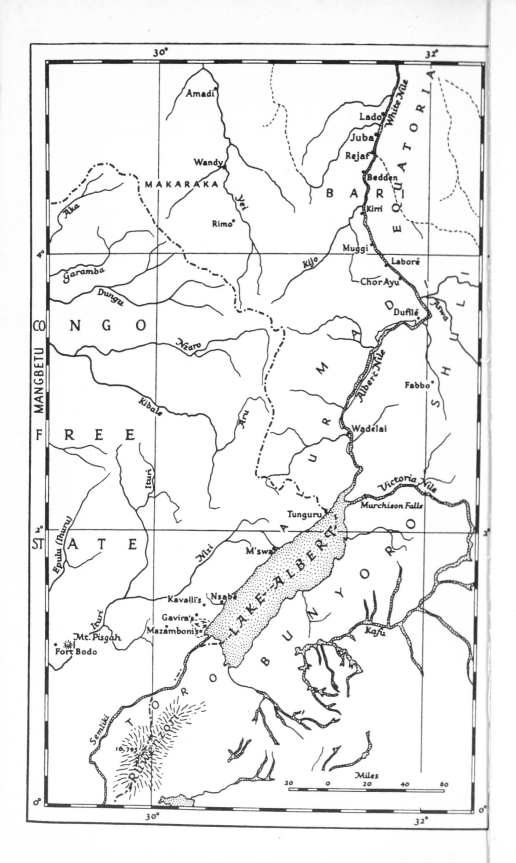

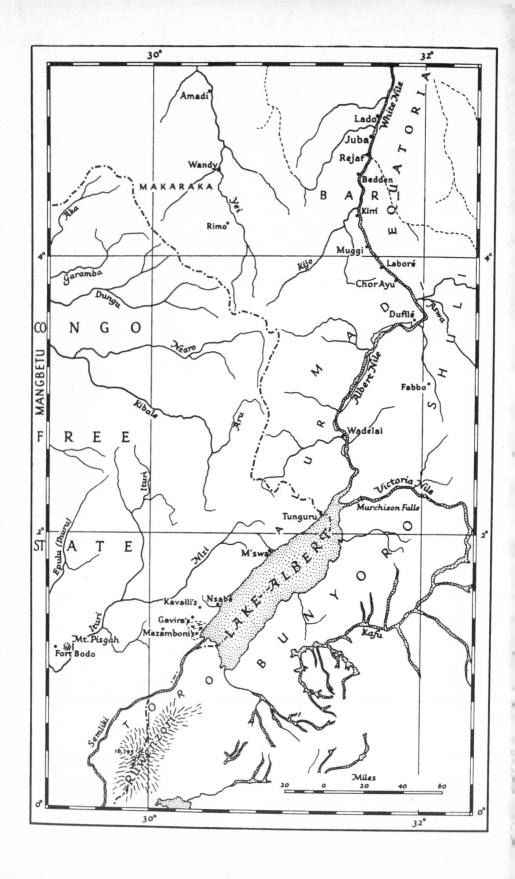